# LOUIS GIANNETTI

*Case Western Reserve University*

**THIRD EDITION**

# Understanding Movies

Prentice-Hall, Inc., Englewood Cliffs, New Jersey   07632

*Library of Congress Cataloging in Publication Data*

GIANNETTI, LOUIS D.
  Understanding movies.

  Includes bibliographies and index.
  1. Moving-pictures. I. Title.
PN1994.G47      1982        791.43        81-13862
ISBN   0-13-936310-6                      AACR2

Editorial/production supervision and interior design by Fred Bernardi
Cover design by Mark Binn
Manufacturing buyer: Harry P. Baisley

Printed in the United States of America

10   9   8   7   6   5   4   3   2

ISBN 0-13-936310-6

PRENTICE-HALL INTERNATIONAL, INC., *London*
PRENTICE-HALL OF AUSTRALIA PTY. LIMITED, *Sydney*
PRENTICE-HALL OF CANADA, LTD., *Toronto*
PRENTICE-HALL OF INDIA PRIVATE LIMITED, *New Delhi*
PRENTICE-HALL OF JAPAN, INC., *Tokyo*
PRENTICE-HALL OF SOUTHEAST ASIA PTE. LTD., *Singapore*
WHITEHALL BOOKS LIMITED, *Wellington, New Zealand*

*Take him and cut him out in little stars,*
*And he will make the face of heav'n so fine*
*That all the world will be in love with Night*
*And pay no worship to the garish Sun.*
　　　**—WILLIAM SHAKESPEARE**

# CONTENTS

v

*"The motion-picture medium has an extraordinary range of expression. It has in common with the plastic arts the fact that it is a visual composition projected on a two-dimensional surface; with dance, that it can deal in the arrangement of movement; with theatre, that it can create a dramatic intensity of events; with music, that it can compose in the rhythms and phrases of time and can be attended by song and instrument; with poetry, that it can juxtapose images; with literature generally, that it can encompass in its sound track the abstractions available only to language."*

MAYA DEREN

# PREFACE

As Maya Deren's observation suggests, analyzing a good movie is no easy task. Because films can express so many ideas and emotions simultaneously, viewers are sometimes overwhelmed by the sheer density of information they're bombarded with. The following chapters may be of use in helping the moviegoer understand some of these complex elements. I entertain no grand pretense at teaching viewers how to respond to movies, only in suggesting some of the reasons they respond as they do. I've been strongly influenced in the rewriting of this text by the letters and comments I have received, especially from teachers who have used the book in their classrooms.

I have retained the same principle of organization from the earlier editions. Each chapter isolates the basic techniques used by filmmakers in conveying meaning. Naturally, the chapters don't pretend to be exhaustive: They're essentially starting points. They progress from the most narrow and specific aspects of cinema ("Photography") to the most abstract and comprehensive ("Theory"). But the eleven chapters aren't tightly interdependent, and can be read out of sequence. Inevitably, such looseness of organization involves a certain amount of overlapping, but I have tried to keep this to a minimum. Technical terms are generally defined when they're first used in the text, but for those who read the chapters out of sequence, the glossary at the end of the book should provide adequate temporary clarifications.

## Acknowledgments

A number of people have helped me in the writing of this book: James Monaco, Floyd C. Watkins, Gerald Barrett, William Bell, Jack Ellis, Jameson Goldner, Herbert Marshall, and Arthur Knight were all generous with their advice and assistance. Ray Kowalski designed the covers: the front cover photo is from *Singin' in the Rain* (MGM, directed by Gene Kelly and Stanley Donen); the rear cover is from *Aguirre, the Wrath of God* (New Yorker Films, directed by Werner Herzog). I'm grateful to Ingmar Bergman, who was kind enough to allow me to use the frame enlargements from *Persona;* and Akira Kurosawa, who graciously consented to my using enlargements from *The Seven Samurai.* I would like to thank my good friend Stefan Czapsky for all his help. As usual, I owe a great debt of gratitude to the Case Western Reserve University Film Society, and to my students, who patiently allowed me to test much of this material on them beforehand. I am very grateful to Fred Bernardi, the editorial-production supervisor of this book, for his patience, commitment, and talent.

I would also like to acknowledge and thank the following individuals and institutions for their assistance in allowing me to use materials under their copyright. Andrew Sarris, for permission to quote from "The Fall and Rise of the Film Director," in *Interviews with Film Directors* (New York: Avon Books, 1967); Svensk Filmindustri, United Artists, and William Pinzler for the use of the frame enlargements from *Persona;* Jonas Mekas, Stan Brakhage, and the New American Cinema Group for permission to quote from *The Film Culture Reader,* edited by P. Adams Sitney (New York: Praeger Publishers, 1970); Kurosawa Productions, Toho International Co., Ltd., and Audio Brandon Films for permission to use the frame enlargements from *The Seven Samurai;* from *North by Northwest,* The MGM Library of Film Scripts, written by Ernest Lehman. Copyright © 1959 by Loews Incorporated. Reprinted by permission of The Viking Press, Inc.; Albert J. LaValley, *Focus on Hitchcock* © 1972. Reprinted by permission of Prentice-Hall, Inc., Englewood Cliffs, New Jersey; Albert Maysles, in *Documentary Explorations,* edited by G. Roy Levin. Garden City: Doubleday & Company, Inc., 1971; Vladimir Nilsen, *The Cinema as a Graphic Art* (New York: Hill and Wang, a Division of Farrar, Straus and Giroux); Maya Deren, "Cinematography: The Creative Use of Reality," in *The Visual Arts Today,* edited by Gyorgy Kepes (Middletown, Conn.: Wesleyan University Press, 1960); Marcel Carné, from *The French Cinema,* by Roy Armes (New York: A. S. Barnes & Co., 1966); Richard Dyer MacCann, "Introduction," *Film: A Montage of Theories* (New York: E. P. Dutton & Co., Inc.), copyright © 1966 by Richard Dyer MacCann, reprinted with permission; V. I. Pudovkin, *Film Technique* (London: Vision, 1954); "The Pusher," by Steppenwolf, Columbia Pictures and Dunhill (ABC Records); André Bazin, *What is Cinema?* (Berkeley: University of California Press, 1967); Michelangelo Antonioni, "Two Statements," in *Film Makers on Film Making,* edited by Harry M. Geduld (Bloomington: Indiana University Press, 1969); Alexandre Astruc, from *The New Wave,* edited by Peter Graham (London: Secker & Warburg,

1968, and New York: Doubleday & Co.); Akira Kurosawa, from *The Movies as Medium,* edited by Lewis Jacobs (New York: Farrar, Straus and Giroux, 1970); Jean Cocteau, from *Jean Cocteau,* by René Gilson (New York: Crown Publishers, Inc., 1969); Pauline Kael, *I Lost It at the Movies* (New York: Bantam Books, 1966); John Grierson, *Grierson on Documentary,* edited by Forsyth Hardy (New York: Harcourt, Brace and Co., 1947).

LOUIS GIANNETTI
*Cleveland, Ohio*

**1**

*"A photograph is by no means a complete and whole reflection of reality: the photographic picture represents only one or another selection from the sum of physical attributes of the object photographed."*

VLADIMIR NILSEN

# PHOTOGRAPHY

## *Realism and Expressionism*

Even before the turn of the last century, movies began to develop in two major directions: the realistic and the expressionistic. In the mid–1890s in France, the Lumière brothers delighted audiences with their short movies dealing with everyday occurrences. Such films as *The Arrival of a Train* fascinated viewers precisely because they seemed to capture the flux and spontaneity of events as they were viewed in real life (9-1). At about the same time, Georges Méliès was producing a number of fantasy films that emphasized purely imagined events. Such movies as *A Trip to the Moon* were typical mixtures of whimsical narrative and trick photography (10-1). In many respects, the Lumières can be regarded as the founders of the realistic tradition of cinema, and Méliès of the expressionistic tradition.

*Realism* and *Expressionism* are merely general rather than absolute terms. When used to suggest a tendency toward either polarity, such labels can be helpful, but in the end they're just labels. Few films are exclusively expressionistic in style, and fewer yet are completely realistic. There is also an important difference between Realism and reality, although this distinction is often forgotten. Realism is a particular style, whereas physical reality is the source of all the raw materials of film, both realistic and expressionistic. Virtually all movie directors go to the photographable world for their subject matter, but what they do with this material—how they shape and manipulate it—is what determines their stylistic emphasis.

1

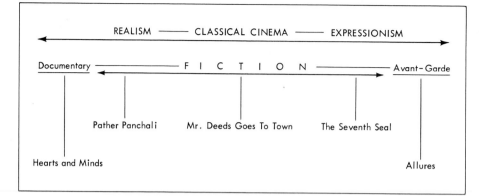

**1-1.**
Film critics and scholars categorize movies according to a variety of criteria, few of them definitive. Two of the most common methods of classification are by style and type. The three major styles—Realism, Classicism, and Expressionism—might be regarded as a continuous spectrum of possibilities, rather than airtight categories. Similarly, the three types of movies—documentaries, fiction, and avant-garde films—are also terms of convenience, for they often overlap. Realistic films like *Pather Panchali* can shade into the documentary; expressionistic movies like *The Seventh Seal* have a personal quality suggesting the traditional purview of the avant-garde. Most fiction films, especially those produced in America, tend to conform to the classical paradigm. Classical cinema can be viewed as an intermediate style which avoids the extremes of Realism and Expressionism—although most movies in the classical form lean toward one or the other style.

Generally speaking, realistic films attempt to reproduce the surface of concrete reality with a minimum of distortion. In photographing objects and events, the filmmaker tries to suggest the copiousness of life itself. Both realist and expressionist film directors must select (and hence, emphasize) certain details from the chaotic sprawl of reality; but the element of selectivity in realistic films is less obvious. Realists, in short, try to preserve the illusion that their film world is unmanipulated, an objective mirror of the actual world. Expressionists, on the other hand, make no such pretense. They deliberately stylize and distort their raw materials so that only the very naive would mistake an expressionistic image of an object or event for the real thing. Details are more rigorously selected, and often they're isolated from their contexts in space and time.

Style in a realistic film is generally unobtrusive. The artist tends to be self-effacing before his or her materials. Such filmmakers are more concerned with *what* is being shown rather than *how* it's manipulated. The camera is used conservatively: it's essentially a recording mechanism that reproduces the surfaces of tangible objects with as little commentary as possible. Some realist filmmakers aim for a rough look in their images, one that doesn't prettify the materials with a self-conscious beauty of form. A high premium is placed on simplicity, spontaneity, and directness. This is not to suggest that these movies lack artistry, however, for at its best, the realistic cinema specializes in an art that conceals art. In the hands of a master of this style—a Jean Renoir, or a Vittorio De Sica—Realism can be profoundly subtle.

Expressionist movies are stylistically flamboyant. Their directors are concerned with expressing their unabashedly subjective experience of reality, not how other people might see it. Expressionists are often concerned with spiritual and psychological truths which they feel can be conveyed best by distorting the surface of the material world. The camera is used as a tool of self-expression, as a method of commenting on the subject matter, a way of emphasizing its essential rather than its objective nature. There's a high degree of manipulation, of re-forming of reality, in expressionistic movies. But it's precisely this "deformed" imagery that can be so artistically striking in such films.

Most realists would claim that their major concern is with *content* rather than *form* or technique. The subject matter is always supreme, and anything that distracts from the content is viewed with suspicion. In its most extreme form, the realistic cinema tends toward documentary, with its emphasis on photographing actual people and events (1-2). The expressionistic cinema, on

**1-2. *Hearts and Minds* (U.S.A., 1975).**
*Directed by Peter Davis.*
The emotional impact of a documentary image usually derives from its truth rather than its beauty. Davis' indictment of America's devastation of Vietnam consists primarily of TV newsreel footage. This photo shows some Vietnamese children running from an accidental bombing raid on their community, their clothes literally burned off their bodies by napalm. "First they bomb as much as they please," a Vietnamese observes, "then they film it." It was images such as these that eventually turned the majority of Americans against the war. Fernando Solanas and Octavio Gettino, Third World filmmakers, have pointed out: "Every image that documents, bears witness to, refutes or deepens the truth of a situation is something more than a film image or purely artistic fact; it becomes something which the System finds indigestible." Paradoxically, in no other country except the United States would such self-damning footage be allowed on the public airwaves—which are controlled, or at least regulated, by governments. No other country has a First Amendment.

the other hand, tends to emphasize form and technique. Expressionists are often called formalists. The most extreme example of this style of filmmaking is found in the avant-garde cinema (1-6). Some of these movies are totally abstract, in which pure forms (that is, nonrepresentational colors, lines, and shapes) constitute the only content.

But these are generalizations only. In the eclectic world of the cinema, there is much overlapping, and many exceptions. For example, a good many documentaries are stylistically expressionistic, and there are some instances of realistic avant-garde films, like the works of Andy Warhol (see Chapter 10, "Avant-Garde"). Most fiction movies fall somewhere between these two extremes, in a mode critics refer to as classical cinema (1-4). Some directors have worked in a variety of styles. For instance, the early works of Federico Fellini—movies like *I Vitelloni* and *The Nights of Cabiria*—would be classified

**1-3. *Pather Panchali* (India, 1955).**
*With Kanu Bannerjee; Directed by Satyajit Ray.*
In most realistic films, there is a close correspondence of the images to everyday reality. This criterion of value necessarily involves a comparison between the internal world of the movie with the external milieu that the filmmaker has chosen to explore. The realistic cinema tends to deal with people from the lower social echelons, and is implicitly ideological, if not overtly didactic. The artist rarely intrudes on the materials, however, preferring to let them speak for themselves. Rather than focusing on extraordinary events, Realism tends to emphasize the basic experiences of life. It is a style that excels in making us feel the humanity of others. Beauty of form is often sacrificed in order to capture the texture of reality as it's ordinarily perceived. Realistic images often seem unmanipulated, haphazard in their design. The story materials are generally loosely organized and include many details that don't necessarily forward the plot, but are offered for their own sake to heighten the sense of authenticity. See also Robin Wood, *The Apu Trilogy* (New York: Praeger, 1971).

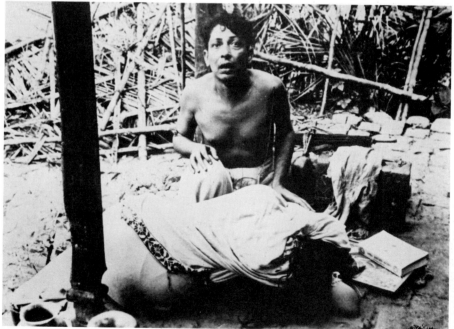

*(Audio-Brandon Films)*

**1-4. *Mr. Deeds Goes to Town* (U.S.A., 1936).**
*With Gary Cooper (with tuba); Directed by Frank Capra.*
Classical cinema avoids the extremes of Realism and Expressionism in favor of a slightly stylized presentation which has at least a surface plausibility. Movies in this form are often handsomely mounted, but the style rarely calls attention to itself. The images are determined by their relevance to the story and characters, rather than a desire for authenticity or formal beauty alone. The implicit ideal is a functional, invisible style: the pictorial elements are subordinated to the presentation of characters in action. Classical cinema is story oriented. The narrative line is seldom allowed to wander, nor is it broken up by authorial intrusions. A high premium is placed on the entertainment values of the story, which is often shaped to conform to the conventions of a popular genre. Often the characters are played by stars rather than unknown players, and their roles are sometimes tailored to showcase their personal charm. The human materials are paramount in the classical cinema. The characters are generally appealing, and slightly romanticized. The audience is encouraged to identify with their values and goals.

within the realistic end of the style spectrum. *La Strada* falls within the purview of classical cinema. *8 1/2* and most of Fellini's subsequent movies have been expressionistic in emphasis. Ingmar Bergman has also worked within this broad range of styles.

Even the terms form and content aren't so clear-cut as they may sometimes seem. In fact, in many respects the terms are synonymous, although they can certainly be useful in suggesting a degree of emphasis. The form of a shot—the way in which a subject is photographed—is its true content, not necessarily what the subject is perceived to be in reality. The communications theorist Marshall McLuhan pointed out that the content of one medium is actually another medium. For example, a photograph (visual image) depicting a man eating an apple (taste) involves two different mediums: each communicates information—content—in a different way. A verbal description of the photograph of the man eating an apple would involve yet another medium (language) which communicates information in yet another manner. In each case, the precise information is determined by the medium, although superficially all three have the same content.

In literature, the naive separation of form and content is called "the heresy of paraphrase." For example, the content of *Hamlet* can be found in a college outline, yet no one would seriously suggest that the play and outline are the same "except in form." To paraphrase artistic information is inevitably to change its content as well as its form. Artistry can never be gauged by subject matter alone. The manner of its presentation—its forms—is the true content of paintings, literature, and plays. The same applies to movies.

The French critic, André Bazin, noted: "One way of understanding better what a film is trying to say is to know how it is saying it." Bazin was putting forth the theory of organic form: the belief that form and content are symbiotic in film as well as any other kind of art. The American critic, Herman G. Weinberg, expressed the matter succinctly: "The way a story is told is part of that story. You can tell the same story badly or well; you can also tell it well enough or magnificently. It depends on who is telling the story."

Form and content are best used as relative terms. They are useful concepts for temporarily isolating specific aspects of art for the purposes of closer examination. Such an unnatural separation is artificial, of course, yet this technique can yield more detailed insights into the work of art as a whole. By beginning with an understanding of the basic components of the film medium—its various languages, as it were—we will see how form and content in the cinema, as in the other arts, are ultimately the same.

**1-5. *The Seventh Seal* (Sweden, 1957).**
*With Max Von Sydow (right) and Bengt Ekerot; Cinematography by Gunnar Fischer; Directed by Ingmar Bergman.*
The expressionist cinema is largely a director's cinema: authorial intrusion is common. There is a high degree of manipulation in the narrative materials, and the visual presentation is stylized. The story is exploited as a vehicle for the filmmaker's personal obsessions. Fidelity to objective reality is rarely a relevant criterion of value. The most artificial genres—musicals, epics, fantasy films—are generally classified as expressionistic. Expressionist movies tend to deal with extraordinary characters and events—such as this mortal game of chess between a medieval knight and the figure of Death. This style of cinema excels in dealing with ideas—political, religious, philosophical—and is often the chosen medium of didactic artists. Its texture is densely symbolic: feelings are expressed through forms, like the dramatic high-contrast lighting of this shot. Expressionism is also rich in visual lyricism. It is the favored idiom of the great stylists of the cinema. See also Jörn Donner, *The Films of Ingmar Bergman* (New York: Dover, 1972).

(Janus Films)

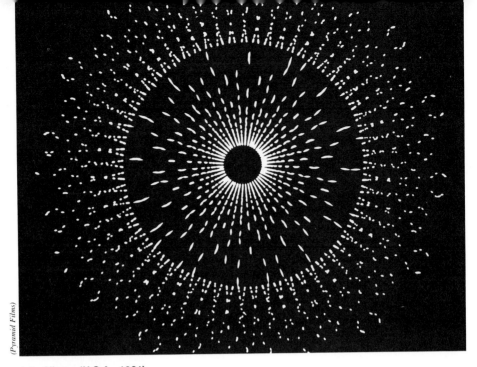

(Pyramid Films)

**1-6. *Allures* (U.S.A., 1961).**
*Directed by Jordan Belson.*
In the avant-garde cinema, subject matter is often suppressed in favor of abstraction and an emphasis on formal beauty for its own sake. Like many artists in this idiom, Belson began as a painter and was attracted to film because of its temporal and kinetic dimensions. He was strongly influenced by such European avant-garde artists as Hans Richter, who championed the "absolute film"—a graphic cinema of pure forms divorced from a recognizable subject matter. Belson's works are inspired by philosophical concepts derived primarily from Oriental religions, but these are essentially private sources and are rarely presented explicitly in the films themselves. Form is the true content of Belson's movies. His animated images are mostly geometrical shapes, dissolving and contracting circles of light, and kinetic swirls. His patterns expand, congeal, flicker, and split off into other shapes, only to reform and explode again. It is a cinema of uncompromising self-expression: personal, often inaccessible, and iconoclastic.

## The Shots and Angles

The different cinematic shots are defined by the amount of subject matter that's included within the frame of the screen. In actual practice, however, shot designations vary considerably: a medium shot for one director might be considered a closeup by another. Furthermore, the longer the shot, the less precise are the designations. In general, shots are determined on the basis of how much of the human figure is in view. The shot is not necessarily defined by the distance between the camera and the object photographed, for in some instances certain lenses distort distances. For example, a telephoto lens can produce a closeup on the screen, yet the camera in such shots is generally quite distant from the subject matter (1-26).

The more area covered by a shot, the less detailed it is, and the more abstract its form. The less area covered, the more disorienting is the image in terms of its physical context. Realist directors generally wish to preserve the spatial integrity of a scene, a sense of where details fit in a given space. Such filmmakers tend to favor the longer shots which preserve the relationships between people and their contexts. Expressionist directors, on the other hand, tend to favor the closer shots. These fragment real space into a series of detailed pieces of the whole. In actual practice, however, the choice of shots is generally a matter of emphasis rather than exclusion, for few directors can dispense with either long or close shots without confusing the audience. Although there are many different kinds of shots in the cinema, most of them are subsumed under the seven basic categories: the extreme long shot, the long shot, the full shot, the medium shot, the closeup, the extreme closeup, and the deep-focus shot.

The *extreme long shot* is taken from a great distance, sometimes as far as a

**1-7. *Intolerance* (U.S.A., 1916).**
*Cinematography by G. W. "Billy" Bitzer; Directed by D. W. Griffith.*
Extreme long shots are almost always exterior shots, showing a vast portion of the locale. They are especially common in epic films in which the dramatic values are sweeping and larger than life. Griffith's monumental exterior set for the Babylonian sequence of this film was the largest and most costly ever constructed in its time. Bitzer, who photographed virtually all of Griffith's movies, is the first great cinematographer of the medium. Together they popularized many standard optical techniques, including the fade-out, the iris-in and iris-out, double and multiple exposures, and all kinds of masking devices to alter the shape of the screen. Griffith and Bitzer developed soft focus and "mist" (filtered) photography, back lighting, side lighting, and tinting. They introduced the point-of-view shot (photographing events as though through a character's eyes), and many types of moving camera shots. See *G. W. Bitzer: His Story* (New York: Farrar, Straus and Giroux, 1973).

*(Museum of Modern Art)*

quarter of a mile away (1-7). It's almost always an exterior shot and shows much of the locale. Extreme long shots also serve as spatial frames of reference for the closer shots, and for this reason are sometimes called establishing shots. If people are included in extreme long shots, they usually appear as mere specks on the screen. The most effective use of these shots is often found in epic films, where locale plays an important role: westerns, war films, samurai films, and historical movies. Not surprisingly, the greatest masters of the extreme long shot are those directors associated with epic genres: D. W. Griffith, Sergei Eisenstein, John Ford, and Akira Kurosawa.

The *long shot* is perhaps the most complex in the cinema, and the term itself one of the most imprecise. In general, however, long shot ranges correspond approximately to the distances between the audience and the stage in the live theatre. The closest range within this category is the full shot which just barely includes the human body in full (1-2). Charles Chaplin favored the full shot because it was best suited to the art of pantomime, yet was close enough to capture at least gross facial expressions (see 6-23). Long shots are favored by most realist directors, since they include a considerable portion of the locale as well as the human body in full. These ranges are ideally suited to those filmmakers who communicate their ideas primarily through their *mise-en-scène*—the arrangement of objects and figures within a unified space.

The *medium shot* contains a figure from the knees or waist up. A functional shot, it's useful for shooting exposition scenes, for carrying movement, and for dialogue. It's also used for transitions between closeups and the longer shots, and for re-establishing a context after a close or long shot. There are several variations of the medium shot. The *two-shot* contains two figures, from the waist up (1-8). The *three-shot* contains three figures; beyond three,

*(Columbia Pictures)*

**1-8. *His Girl Friday* (U.S.A., 1940).**
*With Cary Grant and Rosalind Russell;*
*Directed by Howard Hawks.*
The medium shot is so characteristic of the American cinema that French critics referred to it as "*le plan américain*"—the American shot. It's ideal for witty dialogue comedies like *His Girl Friday*. The medium shot was Hawks' favorite because it preserves the interplay between two personalities: The shot is close enough to allow us to see facial expressions, yet distant enough to capture a player's body language. Hawks' visual style is one of the plainest of the American cinema. "I like to tell a story as simply as possible," he explained, "with the camera at eye level." He disliked virtuoso camerawork and artful lighting effects. "I want to see the scene the way it would look if I were looking at it," he said, and that usually meant medium two-shots. Like most classical stylists, he believed that the best technique is that which seldom calls attention to itself. See also Joseph McBride, ed., *Focus on Howard Hawks* (Englewood Cliffs, N.J.: Prentice-Hall, 1972).

the shot tends to become a full shot, unless the other figures are in the background. The *over-the-shoulder shot* usually contains two figures, one with part of his or her back to the camera, the other facing the camera. This shot is useful as a variation of the standard two-shot, and as a way of emphasizing one person's dominance over another (2-32).

The *closeup* shows very little if any locale, and concentrates on a relatively small object—the human face, for example (1-12). Since the closeup magnifies the size of an object, it tends to elevate the importance of things, often suggesting a symbolic significance. In Hitchcock's *Notorious*, for example, the heroine suddenly realizes that she's gradually being poisoned by her evening coffee.

**1-9. *Citizen Kane* (U.S.A., 1941).**

*With Orson Welles, Joseph Cotten, and Everett Sloane (at far end of table); Cinematography by Gregg Toland; Directed by Welles.*

Much of this film was shot in deep focus, which is meant to be admired for its virtuosity as well as its functionalism. In this shot, the space between Kane (Welles) and his two associates (Cotten and Sloane) suggests a certain estrangement, for they have to shout at each other in order to be heard—a technique the director uses in many scenes. André Bazin, an enthusiastic champion of deep-focus photography, believed that this technique reduces the importance of editing and preserves the cohesiveness of real space and time. Many spatial planes can be captured simultaneously in a single take, maintaining the objectivity of a scene. Bazin felt that audiences were thus encouraged to be more creative—less passive—in understanding the relationship between people and things. Deep focus permits viewers to enjoy the same freedom they enjoy in real life. In this photo, for example, we are free to look at the faces of over two dozen characters. "The public may choose, with its eyes, what it wants to see of a shot," Welles said. "I don't like to force it."

(RKO)

Suddenly, a close shot of the coffee cup appears on the screen—a huge distortion of its real size. The image of the delicate demitasse captures not only the heroine's realization, but also the veneer of elegance that protects her poisoners from being detected. The image functions as a symbol of the "respectable" life style of some Nazi espionage agents near the end of World War II. The extreme closeup is a variation of this shot. Thus, instead of a face, the extreme closeup might show only a person's eyes or mouth.

The *deep-focus shot* is actually a variation of the long shot, consisting of a number of focal distances, and photographed in depth (1-9). Sometimes called a *wide-angle shot*, this technique captures objects at close, medium, and long ranges simultaneously. The shot is useful for preserving the unity of space. The objects in a deep-focus shot are carefully arranged in a succession of planes. By using this layering technique, the director can guide the viewer's eye from one distance to another and to another. Generally, the eye travels from a close range to a medium to a long (see also 7-13). A famous scene from *Citizen Kane* employs the deep-focus shot effectively. Kane's wife has attempted suicide, and is lying on her bed in a darkened room. At the bottom of the screen, in closeup range, stands an empty glass and a vial of medication; in the middle of the screen, in medium range, lies Mrs. Kane in bed; in the upper portion of the screen, in long range, Kane enters through a door. The shot also suggests a kind of cause–effect relationship: (1) the lethal dose was taken by (2) Mrs. Kane because of (3) Kane's inhumanity.

The angle from which an object is photographed can often serve as an authorial commentary on the subject matter. In a sense, angles can be likened to a writer's use of adjectives: they often reflect his or her attitude toward a subject. If the angle is slight, it can serve as a subtle form of emotional coloring. If the angle is extreme, it can represent the major meaning of an image. A picture of a person photographed from a high angle actually suggests an opposite interpretation from an image of the same person photographed from a low angle. The subject matter is identical in each image, yet in terms of the information we derive from both, it's clear that the form *is* the content, the content the form (1-10).

(a)

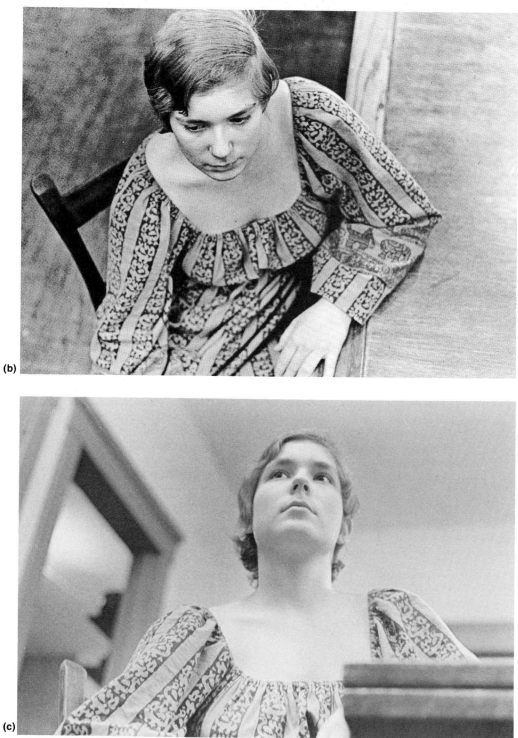

(b)

(c)

**1-10.**
Three angles of the same subject. Photos by Barry Perlus. The angle from which a subject is photographed determines much of its meaning. Here the same subject is captured from eye-level (a), and from high (b) and low (c) angles. Although the person is the same, our reactions to her vary for each angle suggests different meanings.

Directors in the realistic tradition tend to avoid extreme angles. Most of their scenes are photographed from eye level, roughly 5 to 6 feet off the ground—approximately the way an actual observer might view a scene. Usually, these directors attempt to capture the clearest view of an object. *Eye-level shots* are seldom intrinsically dramatic since they tend to be the norm. Virtually all directors use some eye-level shots, particularly in routine expository scenes.

Expressionist directors are not always concerned with the clearest image of an object, but with the image that best captures an object's essence. Extreme angles involve distortions. Yet many directors feel that by distorting the surface realism of an object, a greater truth is achieved—a symbolic truth. Both realist and expressionist directors know that the viewer tends to identify with the camera's lens. The realist wishes to make the audience forget that there's a camera at all; the expressionist is constantly calling attention to it.

There are five basic angles in the cinema: the bird's-eye view, the high angle, the eye-level shot, the low angle, and the oblique angle. As in the case of shot designations, there are many intermediate kinds of angles. For example, there can be a considerable difference between a low- and extreme low-angle shot—although usually, of course, such differences tend to be matters of degree. Generally speaking, the more extreme the angle, the more distracting and conspicuous it is in terms of the subject matter being photographed. In some cases, the commentary of the angle is more significant than the object itself.

The *bird's-eye view* is perhaps the most disorienting angle of all, for it involves photographing a scene from directly overhead (3-3). Since we seldom view events from this perspective, the subject matter of such shots might initially seem unrecognizable and abstract. For this reason, directors tend to avoid this type of camera setup. In certain contexts, however, this angle can be highly expressive. In effect, bird's-eye shots permit us to hover above a scene like all-powerful Gods. The people photographed seem antlike and insignificant. Directors whose themes revolve around the idea of fate—Hitchcock and Fritz Lang, for example—tend to favor high angles. Occasionally these filmmakers use a bird's-eye shot at the moment of destiny's greatest impact—as in the famous stairs murder in *Psycho.*

Ordinary *high-angle shots* are not so extreme, and therefore not so disorienting. The camera is placed on a crane, or some natural high promontory, but the sense of audience omnipotence is not overwhelming. Somewhat akin to the omniscient point of view in literature, high angles give a viewer a sense of a general overview, but not necessarily one implying destiny or fate. In terms of the object photographed, high angles reduce the height of objects. Movement is slowed down: this angle tends to be ineffective for conveying a sense of speed, useful for suggesting tediousness. The importance of setting or environment is increased: the locale often seems to swallow people. High angles reduce the importance of a subject. A person seems harmless and insignificant photographed from above (1-11). This angle is also effective for conveying a character's sense of self-contempt.

**1-11. *Bonnie and Clyde* (U.S.A., 1967).**
*With Warren Beatty and Faye Dunaway; Cinematography by Burnett Guffey; Directed by Arthur Penn.*
High angles tend to suggest powerlessness, entrapment, or assailability. The higher the angle, the more it tends to imply fatality. See also Robin Wood, *Arthur Penn* (New York: Praeger, 1970); and John G. Cawelti, *Focus on Bonnie and Clyde* (Englewood Cliffs, N.J.: Prentice-Hall, 1973).

But dramatic context always takes precedence over formal conventions. In Hitchcock's *North by Northwest,* for example, a high-angle shot produces the opposite effect. The villain has just learned that his mistress is an enemy agent. Within minutes, they will be flying over the ocean on a mission. The villain confides his solution to his henchman: "This matter is best disposed of from a great height . . . over water." As he says this, the camera sweeps up to an extreme high angle. The effect is not to emphasize the villain's vulnerability, but the heroine's. The angle also increases our own sense of insecurity since we identify strongly with her.

There are some directors who avoid angles because they are too manipulative and morally loaded. In the works of the Japanese master, Yasujiro Ozu, the camera is usually placed 4 feet from the floor—where an actual observer would view the events seated Japanese style. Ozu treats his characters as equals, and he discourages us from viewing them either condescendingly or sentimentally. For the most part, they are ordinary people, neither very virtuous nor very corrupt, but Ozu lets them reveal themselves. He believed that value judgments are implied through the use of angles, and kept his camera neutral and dispassionate. *Eye-level shots* permit viewers to make up their own minds about what kind of people are being presented (see 2-4).

*Low angles* have the opposite effect of high: they increase height, and thus are useful for suggesting verticality. More practically, they can increase a short actor's height. Motion is speeded up, and in scenes of violence especially, low angles can capture a sense of confusion. The battle scenes of Kurosawa's *Seven*

**1-12.** *The Loneliness of the Long-Distance Runner* **(Great Britain, 1962).**
*With Tom Courtenay; Cinematography by Walter Lassally; Directed by Tony Richardson.*
Low angles can be used to make characters more heroic, larger than life. Based on a novel by Alan Sillitoe (who also wrote the screenplay), this movie deals with a defiant working-class youth who refuses to be cowed by a system that exploits him.

*(Audio-Brandon Films)*

*Samurai* are magnificently effective, in part because many of them are photographed from low positions. Environment is usually minimized in low angle, and often the sky or a ceiling is the only background (1-12). There are exceptions, however. In *Citizen Kane*, the overhead ceiling is a constant reminder of how Kane is confined by his own possessions, especially his mansion. Lighting for interior low-angle shots can't be from above, its usual position (7-26), since the lights would appear in the picture (7-25). In this case, they are placed in front, on the sides, or behind. Psychologically, low angles heighten the importance of a subject. The figure looms threateningly over the spectator who is made to feel insecure and dominated. A person photographed from below inspires fear, awe, and respect (1-13). For this reason, low angles are often used in propaganda films, or scenes depicting heroism.

*(Janus Films)*

**1-13.** *Nosferatu* **(Germany, 1922).**
*With Max Schreck; Cinematography by Fritz Arno Wagner; Directed by F. W. Murnau.*
When an extreme low angle is combined with a perspective-distorting wide-angle lens, a character can seem threatening, for he looms above the camera—and us—like a towering giant. See also Lotte Eisner, *F. W. Murnau* (Berkeley, Cal.: University of California Press, 1978).

*(Continental 16)*

**1-14.** *The Third Man* **(Great Britain, 1949).**
*Cinematography by Robert Krasker; Directed by Carol Reed.*
By tilting the camera somewhat to its side, the natural horizontal and vertical lines of a scene can be converted into tense diagonals, thus producing a sense of imbalance or impending disaster. Reed uses tilt shots throughout this film, dynamizing the sinister setting—the ruins of war-shattered Vienna. Graham Greene's celebrated screenplay to the film is included in John Russell Taylor, ed., *Masterworks of the British Cinema* (New York: Harper & Row, 1974).

An *oblique angle* involves a lateral tilt of the camera. When the image is projected, the horizon is skewed. A man photographed at an oblique angle will look as though he's about to fall to one side. More prosaically, this angle is sometimes used for point-of-view shots—to suggest the imbalance of a drunk, for example. Psychologically, oblique angles suggest tension, transition, and impending movement. The natural horizontal and vertical lines are forced into unstable diagonals (1-14). Oblique angles are not often used, for they can disorient a viewer. In scenes of violence, however, they can be effective in capturing precisely this sense of visual anxiety.

### Lighting and Color

Generally speaking, the cinematographer is responsible for arranging and controlling the lighting in a film, usually at the specific or general instructions of the director. The illumination of most movies is seldom a casual matter, for lights can be used with pinpoint accuracy. Through the use of spotlights, which are highly selective in their focus and intensity, a director can guide the viewer's eyes to any area of the photographed image. Motion picture lighting is seldom static, for even the slightest movement of the camera or the subject photographed can cause the lighting to shift. Movies take so long to complete in part because of the enormous complexities involved in lighting each new shot. The cinematographer must make allowances for every movement within a continuous take. Each different color, shape, and texture reflects or absorbs differing amounts of light. If an image is photographed in depth, an even greater complication is involved, for the lighting must also be in depth. Furthermore, cinematographers don't have at their disposal most of the dark-room techniques of a still photographer: variable paper, dodging, air-

**1-15. *The Nights of Cabiria* (Italy, 1956).**
*With Giulietta Masina; Cinematography by Otello Martelli; Directed by Federico Fellini.*
Light–dark symbolism is almost inevitable in a film shot in black and white. As Fellini's title suggests, darkness is associated with sexuality, mystery, and fantasy in this movie. Light tends to be associated with clarity, truth, and reality. In this scene, Fellini's symbolism is more complex. The central character (Masina) is an absurdly comical prostitute, who fancies herself as tough, worldly, and self-sufficient. In a seedy side-street theatre she is hypnotized by a magician, and under the glare of a spotlight, she re-enacts her innocent, tender girlhood. The symbolism of the light suggests that what we are seeing is a true picture of Cabiria's nature. But this is an artificial light, one associated with the magician (a common symbol of the artist figure in Fellini's works), and therefore the light suggests an underlying truth rather than a literal one. In Fellini's films, the Italian Catholic Church is often associated with show business. Conversely, show business—even in its tackiest form—is often associated with spirituality and salvation. In this movie, it is the artist–magician who reveals Cabiria's poetic spirituality, not the priests at a religious shrine who seem more concerned with showmanship and theatricality.

*(Audio-Brandon Films)*

brushing, choice of development, enlarger filters, etc. In a color film, the subtle effects of lights and darks are often obscured, for color tends to obliterate shadings and flatten images. Color is also a distracting element. Often an object that dominates a black and white image will recede in importance when photographed in color, and vice-versa.

There are a number of different styles of lighting. Usually the style is geared to the theme and mood of the film. Comedies and musicals, for example, tend to be lit in high key, with bright, even illumination, and few conspicuous shadows (1-16). Tragedies and melodramas are often lit in high

(MGM)

**1-16. *The Wizard of Oz* (U.S.A., 1939).**
*With (left to right) Jack Haley, Ray Bolger, Frank Morgan, Judy Garland, and Bert Lahr; Cinematography by Harold Rosson; Directed by Victor Fleming.*
Unless the story dictated a different type of illumination, high key lighting was the rule at MGM, which prided itself on its cheerful, wholesome entertainment. Life was almost always sunny at Metro. High key lighting is evenly distributed, with no harsh contrasts, the details in clear view. The production values are meant to be admired, not concealed.

contrast, with harsh shafts of lights and dramatic streaks of blackness. Mysteries and thrillers are generally low key, with diffused shadows and atmospheric pools of light. Films shot in studios are generally more stylized and theatrical, whereas location photography tends to use available illumination, with a more natural style of lighting.

Lights and darks have had symbolic connotations since the dawn of man. The Bible is filled with light–dark symbolism; Rembrandt and Caravaggio used light–dark contrasts for psychological purposes as well. In general, artists have used darkness to suggest fear, evil, the unknown. Light usually suggests security, virtue, truth, joy. Because of these conventional symbolic associations, some directors deliberately reverse light–dark expectations. Hitchcock's movies attempt to jolt the viewers by exposing their shallow sense of security. By using many subjective techniques—devices forcing the viewer to identify strongly with the protagonist—Hitchcock strips away our complacency, often in the most terrifying manner. In *North by Northwest,* for example, the hero is stranded in Chicago where sinister shadows seem to threaten him at every turn—yet nothing happens. We laugh at ourselves for our paranoia. Later, the protagonist finds himself in an isolated rural area. There is total visibility for miles, and the sun glows radiantly over the flat terrain. Nothing could be more secure or boring—until suddenly a shocking outrage is committed against the hero in broad daylight. In Hitchcock's universe, paranoia turns out to be the most appropriate adjustment to life.

Lighting can be used realistically or expressionistically. The realist tends to favor available lighting, at least in exterior shots. Even out of doors, however, most directors use some lamps and reflectors, either to augment the natural light, or, on bright days, to soften the harsh contrasts produced by the sun. With the aid of special lenses and more light-sensitive film stocks, some directors have managed to dispense with artificial lighting completely. Avail-

**1-17. *Barry Lyndon* (U.S.A./Great Britain, 1975).**
*With Marisa Berenson and Murray Melvin; Cinematography by John Alcott; Directed by Stanley Kubrick.*
"What I'm after is a majestic visual experience," Kubrick has said of his movies. The visual style of *Barry Lyndon* is modeled on the paintings of the 18th century masters, especially Gainsborough and Watteau. Kubrick is a fanatic about authenticity. Since candlelight was the main source of interior illumination in the 18th century, he wanted no other source of light. He has always preferred available lighting. The lamps in his contemporary stories are not just decorative, but are equipped to provide the major illumination for a scene. He believes that the glare from a recognizable light source can produce dramatic contrasts, or wash out an image in a striking manner. In order to shoot by candlelight in this film, he asked the Zeiss Corporation to adapt a very fast (F 0.7) 50 mm still camera lens for the motion picture camera. The Zeiss Lens is the fastest in existence, and Kubrick had to have a special movie camera built to allow for its use. But he got what he wanted: the glowing interiors of *Barry Lyndon* are stunning in their beauty.

**1-18. *Murmur of the Heart* (France/Italy/West Germany, 1971).**
*With Lea Massari; Cinematography by Ricardo Aronovich; Directed by Louis Malle.*
Realistic cinematography excels in capturing a fleeting instant of beauty. This photo portrays an ordinary occurrence, yet its delicate composition and Vermeer lighting make it suitable for hanging on a museum wall.

able lighting tends to produce a documentary look in the film image, a hard-edged quality and an absence of smooth modeling (but see 1-18 and 1-25). Boris Kaufman's cinematography in *On the Waterfront* and *The Pawnbroker* is deliberately antiromantic in its harshness, largely because of his reliance on available light. Not all exterior shooting is necessarily hard-edged, however. Through the use of special lenses and additional lighting, John Ford and Akira Kurosawa were able to evoke a nostalgic romantic past while still using actual locations. For interior shots, realists tend to prefer images with an obvious light source—a window or a lamp. Or they often use a diffused kind of lighting with no artificial, strong contrasts. In short, the realist doesn't use conspicuous lighting unless its source is contextually probable.

The expressionist uses light less literally. He is guided by its symbolic implications and will often stress these qualities by deliberately distorting natural light patterns (1-19). A face lighted from below almost always appears sinister, even if the actor assumes a totally neutral expression. Similarly, an obstruction placed in front of a light source can assume frightening implications, for it tends to threaten our sense of safety. On the other hand, in some contexts, especially in exterior shots, a silhouette effect can be soft and romantic, perhaps because the open space acts as a counter to the sense of entrapment of a confined interior. When a face is obviously lighted from above, a certain angelic effect is the result. "Spiritual" lighting of this type tends to border on the cliché, however, and only the best cinematographers have handled this technique with subtlety. When a face is lighted only from the front, its sculptural contours tend to be flattened out. Such flat images are seldom found in professionally photographed films and are associated with amateur movie making. Back lighting, which is a kind of semisilhouetting, is soft and ethereal. Love scenes are often photographed with a halo effect

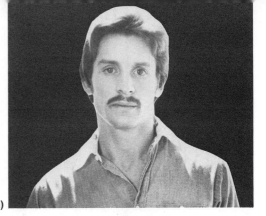

(a)

(b)

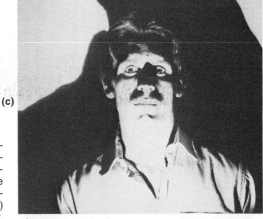

(c)

**1-19.**
Four lighting sources on the same subject. Photos by Evelyn Hayes. The lighting of a subject can be of greater importance than the subject itself. Here are four examples of how form (light) can determine content. Lighting from above (a) tends to create a romantic halo effect, suggesting spirituality. A face half-plunged in darkness (b) can symbolize self-division and ambivalence. Lighting from below (c) generally makes the subject's face appear sinister, eerie. When the subject blocks out the source of light (d), viewers can be made to feel threatened, for we tend to associate light with safety.

(d)

around the heads of the lovers to give them a romantic aura (1-24). Backlighting is especially evocative when used to highlight blonde hair. In the 1930s in Hollywood, this technique was very popular and can be seen throughout the films of Ernst Lubitsch and Josef von Sternberg.

Through the use of spotlights, an image can be composed of violent contrasts of lights and darks. The surface of such images seems disfigured, torn up. The Expressionist director uses such severe contrasts for psychological and thematic purposes (1-20). In *Citizen Kane,* the mixture of decency and corruption in Kane is suggested by the contrasting lights: sometimes his face seems split in half, with one side brightly illuminated, the other plunged in darkness. One of Griffith's most powerful images in *Birth of a Nation* shows the mangled corpses of "war's peace": the grotesquely strewn bodies are lighted in such harsh contrasts that we barely recognize what's being photographed.

**1-20.** *Seven Beauties* **(Italy, 1975).**
*With Giancarlo Giannini and Elena Fiore; Cinematography by Tonino delli Colli; Directed by Lina Wertmüller.*
Light and color are crucial mediums to the expressionist filmmaker. To emphasize the comic grotesqueness of her characters, Wertmüller often uses garish lighting effects, like this glaring overhead lamp. She sometimes floods a scene with a single color—whorish reds, for example—to heighten its luridness. See also Ernest Ferlita and John R. May, *The Parables of Lina Wertmüller* (New York: Paulist Press, 1977).

*(Warner Brothers)*

*(Columbia Pictures)*

**1-21. *Crime and Punishment* (U.S.A., 1935).**

*With Peter Lorre; Cinematography by Lucien Ballard; Directed by Josef von Sternberg.*
Sternberg was a master of atmospheric lighting effects, and closely supervised the photography of his films. His stories are unfolded primarily in terms of light and shade, rather than conventional dramatic means. "Every light has a point where it is brightest, and a point toward which it wanders to lose itself completely," he explained. "The journey of rays from that central core to the outposts of blackness is the adventure and drama of light." Note how the closed form of the mise-en-scène and the light encircling the protagonist (Lorre) produce an accusatory effect, a sense of entrapment.

By deliberately permitting too much light to enter the aperture of the camera, a director can overexpose an image—producing a blanching flood of light over the entire surface of the picture. Overexposure has been most effectively used in nightmare and fantasy sequences. In Fellini's *8 1/2*, for example, the hero's recollections of a traumatic childhood experience are shown in deliberately overexposed images. Sometimes this technique can suggest a kind of horrible glaring publicity, a sense of emotional exaggeration. One sequence from Bergman's *Sawdust and Tinsel* uses overexposure to emphasize a character's anguish over a public humiliation.

Although color in film didn't become commercially widespread until the 1940s, there were many experiments in color before this period. Some of Méliès' movies, for example, were painted by hand in assembly line fashion, with each painter responsible for coloring a minute area of the film strip. The original version of *Birth of a Nation* (1915) was printed on various tinted stocks to suggest different moods: the burning of Atlanta was tinted red, the night scenes blue, the exterior love scenes pale yellow. Sophisticated film color was developed in the 1930s, but for many years a major problem was its tendency to prettify everything. If color enhanced a sense of beauty—in a musical, for example, or an historical extravaganza—the effects were often appropriate. Thus, the best feature films of the early years of color were usually those with artificial or exotic settings. The earliest color processes tended also to emphasize garishness, and often special consultants had to be called in to harmonize the color schemes of costumes, makeup, and decor. Furthermore, each color process tended to specialize in a certain base hue— red, blue, or yellow, for example—while the other colors of the spectrum were somewhat distorted. It was well into the 1950s before these problems were resolved. Compared with the subtle color perceptions of the human eye, however, and despite the apparent precision of most present-day color processing, cinematic color is still a relatively crude approximation. After the 1960s, virtually all fiction films were automatically photographed in color.

**1-22. *Manhattan* (U.S.A., 1979).**
*With Woody Allen and Diane Keaton; Cinematography by Gordon Willis; Directed by Allen.*
Allen wanted this movie to be both a homage to, and a critique of, his loved/hated city. Most of the love is expressed in the romantic Gershwin score and in Willis' rhapsodic photography. This tender silhouette is photographed at dusk in the sculpture garden of the Museum of Modern Art. Willis is one of the most admired of contemporary cinematographers. His artistry is best illustrated by his low-key atmospheric shots. Most of his major assignments have been dark films: *The Godfather, The Godfather Part II, Klute, All the President's Men, Interiors,* and *Stardust Memories.* He works closely with his directors, and tries to make their visual ideas even stronger. He is a precise craftsman, planning every detail in advance and exercising tight control over the shooting. "What is not there is sometimes more interesting than what is," he believes. His most poetic images have a stark simplicity. "In a good movie, you lead the audience along," he has pointed out. "I want the audience to get caught up in the film and not be aware of what we're doing. I don't like tricks, but I like magic. I want magic." See also James Stevenson, "Profiles: Cinematographer Gordon Willis," in *The New Yorker* (October 16, 1978).

(*United Artists*)

Exceptions to this rule, like Mel Brooks' *Young Frankenstein* and Woody Allen's *Manhattan* (1-22), were shot in black and white for nostalgic reasons, to suggest an earlier era of movies.

There are some brilliant cinematographers who have produced relatively realistic color in film, among them Lucien Ballard (*The Wild Bunch*), Sven Nykvist (*The Postman Always Rings Twice*), and Raoul Coutard (*Weekend*). In general, however, the most famous color films tend to be expressionistic. Michelangelo Antonioni's attitude is fairly typical: "It is necessary to intervene in a color film, to take away the usual reality and replace it with the reality of the moment." In *Red Desert* (photographed by Carlo Di Palma), Antonioni spray-painted natural locales to emphasize internal, psychological states. Industrial wastes, river pollution, marshes, and large stretches of terrain were painted gray to suggest the ugliness of contemporary industrial society, and the heroine's drab, wasted existence. Whenever red appears in the film, it suggests sexual passion; yet the red—like the loveless sexuality—is an ineffectual cover up of the pervasive gray.

Psychologically, color tends to be a subconscious element in film: it's strongly emotional in its appeal, expressive and atmospheric rather than con-

**1-23.** *The Lady from Shanghai* **(U.S.A., 1947).**
*With Rita Hayworth, Orson Welles, and Everett Sloane; Cinematography by Charles Lawton, Jr.; Directed by Welles.*
Great stylists like Welles are attracted to expressionistic genres because they offer the maximum opportunity for a display of visual rapture. This shootout in an abandoned fun house takes place in the hall of mirrors—a perfect visual analogue of Welles' themes—the fragmentation of personality, and the treacherous allure of beauty. *The Lady from Shanghai* and its companion piece *Touch of Evil* (7-20) are examples of the expressionistic style French critics called *film noir*—black cinema. See also Charles Higham, *The Films of Orson Welles* (Berkeley, Cal.: University of California Press, 1970).

*(Columbia Pictures)*

scious or intellectual. Psychologists have discovered that most people actively attempt to interpret the lines of a composition, but they tend to accept color passively, permitting it to suggest moods rather than objects. Lines are associated with nouns, color with adjectives. Line is sometimes thought to be masculine, color feminine. Both lines and color suggest meanings, then, but in somewhat different ways.

Since earliest times, visual artists have used color for symbolic purposes. Color symbolism is probably culturally acquired, though its implications are surprisingly similar in otherwise differing societies. In general, cool colors (blue, green, violet) tend to suggest tranquility, aloofness, and serenity. Cool colors also have a tendency to recede in an image. Warm colors (red, yellow, orange) suggest aggressiveness, violence, and stimulation. They tend to come forward in most images. Many film directors have exploited these symbolic and psychological implications. In *A Clockwork Orange,* for example, Stanley Kubrick used orange and blue as thematic motifs. The first "ultra-violent" half of the film deals with the sexual and social aggressions of the protagonist (Malcolm McDowell), and appropriately favors hot colors—oranges, reds, and pinks. The second "weepy-tragic" half shows the protagonist as victim, and most of these sequences feature cool colors, especially blues and grays. Humanity is symbolized by orange, mechanization by its complement, blue. This weird fusion of the human with the mechanical is the theme of Kubrick's film, and is suggested by the very title which was taken from Anthony Burgess' novel, the original source of the movie. Many films are organized around such symbolic color polarities.

Some directors deliberately exploit film color's natural tendency to garishness. Fellini's *Juliet of the Spirits* features many bizarre costumes and settings to suggest the tawdry but fascinating glamor of the world of show

**1-24.** *An Unmarried Woman* **(U.S.A., 1978).**
*With Jill Clayburgh and Alan Bates; Cinematography by Arthur Ornitz; Directed by Paul Mazursky.*
Even within a single film, lighting styles can vary considerably, depending on the mood of a given scene. Most of the earlier portions of this movie are photographed in a documentary style. After the protagonist (Clayburgh) falls in love, the photographic style becomes more romantic. The city's lights are etherealized by the shimmering soft-focus photography. The halo effect around the lovers' heads reinforces the air of enchantment— these are soulmates, not just lovers.

business (1-34). Similarly, the brash colors in Godard's *Weekend* are used to heighten the vulgar materialism of bourgeois life. Bob Fosse's *Cabaret* is set in Germany and shows the early rise of the Nazi party. The colors are somewhat "neurotic," with emphasis on such 1930s favorites as plum, acid green, purple, and florid combinations, like gold, black, and pink.

Directors often complain about the tendency of colors to "run away," to dominate images in a way that was never intended. Hitchcock solved this problem by simply repressing color as much as possible. In two films, he used lack of color as a symbolic comment on the drabness of Communist life. *Topaz* features a credit sequence showing a Soviet military parade in which everything (including people) is photographed in a pervasive blue-gray. Only the red stars of the huge banners and soldiers' caps "enliven" these images—a typical instance of Hitchcockian wit. In *Torn Curtain*, a refugee ex-countess wears a gay splashy scarf which is conspicuously out of keeping with her lacklustre environment, an Eastern European People's Republic. "I am not Communistical," she announces haughtily, not without a touch of pathos.

**1-25. *The Garden of the Finzi-Continis* (Italy, 1970).**
*With Dominique Sanda; Cinematography by Ennio Guarnieri; Directed by Vittorio De Sica.*
De Sica wanted this movie to be ravishingly photographed—a visual correlative to the fragile beauty of the characters and their world. He also wanted the movie to be realistic because the story deals with a shameful chapter of history—the deportation of Italian Jews to Nazi Germany. Guarnieri's cinematography triumphantly fuses these somewhat disparate needs. Even the closeups—which offer few possibilities in the art of composition—are exquisitely designed, almost abstract. Yet they were photographed primarily with available lighting, in actual locations. The photography is beautiful as well as authentic; it is also organic to the dramatic context, and to the character's enigmatic nature. Such is the art of a great cinematographer.

*(Cinema 5)*

Black and white photography in a color film is often employed for symbolic purposes. Some directors alternate whole episodes in black and white with entire sequences in color. The problem with this technique is its facile symbolism: the jolting black and white sequences are too obviously "significant" in the most arty sense. A more effective variation is simply not to use too much color, to let black and white predominate. In Tony Richardson's *Tom Jones*, the luxuriant greens of the countryside are dramatically contrasted with our first glimpse of an eighteenth-century London slum—drained of color, except for a few washed out browns, gray-blues, and yellowish whites. In De Sica's *Garden of the Finzi-Continis*, which is set in Fascist Italy, the early portions of the film are richly resplendent in shimmering golds, reds, and almost every shade of green. As political repression becomes more brutal, these colors almost imperceptibly begin to wash out, until near the end of the film, the images are dominated by whites, blacks, blue-grays, and dull browns (1-25).

## Lenses, Filters, Stocks, and Opticals

Because the camera's lens is a crude mechanism when compared to the human eye, some of the most striking effects in a film image can be achieved through the distortions of the photographic process itself. Particularly with regard to size and distance, the camera lens doesn't make psychological adjustments, but records things literally. For example, whatever is placed closest to the camera's lens will tend to appear larger than an object at a greater distance. In the deep-focus shot of *Citizen Kane* alluded to earlier, the glass and vial of medication are literally larger than Kane himself, for they stand just in front of the lens while Kane is quite distant from it. The context of the scene tells us this size difference is not literally true, of course. The setup allows Welles to convey a symbolic relationship.

Realist directors tend to use "normal" lenses in order to produce a minimum of distortion. These lenses photograph subjects more-or-less as they are perceived by the human eye. Expressionist directors often prefer lenses and filters that intensify given qualities and suppress others. Cloud formations, for example, can be exaggerated threateningly or softly diffused, depending on what kind of lens or filter is used. Different shapes, colors, and lighting intensities can be radically altered through the use of specific optical modifiers. There are literally dozens of different lenses but most of them are subsumed under three major categories: those in the nondistorting range, the telephoto lenses, and the wide-angles (1-26).

(a)

**(b)**

**(c)**

**1-26.**
Three photos of the same subject with different lenses. Photos by Barry Perlus. The camera is at the same distance from the subject in each of these shots. Photo (a) is taken with a normal lens; photo (b) with a wide angle; photo (c) with a telephoto lens. Note how perspective is undistorted in (a), elongated in (b), and flattened in (c).

The *telephoto lens* is often used to get closeups of objects from extreme distances. For example, no cinematographer is likely to want to get close enough to a wild lion to photograph an ordinary closeup. In cases such as these, the telephoto is used, thus guaranteeing the safety of the cinematographer while still producing the necessary closeup. Telephotos also permit them to work discreetly. In crowded urban locations, for example, passersby are likely to stare at a movie camera. The telephoto permits the cinematographer to remain hidden—in a truck, for example—while he or she shoots close shots through the windshield or back window of the truck. In effect, the lens works like a telescope, and because of its long focal length, it is sometimes called a *long lens*.

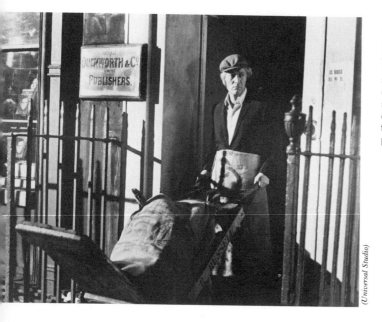

(Universal Studio)

**1-27. Frenzy (U.S.A./Great Britain, 1972).**
*With Barry Foster; Directed by Alfred Hitchcock.*
Some filters can totally transform the essential nature of the subject matter. The day-for-night filter permits a director to shoot a scene in sunlight, but because certain types of light rays are filtered out, the scene looks as though it is taking place at night.

Telephoto lenses produce a number of side effects that are sometimes exploited by directors for symbolic purposes. Most long lenses are in sharp focus on one distance plane only. Objects placed before or beyond that distance blur, go out of focus. The longer the lens, the more sensitive it is to distances, and in the case of extremely long lenses, objects placed a mere few inches away from the selected focal plane can be out of focus. This deliberate blurring of planes in the background, foreground, or both, can produce some striking photographic and atmospheric effects. In *The Garden of the Finzi-Continis*, the wealthy and short-sighted Jewish family of the title are often photographed in this manner, especially when they are in their garden, which suggests an innocent, lush Garden of Eden. The photographic blurring is symbolic of the family's naiveté and lack of political vision. They see only what is immediately before them. Everything outside—in this case, Fascist Italy—remains figuratively and literally out of focus for them.

The focal distance of long lenses can usually be adjusted while actually shooting, and thus the director is able to neutralize planes and guide the viewer's eye to various distances in a sequence—a technique sometimes called rack focusing or selective focusing. In *The Graduate,* Mike Nichols used a slight focus shift instead of a cut when he wanted the viewer to look first at the young heroine, who then blurs out of focus, then at her mother, who is standing a few feet off in a doorway. The focus-shifting technique suggests a cause–effect relationship, and parallels the heroine's sudden realization that her boyfriend's mistress is her mother. In *The French Connection,* William Friedkin used selective focus in a sequence showing a criminal under surveillance. He remains in sharp focus while the city crowds of his environment are an undifferentiated blur. At strategic moments in the sequence, Friedkin shifts the focus plane from the criminal to the dogged detective who is tailing him in the crowd.

Long lenses also flatten images, decreasing the sense of distance between depth planes. Two people standing yards apart might look inches away when photographed with a telephoto lens. With very long lenses, distance planes are so compressed that the image can resemble a flat surface of abstract patterns. When anything moves toward or away from the camera in such shots, the mobile object doesn't seem to be moving at all. In *Marathon Man,* the protagonist (Dustin Hoffman) runs desperately toward the camera, but due to the flattening of the long lens, he seems almost to be running in place rather than moving toward his destination.

The *wide-angle* or so-called *short lenses* have short focal lengths and wide

**1-28. *The Emigrants* (Sweden, 1972).**
*With Liv Ullmann and Max von Sydow; Photographed and directed by Jan Troell.*
If we were to view a scene similar to this in real life, we would probably concentrate most of our attention on the people in the wagon. But there are considerable differences between reality and cinematic Realism. Realism is an artistic style. In selecting materials from the chaotic sprawl of reality, the realist filmmaker necessarily eliminates some details and emphasizes others into a structured hierarchy of visual significance. For example, the stone wall in the foreground of this shot occupies more space than the humans. Visually, this dominance suggests that the rocks are more important than the people. The unyielding stone wall symbolizes divisiveness and exclusion—ideas that are appropriate to the dramatic context. If the wall were irrelevant to the theme, Troell would have eliminated it and selected other details from the copiousness of reality—details which would be more pertinent to the dramatic context.

angles of view. These are the lenses used in deep-focus shots, for they preserve a sharpness of focus on virtually all distance planes. The distortions involved in short lenses are both linear and spatial. The wider the angle, the more lines and shapes tend to warp, especially at the edges of the image. Distances between various depth planes are also exaggerated with these lenses: two people standing a foot away from each other can appear yards apart in a wide-angle image. *Citizen Kane* is filled with such shots. Welles' *The Trial* uses such lenses to emphasize the vast, vacuous distances between people. In closeup ranges, wide-angle lenses tend to make huge bulbs of people's noses, and slanting, sinister slits of their eyes. Welles used several such shots in *Touch of Evil*. Movement toward or away from the camera is exaggerated when photographed with a short lens: two or three ordinary steps can seem like inhumanly lengthy strides—an effective technique when a director wants to emphasize a character's strength, dominance, or ruthlessness. The *fish-eye lens* is the most extreme wide-angle modifier, and it creates such severe distortions that the lateral portions of the screen seem reflected in a sphere, as though we were looking through a crystal ball. John Frankenheimer, in his science-fiction film *Seconds*, used the fish-eye to suggest the protagonist's eerie semiconscious state.

Lenses and filters can be used for purely cosmetic purposes—to make an actor or actress taller, slimmer, younger, or older. Josef von Sternberg sometimes covered his lens with a transluscent silk stocking to give his images a gauzy, romantic aura. A few glamor actresses beyond a certain age even had clauses in their contracts stipulating that only beautifying soft-focus lenses could be used for their closeups. These optical modifiers eliminate small facial wrinkles and skin blemishes.

There are even more kinds of filters than there are lenses. Some trap light and refract it in such a way as to produce a diamondlike sparkle in the image (see 6-10). Many filters are used to supress or heighten certain colors. Color filters can be especially lovely in exterior scenes. The romantic, ethereal images of Bo Widerberg's *Elvira Madigan* were largely the result of expert filtered photography. Robert Altman's *McCabe and Mrs. Miller* (photographed by Vilmos Zsigmond) used green and blue filters for many of the exterior scenes, and yellow and orange for interiors. These filters emphasized the bitter cold of the winter setting, and the communal warmth of the rooms inside the primitive buildings.

Though there are a number of different kinds of film stocks, most of them fall within the two basic categories: fast and slow. Fast stock is highly sensitive to light, and in some cases can register images with no illumination except what's available on location, even in nighttime sequences. Slow stock is relatively insensitive to light and requires as much as ten times more illumination than fast stocks. Traditionally, slow stocks are capable of capturing colors with precision, without washing them out.

Fast stocks were commonly associated with documentary movies, for with their great sensitivity to light, these stocks can reproduce images of events while they're actually occurring. The documentarist is able to photograph people and places without having to set up cumbersome lights. Because of this light sensitivity, fast stocks produce a grainy image in which lines tend to be fuzzy and colors tend to wash out. In a black and white film, lights and darks contrast sharply, and many variations of gray can be lost (1-29).

Ordinarily, technical considerations such as these would have no place in

**1-29. Faces (U.S.A., 1968).**
*With Gena Rowlands and John Marley;
Directed by John Cassavetes.*
Fast film stocks are highly sensitive to
light and can record images with no
additional illumination except with what's
available on a set or location. These
stocks tend to produce harsh light–dark
contrasts, and grainy images. These
characteristics are deliberately heightened in Cassavetes' documentary-like
story of the disintegration of a marriage. The movie was originally shot in 16
mm, then blown up to the standard theatrical gauge of 35 mm—which greatly increased the grain content of the images.

*(The Walter Reade Organization)*

a book of this sort, but the choice of stock can produce considerable
psychological and aesthetic differences in a movie. Since the early 1960s,
many fiction filmmakers have switched to fast stocks in order to give their
images a documentary sense of urgency. Godard particularly favored the use
of fast film, and his cinematographer Raoul Coutard created some striking
effects, notwithstanding the presumed limitations of these stocks (1-33). Gillo
Pontecorvo's *The Battle of Algiers* is so harshly contrasting in its blacks and
whites, so deliberately grainy, and fuzzy in its image resolution, many viewers
assume the movie is a documentary (9-4). Pontecorvo added a title at the
beginning, stating that *all* the images were photographed specially for the
film, and no documentary footage was intercut with his own. The visual
blemishes of fast stock turn out to be aesthetic virtues in this film, for its
immediacy and realism are largely due to these technical characteristics.

   The optical printer is an elaborate machine that produces many special
effects in the cinema. It includes a camera and projector precisely aligned,
and permits the operator to rephotograph all or a portion of an existing
frame of a film. Double exposure, or the superimposition of two images, is
one of the most important of these effects, for it permits the director to
portray two levels of reality simultaneously. For this reason, the technique is

*(Museum of Modern Art)*

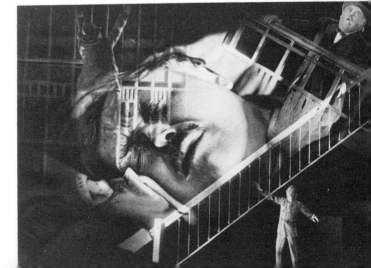

**1-30. *Secrets of a Soul* (Germany,
1926).**
*With Werner Krauss; Directed by G. W.
Pabst.*
The optical printer is an invaluable piece
of equipment, particularly to the expressionist filmmaker, for among other
things, it allows the superimposition of
two or more realities within a unified
space, as in this montage dream sequence.

often used in fantasy and dream sequences, as well as in scenes dealing with the supernatural. The optical printer can also produce multiple exposures or the superimposition of many images simultaneously. Multiple exposures are useful for suggesting mood, time lapses, and any sense of mixture—of time, places, objects, events (1-30).

Negative image—the reversing of lights and darks of the positive, or finished print—has not been much used in the cinema except by avant-garde experimentalists. Movie makers apparently find this technique too flamboyant and obscure for conventional fiction films: the viewer's light–dark expectations are literally reversed, creating a sense of .confusion (1-31). Godard used the technique with considerable effect in *Weekend* and *Alphaville*, where it suggests an x-ray effect, looking beneath the surface of things. Jean Cocteau used negative images to suggest dehumanization, the pervasiveness of death and dying.

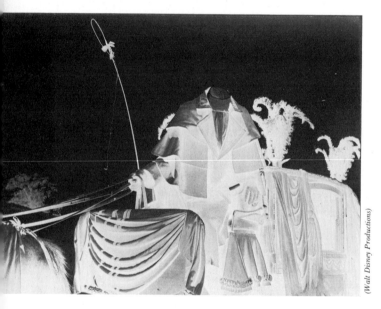

(Walt Disney Productions)

**1-31. *Darby O'Gill and the Little People* (U.S.A., 1959).**
*Directed by Robert Stevenson.*
Although negative images are seldom used in fiction films, they can be highly effective in scenes dealing with the supernatural. Negative images suggest a sense of looking beneath the surface of things and are particularly evocative in portraying ideas of death and dying.

## The Cinematographer

The cinema is a collaborative enterprise, the result of the combined efforts of many artists, technicians, and businesspeople. Because the contributions of these individuals vary from film to film, it's hard to determine who's responsible for what in a movie. Most sophisticated viewers agree that the director is generally the dominant artist in the best films. The principal collaborators—actors, writers, cinematographers—perform according to the director's unifying sensibility. But directorial dominance is an act of faith. Many movies are stamped by the personalities of others—a prestigious star, for example, or a skillful editor who manages to make sense out of a director's botched footage.

Cinematographers sometimes chuckle sardonically when a director's visual style is praised by critics. Some directors don't even bother looking

**1-32. *Metropolis* (Germany, 1926).**
*With Brigitte Helm; Cinematography by Karl Freund and Günther Rittau; Directed by Fritz Lang.*
Like many German filmmakers of his generation, Lang controlled all aspects of the visual style in his movies. He considered himself a formalist, and planned almost every detail in advance. Each night before shooting he worked at least 2 hours planning his angles, lenses, and lighting effects. He always had exact sketches of his sets, and sometimes even small-scale models to work out his shots. "Every picture has a certain rhythm which only one man can give it," Lang explained. "That man is the director. He has to be like the captain of a ship." See also Paul M. Jensen, *The Cinema of Fritz Lang* (New York: A. S. Barnes, 1969); and Frederick W. Ott, *The Films of Fritz Lang* (Secaucus: The Citadel Press, 1979).

through the viewfinder, and leave such matters as composition, angles, and lenses up to the cinematographer. When directors ignore these important formal elements, they throw away some of their most expressive pictorial opportunities and function more like stage directors, who are concerned with dramatic rather than visual values—that is, with the script and the acting rather than the photographic quality of the image itself.

On the other hand, a few cinematographers have been praised for their artistry when in fact the effectiveness of a film's images is largely due to the director's pictorial skills. Even in his earliest years, Hitchcock provided individual frame drawings for most of the shots in his films. His cinematographers framed up according to Hitchcock's precise sketches. Hence, when he claimed that he never looked through the viewfinder, he meant that he assumed his cinematographer had followed instructions. This is not to denigrate the skills of these collaborators—particularly Robert Burks, who photographed many of Hitchcock's best works. But like many cinematographers, Burks' excellence as a craftsman was based mostly on his ability to execute Hitchcock's precise requirements.

Sweeping statements about the role of the cinematographer are impossi-

(Contemporary Films)

**1-33. *Breathless* (France, 1959).**

*With Jean-Paul Belmondo (back to camera); Cinematography by Raoul Coutard; Directed by Jean-Luc Godard.*

Prior to 1959, most fiction movies were photographed with heavy cameras, lots of lights, and large technical crews. The French New Wave changed all that. In order to capture the spontaneity of the moment, Godard and others preferred the newly perfected hand-held camera, with its vastly increased mobility and flexibility. The New Wave directors also preferred fast film stock so they could shoot with available lighting. When Coutard agreed to photograph *Breathless,* Godard said to him: "I want only one thing from you. You must rediscover how to do things simply." Godard detested studio sets and artificial lighting styles, at least in this phase of his career, when he wanted to capture the utmost sense of realism in the photography. Coutard was one of the first masters of the hand-held camera. He was also able to produce striking images using only available lighting. "A film cameraman ought never to let himself forget that the eye of the spectator is naturally tuned to full daylight," Coutard observed. See Raoul Coutard, "Light of Day," in *Jean-Luc Godard* (New York: Dutton, 1968), edited by Toby Mussman; and *The Films of Jean-Luc Godard* (New York: Praeger, 1969), edited by Ian Cameron.

ble to make, for it varies widely from film to film and from director to director. Some cinematographers specialize in realistic photography. James Wong Howe, for example, insisted that all his best work was "naturalistic." Stanley Cortez and Lee Garmes, on the other hand, were at their best in expressionistic styles, with richly textured surfaces, and subtle chiaroscuro effects. In actual practice, however, virtually all cinematographers agree that the style of the photography should be geared to the story, theme, and mood of the film. William Daniels had a prestigious reputation as a glamor photographer at MGM, and for years was known as "Greta Garbo's cameraman" (see 6-13 and 7-24). Yet Daniels also shot Erich von Stroheim's harshly realistic *Greed,* and the cinematographer won an Academy Award for his work in Jules Dassin's *Naked City* which is virtually a semidocumentary. In the films of Antonioni (*La Notte, Il Grido, Eclipse*), the cinematography of Gianni Di Venanzo is austere and realistic; but in the works of Fellini (*8 1/2* and *Juliet of the Spirits*) it's extravagantly romantic (1-34). Similarly, Coutard's work for Godard is relatively

**1-34. Juliet of the Spirits (Italy, 1965).**
With Giulietta Masina (right) and Sandra Milo (center); Cinematography by Gianni Di Venanzo; Directed by Federico Fellini. Di Venanzo was one of the most flexible of cinematographers, equally at home with realistic or expressionistic movies, in the studio or on location. A brilliant colorist, as this film attests, Di Venanzo also photographed the black-and-white Surrealist images of Fellini's *8½*. See also Peter Bondanella, ed., *Federico Fellini: Essays in Criticism* (New York: Oxford University Press, 1978); and Gilbert Salachas, ed., *Federico Fellini: An Investigation into His Films and Philosophy* (New York: Crown Publishers, 1969).

(Rizzoli Films)

documentarylike; but when working for François Truffaut, Coutard's camerawork is noticeably more lyrical, as in *Jules and Jim* (11-16).

Generally speaking, the best directors tend to prefer working with the best cinematographers. The names of some cameramen are inextricably linked with specific directors: Billy Bitzer with D. W. Griffith, Edouard Tissé with Sergei Eisenstein, Sven Nykvist with Ingmar Bergman, Freddie Young with David Lean, Gregg Toland with William Wyler, and many others. Some cinematographers eventually became directors, most notably Jan Troell, George Stevens, Nicholas Roeg, Jack Cardiff, and Haskell Wexler. Lee Garmes and Raoul Coutard both tried their hand at directing, and Josef von Sternberg was a member of the American Society of Cinematographers. Cassavetes and Kubrick shoot a lot of their own footage, as do a number of other filmmakers.

During the halcyon years of the Hollywood studio system—roughly the 1930s and 1940s—some of the best cinematographers were associated with a specific studio and helped establish the semiofficial style of that studio. Each of the major studios had a characteristic "look" during this period, and it was created in part by its lighting cameramen. MGM—the most prosperous studio—was proud of its roster of cinematographers, which included Hal Rosson, William Daniels, and Ray June. At Paramount, Lee Garmes, Karl Struss, Charles B. Lang, and John F. Seitz were the big names. Warner Brothers specialized in moody low-key styles, popularized by Tony Guadio and Sol Polito, who was generally regarded as Hollywood's most gifted cinematographer of mobile camera work. For many years, Twentieth Century-Fox was the employer of Arthur C. Miller and Leon Shamroy—the first to explore Fox's new widescreen process, CinemaScope. Even the smaller studios could boast a few great cameramen, like Columbia's Joseph L. Walker. Lowly Universal had under contract two of the finest artists of the period, Russell Metty and Stanley Cortez. Independent producer Sam Goldwyn gave Gregg Toland virtual *carte blanche* to carry on his elaborate experiments in lighting. (Toland, who died tragically at the age of 44, was described by Orson Welles as the greatest American cinematographer of his generation.)

Many filmmakers understand the technology of cinematography very

**1-35. Production photo of *Deliverance* (U.S.A., 1972).**
*Cinematography by Vilmos Zsigmond (in rubber suit); Directed by John Boorman.* Cinematographers are expected to work under the most dangerous conditions, with cumbersome equipment. Zsigmond and his crew had to work from a rubber raft which swirled precariously in the currents of the wild Chattooga River in Georgia. A superlative stylist, Zsigmond has photographed such visually striking films as *McCabe and Mrs. Miller, The Long Goodbye, Scarecrow, Deliverance, The Deer Hunter,* and *Heaven's Gate.*

*(Warner Brothers)*

well. Others are totally ignorant of such matters and require impossible results. Astonishingly, these artists often manage to deliver. Cinematographers have to be extraordinarily hearty, flexible, and resourceful. Daniels, for example, was required to work in 132° heat for the Death Valley sequences of *Greed.* Cortez had to perform near-miracles for Welles in *The Magnificent Ambersons.* Often cameramen must work under water, in deep dark narrow pits, high overhead on precarious ledges, and in almost every kind of dangerous situation. The marvel is that they manage to live as long as they do, and some of them have been working continuously for five decades.

There are some great films that are photographed competently, but not necessarily with distinction. Realist directors are especially likely to prefer an unobtrusive style. Many of the works of Buñuel, for example, can only be described as "professional" in their cinematography. Buñuel is rarely interested in formal beauty—except occasionally to mock it. Rollie Totheroh, who photographed most of Chaplin's movies, merely set up his camera and let Chaplin the actor take over. Photographically speaking, there are few memorable shots in his films: what makes the images compelling is the genius of Chaplin's acting. This photographic austerity—some would consider it poverty—is especially apparent in those rare scenes when Chaplin is off-camera.

But there are far more films in which the *only* interesting or artistic quality is the cinematography. For every great work like Fritz Lang's *You Only Live Once,* Leon Shamroy had to photograph four or five bombs of the ilk of *Snow White and the Three Stooges.* Lee Garmes photographed several of von Sternberg's visually opulent films, but he also was required to shoot *My Friend Irma Goes West.* Some of James Wong Howe's most brilliant innovations—including deep-focus interior photography and ceilinged sets—were wasted on a potboiler entitled *Transatlantic* which was made ten years before *Citizen Kane,* the film usually cited as the first movie to use interior deep-focus and ceilinged sets.

In this chapter, we've been concerned with visual images largely as they relate to the art and technology of cinematography. But the camera must have materials to photograph—objects, people, settings. Through the manipulation of these materials, the director is able to convey a multitude of ideas and

(Paramount Pictures)

**1-36. Days of Heaven (U.S.A., 1978).**
*Cinematography by Nestor Almendros; Directed by Terrence Malick.*
The Spanish-born Almendros has worked primarily in France, especially with Truffaut and Eric Rohmer. *Days of Heaven* was his first American assignment and won him an Academy Award. Malick wanted the setting to suggest a lush Garden of Eden. He encouraged Almendros to make his cinematography as visually seductive as possible. Whether focusing on a closeup of a locust munching on a stalk of wheat or an extreme long shot of a rural sunrise, the images are ravishing in their lyricism.

emotions spatially. This arrangement of objects in space is referred to as a director's mise-en-scène—the subject of the following chapter.

## Further Reading

ALTON, JOHN, *Painting with Light* (New York: Macmillan, 1949). A study of the art of cinematography, with particular emphasis on lighting.

BAZIN, ANDRÉ, "The Ontology of the Photographic Image," in *What is Cinema?* (Berkeley: University of California Press, 1967). A brief theoretical exploration of the realistic nature of photography.

BIRREN, FABER, *Color, Form, and Space* (New York: Reinhold Publishing, 1961).

CLARKE, CHARLES G., *Professional Cinematography* (Hollywood: American Society of Cinematographers, 1964). A standard reference work.

FIELDING, RAYMOND, *The Techniques of Special Effects Cinematography* (New York: Hastings House, 1965). A standard scholarly study.

HIGHAM, CHARLES, ed., *Hollywood Cameramen* (Bloomington: Indiana University Press, 1970). Interviews with famous American cinematographers, including Shamroy, Garmes, Daniels, Howe, Cortez, Miller, and Karl Struss.

JOHNSON, WILLIAM, "Coming to Terms with Color." *Film Quarterly,* XX, no. 1

(1966). Reprinted in Jacobs, Lewis, ed., *The Movies as Medium* (New York: Farrar, Straus & Giroux, 1970).

KOSZARSKI, RICHARD, compiler, "The Men with the Movie Cameras: Sixty Filmographies," in *Film Comment* (Summer 1972).

MALTIN, LEONARD, ed., *Behind the Camera: The Cinematographer's Art* (New York: New American Library, 1971). Interviews with Miller, Ballard, Hal Mohr, Hal Rosson, and Conrad Hall.

MCLUHAN, MARSHALL, *Understanding Media* (New York: Signet Books, 1964). A philosophical exploration of how film and other mediums convey information and hence alter our everyday lives.

# MISE-EN-SCÈNE

Mise-en-scène (from the French, meaning literally "placing on stage") is a term borrowed from the live theatre. The phrase refers to the arrangement of all the visual elements of a theatrical production within a given space—the stage. This playing area can be defined by the proscenium arch which encloses the stage in a kind of picture frame; or the acting area can be more fluid, extending even into the auditorium. No matter what the confines of the stage may be, its mise-en-scène is always in three dimensions: objects and people are arranged in actual space, which has depth as well as height and width. This space is a continuation of the space the audience occupies, no matter how much a theatre director tries to suggest a separate "world" on the stage.

In film, mise-en-scène is a more complex term, blending the visual conventions of the theatre with the plastic arts. Like the stage director, the filmmaker arranges objects and people within a given three-dimensional space. But once this arrangement is photographed, it's converted into a two-dimensional *image* of the original. The space in the world of the movie is not the same as that occupied by the audience: only the image exists in the same physical area, like a picture in an art gallery. Mise-en-scène in movies resembles the art of painting in that an image of formal patterns is presented on a flat surface and is enclosed by a frame. But because of its theatrical heritage, cinematic mise-en-scène is also an expression of a dramatic idea, unfolding in time, through the deconstruction and reconstruction of the visual materials. In general, realistic films tend to veer toward the theatrical in terms of its visuals: that is, story, character, and dramatic continuity take precedence over

41

(RKO)

**2-1. *Notorious* (U.S.A., 1946).**

*With Ingrid Bergman, Claude Rains, and Leopoldine Konstantine; Directed by Alfred Hitchcock.*
Hitchcock always regarded himself as a formalist, calculating his effects with an extraordinary
degree of precision. He believed that an unmanipulated reality is filled with irrelevancies: "I do not
follow the geography of a set, I follow the geography of the screen," he said. The space around
actors must be orchestrated from shot to shot. "I think only of that white screen that has to be filled
up the way you fill up a canvas. That's why I draw rough setups for the cameraman." Here, the
mise-en-scène is a perfect analogue of the heroine's sense of entrapment, without violating the
civilized veneer demanded by the dramatic context. The dialogue in such instances can be perfectly
neutral, for the psychological tensions are conveyed by the placement of the camera and the way
the characters are arranged in space. See François Truffaut (with the collaboration of Helen G.
Scott), *Hitchcock* (New York: Simon and Schuster, 1967). Truffaut's classic interview is copiously
illustrated with frame enlargements from most of Hitchcock's works.

purely formal beauty. Expressionistic movies tend toward painting, with images of striking pictorial richness and formal complexity—images that aren't necessarily dictated by the narrative context.

## The Frame

Each movie image is enclosed by the frame of the screen, which defines the world of the film from the actual world of the darkened auditorium. Unlike the painter or still photographer, the film director doesn't regard each framed composition as self-sufficient. Like drama, film is a temporal as well as a spatial art, and consequently, the visuals are constantly in flux: the compositions are broken down, redefined, and reassembled before our eyes. A single-frame image from a movie is necessarily an artificially frozen moment which was never intended to be wrenched from its context in time and motion. For critical purposes, it's sometimes necessary to analyze a still frame in

(a)

**2-2. *2001: A Space Odyssey* (U.S.A./
Great Britain, 1968).**
*Directed by Stanley Kubrick.*
The widescreen is particularly suited to
capturing the vastness of a locale. If this
image were cropped to a conventional
aspect ratio (b), much of the feel of the
infinity of space would be sacrificed. We
tend to scan an image from left to right,
and therefore, in Kubrick's composition
(a), the astronaut seems to be in danger
of slipping off into the endlessness of
space. If the composition is turned upside
down, however (c), the astronaut seems
to be coming home into the safety of the
spacecraft. See also Jerome Agel, ed.,
*The Making of Kubrick's 2001* (New
York: A Signet Book, 1970); and Caroline
Geduld, *Filmguide to 2001: A Space
Odyssey* (Bloomington, Ind.: Indiana
University Press, 1973).

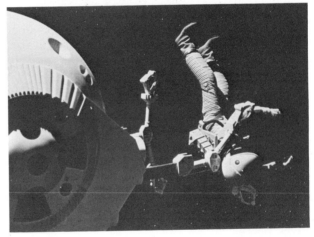

(b)

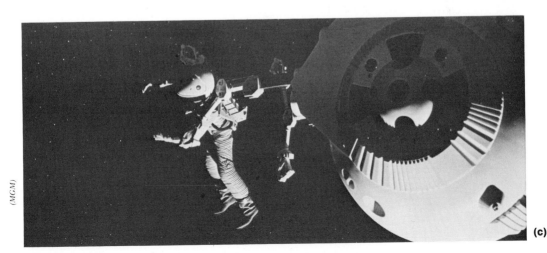

(c)

isolation, but the viewer ought to make due allowances for the dramatic and temporal contexts of the image.

The frame functions as the basis of composition in a movie image. Unlike the painter or still photographer, however, the film director doesn't fit the frame to the composition, but the compositions to a single-sized frame, whose horizontal and vertical ratios remain constant throughout the movie. Screens come in a wide variety of ratios, especially since the introduction of widescreen in the early 1950s, but most conventionally shaped frames have a ratio of approximately 4 by 3. Widescreens are roughly 5 by 3, although they can be as extreme as 2.5 by 1—as in the movies of the Hungarian director, Miklós Jancsó, for example. In such instances, the screen shape can be likened more to a long narrow mural than to a conventional painting.

Some films originally photographed in widescreen are cropped down to a conventional aspect ratio after their initial commercial release. This appalling practice is commonplace in movies which are reduced from 35 mm to 16 mm, the standard gauge used in most noncommercial exhibitions, like those at colleges and museums. Needless to say, the more brilliantly the widescreen is used, the more a movie is likely to suffer when its aspect ratio is diddled with in this manner. Generally, at least a third of the image is hacked away by lopping off the lateral edges of the frame. This kind of cropping can result in many visual absurdities: a speaker at the edge of the frame might be totally absent in the "revised" composition, or an actor might react in horror at something that never even comes into view. When shown on television—which has a 4 by 3 aspect ratio—some of the greatest widescreen films can actually look poorly composed. A few movies—like Kubrick's *2001* and Jancsó's *The Red and the White*—probably wouldn't even make sense on TV, so subtly is the mise-en-scène distributed over the entire surface of the widescreen.

*(Universal Pictures)*

**2-3. *The Incredible Shrinking Man* (U.S.A., 1957).**
*With Grant Williams; Directed by Jack Arnold.*
The mise-en-scène of the live theatre is scaled in proportion to the human figure. Cinematic mise-en-scène can be microscopic or cosmic (2-2) with equal ease, thanks to the magic of special effects. In this photo, for example, the mise-en-scène represents only a few inches of space: its scale is defined not by the human figure, but by the box of matches and the size of the common pin which the dwindling hero is attempting to convert into a weapon.

In the plastic arts, frame dimensions are governed by the nature of the subject matter. Thus, a painting of a skyscraper is likely to be vertical in shape, and would be framed accordingly. Similarly, a vast panoramic scene would probably be more horizontal in its dimensions. But in movies, the frame ratio is externally imposed, and isn't necessarily governed by the intrinsic nature of the materials photographed. This is not to say that all film images are therefore inorganic, however, for in this regard, the filmmaker can be likened to a sonneteer who chooses this rigid form precisely because of the technical challenges it presents. Much of the enjoyment we derive from reading a sonnet results from the tension between the content and the form—which consists of fourteen intricately rhymed lines. When technique and subject matter are perfectly fused in this way, our aesthetic pleasure is heightened. The same principle can be applied to framing in film.

The constant size of the movie frame is especially difficult to overcome in vertical compositions: a sense of height must be conveyed in spite of the dominantly horizontal shape of the screen. One method of overcoming this problem is through masking. In *Intolerance,* for example, D. W. Griffith blocked out portions of his images through the use of black masks, which in effect connected the darkened portion of the screen with the darkness of the auditorium. To emphasize the steep fall of a soldier from a wall, the sides of

**2-4.** *Tokyo Story* **(Japan, 1953).**
*With Chishu Ryu (second from left) and Setsuko Hara (second from right); Directed by Yasujiro Ozu.*
Ozu's mise-en-scène is usually formal, its compositional weights balanced with exquisite delicacy. Note how the diagonal thrust of the tree branches (in an image otherwise composed of stately verticals and horizontals) counteracts the weight of the three figures on the right. The scene is staged within a prosceniumlike enclosure—a frame within a frame—reinforcing its ceremonial dignity. Ozu exploits these formal compositions as ironic foils to the human materials: the intense emotions of the characters are often at odds with the decorum prescribed by such social rituals. "The Ozu scene is balanced, asymmetrical, pleasing to the eye; it is at the same time rigid and uncompromising, as all empty compositions are," Donald Richie has pointed out. "When the actor enters and behaves in a way contrary to the expectations created by such a formal decor, the result is an often touching spontaneity. This composition, then, exists but to be broken." See also 6-27. The definitive study in English of Ozu's art is Donald Richie, *Ozu* (Berkeley, Cal.: University of California Press, 1974).

(New Yorker Films)

the image were masked out. To stress the vast horizon of a location, Griffith masked out the lower third of the image—thus creating a widescreen effect. Many kinds of masks are used in this film, including diagonal, circular, and oval shapes. Some years later, the Soviet director Eisenstein urged the adoption of a square screen, on which masked images could be projected in whatever shape was appropriate to the subject matter.

In the days of silent movies, the iris (a circular or oval mask which can open up or close in on a subject) was rather overused. In the hands of a master, however, the iris can be a powerful dramatic statement. In *The Magnificent Ambersons,* for example, Orson Welles irised in on a primitive auto chugging precariously over a hill, the camera at an extreme long shot range. The iris suggests a snuffing out of such nostalgic scenes, a zeroing-in effect, as though the open-air auto were being squeezed into a tunnel of constricting darkness. In *The Wild Child,* François Truffaut used an iris to suggest the intense concentration of a young boy: the surrounding blackness is a metaphor of how the youngster blocks out his social environment while focusing on an object immediately in front of him. Iris shots of this kind can suggest symbolic ideas precisely because the odd shape of the screen violates our expectations of a stable frame ratio (2-5).

(Twentieth Century-Fox)

**2-5. The Stunt Man (U.S.A., 1980).** *Directed by Richard Rush.* Although extremely popular during the silent period, iris shots were rarely used after the advent of talkies. Contemporary directors occasionally use this technique for nostalgic reasons, to suggest an earlier era of filmmaking. For example, among other things, this movie deals with the making of a World War I aviation picture.

Masking shots fell from favor in the late 1920s, perhaps because this technique tends to call attention to itself. Realist directors are especially wary of such authorial intrusions, which they regard as too flamboyant a distortion of the frame size. Such filmmakers tend to prefer a more subtle and natural type of mask. By placing a tall object between two framing devices (in a doorway, for example, or between two trees), the lateral portions of the composition are in a sense neutralized, and the resultant visual effect is vertical. Low angles and a profusion of vertical lines also tend to counteract the horizontal dominance of the frame.

As an aesthetic device, the frame performs in several ways. The sensitive director is just as concerned with what's left out of the frame as with what's included. The frame selects and delimits the subject, editing out all irrelevancies, and presenting us with only isolated fragments of reality. The materials included within a shot are unified by the frame which in effect imposes an order on them—the order that art carves out of the chaos of reality. The frame also functions as an emphatic technique which permits the director to confer special attention on what might otherwise be overlooked in a wider context. Especially in closeups, the enclosing frame can pinpoint the most minute details.

The movie frame can function as a symbol of other types of enclosures. Some directors use it voyeuristically. In many of the films of Hitchcock, for example, the frame is likened to a window through which the audience may satisfy its impulse to pry into the intimate details of the characters' lives. In fact, *Psycho* and *Rear Window* employ this peeping technique literally. Other directors use the frame in a less snooping manner. In Jean Renoir's *The Golden Coach,* for instance, the frame suggests the proscenium arch of the theatre, and appropriately so, since the controlling metaphor of the movie centers on the idea of life as a stage.

Most of the metaphors and symbols in the cinema derive from the physi-

**2-6. *Greed* (U.S.A., 1924).**
*With Gibson Gowland (left) and Jean Hersholt; Directed by Erich von Stroheim.*
Highly symmetrical designs are generally employed when a director wishes to stress stability and harmony. In this photo, for example, the carefully balanced weights of the design reinforce these (temporary) qualities. The visual elements are neatly juxtaposed in units of twos, with the two beer-filled glasses forming the focal point. The main figures balance each other, as do the two converging brick walls, the two windows, the two people in each window, the shape of the picture above the men, and the shape of the resting dog below them. See also Thomas Quinn Curtiss, *Von Stroheim* (New York: Vintage Books, 1973); and Joel W. Finler, *Stroheim* (Berkeley, Cal.: University of California Press, 1968).

(MGM)

cal properties of the medium. For example, certain areas within the frame can suggest symbolic ideas. By placing an object or actor in a particular location within the frame, the director can comment on that object or character. Placement within the frame is another instance of how form is actually content. Each of the major portions of the frame—center, top, bottom, and edges—can be exploited for such symbolic purposes.

The central portions of the screen are generally reserved for the most important visual elements. This area is regarded by most people as the intrinsic center of interest. When we take a snapshot of a friend, we generally center his or her figure within the confines of the viewfinder. Since childhood, we have been taught that a drawing must be balanced, with the middle serving as the focal point. The center, then, is a kind of norm: we expect dominant visual information to be placed there. Precisely because of this expectation, objects placed in the center tend to be visually undramatic. Realist filmmakers favor central dominance because formally it's the most unobtrusive kind of framing, and the viewer is allowed to concentrate on the subject matter without being distracted by peripheral visual elements. However, even expressionists use the middle of the screen for dominance in routine expository shots.

**2-7. *Midnight Express* (U.S.A., 1978).**
*With Brad Davis (hands raised); Directed by Alan Parker.*
All of the compositional elements in this shot contribute to a sense of entrapment. The protagonist is totally surrounded, not only by the ring of soldiers who have their guns poised for a kill, but also by an outer ring of compositional weights—the airplane above, the stairs and railing to the left, the bench and huddled bystanders at the lower portions of the frame, and the three gunmen sealing off the right. The gridlike lines of the concrete runway also reinforce the sense of entrapment. The image might almost be entitled No Exit.

The area near the top of the frame can suggest ideas dealing with power and aspiration. A figure placed here seems to control the visual elements below, and for this reason authority figures are often photographed in this manner. In images suggesting spirituality, the top of the frame can be exploited to convey a Godlike splendor. This grandeur can also apply to objects—a palace, for example, or the top of a mountain. If an unattractive character is placed near the top of the screen, he or she can seem threatening and dangerous, being in a position of superiority over the other figures within the frame (2-34). However, these generalizations are true only when the other figures are approximately the same size or smaller than the dominating figure.

The top of the frame is not always used in this symbolic manner. In some instances, this is simply the most sensible area to place an object. In a medium shot of a figure, for example, the person's head is going to be near the top of

**2-8. *The General* (U.S.A., 1926).**
*With Buster Keaton; Directed by Keaton and Clyde Bruckman.*
Keaton was a master of classical composition. His visual style is sophisticated and elegant, yet at the same time functional, simple, direct. His comedy is essentially spatial, and derives its humor from the way in which Buster masters—or is mastered by—objects in a unified space. Keaton's visual gags are impeccably framed, without an inch of wasted space. Almost any random shot demonstrates an acute sensitivity to how much—or how little—visual information is necessary to maximize the shot's impact. See also *Buster Keaton's The General,* Richard J. Anobile, ed. (New York: Crown Publishers, 1976), a continuity of frame enlargements from the film; E. Rubinstein, *Filmguide to The General* (Bloomington, Ind.: Indiana Univ. Press, 1973); George Wead and George Lellis, *The Film Career of Buster Keaton* (Boston: G. K. Hall, 1977).

(Audio Brandon Films)

the screen, but obviously this kind of framing is not meant to be symbolic—it's merely logical, since that's where we would expect the head to appear in most medium shots. Indeed, mise-en-scène is essentially an art of the long and extreme long shot. When the subject matter is detailed in closer shots, the director has fewer options concerning the distribution of visual elements. In a closeup, for example, it's virtually impossible to exploit areas within the frame for symbolic purposes because such symbolism usually requires a certain amount of contrast with other elements within the frame.

The areas near the bottom of the frame tend to suggest opposite meanings from the top: subservience, vulnerability, and powerlessness. Objects and figures placed in these positions seem to be in danger of slipping out of the frame entirely. For this reason, these areas are often exploited symbolically to suggest danger. When there are two or more figures in the frame and they are approximately the same size, the figure nearer the bottom of the screen tends to be dominated by those from above. Even when the top and middle portions of the screen are empty, figures placed near the lower part of the frame can seem vulnerable, perhaps because we expect something or someone to fill in the space above the figures. Art as well as nature abhors a vacuum.

The left and right edges of the frame tend to suggest insignificance since these are the farthest removed areas from the center of the screen. Many mediocre films shot in widescreen can be cropped to a conventional aspect ratio precisely because their directors place only incidental details in these portions of the screen. But when images can be de-scoped without significant visual damage, we can be reasonably assured that the director had only pedestrian pictorial talents to begin with, for there's not much point in using widescreen unless one plans to exploit its artistic advantages. Objects and figures placed near the edges of the screen are literally close to the darkness outside the frame. Many directors use this darkness to suggest ideas traditionally associated with the lack of light—the unknown, the unseen, and the fearful. In some instances, the blackness outside the frame can symbolize oblivion or even death. In films about people who want to remain anonymous and unnoticed, the director sometimes deliberately places them off-center, near the "insignificant" edges of the screen. Michelangelo Antonioni uses this technique throughout much of *Red Desert*.

Finally, there are some instances when a director places the most important visual elements completely off-frame. Particularly when a character is associated with darkness, mystery, or death, this technique can be highly effective, for the audience is most fearful of what it can't see. In the early portions of Fritz Lang's *M*, for example, the psychotic child-killer is never seen directly. We can only sense his presence, for he lurks in the darkness outside the frame. Occasionally, we catch a glimpse of his shadow streaking across the set, and we're aware of his presence by the eerie tune he whistles off-screen when he is excited or upset.

There are two other off-frame areas which can be exploited for symbolic purposes: the space behind the set and the space behind or just before the camera. By not showing us what is happening behind a closed door, the filmmaker can pique the viewer's curiosity, creating an unsettling effect, for we tend to fill in such vacuums with vivid imaginings. The final shot from Hitchcock's *Notorious* is a good example. The hero helps the drugged heroine past a group of Nazi agents to a waiting auto. The rather sympathetic villain

(Claude Rains) escorts the two, hoping his colleagues will not become suspicious. In a deep-focus long shot, we see the three principals in the foreground while the Nazi agents remain near the open door of the house in the upper background—watching, wondering. The hero maliciously locks the villain out of the car, which then drives out of frame, leaving the villain stranded without an explanation. His colleagues call out his name, and he is forced to return to the house, dreading the worst. He climbs the stairs and re-enters the house with the suspicious agents, who then close the door behind them. Hitchcock never shows what happens behind the door. The area behind the camera can also create unsettling effects of this sort. In John Huston's *The Maltese Falcon*, for example, we witness a murder without ever seeing the killer. The victim is photographed in a medium shot as a gun enters the frame from just in front of the camera. Not until the end of the movie do we discover the identity of the off-frame killer.

## Composition

Although the photographable materials of movies exist in three dimensions, one of the primary problems facing the film director is much like that confronting the painter: the arrangement of shapes, colors, lines, and textures on a flat rectangular surface. In the classical cinema, this arrangement is generally held in some kind of balance, or harmonious equilibrium. The desire for balance is analogous to people balancing on their feet, and indeed to most man-made structures which are balanced on the surface of the earth. Instinctively, we assume that balance is the norm in most human enterprises.

In movies, however, there are some important exceptions to this rule. When a visual artist wishes to stress a *lack* of equilibrium, many of the standard conventions of classical composition are deliberately violated. In movies, the dramatic context is usually the determining factor in composition. What is superficially a bad composition might actually be highly effective, depending on its psychological context. Many films are concerned with neurotic characters or events that are out of joint. In such cases, the director might well ignore the conventions of classical composition. Instead of centering a character in the image, his or her spiritual maladjustment can be conveyed symbolically, by photographing the subject at the edge of the frame. In this manner, the director throws off the visual balance and presents us with an image that's psychologically more appropriate to the dramatic context. There are no set rules about these matters. Classical filmmakers like Buster Keaton and John Ford used mostly balanced compositions. Filmmakers outside the classical tradition tend to favor compositions that are asymmetrical or off-center. In movies there are a variety of techniques to convey the same ideas and emotions. Some filmmakers favor visual methods, others favor dialogue, still others editing or acting. Ultimately, whatever *works* is right.

The human eye automatically attempts to harmonize the formal elements of a composition into a unified whole. The eye can detect as many as seven or eight major elements of a composition simultaneously. In most cases, however, the eye doesn't wander promiscuously over the surface of an image, but is guided to specific areas in sequence. The director accomplishes this through the use of a *dominant contrast*, which is also known as the *dominant*.

(Columbia Pictures)

**2-9. *Macbeth* (U.S.A./Great Britain, 1971).**
*With Francesca Annis and Jon Finch; Directed by Roman Polanski.*
Movie images are generally scanned in a structured sequence of eye-stops. The eye is first attracted to a dominant contrast which compels our most immediate attention by virtue of its conspicuousness, and then travels to the subsidiary areas of interest within the frame. In this photo, for example, the eye is initially attracted to the face of Lady Macbeth, which is lit in high contrast and is surrounded by darkness. We then scan the brightly lit "empty" space between her and her husband. The third area of interest is Macbeth's thoughtful face which is lit in a more subdued manner. The visual interest of this photo corresponds to the dramatic context of the film, for Lady Macbeth is slowly descending into madness and feels spiritually alienated and isolated from her husband.

The dominant is that area of an image which immediately attracts our attention because of a conspicuous and compelling contrast. It stands out in some kind of isolation from the other elements within the image. In black and white movies, the dominant contrast is generally achieved through a juxtaposition of lights and darks. For example, if the director wishes the viewer to look first at an actor's hand, rather than his face, the lighting of the hand would probably be harsher than the face, which would be lit in a more subdued manner. In color films, the dominant is often achieved by having one color stand out from the others. Virtually any formal element can be used as a dominant contrast: a shape, a line, a texture, and so on.

After the viewer takes in the dominant contrast, his eye then scans the subsidiary contrasts which the artist has arranged to act as counterbalancing devices to the dominant. Our eyes are seldom at rest with visual compositions, then, even with paintings or still photographs. We look somewhere first, then we look at those areas of diminishing interest. None of this is accidental, for visual artists deliberately structure their images so that a specific temporal sequence is followed. In short, movement in film isn't confined only to objects and people that are literally in motion.

In most cases, the visual interest of the dominant corresponds with the dramatic interest of the image. Since films have temporal and dramatic contexts, however, the dominant is often movement itself and what some aestheticians call intrinsic interest. Intrinsic interest simply means that the audience, through the context of a story, knows that an object is more important dramatically than it appears to be visually. Thus, despite the fact that a gun might occupy only a small portion of the surface of an image, if we know that the gun is *dramatically* important, it will assume dominance in the picture despite its visual insignificance. In *The Pawnbroker*, for example, Sidney Lumet wanted to show the relative indifference of city dwellers to a murder that has just taken place. A youth's body lies bleeding on the sidewalk, while people pass by or stare impassively. In a number of shots, his body isn't even visible to the viewer, but because of its intrinsic interest, it takes over as the dominant of these images (2-10).

**2-10. *The Pawnbroker* (U.S.A., 1965).**
*Directed by Sidney Lumet.*
The dominant contrast of this shot would ordinarily be the police car, since it constitutes the area of greatest visual contrast. In this shot, however, the intrinsic interest of the wounded youth (hidden by the crowd) is the dominant. The dramatic context of a movie always takes precedence over formal considerations.

*(Audio Brandon Films)*

Even a third-rate director can guide the viewer's eyes through the use of movement, for motion is almost always an automatic dominant contrast. For this reason, lazy directors ignore the potential richness of their images, and rely solely on movement as a means of capturing the viewer's attention. On the other hand, most directors will vary their dominants, sometimes emphasizing motion, other times using movement as a subsidiary contrast only. The importance of motion varies with the kind of shot used. Movement tends to be less distracting in the longer shots, and highly conspicuous in the closer ranges.

Unless the viewer has time to explore the surface of an image at leisure, visual confusion can result when there are more than eight or nine major compositional elements. If visual confusion is the deliberate intention of an image—as in a battle scene, for example—the director will sometimes overload the composition in order to produce this effect (2-11). In general, the eye

**2-11.** *The Apprenticeship of Duddy Kravitz* (Canada, 1974).
*With Richard Dreyfuss; Directed by Ted Kotcheff.*
In shots emphasizing disorder or confusion, the film director sometimes deliberately overloads the composition in order to produce a corresponding sense of visual chaos. In this photo, for example, the lines, shapes, and compositional weights form no discernible design: the protagonist seems to be sinking into a morass of clutter.

*(Paramount Pictures)*

struggles to unify various elements into an ordered pattern. For example, even in a complex design, the eye will connect similar shapes, colors, textures, etc. The very repetition of a formal element can suggest the repetition of an experience (3-6). These connections form a visual rhythm, forcing the eye to leap over the surface of the design in order to perceive the overall balance.

Visual artists often refer to compositional elements as weights. In most cases, especially in classical cinema, the artist distributes these weights harmoniously over the surface of the image. In a totally symmetrical design—almost never found in fiction movies—the visual weights are distributed evenly, with the center of the composition as the axis point (see 1-6). Since most compositions are asymmetrical, however, the weight of one element is counterpoised with another. A shape, for example, counteracts the weight of a color. Psychologists and art theorists have discovered that certain portions of a composition are intrinsically weighted. The German art historian Wölfflin,

**2-12.** *Superman* **(U.S.A./Great Britain, 1978).**

*With Glenn Ford; Directed by Richard Donner.*

Because the top half of the frame tends to be intrinsically heavier than the bottom, directors usually keep their horizon well above the middle of the composition. They also place most of the visual weights in the lower portions of the screen. When a filmmaker wishes to emphasize the vulnerability of the characters, however, the horizon is often lowered, and sometimes the heaviest visual elements are placed above the characters. In this witty shot, for example, the parents of little Clark Kent are astonished—and visually imperiled—by the superhuman strength of their adopted son.

*(Warner Brothers)*

for instance pointed out that we tend to scan pictures from left to right, all other compositional elements being equal. Especially in classical compositions, the image is often more heavily weighted on the left to counteract the intrinsic heaviness of the right.

The upper part of the composition is heavier than the lower. For this reason, skyscrapers, columns, and obelisques taper upward or they would appear top-heavy. Images seem more balanced when the center of gravity is kept low, with most of the weights in the bottom portion of the screen. A landscape is seldom divided horizontally at the midpoint of a composition, or the sky would appear to oppress the earth. Epic directors like Eisenstein and Ford create some of their most disquieting effects with precisely this technique: they let the sky dominate through its intrinsic heaviness. The terrain and its inhabitants seem overwhelmed from above (2-12, 2-33).

Isolated figures and objects tend to be heavier than those in a cluster. Sometimes one object—merely by virtue of its isolation—can balance a whole group of otherwise equal objects. In many films, the protagonist is shown apart from a hostile group, yet the two seem equally matched despite the arithmetical differences. This effect is conveyed through the visual weight of the hero in isolation (3-14).

Psychological experiments have revealed that certain lines suggest directional movements. Although verticals and horizontals seem to be visually at rest, if movement *is* perceived, horizontal lines tend to move from left to right, vertical lines from bottom to top. Diagonal or oblique lines are more dynamic—that is, in transition. They tend to sweep upward. These psychological phenomena are important to the visual artist, especially the filmmaker, for often the dramatic context is not conducive to an overt expression of emotion (2-13). For example, if a director wishes to show a character's inward

**2-13. *The 400 Blows* (France, 1959).**
*With Jean-Pierre Léaud; Directed by François Truffaut.*
Often the context of a scene does not permit a director to express emotions dramatically. Here, the boy's anxiety and tenseness are expressed in purely visual terms. His inward agitation is conveyed by the diagonal lines of the fence. His sense of entrapment is suggested by the tight framing (sides, top, bottom), the shallow focus (rear), and the obstruction of the fence itself (foreground). See also C. G. Crisp, *François Truffaut* (New York: Praeger, 1972); Graham Petrie, *The Cinema of François Truffaut* (New York: A. S. Barnes, 1970); and Don Allen, *Truffaut* (New York: Viking Press, 1974).

agitation within a calm context, this quality can be conveyed through the dynamic use of line: an image composed of tense diagonals can suggest the character's inner turmoil, despite the apparent lack of drama in the action. Some of the most expressive cinematic effects can be achieved precisely through this tension between the compositional elements of an image and its dramatic context (2-4).

A skeletal structure underlies most visual compositions. Throughout the ages, artists have particularly favored S and X shapes, triangular designs, and circles. These designs are often employed simply because they are thought to be inherently beautiful. The famous S-curve, for example, is regarded as a graceful and feminine design, and is particularly common in Japanese cinema, most notably in the films of Kenji Mizoguchi, which usually feature female protagonists. Design is usually fused with a thematic idea, at least in the best movies. In *Jules and Jim*, for example, Truffaut consistently used triangular designs, for the film deals with a trio of characters whose relationships are constantly shifting, yet always interrelated. The form of the images in this case is a symbolic representation of the romantic triangle of the dramatic content. These triangular designs dynamize the visuals, keeping them off-balance, subject to change. Generally speaking, designs consisting of units of three, five, and seven tend to produce these effects (2-14); whereas those

**2-14. *Semi-Tough* (U.S.A., 1977).**
*With Burt Reynolds, Jill Clayburgh, and Kris Kristofferson; Directed by Michael Ritchie.*
Compositions grouped into units of three, five, and seven tend to suggest dynamic, unstable relationships. Those organized in units of two, four, or six, on the other hand, tend to imply fixed, harmonious relationships. This triangular composition is organically related to the theme of the film, which deals with the shifting love relationships between the three characters. The hero (Reynolds) is trapped between the loyalty he owes his best friend and the love he feels for his friend's fiancée.

composed of units of two, four, or six seem more static, stable, and balanced (2-6).

In *The Seven Samurai,* Kurosawa used circular designs with rich symbolic density. This circular motif is directly related to the theme of the film which is a recurring preoccupation of the Japanese cinema: the need for the individual to act in harmony with the needs of his or her society. The movie is set in the Sengoku period of 16th century Japan—a period of class breakdowns and violent social upheavals. During this era, the traditionally revered ideals of social cooperation and consensus were not much in evidence in Japan. In Kurosawa's film, marauding hoards of bandits terrorize the countryside without obstruction—pillaging the villages, raping women, and confiscating the meager harvests. In desperation, some peasant farmers hire seven down-on-their-heels samurai warriors to protect their village. (Traditionally, the samurai caste served as retainers to the aristocracy, and in terms of class, were just beneath royalty in the social hierarchy of Japan. During the period of the film, however, the samurai class had fallen on hard times, and many samurai were wandering the countryside, masterless. A good number of them turned to robbing and pillaging like common bandits.) Throughout the movie, Kurosawa differentiates the three groups—farmers, bandits, and samurai—and each is characterized by its own type of music.

The circle motif is introduced at the beginning of the film when we see the village huts constructed in a circle: only three of them lie outside this cluster (2-15a). We then see the villagers, huddled together in a circle, kneeling on the ground, and lamenting their fate at the hands of the merciless bandits (b). After seven "hungry" samurai are hired, one of them (Toshiro Mifune) turns out to be a fake. He is actually the son of a farmer—a considerable comedown in social class. As a joke, the official flag of the village consists of six circles (one for each samurai), a written character representing the farming village, and a triangle representing the phony samurai-peasant, who is neither fish nor fowl, although eventually he turns out to be one of the most flexible and intelligent of the major characters (c). Circles are used to symbolize both the individual and the ideal of social unity—the microcosm and

**2-15. *The Seven Samurai* (Japan, 1954).**
*Directed by Akira Kurosawa.*
Throughout this movie, Kurosawa employs circular designs to symbolize both the individual and the ideal of social unity. See also Donald Richie, *Japanese Cinema* (Garden City, N.Y.: Doubleday, 1971); and Joseph L. Anderson and Donald Richie, *The Japanese Film* (New York: Grove Press, 1960).

(a) (b) (c) (d)

(Kurosawa Productions, Toho International, and Audio-Brandon Films)

(e)

(f)

(g)

(h)

(i)

(j)

the macrocosm. The villagers gather in a circle to be instructed, their individual spears arranged like spokes on a wheel (d). In the center of the circle, the chief samurai (Takashi Shimura) stresses the need for the farmers to act as a unified group rather than as individuals (e). During this scene, Kurosawa circles his circle by moving the camera around the periphery of the group, thus emphasizing its unity (f). When a few farmers refuse to sacrifice the three outlying huts, the chief samurai forces the rebels back into the circle. On the back of his robe, we can see the circular yin-yang emblem, a Buddhist symbol of mystical unity, of the reconciliation of opposites (g). The village has a mill wheel which is attached to one of the outlying huts. This wheel is the dominant symbol of social unity in the film (h). Later, during a bandit attack, a farmer refuses to obey orders and rushes off to the mill. His act of individualism costs him his life, and the mill and wheel are set afire by the bandits (i). Kurosawa uses the image of the burning wheel as a symbolic warning of what could happen to the community if individuals refuse to act in concert with each other. The bandits are ultimately defeated, precisely because the strategy of the samurai leader is to isolate one or a few of the bandits from the main group. Each time one of the forty bandits is killed, the samurai chief crosses off an individual circle on his tally sheet (j).

As we can see, some types of designs can suggest intrinsic ideas, but the dramatic context is all important in a movie. Thus, in most American westerns, the circle formed by wagon trains when attacked by Indians suggests the same symbolic ideas of unity and security as Kurosawa's movie. But in *Psycho*, circular designs suggest quite different ideas. Hitchcock's theme deals with the guilt and corruption of virtually all the characters—even the nominally innocent ones. Like many of Hitchcock's works, *Psycho* also deals with the idea of voyeurism—indeed, with the idea of cinema as artistic voyeurism. In the

**2-16.** *Last Tango in Paris* **(Italy/France, 1973).**
*With Marlon Brando and Maria Schneider; Directed by Bernardo Bertolucci.*
Visual motifs, like symbols, derive their significance from the dramatic context of a film. In this movie, Bertolucci associates circular light globes with sexual fantasies. The motif is found in a number of scenes and is associated with various characters in different locations. The motif first appears in the lobby of the apartment house where the two lovers (Brando and Schneider) meet for their sexual trysts. A similar light globe is found in the lobby of the hotel of Brando's deceased wife. Her lover also has a circular globe in his room where he and his mistress met for their liaisons. The same type of light fixture is found in the apartment belonging to Schneider's mother: both of these women use the military gear which once belonged to the *pater familias* as sexual fetishes. The globe motif proliferates lyrically on the screen in the famous tango sequence, shown here. Almost all of Bertolucci's movies contain dance scenes.

opening sequence of the film, the "eye" of the camera enters a window of a hotel room where we witness a scene between two semiclad illicit lovers. Throughout the movie, Hitchcock equates images of human eyes with other circular eye-shaped objects: sinks, bathtub drains, toilets, the empty sockets of a human skull. A profoundly pessimistic work, *Psycho* suggests that behind every human eye lies a psychological sewer, a malign repository of corruption and guilt. In another context, such as *Last Tango in Paris,* circular shapes can have totally different implications (2-16).

## Territorial Space and Proxemic Patterns

Thus far, we've been concerned with the art of mise-en-scène primarily as it relates to the structuring of patterns on a two-dimensional flat surface. But since most movie images deal with the illusion of volume and depth, the film director must keep these theatrical considerations in mind while composing the visuals. It's one thing to construct a pleasing arrangement of shapes, lines, colors, and textures, but movie images must also tell a story in time, a story that generally involves human beings and their problems. In a sense, striking compositions in movies are something extra, for the basic function of these formal elements is to embody concrete objects and characters. Unlike notes of music, then, forms in film are not usually pure—they refer specifically to objects in reality.

Directors generally emphasize volume in their images precisely because they wish to avoid an abstract, flat look in their compositions. In most cases, filmmakers compose on at least three visual planes: the middleground, the foreground, and the background. Not only does this technique suggest a sense of depth, it can also radically alter the dominant contrast of an image, serving as a kind of qualifying characteristic, either subtle or conspicuous. For example, a figure is often placed in the middleground of a composition. Whatever is placed in the foreground will comment on the figure in some way (2-17). Some foliage, for instance, is likely to suggest a certain naturalness and

**2-17.**
*Different foregrounds with the same subject. Photos by Evelyn Hayes.*
The foreground information of a visual image acts as a commentary on the subject matter found in the middle distances and the background.

(a)

(b)

(c)

(d)

blending with the environment of nature. Many of the shots of the protagonists in George Roy Hill's *Butch Cassidy and the Sundance Kid* are photographed in this manner. A gauzy curtain in the foreground can suggest mystery, eroticism, and femininity; the crosshatching of a window frame can suggest self-division; and so on, with as many foreground qualifiers as the director and cinematographer can think of. These same principles apply to backgrounds, although objects placed in these areas tend to yield in dominance to middle- and foreground ranges.

One of the most elementary yet crucial decisions the film director makes is what shot to employ vis-à-vis the materials photographed. That is, how much detail should be included within the frame? How close should the camera get to the subject—which is another way of saying how close should we get to the subject since the viewer's eye tends to identify with the camera's lens in a movie. These are not casual problems, for the amount of space included within the frame can radically affect our response to the photographed materials. With any given subject, the film director can employ a variety of shots, each of which includes or excludes a given amount of surrounding space. But how much space is just right in a shot? What's too much or too little?

Space is a medium of communication, and the way we respond to objects and figures within a given area is a constant source of information in life as well as art. In virtually any social situation, we receive and give off signals relating to our use of space and those people who share it. Most of us aren't particularly conscious of this medium, but we instinctively become alerted whenever we feel that certain social conventions about space are being violated. For example, when people enter a movie theatre, they tend to seat themselves at appropriate intervals from each other. But what's appropriate? And who or what defines it? Why do we feel threatened when someone takes a seat next to us in a nearly empty theatre? After all, the seat isn't ours, and the

**2-18.** *Alien* (U.S.A., 1979).

*With Tom Skerritt; Directed by Ridley Scott.*

Viewers can be made to feel insecure or isolated when a hostile foreground element (like this gloopy creature) comes between us and a figure we identify with.

(Twentieth Century-Fox)

*(Twentieth Century-Fox)*

**2-19. *The Gambler* (U.S.A., 1974).**
*With James Caan; Directed by Karel Reisz.*
Background elements can often be exploited for symbolic purposes. In this shot, the protagonist is exhilarated by his winning streak in a Las Vegas gambling casino. The neon ceiling fixture behind him produces a sunburst effect, making him look like a radiant sun god. Symbolism of this kind is determined in large part by the dramatic context.

other person has paid for the privilege of sitting wherever he wishes. Is it paranoid to feel anxiety in such a situation, or is it a normal instinctive response?

A number of psychologists and anthropologists—including Konrad Lorenz, Robert Sommers, and Edward T. Hall—have explored these and related questions. Their findings are especially revealing in terms of how space is used in the cinema. In his study *On Aggression,* for example, Lorenz discusses how most animals—including humans—are territorial. That is, they lay claim to a given area and defend it from outsiders. This territory is a kind of personal haven of safety and is regarded by the organism as an extension of itself. When living creatures are too tightly packed into a given space, the result can be stress, tension, and anxiety. In many cases, when this territorial imperative is violated, the intrusion can provoke aggressive and violent behavior, and sometimes a battle for dominance ensues over control of the territory.

Peckinpah's *Straw Dogs* demonstrates Lorenz's hypothesis dramatically (2-20). A young American college professor (Dustin Hoffman) exiles himself and his sexy wife to a remote English village where she was raised and where

**2-20. *Straw Dogs* (U.S.A., 1972).**
*With Dustin Hoffman; Directed by Sam Peckinpah.*
Peckinpah's movie is a virtual dramatization of the territorial imperative. Throughout the film, the resentful villagers close in around the intellectual hero (Hoffman) who refuses to read their signals. Their attack begins at the periphery of his existence, but they soon invade his immediate environment. Meeting only token resistance (pictured), they eventually move in for the kill. Shattered glass is used as a motif in a number of scenes. The hero's eye glasses serve as an ironic symbol of his refusal to see what is really happening. When his glasses are broken during a vicious attack, he is forced to rely on his animal instincts in order to survive.

her husband hopes to escape the social and political stresses raging in the United States at the time. The provincial villagers dislike the foreigner whom they regard as a snotty intruder. They insult and threaten him, subtly at first, then more openly. But he always responds in the same way—by retreating within himself and the home he has rented for complete privacy. Only when his home is attacked by some drunken villagers does the professor react, and then with such ferocity that the aggressive behavior of the villagers seems almost mild in comparison.

Psychological and anthropological studies have revealed that a given territory tends to be occupied according to a heirarchy of power. That is, the most dominant organism of a community is literally given a wide berth, whereas the less dominant are crowded together. The amount of space an organism occupies is generally proportioned to the degree of control it enjoys within a given territory. These spatial principles can be seen in many human communities as well. A classroom, for example, is usually divided into a teaching area and a student seating area, but the proportion of space alloted to the authority figure is greater than that alloted to each of those being instructed. The spatial structure of virtually any kind of territory used by humans betrays a discernable concept of power and authority. No matter how egalitarian we might like to think ourselves, most of us conform to these spatial conventions. When a distinguished person enters a crowded room, for example, most people instinctively make room for him—in fact, they're giving him far more room than they themselves occupy.

But what has all this got to do with movies? A great deal, for space is one of the principal mediums of communication in film, and the way that people are arranged in space can tell us a lot about their social and psychological

(Janus Films)

(Warner Brothers)

**2-21a.** *The Blue Angel* **(Germany, 1930).**
*With Marlene Dietrich; Directed by Joseph von Sternberg.*
**2-21b.** *THX 1138* **(U.S.A., 1970).**
*With Robert Duvall and Donald Pleasence; Directed by George Lucas.*
The degree of density in the texture of the mise-en-scène is often a symbolic analogue of the quality of life in the world of the film. The cheap cabaret setting of *The Blue Angel* is chaotic and packed, swirling in smoke and cluttered with tawdry ornaments. The futuristic world of *THX 1138* is sterile, empty.

relationships. In film, dominant characters are almost always given more space to occupy than others—unless the film deals with the loss of power or the social insignificance of a character. The amount of space taken up by a character in a movie does not necessarily relate to that person's actual social dominance; but to his or her dramatic importance. Authoritarian figures like kings and royalty generally occupy a larger amount of space than peasants and underlings; but if a film is primarily about the peasant, the peasant will tend to dominate spatially. In short, dominance is defined *contextually* in film—not necessarily the way it's perceived in reality.

The movie frame is also a kind of territory, albeit a temporary one which exists only for the duration of the shot. The way space is shared within the frame is one of the major tools of the metteur-en-scène, who can define, adjust, and redefine human relationships by exploiting spatial conventions. Furthermore, once a relationship has been established, the director can go on to other matters simply by changing the camera setup. The film director, in short, is not confined to a spatial area that is permanent throughout the scene. A master of mise-en-scène can express shifting psychological and social nuances within a single shot: by exploiting the space between characters, the depth planes within the image, and the intrinsically weighted areas of the frame.

The amount of space within the territory of the frame can be exploited for symbolic purposes. Generally speaking, the closer the shot, the more confined the photographed figures appear to be. Such shots are usually referred to as tightly framed. Conversely, the longer, loosely framed shots tend to suggest freedom. Prison films often employ tightly framed closeups and medium shots because the frame functions as a kind of symbolic prison. In Robert Bresson's *A Condemned Man Escapes*, for example, the director begins the movie with a closeup of the protagonist's hands which are bound by a pair of handcuffs. Throughout the film, the prisoner makes elaborate preparations to escape, and Bresson preserves the tight framing to emphasize the sense of claustrophobia that the hero finds unendurable. This spatial tension

*(Janus Films)*

**2-22. *Grand Illusion* (France, 1938).**
*With (center to right) Erich von Stroheim, Pierre Fresnay, and Jean Gabin; Directed by Jean Renoir.*
Tight framing allows for relatively little freedom of movement. The frame, in effect, becomes a symbolic prison, a useful technique in films dealing with entrapment, confinement, or literal imprisonment, like Renoir's World War I masterpiece. See also Pierre Leprohon, ed., *Jean Renoir: An Investigation into his Films and Philosophy* (New York: Crown Publishers, 1971).

is not released until the end of the movie when the protagonist disappears into the freedom of the darkness outside the prison walls. His triumphant escape is photographed in a loosely framed long shot—the only one in the film—which also symbolizes his sense of spiritual release. Framing and spatial metaphors of this kind are common in films dealing with the theme of confinement—either literal, as in Renoir's *Grand Illusion* (2-22), or psychological, as in Zinnemann's *The Member of the Wedding* (7-11).

Often a director can suggest ideas of entrapment by exploiting perfectly neutral objects and lines on the set. In such cases, the formal characteristics of these literal objects tend to close in on a figure, at least when viewed on the flat screen. In *Red Desert,* for instance, the heroine (Monica Vitti) describes a mental breakdown suffered by a friend she once knew. The audience suspects she's speaking of her own breakdown, however, for the surface of the image implies constriction: while she talks, she's riveted to one position, her figure framed by the lines of a doorway behind her, suggesting a coffinlike enclosure. When figures are framed within a frame in this manner, a sense of confinement is usually emphasized.

**2-23. *Joseph Andrews* (Great Britain, 1976).**
*With John Bull (in sedan chair), Ann-Margret, and Peter Firth; Directed by Tony Richardson.*
Like its companion piece *Tom Jones* (which is also based on a classic novel by Henry Fielding), this movie often employs open forms to suggest the tumultuous sprawl of its eighteenth-century setting. Richardson shot many of the scenes with a hand-held camera in a documentary style. He avoided the elegant formality of most eighteenth-century English paintings in favor of the malicious intimacy of Hogarth's satirical engravings, like *Rake's Progress* and *Gin Lane*.

*(Paramount Pictures)*

Territorial space within the frame can be exploited with considerable psychological complexity. When a figure leaves the frame, for example, the camera can adjust to this sudden vacuum in the composition by panning slightly to make allowances for a new balance of weights. Or the camera can remain stationary, thus suggesting a sense of loss which is symbolized by the empty space which the character formerly occupied (3-13). Hostility and suspicion between two characters can be conveyed by keeping them at the edges of the composition, with a maximum of space between them (2-9), or by having an intrusive character force his or her physical presence into the other character's territory, which is temporarily defined by the confines of the frame (2-24).

**2-24. *Bananas* (U.S.A., 1971).**
*With Woody Allen; Directed by Allen.*
Incongruous proxemic juxtapositions are the source of many visual gags in Allen's political spoof. Pictured here, a friendly F.B.I. agent keeps the disguised hero under tight surveillance while he takes a shower.

*(United Artists)*

Spatial conventions vary from culture to culture, as anthropologist Edward T. Hall has demonstrated in such studies as *The Hidden Dimension* and *The Silent Language.* Hall discovered that *proxemic patterns*—the relationships of organisms within a given space—can be influenced by external considerations. Climate, noise level, and the degree of illumination all tend to alter the space between individuals. People in Anglo-Saxon and Northern European cultures tend to use more space than those in warmer climates. A great deal of noise, danger, and lack of light tend to make people move closer together. Taking these cultural and contextual considerations into account, Hall subdivides the way people use space into four major proxemic patterns: the intimate, personal, social, and public distances.

Hall defines as intimate those distances that range from skin contact to about 18 inches away. This is the distance of physical involvement—of love, comfort, and tenderness between individuals. With strangers, such distances would be regarded as intrusive—most people would react with suspicion and hostility if their space were invaded by someone they didn't know very well. In many cultures, maintaining an intimate distance in public is considered bad taste.

The personal distance ranges roughly from 1½ feet away to about 4 feet away. Individuals can touch if necessary, since they are literally an arm's-length apart. These distances tend to be reserved for friends and acquaintances rather than lovers or members of a family. Personal distances preserve the privacy between individuals, yet these ranges don't necessarily suggest exclusion, as intimate distances almost always do.

Social distances range from 4 feet to about 12 feet. These are the distances usually reserved for impersonal business and casual social gatherings. It's a friendly range in most cases, yet somewhat more formal than the personal distance. Ordinarily, social distances are necessary when there are more than three members of a group. In some cases, it would be considered rude for two individuals to preserve an intimate or personal distance within a social situation. Such behavior might be interpreted as standoffish and exclusive.

Hall defines as public those distances that extend from 12 feet to 25 feet and more. These ranges tend to be formal and rather detached. Displays of

**2-25. Grease (U.S.A., 1977).**
*With John Travolta (extreme right); Musical sequences staged by Patricia Birch; Directed by Randal Kleiser.*
In stylized genres, such as the musical, the proxemic conventions of everyday reality are usually violated in favor of a striking visual effect. Space, in such instances, functions as an abstract ground for the figures.

*(Paramount Pictures)*

emotion are considered bad form at these ranges. Important public figures are generally seen in the public distances, and because a considerable amount of space is involved at these ranges, people generally must exaggerate their gestures and raise their voices in order to be understood clearly.

All of these proxemic patterns are approximate, and Hall stresses their variability from culture to culture. What may be regarded as a personal distance in Egypt or Algeria would probably be regarded as intimate in Sweden or England. Furthermore, most people adjust to proxemic patterns instinctively; we don't usually say to ourselves "This guy is invading my intimate space" when a stranger happens to stand 18 inches away from us. However, unless we're in a combative mood, we involuntarily tend to step away in such circumstances. Obviously, social context is also a determining factor in proxemic patterns. In a crowded subway car, for example, virtually everyone is in an intimate range, yet we generally preserve a public attitude by not speaking to the person whose body is literally pressed against our own.

Proxemic patterns are perfectly obvious to anyone who has bothered to observe the way people obey certain spatial conventions in actual life. But in the cinema, these patterns are also related to the shots and their distance ranges. Although shots are not necessarily defined by the literal space between the camera and the object photographed, in terms of psychological effect, shots tend to suggest physical distances. Politicians who appear on television are often their own worst enemies because of their inability to adjust to different proxemic patterns. Old-time politicians sometimes appear pompous on TV because they are used to speaking to vast audiences which are in the public proxemic ranges. When the TV camera moves in to the personal range, however, their florid gestures and loud speaking voices can seem insincere and rhetorical, even to sympathizers. On the other hand, younger politicians tend to be more sophisticated in their knowledge of the psychological effects of proxemic ranges. Their TV political appearances usually seem smoother, more polished, and sincere—even to their detractors.

Often film directors have a number of options concerning what kind of shot to use to convey the action of a scene. What determines their choice—though usually instinctively rather than consciously—is the emotional impact of the different proxemic ranges. Each proxemic pattern has an approximate shot equivalent (2-26). The intimate distances, for example, can be likened to the close and extreme close shot ranges; the personal distance is approximately a medium close range; the social distances correspond to the medium and full shot ranges; and the public distances are roughly within the long and extreme long shot ranges. Since our eyes identify with the camera's lens, in effect we are placed within these various ranges vis-à-vis the subject matter. When we are offered a closeup of a character, for example, in a sense we feel that we're in an intimate relationship with that character. In some instances, this technique can bind us to the character, forcing us to care about him, and to identify with his problems. If the character is a villain, the closeup can produce an emotional revulsion in us, for in effect, the character is seen to be invading our space. Sergio Leone uses this technique effectively in the closeups of his various villains in *Once Upon a Time in the West.*

In general, the greater the distance between the camera and the subject, the more emotionally neutral we remain. Public proxemic ranges tend to encourage a certain detachment. Conversely, the closer we are to a character,

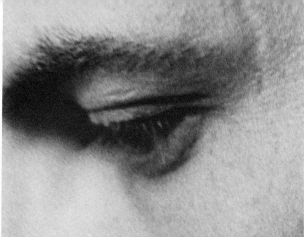

**(a)**

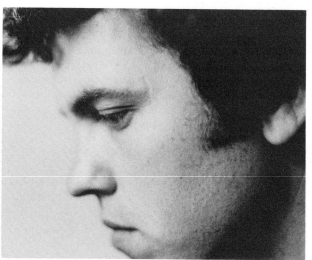

**(b)**

**(c)**

**2-26.**
*Proxemic ranges of the camera. Photos by Evelyn Hayes.*
The director usually has a number of options in the selection of shots. The placement of the camera in relationship to the subject matter is often a matter of instinct, of what *feels* right. These instincts are determined in part by the emotional effects of the different proxemic ranges. The more distant the camera is from the subject, the more objective and detached our response is likely to be, for these are the public and social ranges. When the camera moves closer to the subject matter, our emotional involvement tends to increase, for these are the personal and intimate proxemic ranges. In each of these photos, the true content is determined by the proxemic implications of the shot, not merely by the subject matter alone.

(d)

(e)

the more we feel that we're in proximity with him, and hence, the greater our emotional involvement. "Long shot for comedy, closeup for tragedy" was one of Chaplin's most famous pronouncements. The proxemic principles are sound, for when we are close to an action—a person slipping on a banana peel, for example—it's seldom funny, for we are concerned for the person's safety. If we see the same event from a greater distance, however, it often strikes us as comical. Chaplin used closeups sparingly for this very reason: so long as Charlie remains in long shots, we tend to be amused by his antics and absurd predicaments. In scenes of greater emotional impact, however, Chaplin resorted to closer shots, and their effect is often devastating on the audience. We suddenly realize that the situation we've been laughing at is no longer funny. We feel "closer" to Charlie and identify with his feelings (2-27).

Perhaps the most famous instance of the power of Chaplin's closeups is found at the conclusion of *City Lights*. Charlie has fallen in love with an impoverished flower vendor who is blind. She believes him to be an eccentric millionaire, and out of vanity he allows her to continue in this delusion. By engaging in a series of monumental labors—love has reduced him to work—

he manages to scrape together enough money for her to receive an operation which will restore her sight. But he is dragged off to jail before she can scarcely thank him for the money. The final scene takes place several months later. The young woman can now see and owns her own modest flower shop. Charlie is released from prison, and disheveled and dispirited, he meanders past her shop window. She sees him gazing at her wistfully and jokes to an assistant that she's apparently made a new conquest. Out of pity she goes out to the street and offers him a flower and a small coin. Instantly she recognizes his touch, and scarcely able to believe her eyes, she can only stammer, "You?" In a series of alternating closeups, their embarrassment is unbearably prolonged. Clearly he is not the idol of her romantic dreams, and he is painfully aware of her disappointment. Finally he stares at her with an expression of

**(a)**                                                     *(rbc Films)*

**(b)**                                                     *(rbc Films)*

**2-27a.** *The Gold Rush* **(U.S.A., 1925).** *With Charles Chaplin and Georgia Hale; Directed by Chaplin.*

**2-27b.** *City Lights* **(U.S.A., 1931).** *With Charles Chaplin; Directed by Chaplin.*

Both these scenes involve a fear of rejection by a woman Charlie holds in awe. The scene from *The Gold Rush* is predominantly comical. The tramp has belted his baggy pants with a piece of rope, but doesn't realize it is also a dog's leash, and while dancing with the saloon girl, Charlie is yanked to the floor by the jittery dog at the other end of the rope. Because the camera remains relatively distant from the action, we tend to be more objective, detached, and laugh at his futile attempts to preserve his dignity. On the other hand, the famous final shot from *City Lights* isn't funny at all, and produces a powerful emotional effect. Because the camera is in close, *we* get close to the situation. The proxemic distance between the camera and the subject forces us to identify more with his feelings which we can't ignore at this range. See also Peter Cotes and Thelma Niklaus, *The Little Fellow* (New York: The Citadel Press, 1965); Donald McCaffrey, ed., *Focus on Chaplin* (Englewood Cliffs, N.J.: Prentice-Hall, 1971); and Timothy J. Lyons, *Charles Chaplin: A Guide to References and Resources* (Boston: G. K. Hall, 1978).

shocking emotional nakedness. The film ends on this image of sublime vulnerability.

The choice of a shot is generally determined by practical considerations. Usually the director selects the shot that most clearly conveys the dramatic action of a scene. If there is a conflict between the effect of certain proxemic ranges and the clarity needed to convey what's going on, most directors will opt for the latter and gain their emotional impact through some other means. But there are many times when shot choice isn't necessarily determined by functional considerations. For example, if a scene calls for a shot of a man reading alone at a table, the director has a number of options which are determined at least in part by proxemic considerations. A functional stylist like Howard Hawks would probably have photographed the scene in a medium shot, showing the upper part of the man's body and the table top. A comic realist like Chaplin would probably have used a full or long shot to prevent the audience from identifying too much with the character and to permit us to see the social context. A predominantly expressionistic director like Hitchcock usually wanted the audience to identify with his protagonists, and he probably would have offered us a number of closeups of the man's face and the objects on the table to emphasize an emotional sequence of ideas. A director like Antonioni might portray the scene in an extreme long shot to suggest the man's loneliness and alienation. As with virtually every other cinematic technique, then, the dramatic context determines the choice of shot and its proxemic effects.

## Open and Closed Forms

The concepts of *open* and *closed forms* are generally employed by art historians and critics, but these terms can also be useful in film analysis. Like most theoretical constructs, these are best employed in a relative rather than absolute sense. There are no movies that are completely open or closed in form, only works that tend toward these polarities. Unfortunately, many critics have a way of smoothing over the rough edges of film art, ignoring the deliberate contradictions, paradoxes, and inconsistencies in a movie in order to make it conform to a tidy critical category. But great films manage to defy these facile formulations. Like other critical terms, then, open and closed form should be applied only when such concepts are relevant and helpful in understanding what actually exists in a movie. If the concepts do not seem relevant, they ought to be discarded and replaced with something that is. Criticism should be the handmaiden of art, not vice-versa.

Open and closed forms are not only stylistic polarities, each with its technical emphases, but also two distinct attitudes about reality. Open and closed forms can determine a film director's artistic vision, his or her philosophical universe. The two terms are also loosely related to the concepts of Realism and Expressionism as they have been defined in these chapters. In general, Realist filmmakers tend to employ open forms, while Expressionists veer toward closed. Open forms tend to be stylistically recessive, whereas closed forms are generally selfconscious and conspicuous.

In terms of visual design, open form emphasizes informal, unobtrusive compositions. Often such images seem to have no discernible structure, and suggest a random form of organization. Objects and figures seem to have

**2-28. *The Garden of the Finzi-Continis* (Italy, 1970).**
*With Dominique Sanda (center); Directed by Vittorio De Sica.*
Realist directors are more likely to prefer open forms which tend to suggest fragments of a larger external reality. Design and composition are generally informal. Influenced by the aesthetic of the documentary, open form images seem to have been discovered rather than arranged. Excessive balance and calculated symmetry are avoided in favor of an intimate and spontaneous effect. Still photos in open form are seldom picturesque or obviously artful. Instead, they suggest a frozen instant of truth—a snapshot wrested from the fluctuations of time.

been found, rather than deliberately arranged (2-28). Closed form emphasizes a more stylized design. While such images can suggest a superficial realism, seldom do they have that accidental, discovered look that typifies open forms. Objects and figures are more precisely placed within the frame, and the balance of visual weights is elaborately worked out.

Open forms stress apparently simple techniques because with these unselfconscious methods, the filmmaker is able to emphasize the immediate, the familiar, the intimate aspects of reality. Sometimes such images are photographed in only partially controlled situations, and these aleatory conditions can produce a sense of spontaneity and directness that would be difficult to capture in a rigidly controlled context. Closed forms are more likely to emphasize the unfamiliar. The images are rich in textural contrasts and compelling visual effects. Because the mise-en-scène is more precisely controlled and stylized, there is often a deliberate artificiality in these images—a sense of visual improbability, of being one remove from reality. Closed forms also tend to be more densely saturated with visual information; richness of form takes precedence over considerations of surface realism. If a conflict should arise, formal beauty is often sacrificed for truth in open forms; in closed forms, literal truth is sometimes sacrificed for beauty.

Compositions in open and closed forms exploit the frame differently. In open form images, the frame tends to be de-emphasized. It suggests a window, or a temporary masking, and implies that more important information lies outside the edges of the composition. Space is continuous in these shots, and to emphasize its continuity outside the frame, directors often favor panning their camera across the locale. In open form, the shot seems inadequate, too narrow in its confines to contain the copiousness of the subject matter. Like many of the paintings of Edgar Degas (who usually favored open forms), objects and even figures are arbitrarily cut off by the frame to reinforce the continuity of the subject matter beyond the formal edges of the composition. In closed form, the shot represents a kind of miniuniverse, with all the necessary information carefully structured within the confines of the frame. Space seems enclosed and self-contained rather than continuous. Elements outside the frame are irrelevant, at least in terms of the formal properties of the individual shot, which is isolated from its context in space and time (2-29).

For these reasons, still photographs taken from movies that are predomi-

**2-29. *The Life of Oharu* (Japan, 1952).**
*With Kinuyo Tanaka (lower left); Directed by Kenji Mizoguchi.*
In closed form, the frame is a self-sufficient miniature universe with all the formal elements held in careful balance. Though there may be more information outside the frame, for the duration of any given shot, this information is visually irrelevant. Closed forms are often employed in scenes dealing with entrapment and constriction.

nantly in open form often seem unimpressive, for they're not intrinsically striking or eye-catching. Books about movies tend to favor photographs in closed form: even these isolated fragments seem more obviously artistic because of their formal beauty. The beauty of an open form image, on the other hand, is more elusive, and can be likened to a snapshot which miraculously preserves some candid expression, a kind of haphazard instant of truth. Open form also tends to value a certain visual ambiguity. Often the charm of such images lies precisely in their impenetrability—a mysterious half smile on the face of a character, for example, or an evocative shadow which casts a strange pattern across the set.

In open form movies, the dramatic action generally leads the camera. In such films as *Faces* and *Husbands,* for example, John Cassavetes emphasized the fluidity of the camera: it dutifully follows the actors wherever they wish to go, seemingly placed at their disposal. Such films suggest that chance elements play an important role in determining visual effects (see also 2-30). Needless

**2-30. *Black Gun* (U.S.A., 1972).**
*Directed by Robert Hartford-Davis.*
Movies in open form tend to exploit the frame as a temporary masking that's too narrow in its scope to include all the relevant information. Often the frame seems to cut figures off in an arbitrary manner, suggesting that the action is continued off-screen. In action films, open forms can suggest newsreel footage that was fortuitously photographed by a cameraman who was unable to superimpose an artistic form over his runaway materials.

(Columbia Pictures)

to say, it's not what actually happens on a set that's important, but what *seems* to be happening on the screen: many of the most "simple" effects in an open form movie are achieved after much painstaking labor and manipulation.

In closed form films, on the other hand, the camera often anticipates the dramatic action. Objects and actors are visually choreographed within the confines of a predetermined camera setup. Anticipatory setups tend to imply fatality or determinism, for in effect, the camera seems to know what will happen even before it occurs. In the films of Fritz Lang, for example, the camera often seems to be waiting in an empty room: the door opens, the characters enter, and the action then begins. In some of Hitchcock's movies, a character is seen at the edge of the composition, and the camera seems to be placed in a disadvantageous position, too far removed from where the action is apparently going to occur. But then the character decides to return to that area where the camera has been waiting. When such setups are used in a film, the audience also tends to anticipate actions. Instinctively, we expect something or someone to fill in the visual vacuum of the shot. Philosophically, open forms tend to suggest freedom of choice and the multiplicity of options open to the characters. Closed forms, on the other hand, tend to imply destiny and the futility of the will: the characters don't seem to make the important choices, the camera does—and in advance.

Needless to say, open and closed forms are most effective in movies

**2-31.** *The End of August at the Hotel Ozone* (Czechoslovakia, 1966).
*Directed by Jan Schmidt.*
Open and closed forms aren't intrinsically meaningful, but derive their significance from the dramatic context. In some cases, closed forms can suggest entrapment (2-29); in other cases, such as this photo, closed form implies security. The film deals with a handful of women who somehow survived a nuclear holocaust and are wandering through a radioactive landscape in search of other survivors. These scenes are mostly in open form, capturing the vast stretches of barren terrain and the unrestricted freedom of the young women who are portrayed almost like savages of the wilderness. Eventually they discover a gentle older man who has been living alone for years in a former luxury hotel. The hotel scenes are mostly in closed form, suggesting the shelter of a lost civilization. In this dinner scene, for example, the visual weights are symmetrically balanced, the outer chaos sealed off by the edges of the frame.

(New Line Cinema)

where these techniques are appropriate to the subject matter. A prison film employing mostly open forms is not likely to be emotionally convincing. Most movies employ both open and closed forms, depending on the specific dramatic context. Renoir's *Grand Illusion,* for example, uses closed forms for the prison camp scenes, and open forms after two of the prisoners escape. Also, directors do not necessarily use the same forms for every film. The earlier works of Bergman—movies like *Wild Strawberries* and *The Seventh Seal*—are predominantly closed in form. Bergman's later works, such as *The Shame* and *The Passion of Anna,* are mostly in open forms.

Like most cinematic techniques, open and closed forms have certain limitations as well as advantages. When used to excess, open forms can seem sloppy and naive, like an artless home movie. Too often open forms seem uncontrolled, unfocused, and even visually ugly. Occasionally, these techniques are so blandly unobtrusive that the visuals are boring. On the other hand, closed forms can seem arty, so unspontaneous that their visual elements look computer-programmed. Many viewers are turned off by the stagey flamboyance of some closed form films. At their worst, these movies seem overwrought and decadent—all icing and no cake.

(Paramount Pictures)

**2-32. *Chinatown* (U.S.A., 1974).**
*With Jack Nicholson; Directed by Roman Polanski.*
Tightly framed compositions are usually in closed form, but not always. In this over-the-shoulder shot, for example, the framing is tight, but the form is open. The figure on the right is only partially in view, even though he is important to the dramatic context. See also Leo Braudy, "Varieties of Visual Coherence," in *The World in a Frame* (Garden City, N.Y.: Doubleday, 1976).

In these first two chapters, we have been concerned with the most important source of meaning in the cinema—the visual image. But of course movies exist in time, and have many other ways of communicating information. For this reason, a film image must sometimes be restrained, or less saturated with meanings than a painting or still photograph in which all the necessary information is contained within a single image. The principles of variation and restraint exist in all temporal arts. In movies, these principles can be seen in those images which seem rather uninteresting, usually because the dominant contrast is found elsewhere. Such deliberate pictorial anticlimaxes are neces-

**2-33. *Stagecoach* (U.S.A., 1939).**
*Directed by John Ford.*
Loose framing usually implies open form; but in this classically composed shot, the coach and horses occupy only a small portion of the image (loose framing), yet the composition is totally self-contained in terms of its visual balance of weights (closed form). Ford contrasts the epic grandeur of Monument Valley Utah with the rickety fragility of the coach as it makes its way across the enormous expanse of desert. See also Richard J. Anobile, ed., *John Ford's Stagecoach* (New York: Flare Books, 1975), a reconstruction of the film with over 1200 frame enlargements; and J. A. Place, *The Western Films of John Ford* (New York: Citadel Press, 1974).

sary in the cinema because of its temporal nature and its enormous technical range of expression. In a sense, these anticlimaxes are visual rest areas.

A movie director has literally hundreds of different ways to convey meanings. Like the painter or still photographer, the filmmaker can emphasize visual dominant contrasts. In a scene portraying violence, for example, he can use diagonal and zig-zagging lines, aggressive colors, closeups, extreme low angles, harsh lighting contrasts, unbalanced compositions, large shapes, and so on. Unlike most other visual artists, the movie director can also suggest violence through movement, either of the subject itself or of the camera. The film artist can suggest violence through editing. Furthermore, through the use of the soundtrack, violence can be conveyed by loud or rapid dialogue, harsh sound effects, or strident music. Precisely because there are so many ways to convey a given effect, the film director will vary his emphases, sometimes stressing image, sometimes movement, other times sound. Occasionally,

**2-34.** *M* **(Germany, 1931).**
*Directed by Fritz Lang.*
A mise-en-scène analysis involves a breakdown of the major components of a film image in relation to its dramatic context. For example, this shot takes place near the end of the movie. A psychotic child killer (Peter Lorre, extreme right) has been hunted down by the members of the underworld. These "normal" criminals have taken him to an abandoned warehouse where they intend to try and execute the psychopath for his heinous crimes—in order to take the police heat off themselves. In this scene, the killer is confronted by a witness (center) who holds an incriminating piece of evidence—a balloon. The components of the scene include: (1) the shot is at eye level, slightly more distant than the full shot range; (2) a nondistorting lens is used, with no filters; (3) the dominant is the balloon, the brightest object in the frame (by turning the photo upside down and converting it to a pattern of abstract shapes, its dominance is more readily discernable; (4) the principal subsidiary contrasts are the figures of the killer, the witness, and the two criminals in the upper left; (5) the composition is divided into three general areas—left, center, and right—suggesting instability; (6) the framing is tight: the killer is trapped in the same territory with his threatening accusers; they tower above him, sealing off any avenue of escape, while he cowers below at the extreme right edge (the most vulnerable position), almost falling into the symbolic blackness outside the frame; (7) the proxemic ranges within the photo range from personal to social, like the camera vis-à-vis the materials photographed—a relatively objective distance; (8) the texture is dense, with high-contrast flickering lights and shadows tearing up the image surface; (9) the form is definitely closed, the frame suggesting a constricting cell.

especially in climatic scenes, he will employ all three. Even the greatest movies, then, have some images of only routine interest, especially when the dramatic context calls for a nonvisual dominant.

## Further Reading

ARNHEIM, RUDOLF, *Art and Visual Perception: A Psychology of the Creative Eye* (Berkeley: University of California Press, 1954). Primarily about paintings and drawings.

_____, *Towards a Psychology of Art* (Berkeley: University of California Press, 1966). A theoretical discussion emphasizing a gestalt approach.

_____, *Visual Thinking* (Berkeley: University of California Press, 1969). How we apprehend visual information.

FREEBURG, VICTOR O., *Pictorial Beauty on the Screen* (New York: Macmillan, 1923). A discussion of the conventions of classical composition.

HALL, EDWARD T., *The Hidden Dimension* (Garden City: Doubleday, 1969). How humans and other animals use space.

_____, *The Silent Language* (Greenwich, Conn.: A Fawcett Premier Book, 1959). How people communicate without the use of words.

LORENZ, KONRAD, *On Aggression* (New York: Harcourt, Brace, Jovanovich, 1966). How animals and humans respond when space is redefined for them.

NILSON, VLADIMIR, *The Cinema as a Graphic Art* (New York: Hill and Wang, 1959). How reality is shaped by form, with major emphasis on classical composition.

RUESCH, JURGEN, AND WELDON KEES, *Nonverbal Communication* (Berkeley: University of California Press, 1966).

SOMMER, ROBERT, *Personal Space* (Englewood Cliffs, N.J.: Prentice-Hall, 1969). How individuals use and abuse space.

3

# MOVEMENT

"Movies," "motion pictures," "moving pictures"—all of these phrases suggest the central importance of motion in the art of the film. "Cinema" derives from the Greek word for "movement," as do the words "kinetic," "kinesthesia," and "choreography"—terms usually associated with the art of the dance. Yet oddly enough, filmgoers and critics give surprisingly little consideration to movement *per se* as a medium of communication. Like the image itself, motion is usually thought of in terms of gross subject matter: we tend to remember "what happens" only in a general sense. If we were to describe a sequence from a ballet in such vague terms, our discussion would certainly strike the sophisticated dance enthusiast as naive. Yet cinematic sequences—which can be choreographed with just as much or even greater complexity—are seldom appreciated for their kinetic richness and beauty.

## Kinesthesia

Like images, movement can be literal and concrete, or highly stylized and abstract. In the kinetic arts—pantomime, mime, ballet, modern dance, etc.—we find a wide variety of movements, ranging from the realistic to the expressionistic. This stylistic spectrum can also be seen in film. For example, a naturalistic actor like Spencer Tracy employed only realistic movements, the same sort that could be observed in actual life. Pantomimists are more stylized

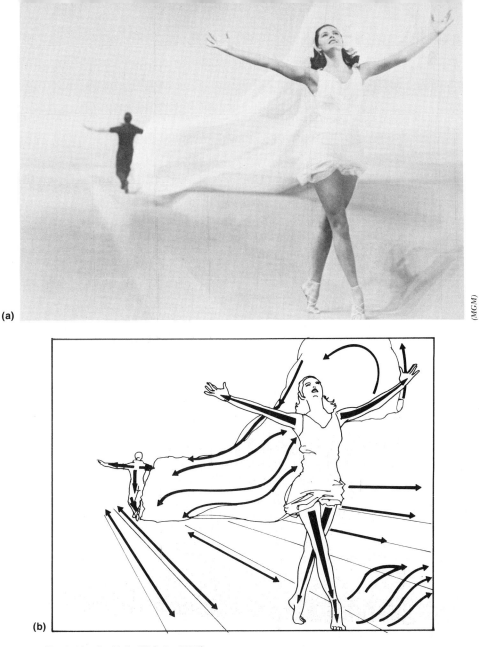

(a)

(b)

**3-1. *Singin' in the Rain* (U.S.A., 1952).**
*With Gene Kelly and Cyd Charisse; Choreography by Kelly; Directed by Kelly and Stanley Donen.*
The art of choreography often exploits objects—such as the billowing veil—as well as dancers' movements to express emotions. In effect, the fabric becomes an extension of the body. In this sequence, the movements of the dancers suggest isolated kinetic explosions, symbolizing the essentially private exaltation of love—yet the two lovers are tenuously connected by the swirling veil which binds them together. Kelly's mastery of the crane shot allowed him to create a choreography of rapturous extravagance, the camera whirling ecstatically, complementing or counterpointing the movements of the dancers.

in their movements. Chaplin, for example, tended to employ motion more symbolically: a swaggering gait and a twirling cane symbolized Charlie's (usually fleeting) arrogance and conceit.

Even more stylized are the movements of performers in a musical. In this genre, characters express their most intense emotions through song and dance. A dance number is seldom meant to be taken literally: it's a stylized convention which we accept as a symbolic expression of certain feelings and ideas. In *Singin' in the Rain,* for example, Gene Kelly does an elaborate dance routine in a downpour. He twirls around street lamps, splashes through puddles like a happy idiot, and leaps ecstatically through a pelting rain—literally nothing can dampen the exhilaration of his love. A wide gamut of emotions is expressed in this sequence, with each kinetic variation symbolizing the character's feelings about his girl: she can make him feel dreamy, childlike, erotically stimulated, brave and forthright, dopey and moonstruck, and finally wild with joy (front cover). In some kinds of action genres, physical contests are stylized in a similar manner. Samurai and kung-fu films, for example, often feature elaborately choreographed sequences (3-2).

Ballet and the art of mime are even more abstract and stylized. A great mime like Marcel Marceau is not so much concerned with expressing literal ideas (which is more properly the province of pantomime) as the *essence* of an

**3-2. *Enter the Dragon* (Hong Kong/U.S.A., 1973).**
*With Bruce Lee (dark trousers); Directed by Robert Clouse.*
Physical contests such as brawls, sword fights, and oriental self-defense methods can be choreographed with considerable kinetic grace. The kung-fu sequences staged by Bruce Lee are particularly stylized, almost like an acrobatic dance.

(a)

(b)

(c)

(d)

*(Warner Brothers)*

idea, stripped of superfluities. A twisted torso can suggest an ancient tree, bent elbows its crooked branches, fluttering fingers the rippling of its leaves. In ballet, movements can be so stylized that we cannot always assign a discernible content to them, although the narrative context generally provides us with at least a vague sense of what the movements represent. On this level of abstraction, however, movements acquire self-justifying characteristics. That is, we respond to them more for their own beauty than for their function as symbolic expressions of ideas (see also 3-3).

**3-3. *Dames* (U.S.A., 1934).**
*Choreography by Busby Berkeley; Directed by Ray Enright.*
Berkeley liberated the camera from the tyranny of the proscenium arch. He often photographed his dancers from unusual angles, like this bird's-eye shot. His style was the most abstract of all American choreographers. He sometimes didn't even bother using dancers, preferring a uniform contingent of comely maidens who are used as camera material, like bits of glass in a shifting kaleidoscope of formal patterns.

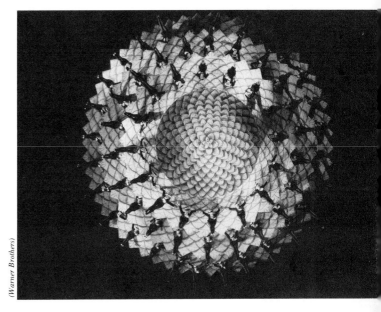

(Warner Brothers)

This concern with kinetic beauty for its own sake can be seen in certain schools of modern dance. Many of the choreographies of Merce Cunningham and Erick Hawkins, for example, are not meant to symbolize anything of a narrative nature. Abstract motion is presented for its own sake, somewhat in the same manner that pure colors, shapes, and lines are offered for their own sakes in nonrepresentational paintings. In movies, nonrepresentational movements are most often found in avant-garde films, in which narrative ideas are deliberately suppressed.

In dance, movements are defined by the space that encloses the choreography—a three-dimensional stage. In film, the frame performs a similar function; however, with each setup change, of course, the cinematic "stage" is redefined. The intrinsic meanings associated with various portions of the frame are closely related to the significance of certain kinds of movements. For example, with vertical movements, an upward motion seems soaring and free because it conforms to the eye's natural tendency to move upward over a composition. Movements in this direction often suggest aspiration, power, and authority—precisely those ideas that are associated with the superior portions of the frame.

Downward movements suggest opposite ideas: grief, death, insignificance, depression, weakness, and so on. In some instances, movement from the top to the bottom of the frame can result in the sensation of being cramped or squeezed. Joseph Mankiewicz's *Suddenly Last Summer* exploits this psychological sensation effectively. Early in the film, several people are waiting for the mistress of the house (Katharine Hepburn) to descend in an elevator. Suddenly, she begins to address the visitors even as the elevator descends. Because the shot is from a low angle, the elevator seems to be slowly crushing the visitors. During the course of the movie, we discover that our first impression of the lady was correct, for she ruthlessly attempts to destroy the lives of several characters in this earlier scene.

Since the eye tends to read a picture from left to right, physical movement in this direction seems psychologically natural, whereas movement from the right to left often seems inexplicably tense and uncomfortable. The sensitive filmmaker exploits these psychological phenomena to reinforce the dramatic ideas. Frequently the protagonists of a movie travel toward the right of the screen, while the antagonists move toward the left. In John Huston's *The Red Badge of Courage*, the hero moves from right to left when he runs away from a battle in fear. Later, when he courageously joins an infantry charge, his movement is from left to right.

Movement can be directed toward or away from the camera. Since we identify with the camera's lens, the effect of such movements is somewhat like a character moving toward or away from us. If the character is a villain, walking toward the camera can seem aggressive, hostile, and threatening, for in effect, he's invading our space (3-4). If the character is attractive, move-

**3-4. *Man Hunt* (U.S.A., 1941).**
*Directed by Fritz Lang.*
When unattractive characters move toward the camera—toward us—the movement is perceived as threatening and hostile. In this shot portraying a posse in pursuit of the protagonist, the yelping dogs and their masters seem to invade our personal space, violating our sense of security.

(Twentieth Century-Fox)

ment toward the camera seems friendly, inviting, sometimes seductive. In either case, movement toward the audience is generally strong and assertive, suggesting confidence on the part of the moving character.

Movement away from the camera tends to imply opposite meanings. Intensity is decreased and the character seems to grow remote as he or she withdraws from us. Audiences feel safer when a villain moves away in this manner, for he thereby increases the protective distance between us and him. In some contexts, such movements can seem weak, fearful, and suspicious. Most movies end with a withdrawal of some sort, either of the camera from the locale, or of the characters from the camera. The final shot of Vittorio De Sica's *Bicycle Thief* shows the two humiliated protagonists walking away from the camera into a moving crowd: the effect is one of great delicacy and restraint, as if to show that further pursuit of these characters would be an invasion of their privacy.

There are considerable psychological differences between lateral movements on the screen and movements toward or away from the camera. A script might simply call for a character to move from one place to another, but *how* the director chooses to photograph this movement will determine most of its psychological implications. Generally speaking, if the character moves from right to left (or vice-versa) he or she will seem determined and efficient, a person of action (3-5). Unless the camera is at extreme long shot range, these

**3-5. *Slow Dancing in the Big City* (U.S.A., 1978).**
*With Anne Ditchburn and Hector Jaime Mercado; Choreography by Robert North; Directed by John Avildsen.*
Lateral movements tend to emphasize speed, decisiveness, and excitement. Such shots are usually brief, for the amount of time required to move from one side of the frame to the other is minimal.

(United Artists)

movements are necessarily photographed in brief takes—shots lasting only a few seconds. Since lateral movements tend to emphasize speed and efficiency, they are often used in action movies.

On the other hand, when a character moves in or out of the depth of a scene, the effect is often one of slowness. Unless the camera is at close range or

(a)

(b)

*(Janus Films)*

### 3-6. *L'Avventura* (Italy, 1960).

*With Monica Vitti; Directed by Michelangelo Antonioni.*

Psychological films often employ movements in and out of the depth of an image, especially to create a sense of tediousness and exhaustion. Shots of this sort require anticipatory setups which reinforce these qualities, for we see the destination of a character's movement long before it's completed. Here, the heroine's search for her lover in the corridors of a hotel suggests the futility of her love affair. The endless succession of doors, fixtures, and hallways implies, among other things, the repetition of the frustration she is now experiencing. Much of the meaning of shots such as these lies in their duration: space is used to suggest time. Needless to say, Antonioni's movies are among the slowest paced of the contemporary cinema: long after the viewer has had time to absorb the visual information of a shot, it continues on the screen. When this film was originally shown at the Cannes Film Festival, an audience of hostile critics kept shouting "Cut! Cut!" at the screen. The shots were so lengthy and the pace so slow that viewers assumed the director was inept at editing. But like many of Antonioni's works, this is about enervation, and the movie's slow rhythm is organically related to this theme.

an extreme wide angle lens is used, movements toward or away from the camera take longer to photograph than lateral movements. With a telephoto lens, such movements can seem hopelessly dragged out. Furthermore, when depth movement is photographed in an uninterrupted lengthy take, the audience tends to anticipate the conclusion of the movement, thus intensifying the sense of tedium while we wait for the character to arrive at his destination. Especially when a character's physical goal is apparent—the length of a long corridor, for example—audiences generally grow restless if they are forced to view the entire movement (3-6). Most directors would photograph the action in several different setups, thus compressing the time and space from the inception of the movement to its conclusion.

The distance and angle from which movement is photographed determines much of its meaning. In general, the longer and higher the shot, the slower the movement tends to appear. If movement is recorded from close and low angles, it seems intensified and speeded up. A director can photograph the same subject—a running man, for example—in two different setups and produce opposite meanings. If the man is photographed in an extreme long shot from a high angle, he will seem ineffectual and impotent. If he's photographed from a low angle in a medium shot, he will seem a dynamo of energy. Despite the fact that the subject matter in each setup is absolutely identical, the true content of each shot is its form.

Many viewers, oblivious to these perceptual relationships, tend to think of movement only in terms of gross physical action. The result has been a good deal of naive theorizing on what is "intrinsically cinematic." Such viewers tend to think that the more the movement would be perceived as extravagant in real life, the more filmic it becomes. Subject matter that emphasizes epic events and exterior locations are presumed to be fundamentally more suited to the medium than intimate, restricted, or interior subjects. Such views are based on a misunderstanding of movement in film. To be sure, one can use the terms epic and psychological in describing the general emphasis of a movie. Even on this general level, however, arguments about intrinsically cinematic subjects are usually spurious. Few would claim that Tolstoy's *War and Peace* is intrinsically more novelistic than Dostoyevsky's *Crime and Punishment,* although we may refer to one as an epic and the other as a psychological novel. In a similar vein, only a naive viewer would claim that Michelangelo's *Sistine Ceiling* is intrinsically more visual than a Vermeer domestic scene. They are different, yes. But not necessarily better or worse, and certainly not through any intrinsic quality. In short, there are some good and bad epic works of art, and some good and bad psychological works. It's the treatment that counts, not the material per se.

Movement in film is a subtle issue, for it's necessarily dependent upon the kind of shot employed. The cinematic closeup can convey as much movement as the most sweeping vistas in extreme long shot. In fact, in terms of the area covered on the screen's surface, there is actually more movement in a closeup showing tears running down a person's face than there is in an extreme long shot of a car traveling fifty feet. Cinematic movement is always relative to the shot. An epic film like Lean's *Lawrence of Arabia* might appear to have more movement than a psychological film like Carl Dreyer's *The Passion of Joan of Arc,* but, in fact, Dreyer's film is photographed mostly in closeup: the movement of a feature might literally cover yards of space on the screen's surface.

(RKO)

**3-7. *Top Hat* (U.S.A., 1935).**

*With Fred Astaire and Ginger Rogers; Choreography by Astaire and Hermes Pan; Directed by Mark Sandrich.*

Astaire's dancing style is the epitome of cool—elegant, debonair, effortless. He has influenced such classical choreographers as Jerome Robbins and George Balanchine, and such dancers as Rudolf Nureyev who described Astaire as "the greatest dancer in American history." His range is extraordinarily broad, encompassing the wit and speed of tap, the airy romanticism of ballroom styles, and later in his career, the ethereal lyricism of modern dance. He insisted on artistic control over his dance numbers. A perfectionist, he also insisted on a six-week rehearsal period before production began. In his nine RKO musicals, he and Hermes Pan worked out the choreography, then taught the steps to Ginger Rogers who usually came in shortly before production. The camera is essentially functional: it records the movements of the dancers in lengthy takes, at full shot range, panning and tilting after them as unobtrusively as possible. Their dance numbers are actually love scenes: he woos his lady kinetically. In fact, they rarely even kiss on screen. She is usually reluctant, cool to his verbal advances, but once the music begins, their bodies undulate and sway in rhythmic syncopation, and soon she's a lost creature, yeilding completely to her kinesthetic destiny. See also Arlene Croce, *The Fred Astaire & Ginger Rogers Book* (New York: Vintage Books, 1977).

**3-8. *An American in Paris* (U.S.A., 1951).**
*With Gene Kelly (center); Choreographed by Kelly; Directed by Vincente Minnelli.*
Like his greatest rival and lifelong friend Fred Astaire, Kelly worked in a broad range of styles. He is a vigorous hoofer, earthy rather than airborne, like Astaire. Kelly's tap dancing is muscular, gymnastic, and virile rather than light or nonchalant. He was fond of incorporating lengthy ballet sequences in his films, like this famous Gershwin number extolling such French painters as Utrillo, Toulouse-Lautrec, and (pictured) Raoul Dufy. Above all, Kelly's dancing is sexy, with an emphasis on pelvic movements, tensed loins, twisting torsos, and erotic, close-to-the-floor gyrations. He usually wore close-fitting costumes to emphasize his well-muscled body. He also allowed his personality to shine through, breaking the formality of the choreography with a cocky grin or an ecstatic smile that's as hammy as it is irresistible.

Epic and psychological films employ movement in different ways, with emphasis on different shots. In general, epic movies depend on the longer shots for their effects, whereas psychological films tend to employ the closer shots. Epics are concerned with a sense of sweep and breadth, psychological movies with depth and detail. Epics often emphasize events, psychological films the implications of events. In good movies, as in good novels and plays, these characteristics are matters of emphasis, not exclusion. Shakespeare's *Henry V*—which in a sense is conceived in "long shot"—is not devoid of psychological detail. Nor is Chekhov's *The Cherry Orchard*—conceived in "closeup"—lacking in action. Similarly, *Lawrence of Arabia* is both an epic and a complex character study (3-9).

Two directors can approach the same material and produce totally different results. *Hamlet* is a good example. Laurence Olivier's film version of this play is essentially an epic, with emphasis on the longer shots. Tony

(Columbia Pictures)

**3-9. *Lawrence of Arabia* (Great Britain/U.S.A., 1962).**
*Cinematography by Freddie Young; Directed by David Lean.*
In order for movement to dominate in extreme long shots, it must be presented in epic proportions—as in Lean's desert saga of the enigmatic T. E. Lawrence, alias T. E. Shaw, alias Lawrence of Arabia.

**3-10. *The Wild Child* (France, 1970).**
*With Jean-Pierre Cargol; Directed by François Truffaut.*
Unlike the dance or the live theatre, cinematic movement is always relative: only gross movements are likely to be perceived in an extreme long shot, whereas the path of the tear in this photo covers over half the height of the screen. See also Annette Insdorf, *François Truffaut* (New York: William Morrow, 1979).

(United Artists)

Richardson's version is primarily a psychological study, dominated by close and medium shots. Olivier's movie emphasizes costume and setting. There are many long shots, especially of the brooding castle of Elsinore. Much is made of Hamlet's interaction with this moody locale. We are informed at the beginning of the film that the story is about "a man who could not make up his mind." The long shots are used to emphasize this interpretation visually. Most of them are loosely framed, suggesting that Hamlet (played by Olivier) has considerable freedom of movement, freedom to act. But he refuses to use this freedom, preferring to sulk in dark corners, paralyzed with indecision. When he does move, the motion is generally recorded from long distances, thus reinforcing the impotence of the protagonist in relationship to his environment.

Richardson's *Hamlet* is relatively unconcerned with costumes and decor. The protagonist (Nicol Williamson) is almost always seen in tightly framed close shots. Unlike Olivier's indecisive and contemplative Hamlet, Williamson's is impulsive and rash, a man who often acts before he thinks. Imprisoned by the confining closeups, the tortured hero virtually spills off the edges of the frame into oblivion. The unstable hand-held camera can barely keep up with him as he lunges hyperkinetically from place to place. If the same movements were photographed from a long shot range, of course, the character would seem to move more normally. In the live theatre, these two interpretations would have to be achieved through other means. Although drama is in part a visual medium, the "frame" size (the confines of the set, or the proscenium arch) remains the same for the duration of the play. The

**3-11. *Two Tars* (U.S.A., 1928).**
*With Stan Laurel and Oliver Hardy; Directed by James Parrott.*
The comedy of Laurel and Hardy—like that of most slapstick comedians—is quintessentially kinetic. They were unrivalled in their ability to swell a tiny gesture into an apocalyptic orgy of destruction. Their comedies are filled with rituals of revenge and slow escalations of hostility, snowballing finally into total mass demolition—a story formula they employed many times with brilliant results. See John McCabe, *Mr. Laurel and Mr. Hardy* (New York: Signet, 1968); and Charles Barr, *Laurel & Hardy* (Berkeley, Cal.: University of California Press, 1968).

(MGM)

theatre, in short, is restricted to "long shots," where such distortions of movement are virtually impossible.

If there is a great deal of movement in the closer shots, its effect on the screen will be exaggerated, perhaps even disorienting. For this reason, directors tend to employ these ranges for relatively static scenes. The animation of two people talking and gesturing, for example, is enough movement to prevent most medium shots from appearing static. A memorable two-shot sequence from Elia Kazan's *On the Waterfront* takes place in the cramped back seat of a taxicab. Two brothers (Marlon Brando and Rod Steiger) engage in some masculine small talk. Before long, Brando painfully reminds the older brother that he (Brando) might have been a big-time prize fighter had the older brother not interfered by fixing the match. The facial expressions and gestures of the two men represent the only significant movement in the scene. Yet it seems almost electric with energy, mostly because of the brilliance of the two actors. Brando's pained resentment, restrained by love, is conveyed by the subtle modulations of his face. His clumsy embarrassment is reflected in his tentative hand gestures. Steiger's uptight fury gradually diminishes into remembrance and shame: wild-eyed and trembling, he avoids Brando's face. Finally, recognizing his guilt, Steiger seems almost to collapse, yet the actual movement is minimal: a sigh and a slight lowering of the head and shoulders.

**3-12. *All That Jazz* (U.S.A., 1979).**
*With Roy Scheider (in hospital bed); Choreographed and directed by Bob Fosse.*
Fosse's musical autobiography is unfolded almost exclusively through dance. Three of his idols are Busby Berkeley, Fred Astaire, and Gene Kelly. In fact, Fosse's own choreographic style might be viewed as a synthesis of these three influences. Like Berkeley, he choreographs for the camera, not an imaginary spectator immobilized in front of a proscenium arch. Fosse often photographs his dancers in a series of quick shots from unusual angles, stressing an abstract look in the mise-en-scène. He also shares Berkeley's delight in campy accessories, like tinsel, gaudy feathers, and scanty, sequin-studded costumes. Like Astaire, Fosse is witty and inventive in his integration of dance with locale. This sequence takes place in the intensive-care unit of a hospital where the jaded hero sucks his final breaths before departing for the great terpsichorean stage in the sky. Fosse's spontaneity and speed are also Astairean. Gene Kelly's delirious crane shots exerted a strong influence on Fosse's style. Like Kelly too, Fosse's choreography is muscular and crotchy—almost kinky in its eroticism. Fellini is another Fosse idol, and in this movie and others, he draws heavily from the maestro's works, especially *8½*. Fosse insisted on hiring Fellini's usual cinematographer Giuseppe Rotunno to photograph *All That Jazz*.

*(Twentieth Century-Fox and Columbia Pictures)*

Closeups are even more subtle in their recording of movement. The so-called chamber films of Bergman—*Scenes from a Marriage* and *Autumn Sonata,* for example—are heavily dependent on close shots. These movies are restricted by cramped interiors, small casts, and static situations. Robert Bresson and Carl Dreyer extract both broad and subtle movements by photographing an expressive face in closeup. In fact, these two directors have referred to the human face as a spiritual "landscape." In Dreyer's *Passion of Joan of Arc,* for instance, one of the most powerful scenes is a close shot of Joan (Falconetti) as a tear slowly trickles down her face. Expanded thousands of times by the closeup, the path of the tear represents a cataclysmic movement on the screen, far more effective than the inane cavalry charges and clashing armies of conventional epic films.

Hackneyed techniques are almost invariably the sign of a second-rate director. Certain emotions and ideas—like joy, love, hatred, etc.—are so prevalent in the cinema that serious artists are constantly searching for new methods of presentation, methods which confer uniqueness to the commonplace, transforming the familiar into something fresh and unexpected. For example, death scenes are common in movies. But because of their frequency, they are often presented tritely. Certainly death remains a universal concern, one that can still move audiences if handled with any degree of originality and imagination.

One method of avoiding staleness is to convey emotions through kinetic symbolism. Like the choreographer, the film director can exploit the intrinsic meanings inherent in certain types of movements. Even so-called abstract motions tend to suggest ideas and feelings. Some movements strike us as soft and yielding, for example, while others seem harsh and aggressive. Curved

**3-13. *Lightning Swords of Death* (Japan, 1973).**
*With Tomisaburo Wakayama; Directed by Kenji Misumi.*
Film directors often exploit empty or "negative space" to suggest ideas dealing with loss, both physical and psychological. In this image, the decapitated victim's sudden death is viscerally reinforced by the empty space that fills his half of the screen. The symmetrical balance of the composition is destroyed with the victim's fall, releasing the tensions of the tight frame, and creating a sudden vacuum which accompanies the protagonist's victory over his enemy.

*(Columbia Pictures)*

(Janus Films)

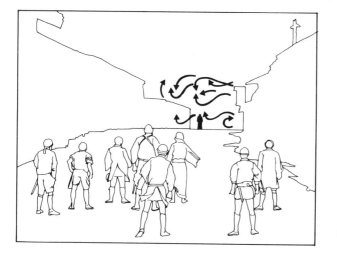

**3-14.** *Yojimbo* **(Japan, 1961).**
*Directed by Akira Kurosawa.*
Kurosawa's movies are rich in symbolic kinetic techniques. He often creates dramatic tensions by juxtaposing static visual elements with a small but dynamic whirlpool of motion. In this scene, for example, the greatly out-numbered protagonist (Toshiro Mifune) prepares to do battle with a group of vicious hoodlums. In static visual terms, the samurai hero seems trapped by the enclosing walls and the human wall of thugs who block off his space. But surrounding the protagonist is a furious whipping wind (the dominant contrast of the shot) which symbolizes his fury and physical power. See also Audie Bock, *Japanese Film Directors* (New York: Harper & Row, 1978).

and swaying motions are generally graceful and feminine. Those that are straight and direct strike us as intense, stimulating, and powerful. Movements can seem wispy, jerky, exploding, withering, and so on. Furthermore, unlike the choreographer, the filmmaker can exploit these symbolic movements without even having to use people to perform them.

If a dancer were to convey a sense of grief at the loss of a loved one, his or her movements would probably be implosive, withdrawn, with an emphasis on slow, solemn, downward movements. A film director might exploit this same kinetic principle but in a totally different physical context. For instance, at the

**3-15. *The French Connection* (U.S.A., 1971).**

*Directed by William Friedkin.*

Expansive outward movements and sunburst effects are generally associated with explosive emotions, like joy or terror. In this shot, however, the symbolism is more complex. The scene occurs at the climax of a furious chase sequence in which the much-despised protagonist (Gene Hackman, with gun) finally triumphs over a vicious killer by shooting him—just as he seems on the verge of eluding the dogged police officer once again. This kinetic outburst on the screen symbolizes not only the bullet exploding in the victim's body, but a joyous climax for the protagonist after his humiliating and dangerous pursuit. The kinetic "ecstasy of death" also releases the dramatic tension that has built up in the audience during the chase sequence: in effect, we are seduced into sharing the protagonist's joy in the kill.

beginning of *Citizen Kane,* we realize that Kane has died when we see a fragile glass globe crash to pieces on the floor. This downward motion is followed by a shot of a window shade in Kane's sickroom slowly being lowered, an act which snuffs out the light. In Walter Lang's *The King and I,* we realize that the seriously ailing King (Yul Brynner) has died when we see a closeup of his hand slowly slipping toward the bottom of the frame, disappearing finally off the lower edge into the darkness. In Eisenstein's *Old and New* (also known as

*The General Line*), a valuable stud bull dies, and its death has serious consequences for the agricultural commune which has purchased the animal. These consequences are expressed through two parallel shots emphasizing the same kinetic symbolism. First Eisenstein shows us an extreme closeup of the dying bull's eye as it slowly closes: the mournful lowering of the eyelid is

(a)

(b)

(United Artists)

**3-16. *High Noon* (U.S.A., 1952).**
*With Gary Cooper; Directed by Fred Zinnemann.*
The closer and tighter the shot, the more the motion dominates. In longer, more loosely framed shots, movement tends to recede in importance, usually in direct proportion to the distance of the kinetic action from the camera. Even the slightest alterations in framing can affect our reactions. The two fight sequences portrayed here, for example, imply subtle differences. The closer, tighter framed shot (a) suggests more danger and desperation, for the antagonist (Lloyd Bridges) almost manages to pull the protagonist off-screen right. In the somewhat longer, looser shot (b), the protagonist's control over his adversary is reinforced by the amount of space allowed for the hero's movements. By allowing more space and distance, the director is able to present the fight scene with a greater degree of stylization and objectivity: in effect, the control of the visual elements within the frame becomes a spatial metaphor for the protagonist's control over his antagonist. See also Louis Giannetti, "Fred Zinnemann's *High Noon*," in *Film Criticism* (Winter, 1976).

magnified many times by the closeness of the shot. Eisenstein then cuts to a shot of the sun lowering on the horizon, its streaming shafts of light slowly retracting as the sun sinks below the earth's rim. Trivial as a bull's death might seem, to the hardworking members of the commune, it suggests an almost cosmic significance. Their hopes and dreams for a better future die with the animal.

Of course context is everything in movies. The kind of symbolism in *Old and New* would probably seem pretentious and arty in a more realistic film. However, the same kinetic *principle* can be used in almost any kind of context. In Norman Jewison's *In the Heat of the Night,* for example, a police officer (Sidney Poitier) must inform a woman (Lee Grant) that her husband has been brutally murdered. When she hears the news, the woman shields her body with her arms in a kind of shrivelling, implosive gesture. In effect, she withdraws into herself, her body withering as the news sinks in. She will not permit even the sympathetic officer to touch or comfort her in any way.

In Charles Vidor's *Ladies in Retirement,* these same kinetic principles are employed in a totally different context. An impoverished housekeeper (Ida Lupino) has asked her aging employer for financial assistance to prevent the housekeeper's two retarded sisters from being put away in an asylum. The employer, a vain selfish woman who acquired her wealth as the mistress of a rich man, refuses to help her employee. As a last resort, the desperate housekeeper decides to kill the old woman and use her isolated cottage as a refuge for the good-naturedly dotty sisters. The murder scene itself is conveyed through kinetic symbolism. We see the overdressed dowager playing a ditty at her piano. The housekeeper, who plans to strangle the woman from behind,

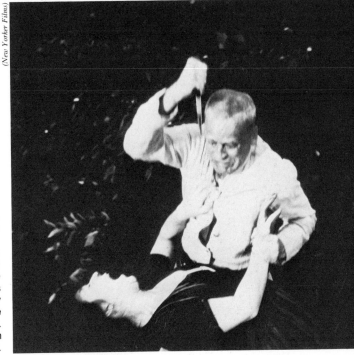

(New Yorker Films)

**3-17. Woyzeck (West Germany, 1978).**
*With Klaus Kinski and Eva Mattes; Directed by Werner Herzog.*
Kinetic symbolism is often integrated with the symbolic associations of off-frame darkness. In this scene, for example, the crazed protagonist stabs his faithless wife—but she refuses to die, repeatedly pulling herself up from the out-of-frame darkness as he strikes again and again. Finally, her fingers loosen their grasp on his shirt, and her body slips out of frame.

slowly creeps up while she is singing. But instead of showing us the actual strangulation, Vidor cuts to a medium close shot of the floor where, one by one, the dowager's pearls drop to the floor. Suddenly a whole clump of pearls splatter near the old lady's now motionless feet. The symbolism of the dropping pearls is appropriate to the context, for they embody not only the woman's superfluous wealth, but her vanity and selfishness as well. Each falling pearl suggests an elegantly encrusted drop of blood. Drop by drop, her life ebbs away, until the remaining strands of pearls crash to the floor, and the wretched creature is dead. By conveying the murder through this kinetic symbolism, Vidor prevents us from witnessing the actual event which probably would have lost the audience's sympathy for the housekeeper. In fact, his presentation actually encourages the audience to identify with her since her motives are selfless.

In each of these instances, the directors—Welles, Lang, Eisenstein, Jewison, and Vidor—were faced with a similar problem: how to present a death scene with freshness and originality. Each director solved the problem by exploiting similar kinetic movements: a slow, contracting, downward motion—the same kind of movement that a dancer would employ literally on a stage.

Kinetic symbolism can be used to suggest other ideas and emotions as well. For example, ecstasy and joy are frequently expressed by expansive motions, fear by a variety of tentative or trembling movements. Eroticism can be conveyed through the use of undulating motions. In Kurosawa's *Rashomon*, for example, the provocative sexuality of a woman is suggested by the sinuous motions of her silk veil—a movement so graceful and tantalizing that the protagonist (Toshiro Mifune) is unable to resist her erotic allure. Since most Japanese viewers regard overt sexuality in the cinema as tasteless—even kissing is rare in their movies—sexual ideas are often expressed through these symbolic methods (see also 7-31).

Every art form has its rebels, and cinema is no exception. Because movement is almost universally regarded as basic to film art, a number of directors have experimented with the idea of stasis. In effect, these filmmakers are deliberately working against the nature of their medium—stripping it of all but the most essential motions (3-18). Such filmmakers as Bresson, Ozu, and Dreyer have been described as minimalists because their kinetic techniques

**3-18. The Last Picture Show (U.S.A., 1971).**
*With Timothy Bottoms and Cloris Leachman; Directed by Peter Bogdanovich.*
Film directors occasionally use stasis or lack of movement to suggest ideas such as exhaustion, spiritual paralysis, and even death. In such instances, even the slightest movement—such as the motion of the woman's comforting arm—tends to acquire magnified significance.

are so austere and restrained. When virtually nothing seems to be moving in an image, even the slightest motion can take on enormous significance. In many cases, this stasis is exploited for symbolic purposes: lack of motion can suggest spiritual or psychological paralysis, as in the movies of Antonioni, for example. Andy Warhol, the *enfant terrible* of the avant-garde cinema, reduced this principle of minimalism to an aesthetic joke. With impish perversity, Warhol made an eight-hour movie, *Empire,* which consists of a single stationary shot of the Empire State Building (see Chapter 10, "Avant-Garde").

## The Moving Camera

Before the 1920s, directors tended to confine movement to the subject photographed. There were relatively few who moved their cameras during a shot, and then usually to keep a moving figure within the frame. In the 1920s such German filmmakers as F. W. Murnau and E. A. Dupont moved the camera within the shot not only for physical reasons, but for psychological and thematic reasons as well. Some of these directors got a bit carried away. In Dupont's *Variety,* for instance, the camera seems never to be still, and the effectiveness of the technique eventually diminishes into tediousness. There are several instances in Murnau's otherwise excellent *The Last Laugh* when a straight cut would probably have been more effective. In general, however, the German experiments permitted subsequent directors to use the mobile camera to communicate subtleties previously considered impossible. Although editing might be faster, cheaper, and less distracting, the straight cut (that is, moving the camera *between* shots) does not always suit the purpose.

A major problem of the moving camera involves time. Films that employ this technique extensively tend to seem slow moving, since moving in or out of a scene is considerably more time consuming than a straight cut. A director must decide whether moving the camera is worth the film time involved, and whether the movement warrants the additional technical and budgetary complications. If a director decides to move the camera, he or she must then decide how. Should it be mounted on a vehicle or simply moved around the axes of the tripod? Each major type of movement implies different meanings, some obvious, some subtle. Directors can choose from four basic kinds of camera movements: pans, tilts, crane shots, and dolly shots. The zoom lens, the hand-held camera, and aerial shots are variations of these basic four.

*Pan* and *tilt shots*—those movements of the camera that scan a scene either horizontally or vertically—are taken from a stationary axis point, with the camera mounted on a tripod of some kind. Such shots are time consuming since the camera's movement must ordinarily be smooth and slow to permit the images to be recorded clearly. Pans are also unnatural in a sense, for when the human eye moves in a similar manner, it jumps from one point to another, skipping over the intervals between points.

The most common use of a pan is to keep the subject within frame. If a man moves from one position to another, the camera moves horizontally to keep him in the center of the composition. Pans in extreme long shot are especially effective in epic films where an audience can experience the vastness of a locale. John Ford, for example, often panned over long stretches of desert before finally settling on some pilgrims as they make their way across

**3-19. Production photo of *Medium Cool* (U.S.A., 1969).**
*Photographed and directed by Haskell Wexler (behind camera).*
The so-called crab dolly (pictured) does not require tracks and can move on the ground in any direction. Note the technician's hands pulling the dolly in this traveling shot. Even on location, most directors prefer to record the sound. The overhead boom, of course, would not appear in the frame of the finished shot.

the sweeping terrain. But pans can be just as effective at medium and close ranges. The so-called reaction pan, for instance, is a movement of the camera away from the central attraction—usually a speaker—in order to capture the reaction of an onlooker or listener. In such cases, the pan is an effective way of preserving the cause–effect relationship between the two subjects. A straight cut from one shot to another would tend to emphasize their separateness.

Pans can also be used to emphasize solidarity and psychological rapport among people. In Truffaut's *Jules and Jim*, for example, the camera pans rather than cuts between three characters in a scene. A woman is loved by two men: one her husband, the other his best friend. She stands in the middle of the frame, while the men sit at either side of her. There is a genuine sense of love that binds the three together, despite their legal and moral entanglements. To emphasize these complex interrelationships, the director first pans to one character, then to another, and then to a third, and back and forth again for the duration of the shot. The characters are engaged in a rather strained conversation all the while. Since the scene is photographed from a medium-long range, the pan is too conspicuous to pass unnoticed—Truffaut's way of emphasizing the awareness of the characters of this awkward *ménage à trois.*

The *swish pan* (also known as a *flash pan* and a *zip pan*) is a variation of this technique and is often used for transitions between shots—as a substitute cut. What the swish pan involves is a whirling of the camera at a speed so rapid that only blurred images are recorded. Despite the fact that it actually takes more time than a cut, swish pans connect one scene to another with a greater sense of simultaneity than a cut can suggest. For this reason, flash pans are often used to connect events at different locales which might otherwise appear remote from each other. In *The Wild Bunch,* Sam Peckinpah used zip pans for reaction shots within the same scene. The effect is one of great violence, rapidity, and simultaneity.

Because a pan shot tends to emphasize connectedness, some directors have used such shots to suggest symbolic rather than literal connections. In *The Manchurian Candidate,* for example, John Frankenheimer used a 360-degree pan with great daring and wit during several dream sequences. Some American prisoners of the Korean War have been brainwashed and are being exhibited to a group of Communist observers in a laboratory amphitheatre. During the sequences, we also see what the brainwashed soldiers *think* is going on— that they are temporarily detained in a New Jersey hotel, listening half-heartedly to a lecture on horticulture which is being presented to a group of genteel dowagers. Several times Frankenheimer circles the entire assembly by beginning with the speaker's platform, scanning the audience, then circling back to the other end of the platform. Throughout these traveling shots, two "realities" are intercut: genteel ladies are incongruously linked with Communist observers. The dreamers (who are still partially brainwashed many months later) are unable to make sense out of these weird mixtures of settings, characters, and events. Frankenheimer uses the circular motif as a metaphor of psychological determinism, a programmed pattern that begins to "short circuit" after the prisoners are released and sent back to America. The metaphor of circuitry is used several times in the dialogue as well. ("The wires have been pulled, Raymond—you're free.")

These same principles apply to most tilt shots, or the vertical movement of the camera around a stationary horizontal axis. Tilts can be used to keep subjects within frame, to emphasize spatial and psychological interrelationships, to suggest simultaneity, and to emphasize cause–effect relationships. Tilts, like pans, can also be used subjectively in point-of-view shots: the camera can simulate a character's looking up or down a scene, for example. Since a tilt is a change in angle, it is often used to suggest a psychological shift within a character: when an eye-level camera tilts downward, for instance, the person photographed suddenly seems vulnerable.

*Dolly shots,* sometimes called *trucking* or *tracking shots,* are taken from a moving vehicle (dolly) of some kind. The vehicle literally moves in, out, or with a scene while the action is being photographed. Tracks are sometimes laid on the set to permit the vehicle to move smoothly—hence, the term tracking shot. If these shots involve long distances, the tracks have to be laid or withdrawn while the camera is moving in or out. Today, any vehicular movement of the camera can be referred to as a dolly shot. The camera can be mounted on a car, a train, even a horse. One of the most effective dolly shots in *Jules and Jim* was taken from a moving bicycle: the scene itself is a bicycle outing in the country, and to capture the lyrical, graceful movements of the

**3-20. *Breathless* (France, 1959).**
*With Jean-Paul Belmondo and Jean Seberg; Directed by Jean-Luc Godard.* As this famous low-budget film demonstrates, dolly shots need not be elaborate. To save money and permit himself greater freedom of movement, Godard strapped his cinematographer (Raoul Coutard) in a wheelchair, and pushed this improvised dolly manually. Many of the long tracking shots in this movie were taken on the busy boulevards of Paris. See also Royal S. Brown, ed., *Focus on Godard* (Englewood Cliffs, N.J.: Prentice-Hall, 1972); and Richard Roud, *Godard* (Garden City, N.Y.: Doubleday, 1968).

*(Contemporary Films)*

characters on their bikes, Truffaut's cinematographer, Raoul Coutard, mounted the camera on a similar vehicle (see also 3-20).

Tracking is a useful technique for point-of-view shots, to capture a sense of movement in or out of a scene. If a director wants to emphasize the destination of a character's movement, he is more likely to use a straight cut between the initiation of the movement and its conclusion. If the experience of the movement itself is important, the director is more likely to dolly. Thus, if a character is searching for something, the time-consuming point-of-view dolly helps to elongate the suspense of the search. Similarly, the pull-back dolly is an effective technique for surprising the character (and audience) with a sudden revelation: by moving back, the camera reveals something startling—a corpse, for example.

A common function of dolly shots is to provide an ironic contrast with dialogue. In Jack Clayton's *The Pumpkin Eater,* a distraught wife (Anne Bancroft) returns to an ex-husband's house where she has an adulterous liaison with him. As the two lie in bed, she asks him if he had been upset over their divorce, and whether or not he missed her. He assures her that he wasn't in the least upset, but while their voices continue on the soundtrack, the camera belies his words by slowly dollying through his living room, revealing pictures, memorabilia, and mementos of the ex-wife. The shot is a kind of direct communication between the director and the audience. In a sense, shots of this kind can be compared with an omniscient narrator in a novel, providing the reader with information which the characters lack. These techniques are deliberate authorial intrusions, and are favored by filmmakers who view their characters with skepticism or irony—Lubitsch and Hitchcock, for example.

One of the most common uses of dolly shots is to emphasize psychological rather than literal revelations. By slowly tracking in on a character, the director is getting close to something crucial. The movement acts as a signal to the audience, suggesting, in effect, that we are about to witness something important. A cut to a closeup would tend to emphasize the rapidity of the discovery, but a slow dolly shot suggests a more gradual revelation. For example, in Clive Donner's *The Caretaker* (also known as *The Guest*), this technique is used several times. Based on Harold Pinter's play, the film concerns two brothers and an old tramp who tries to set one brother against the other. The dialogue, as is often the case in a Pinter script, is evasive and not very helpful in providing an understanding of the characters. Whole speeches seem to be wasted on irrelevant subjects. The brothers are dissimilar in most respects. Mick (Alan Bates) is materialistic and aggressive; Aston (Robert Shaw) is gentle and withdrawn. Each brother has a crucial scene in the film in which the camera slowly tracks from a long range to a closeup. During these two shots, the camera gradually probes the psychological essence of the characters: with Mick, his obsessive preoccupation with decorating his grubby properties; with Aston, his horrifying experience in a mental hospital where he received shock treatments which were to make him "like other people." Neither of the speeches is really very informative, at least not on a literal level. It is in the juxtaposition of the dialogue with the implications of the dolly shot that the audience feels it has finally "arrived" at an understanding of each character.

A stationary camera tends to convey a sense of stability and order, unless there is a great deal of movement within the frame. The moving camera—by

**(a)**

*(Warner Brothers)*

**(b)**

**3-21.** *A Clockwork Orange* **(U.S.A.,/ Great Britain, 1972).**
*With Malcolm McDowell; Directed by Stanley Kubrick.*
The pull-back dolly is often used to establish important psychological as well as physical information. Kubrick's movie opens with a closeup of the protagonist (McDowell) staring brazenly at the camera. On the soundtrack, we hear his confidential commentary which establishes an intimate if uneasy rapport between him and us: we become his confidents. Once this intimacy is established, Kubrick pulls back and offers us a wider and longer view of the protagonist's physical surroundings—a weird "milk bar" where he and his "droogs" sit in a drug-induced stupor.

*(Warner Brothers)*

**3-22. *Rope* (U.S.A., 1948).**
*With James Stewart (left), Farley Granger (right), and John Dall (second from right); Directed by Alfred Hitchcock.*
An incorrigible experimenter in form, Hitchcock shot this film in a single uninterrupted take, the camera and characters choreographed so that the size of the images could be varied from closeups to long shots. During shooting, whenever the camera had to be reloaded (every 10 minutes), he devised ways to mask the cut between shots, such as having a character's back momentarily darken the screen, and continuing the "uninterrupted" scene when the character moves away from the lens. The film is one of the few examples of a literal adherence to the unities of time, place, and action.

its very instability—can create ideas of vitality, flux, and sometimes disorder. Orson Welles has exploited the mobile camera to suggest a character's dynamic energy. In his *Othello,* for example, the dolly shot becomes a thematic motif. The confident moor is often photographed in traveling shots, especially at the beginning of the movie. In the ramparts scene, he and Iago walk with military briskness as the camera moves with them at an equally energetic pace. When Iago tells him of his suspicions, the camera slows down, then comes to a halt. Once Othello's mind has been poisoned, he is photographed mostly from stationary setups: not only has his confident energy drained away, but a spiritual paralysis invades his soul. In the final shots of the film, he barely moves, even within the still frame. This paralysis motif is completed when Othello kills himself.

When the camera literally follows a character, the audience implicitly assumes that it will discover something along the way. A journey, after all, usually has a destination. But traveling shots are often symbolic rather than literal. In Federico Fellini's *8 1/2,* for example, the moving camera is used to suggest a variety of thematic ideas. The protagonist Guido (Marcello Mastroianni) is a film director who is trying to put together a movie near a bizarre health spa. Everywhere he turns, he's confronted by memories, fantasies, and realities more fantastic than anything he can imagine (see also 4-9). But he is paralyzed by indecision. What, if anything, from all this copious flux and superabundance will he select for his movie? He can't use it all, for it won't fit together, the materials are too sprawling. Throughout the film, the camera wanders restlessly, prowling over the fantastic locale, compulsively hoarding images of faces, textures, and shapes. All are absorbed by Guido, but he is unable to detach them from their contexts to form a meaningful artistic structure.

The film's traveling shots function on several levels. They are used to suggest Guido's increasingly desperate search for a theme, a story, or a cinematic structure of some kind. They are also analogues of Guido's passive receptivity: he is like a walking recording machine, seeking out and storing image upon image for their own sake. The traveling shots, in conjunction with the movement of people, processions, and traffic, are also analogues for the unbroken flow of experiences that comprise Guido's reality—a reality he finally refuses to simplify for the sake of producing a tidy little movie. But where Guido fails, Fellini succeeds triumphantly. The final sequence of the film (which takes place in Guido's imagination) emphasizes the continuity and coherence of *all* his experiences. The characters from his life—including those of Guido's past and fantasies—join hands and dance joyously around a circus ring, a ritual celebration of the limitlessness of the artistic imagination. The ring is a visual symbol of Fellini's conception of life's infinite flow which has no beginning or end.

**3-23.** *La Ronde* **(France, 1950).**
*With Simone Signoret (right); Directed by Max Ophüls.*
"There is no escape from the trap of time," Andrew Sarris has observed of the traveling shots in the films of Ophüls. "'*Quelle heure est-il?*' ask the characters in *La Ronde,* but it is always too late, and the moment has always passed." Sarris has also noted that the director usually tells his stories from the woman's point of view, and "the fluidity of his camera serves to hasten his heroines to their disillusioning rendezvous with reality. . . . As we follow the Ophülsian characters, step by step, up and down stairs, and up and down streets, and round and round the ballroom, we realize their imprisonment in time." See Andrew Sarris, "Max Ophüls," in *Interviews with Film Directors* (New York: Avon Books, 1967).

(Janus Films)

A number of film theorists have discussed the unique capacity of the cinema to convert space into time and time into space. The amount of time it takes to photograph concrete objects can be the main purpose of a shot, particularly a traveling shot. In other words, some directors exploit the dolly shot as a consumer of time. This is particularly true in some of the films of Alain Resnais and Bernardo Bertolucci, whose movies often revolve around temporal themes. The acknowledged master of these types of dolly shots was Max Ophüls (3-23). In such films as *Letter From an Unknown Woman* and *The Earrings of Mme. de . . .* , the heroines throw themselves into imprudent but glorious love affairs. The camera tracks relentlessly, as the women become more irrevocably involved with their lovers. As Andrew Sarris has pointed out, Ophüls uses his dolly shots as metaphors of time's cruel prodigality. His world is one of tragic flux and instability in which love is destined to run its eventually bitter course. These lengthy tracking shots preserve the continuity of time by preserving the continuity of space. There is no time for pause and reflection "between shots" in these films. Ophüls' temporalization of space can be overlooked by the casual viewer, for the dolly shots are at least to some degree functional. They follow characters in their daily rounds of activities. But a stationary camera would be just as functional (not to mention less expensive), for the characters could move toward or away from a fixed setup.

In the 1950s, the perfection of a new lightweight hand-held camera permitted directors to move in or out of scenes with greater flexibility. Originally used by documentarists to permit them to shoot in nearly every kind of location, these cameras were quickly adopted by many fiction film directors as well. Hand-held shots are often jumpy and ragged. The camera's rocking is hard to ignore, for the screen exaggerates these movements, especially if the shots are taken from close ranges. For this reason, directors often use the hand-held camera for point-of-view shots. In Mike Nichols' *The Graduate,* a hand-held shot is used to simulate the hero's attempts to maneuver through a crowded room of people. Most cinematographers can manipulate a lightweight camera as steadily as a dolly if the situation requires.

*Crane shots* are essentially airborne dolly shots. A crane is a kind of mechanical arm, often more than twenty feet in length. It can lift a cinematographer and camera in or out of a scene. It can move in virtually any direction: up, down, diagonally, in, out, or any combinations of these. In many respects, the crane resembles those used by the telephone company to repair lines. Because of this flexibility, a crane shot can suggest a number of complex ideas. It can move from high long distances to low close ones, as it does in Hitchcock's *Notorious,* where the camera sweeps from an extreme high-angle long shot of a ballroom to an extreme closeup of the hand of the heroine (Ingrid Bergman) clasping a small key.

Because the camera can move in space, a number of filmmakers have used crane shots as metaphors of penetration. In the first Susan Alexander sequence of *Citizen Kane,* Welles used a spectacular crane shot that was criticized for its flashiness by some critics. Through a downpouring rain, the camera cranes up to the roof of a seedy nightclub where the wretched Susan is performing, plunges through a neon sign advertising her engagement, then sinks down through the skylight of the nightclub where Susan has collapsed in a drunken stupor. The camera's penetrating movement parallels the reporter's probe into Kane's personality. Both the camera and the reporter encounter numerous obstacles—the rain, the sign, the very walls of the building

**3-24. *Shame* (Sweden, 1968).**
*With Max von Sydow and Liv Ullmann; Directed by Ingmar Bergman.*
Particularly at close ranges, the hand-held camera tends to be unsteady. Here the rocking suggests the motion of the boat. Shots like these almost always symbolize instability, impermanence, and transition. See also *Persona and Shame: The Screenplays of Ingmar Bergman* (New York: Grossman, 1972).

must be penetrated before we can even see Susan, much less hear her speak. The shot also embodies a brutal invasion of privacy, a disregard for the barriers Susan has placed around her in her grief.

Like dolly shots, crane shots can be used to temporalize space. In the final sequence of Lumet's *Long Day's Journey Into Night*, the camera begins with a closeup and ends in an extreme long shot. The setting is the family living room, late at night. The mother, who is hopelessly addicted to morphine, is oblivious to her despairing family. She is vaguely reminiscing about her childhood experiences in a convent school, speaking more to herself than to the others. As she takes her journey into the past, the camera slowly moves back and up, from a close shot of the mother's face to a high extreme long shot of the entire living room. At the end of the crane's movement, the room is a dimly lit white area, taking up less than a tenth of the screen and surrounded

(Paramount Pictures)

**3-25.** *The Conformist* (Italy/France, 1970).
*With Jean-Louis Trintignant (left); Directed by Bernardo Bertolucci.*
Bertolucci's traveling shots are personal, eccentric, even perverse. Often the camera lunges forward, sideways, or up and away—even in the middle of dialogue sequences. These spontaneous eruptions destabilize the visual materials, infusing the action with a surge of kinetic energy. Bertolucci's favorite cinematographer Vittorio Storaro is regarded as an unsurpassed master of mobile camera work. See also 2-16.

by total darkness. The shot carries a multitude of meanings, all implied by the title. The journey is into the past, not only the mother's, but the rest of the family's as well. The mother's journey into night is her increasing sense of isolation and oblivion, brought on by the drugs. The journey is also taken by the other members of the family, for the mother's night plunges the rest of the family into the same black despair. In short, the movement of the crane shot is an embodiment of the temporal implications of Eugene O'Neill's symbolic title.

The use of a zoom lens doesn't usually involve the actual movement of the camera, but its effect on the screen is very much like an extremely fast tracking or crane shot. The zoom is a combination of lenses, which are continuously variable, permitting the camera to change from close wide-angle distances to extreme telephoto positions (and vice versa) almost instantaneously. The effect of the zoom is a breathtaking sense of being plunged into a scene, or an equally jolting sense of being plucked out of it. Zoom shots are used instead of dolly or crane shots for a number of reasons. They can zip in or out of a scene much faster than any vehicle. From the point of view of economy, they are cheaper than dolly and crane shots since no vehicle is necessary. When filming in crowded locations, zoom lenses can be useful for photographing from long distances, away from the curious eyes of passersby. With a single setup of the camera, the zoom can switch from close to long ranges (and vice versa) with rapid ease. Much of the location shooting of *The French Con-*

*nection* required the presence of actual city crowds. Friedkin shot these scenes from long unobtrusive distances; but with the help of the zoom lens, he was able to photograph close shots as well as long.

There are certain psychological differences between zoom shots and those involving an actual moving camera. Dolly and crane shots tend to give the viewer a sense of entering into or withdrawing from a set: furniture and people seem to stream by the sides of the screen, as the camera penetrates a three-dimensional space. Zoom lenses forshorten people and flatten space. The edges of the image simply disappear at all sides: the effect is one of sudden magnification. Instead of feeling as though we are entering a scene, we feel as though a small portion of it has been thrust toward us. In shots of brief duration, these differences tend to be insignificant, but in lengthier shots, the psychological differences can be pronounced.

Since the early 1960s, the zoom has been one of the most abused devices in the cinema—mostly through overuse. Hack directors use zoom shots to zap up their materials—to lend dull scenes a sense of urgency. Some television adventure series would be impossible without the indispensible zoom, for these programs consist mostly of banal events which are made to seem cataclysmic by the rapid zooming in and out on essentially static scenes. A sign of a desperate director is the arbitrary and frequent use of zoom shots.

In the hands of a master, however, zooms can be richly expressive and even subtle. In *The Wild Bunch,* Peckinpah used a slight zooming in and out as metaphors of psychological tension and release. The wild bunch are in the process of transporting a wagonload of weapons and munitions when they're ambushed by Mexican soldiers. Rather than give up the load to the soldiers, the bunch threaten to blow it up—and themselves with it. The decision rests with the Mexican officer in charge of the ambush. As he quickly sizes up the

**3-26. *Mean Streets* (U.S.A., 1973).**
*With Robert De Niro, Amy Robinson, and Harvey Keitel; Directed by Martin Scorsese.*
In scenes of violence, a wildly lurching hand-held camera can kineticize the visual materials with a terrifying quicksilver instability.

(Warner Brothers)

situation, the camera zooms in slightly, framing the officer in a tighter composition. Realizing that he's been outwitted, he smiles ironically, and agrees to let the bunch pass with their wagon. As he does so, the camera zooms back to its former position, thus releasing the tensions of the tight frame. The shot functions almost like a screw, which turns in on the officer while he's under pressure to make a quick decision, then loosens up after he decides.

Aerial shots, usually taken from a helicopter, are really variations of the crane shot. Like the crane, the helicopter can move in virtually any direction. When a crane is impractical—usually on exterior locations—an aerial shot can duplicate the effect. The helicopter shot can be much more extravagant, of course, and for this reason, is occasionally used to suggest a swooping sense of freedom. In *Jules and Jim*, an aerial shot conveys Jim's lyrical exhilaration when, after many years, he plans to visit his friend Jules and his wife in Germany. In *Apocalypse Now*, Coppola used aerial shots to produce a God-like sense of inexorability as swirling American helicopters annihilate a Vietnamese village (3-27).

**3-27. Apocalypse Now (U.S.A., 1979).** *Cinematography by Vittorio Storaro; Directed by Francis Ford Coppola.*
The famous helicopter attack sequence in this film is a kinetic tour-de-force, suffusing the action with a sense of exhilaration—and horror. Virtually every shot in this brilliantly edited sequence contains a forward rush, a sense of being swept up by events out of control. Coppola often juxtaposes religious scenes with scenes of violence in his movies. In this shot, for example, attack helicopters swirl overhead in the smoke of battle while American soldiers participate in Holy Communion services.

*(United Artists)*

### Mechanical Distortions of Movement

Movement in film is not a literal phenomenon, but an optical illusion. Present-day cameras record movement at 24 frames per second. That is, in each second, 24 separate still pictures are photographed. When the film is shown in a projector at the same speed, these still photographs are mixed instantaneously by the human eye, giving the illusion of movement. This phenomenon is called the persistence of vision. By simply manipulating the timing mechanism of the camera and/or projector, a filmmaker can distort movement on the screen. Even at the turn of the century, Méliès was experimenting with various kinds of trick photography, and while most of these experiments were just clever stunts, subsequent directors have used these discoveries with artistic results. There are five basic distortions of this kind: animation, fast motion, slow motion, reverse motion, and freeze frames.

There are two fundamental differences between animation and live-action movies. In *animation sequences,* each frame is photographed separately rather than continuously at the rate of 24 frames per second. Another difference is that animation, as the word implies, doesn't ordinarily involve the photographing of subjects that move by themselves. The subjects photographed are generally drawings or static objects. Thus, in an animated movie, thousands of frames are separately photographed. Each frame differs from its neighbor only to an infinitesimal degree. When a sequence of these frames is projected at 24 fps, the illusion is that the drawings or objects are moving, and hence, are "animated."

The common denominator of both animated and live-action film procedures is the use of the camera, the photographic process. In a sense, animation has greater affinities with the graphic arts, whereas ordinary fiction films have closer ties with the live theatre. But in both cases, the recording camera acts as an intermediary between the subject and the audience. Even animated films, however, have different emphases. Many of the features of Walt Disney, for instance, are as dramatic as ordinary fiction films. In fact, a number of parents have considered Disney's *Bambi* too frightening and violent for children. On the other hand, some of the brilliant animated films of the Canadian Norman McLaren and the Yugoslavian Zagreb School are virtually abstract expressionist paintings on celluloid.

A popular misconception about animated movies is that they are intended primarily for the entertainment of children—perhaps because the field was dominated for so many years by Disney. In actuality, the gamut of

**3-28. *Pinocchio* (U.S.A., 1940).**
*By Walt Disney.*
Beginning with the "Silly Symphonies" of the early 1930s, the field of animation was dominated for many years by Disney whose movies were ostensibly aimed at children. Disney's great feature length films—*Snow White and the Seven Dwarfs, Fantasia, Pinocchio, Bambi,* and *Dumbo*—are classics of the cinema and appeal to adults as well. See also Christopher Finch, *The Art of Walt Disney* (New York: Abrams, 1973); and Richard Schickel, *The Disney Version* (New York: Simon and Schuster, 1969).

(© Walt Disney Productions)

sophistication in this genre is as broad as in live-action fiction films. The works of Disney and the puppet films of the Czech Jiri Trnka appeal to both children and adults. Some of the great Yugoslavian animated movies are likely to appeal primarily to adults—Ante Bajaja's *Justice,* for example. A few of these films are as sophisticated as the drawings of Paul Klee. There are even some X-rated animated films, most notably Ralph Bakshi's *Fritz the Cat* and *Heavy Traffic* (3-29). The computer-animated films of John and James Whitney are formally complex and are not likely to appeal to children. Nor are youngsters likely to be attracted to the mystical abstract works of Jordan Belson (1-6).

Another popular misconception about animated movies is that they are more simple than live-action films. The contrary is usually the case. For every second of screen time, 24 separate drawings usually have to be photographed. Thus, in an average 90-minute feature, over 1,296,000 drawings are necessary. Furthermore, some animators use transparent plastic sheets (called cels) which they layer over each other in order to give the illusion of depth to their drawings. Some single frames consist of as many as three or four layers of cels. Most animated films are short precisely because of the overwhelming difficulty of producing all the necessary drawings for a longer movie. Feature-length animated movies are usually produced assembly-line fashion, with dozens of draftsmen drawing thousands of separate frames. The animated Beatles film *The Yellow Submarine* was drawn by many different artists, although the guiding sensibility was that of the Canadian animator, George Dunning.

**3-29. *Heavy Traffic* (U.S.A., 1973).**
*By Ralph Bakshi.*
Many animated films are too mature or sophisticated, either in subject matter or technique, to be appreciated by young children. Bakshi's witty social satire is deliberately gross and raunchy, and was accordingly awarded an X rating. See also Ralph Stephenson, *The Animated Film* (New York: A. S. Barnes, 1973).

*(American International Pictures)*

Technically, animated films can be as complex as live-action movies. The same techniques can be used in both forms: traveling shots, zooms, angles, various lenses, editing, dissolves, etc. The only difference is that animators *draw* these elements into their images. Furthermore, animators also can use most of the techniques of the painter: different kinds of paints, pens, pencils, pastels, washes, acrylics, and so on.

Some filmmakers have even combined the techniques of live-action with animation. In *Neighbors,* for example, McLaren used a technique called *pixillation* which involves photographing live actors frame by frame, a method sometimes called *stop-motion photography* (10-10). When the sequence is projected on the screen, the actors move in abrupt, jerky motions, suggesting a primitive cartoon figure. Other filmmakers have combined animation and theatrical film techniques within the same frame. This mixture is accomplished with the aid of the optical printer. Two film strips are superimposed—one consisting of animated frames, the other of photographs of actual people and things. Mattes are used to block out certain areas of the real scene where the animated drawings will appear in the finished print (3-30). Disney used this technique in many of the sequences of *Song of the South* and *Mary Poppins.* The technique is not always successful, for the reality of one style tends to contradict the plausibility of the other. The animated world has a kind of reality that sometimes doesn't mesh with photographs of actual people and things.

**3-30. *King Kong* (U.S.A., 1933).**
*With Fay Wray; Special effects by Willis H. O'Brien; Directed by Merian C. Cooper and Ernest B. Schoedsack.*
O'Brien was a specialist in model animation, which uses stop-motion photography on miniature models with malleable parts. When animated, these models become giant prehistoric creatures. Actually, a variety of special effects was used in the film, including matte and process shots and composite shots produced by the optical printer. In this "realistic" shot, for example, a live-action print was fused with an animated print using an 18-inch model of Kong. There were six miniature models in all, plus a 20-foot bust of Kong's head and shoulders, and an 8-foot long mechanized hairy hand which could lift the screaming Miss Wray up, down, and away. See also 7-7.

*(RKO)*

*Fast motion* is achieved by having events photographed at a slower rate than 24 fps. Ordinarily, the subject photographed moves at a normal pace. When the sequence is projected at 24 fps, the effect is one of acceleration. This technique is sometimes used to intensify the natural speed of a scene— one showing galloping horses, for example, or cars speeding past the camera.

Early silent comedies were photographed before the standardization of cameras and projectors at 24 fps, and therefore their sense of speed is exaggerated at present-day projector speeds. Even at 16 or 20 fps, however, many of these early directors employed fast motion for comic effects. Without the use of acceleration, the comedies of Mack Sennett would lose much of their loony vitality.

According to the French aesthetician, Henri Bergson, when people act mechanically, rather than flexibly, comedy is the result. People, unlike machines, can think, feel, and act reasonably. A person's intelligence is mea-

**3-31.** *Frank Film* **(U.S.A., 1973).** *By Frank Mouris.* Avant-garde filmmakers have used stop-motion photography and animation since the time of Méliès, in part because such techniques decrease the artist's dependence on collaborators. Mouris' droll autobiography consists almost entirely of magazine cut-outs which are ludicrously choreographed through stop-motion photography.

(Pyramid Films/American Federation of Arts)

sured by his or her ability to be flexible. When behavior becomes machinelike and inflexible, we find it laughable. One aspect of machinelike behavior is speed: when a person's movements are speeded up on film, he or she seems inhuman, ridiculous. Dignity is difficult in fast motion, for acceleration robs us of our humanity. In Richard Lester's *A Hard Day's Night,* acceleration is merely one of the dozens of visual gags in the film. Other directors use this technique for thematic purposes or as an aspect of characterization. The Upton Inn mixup in Richardson's *Tom Jones* is funny precisely because the fast motion captures the machinelike predictability of all the characters: Tom flies from Mrs. Waters' bed, Mr. Fitzpatrick flies off the handle, Squire Weston screams for his daughter, and the servants scream for their lives.

*Slow motion* sequences are achieved by photographing events at a faster rate than 24 fps, and projecting the film strip at the standard speed. Slow motion tends to ritualize and solemnize movement. Even the most commonplace actions take on a choreographic gracefulness in slow motion. Where speed tends to be the natural rhythm of comedy, slow, dignified movements

**3-32. *Allegro Non Troppo* (Italy, 1977).** By Bruno Bozzetto. Bozzetto is Italy's most famous animator, wry, spritely, and sophisticated. This affectionate spoof of *Fantasia* is a virtual homage to Bozzetto's idol, Walt Disney.

*(New Line Cinema)*

tend to be associated with tragedy. In *The Pawnbroker,* Sidney Lumet used slow motion in a flashback sequence, showing the protagonist as a young man on an idyllic country outing with his family. The scenes are lyrical and otherworldly—too perfect to last. Luis Buñuel's *Los Olvidados* employs this technique in a dream sequence where the throbbing undulations of a raw piece of meat are almost hallucinatory.

When violent scenes are photographed in slow motion, the effect is paradoxically beautiful. In *The Wild Bunch,* Peckinpah used slow motion to photograph the grisliest scenes of horror—flesh tearing, blood splattering, horses toppling, an almost endless variety. By aestheticizing these scenes of ugliness, Peckinpah demonstrates why the men are so addicted to a life of violence when it seems so profitless. Violence becomes almost an aesthetic credo, somewhat like the way it's portrayed in the fiction of Hemingway. Slow-motion violence became virtually a trademark in the works of Peckinpah; but after the late 1960s, other directors reduced it to a cinematic cliché.

*Reverse motion* simply involves photographing an action with the film running reversed. When projected on the screen, the events run backward. Since Méliès' time, reverse motion has not progressed much beyond the gag stage. In *A Hard Day's Night* Lester used reverse motion as a comic choreographic retake; in *The Knack,* for a quick laugh when an egg "returns" to its shell. One of the most expressive uses of reverse motion—combined with slow motion—is in Jean Cocteau's *Orpheus.* The protagonist has taken a journey into Hell, to regain his lost wife. He makes a serious blunder while there and expresses a wish to return to his original point of decision to correct his mistake. Magically, he is whisked into the past before our eyes, as the previous sequence unfurls backwards in slow motion—to the physical setting where the fateful decision was made. The reverse motion in this sequence is a good instance of how space can be temporalized and time spatialized in the cinema.

A *freeze frame* suspends all movement on the screen. A single image is selected and reprinted for as many frames as is necessary to suggest the halting of motion. By interrupting a sequence with a freeze shot, the director calls attention to an image—offering it, as it were, for our delectation (3-34).

**3-33. *Hair* (U.S.A., 1979).**
*Choreography by Twyla Tharp; Directed by Milos Forman.*
Slow motion etherealizes movement, lending it a dreamy, other-worldly grace. Throughout this musical, slow motion is used in the dance numbers to emphasize the individuality rather than the uniformity of the dancers. Twyla Tharp's choreography is organic to the story, which deals with the free-wheeling lifestyle of some 1960s hippies. The dance numbers are loose and spontaneous, with each dancer doing his or her own thing—like jiggling links in a chain.

Sometimes the image is a fleeting moment of poignance which is over in a fraction of a second, as in the final shot of Truffaut's *The 400 Blows.* Directors also use freeze frames for comic purposes. In *Tom Jones,* Richardson freezes the shot of Tom dangling on a noose while the off-screen narrator urbanely explains to the audience why Tom should not hang until his tale is finished.

In other instances, the freeze frame can be used for thematic purposes. The final image of Richardson's *The Loneliness of the Long Distance Runner* is frozen to emphasize the permanence of the protagonist's status at the end of the picture. Freeze frames are ideal metaphors for dealing with time, for in effect, the frozen image permits no change. Near the end of *True Grit,* for example, Henry Hathaway froze a shot of the protagonist (John Wayne) and his horse leaping over a fence. By halting the shot at the crest of the leap, Hathaway creates a metaphor of timeless grandeur: the image suggests a heroic equestrian statue, immune from the ravages of time and decay. Of course, the total absence of movement is often associated with death, and Hathaway's freeze frame also implies this idea. Perhaps a more explicit metaphor of death can be seen in the conclusion of George Roy Hill's *Butch Cassidy and the Sundance Kid* where the two heroes (Paul Newman and Robert Redford) are "frozen" just before they are shot to death. Like Hathaway's freeze frame, Hill's suggests an ultimate triumph over death.

Most of the mechanical distortions mentioned above were discovered by Méliès. For many years after, they were largely ignored by the majority of

**3-34. *Viridiana* (Mexico/Spain, 1961).**
*Directed by Luis Buñuel.*
This famous freeze-frame parody of Leonardo's *Last Supper* is only one example of Buñuel's savage assault on the Church, sentimental liberalism, and middle-class morality. His sardonic wit is often shocking, blasphemous. For example, the context of this freeze frame is a drunken orgy of beggars who pose for a group photo to the accompaniment of Handel's *Messiah*. A reeling reveler snaps the picture not with a camera but her genitals. This raucous gesture throws the "disciples" into paroxysms of laughter. Though a nonbeliever, Buñuel is able to infuse a sense of scandal in these sacrilegious jokes. ("Thank God I am still an atheist," he once sighed.)

commercial filmmakers until the late 1950s, when the French New Wave directors revived them. Since then, many of these techniques have been used promiscuously. Zooms, freeze frames, and slow-motion sequences became almost *de rigueur* in the 1960s. In many cases, they degenerated into clichés—modish flourishes which were tacked on to the materials, regardless of whether the techniques were organic to the spirit of the subject.

Movement in film is not simply a matter of "what happens." The director has dozens of ways to convey motion, and what differentiates a great director from a merely competent one is not so much a matter of what happens, but *how* things happen—how suggestive and resonant are the movements in a given dramatic context? Or, how effectively does the form of the movement embody its content?

## Further Reading

BACHER, LUTZ, *The Mobile Mise en Scène* (New York: Arno Press, 1978). Primarily on lengthy takes and camera movements.

DAVIS, JAMES E., "The Only Dynamic Art," in *Introduction to the Art of the Movies*, Lewis Jacobs, ed. (New York: The Noonday Press, 1960). A collection of articles.

DEREN, MAYA, "Cinematography: The Creative Use of Reality," in *The Visual Arts Today,* Gyorgy Kepes, ed. (Middletown, Conn.: Wesleyan University Press, 1960). A discussion of dance and documentary in film.

GIANNETTI, LOUIS D., "The Aesthetic of the Mobile Camera," in *Godard and Others: Essays in Film Form* (Cranbury, N.J.: Fairleigh Dickinson University Press, 1975). Symbolism and the moving camera.

HALAS, JOHN, AND ROGER MANVELL, *Design in Motion* (New York: Focal Press, 1962). Movement and Mise-en-scène.

HOLLOWAY, RONALD, *Z is for Zagreb* (New York: A. S. Barnes, 1972). A discussion of the famous Zagreb animators.

HOLMAN, BRUCE L., *Puppet Animation in the Cinema* (New York: A. S. Barnes, 1975). Emphasis on Czech and Canadian animators.

JACOBS, LEWIS et al., "Movement," in *The Movies as Medium,* Lewis Jacobs, ed. (New York: Farrar, Straus, & Giroux, 1970). A collection of essays.

KNIGHT, ARTHUR, "The Street Films: Murnau and the Moving Camera," in *The Liveliest Art* (New York: Mentor, rev. ed. 1979). The German school of the 1920s.

LINDSAY, VACHEL, *The Art of the Moving Picture* (New York: Liveright, 1970). Reprint of an early classic study.

4

*"The foundation of film art is editing."*
V. I. PUDOVKIN

# EDITING

We have been concerned thus far with cinematic communication as it relates to the single shot, the basic unit of construction in film. Except for traveling shots and lengthy takes, however, shots in movies tend to acquire meaning when they are juxtaposed with other shots, when they are structured into a coherent edited sequence. Physically, editing is simply joining one strip of film (shot) with another. Shots are joined into scenes and scenes into sequences. On the most mechanical level, editing eliminates unnecessary time and space. Through the association of ideas, editing connects one shot with another, one scene with another, and so on. Simple as this may now seem, the convention of editing represents the first cornerstone of film art. In fact, Terry Ramsaye, an early film critic, referred to editing as the "syntax" of cinema, its grammatical language. Like linguistic grammar, the syntax of editing must be learned—we don't possess it innately.

From its primitive beginnings in the early part of the twentieth century, editing has evolved into an art of great complexity, nearly every decade providing new variations and possibilities. Before the turn of the century, most movies consisted of short anecdotes photographed in long shot in a single take. When the film stock was nearly exhausted, the event would be quickly concluded. The duration of the shot and the scene were equal. Essentially, these early movies were little more than stage playlets recorded on celluloid: the camera was stationary; the actors remained in long shot; the scene ran continuously with screen time and real time roughly the same. For example, the central idea of one early film involves a man throwing a party for several girls. They engage in a number of comic bits—flirtations, spilling drinks, and so on. Then the party ends with the entire cast boisterously leaving the set. Great cinema it wasn't.

After 1900, things improved. In France, England, and America, crude narratives made their first appearance. No longer merely situations, but stories, with a beginning, middle, and end, these movies demanded more than a single set and one continuous shot. The problem was continuity. Odd as it may now seem, the filmmakers of this period were worried that audiences wouldn't see the relationship between one segment (shot) of the story and another. To solve their problem, they may have turned to the live theatre for help. Here, the curtain was an accepted convention, implying a transition in time and/or place. The curtain, in effect, connected the various scenes and acts into a coherent whole. The fade was to film what the curtain was to drama. Quite simply, what a fade involved was the diminishing of light at the conclusion of a scene until the screen went black. The next scene would then fade in, often revealing a different location at a different time. Usually the two scenes were unified by the presence of the same actor. As early as 1899, the

**4-1. *The Deer Hunter* (U.S.A., 1978).**
*Directed by Michael Cimino.*
Editing is an art as well as a craft. Like all art, it's not beholden to mechanical formulations. In some cases, instinct takes precedence over logic. For example, when sneak preview audiences were asked for their reactions to this 3-hour long film, most viewers responded enthusiastically, but felt the hour-long wedding sequence of the opening could have been cut down. In terms of its story content, the sequence could be condensed to a few minutes of screen time—which is exactly what its makers did. When the shortened version was shown to audiences, reactions were negative. Cimino and his editor, Peter Zinner, restored the cut footage. The long wedding sequence is necessary not for its intellectual content so much as for its *experiential* value. It provides the movie with a sense of moral balance. The community solidarity of the sequence is what the characters fight for in the subsequent portions of the film.

Frenchman, George Méliès, made a short movie, *Cinderella,* in twenty "arranged scenes."

Before long, directors began cutting within scenes as well as between them. The American, Edwin S. Porter, is usually credited with this innovation, although, in fact, as early as 1900 the Englishman G. A. Smith inserted a closeup within a scene. At about the same time, his countryman, James Williamson, featured an intercut chase sequence within one of his movies. These innovations were largely ignored, however, until Porter arrived at them independently somewhat later. Porter's *The Life of an American Fireman* (1903) pushed the concept of editing a step further. A simple story of a fireman's rescue of a woman and her child, Porter's film contained seven scenes. The last featured three different shots: the firetruck arriving at the burning building; an interior shot of a woman and her child trapped in the burning building; and an exterior shot of the fireman carrying the woman down the ladder. This last action was repeated in the rescue of the child.

Traditionally, scene seven would have been filmed in one continuous take. By breaking up the scene into three different shots, Porter established the shot, and not the scene, as the basic unit of film construction. This new editing concept also introduced the idea of shifting points of view in film. Until that time, most movies were shot in stationary long shot—roughly the position a close observer would have in the live theatre. The duration of a scene corresponded to the actual event. But with the breakup of shots into both exterior and interior positions, the observer is, in effect, at both places at once. Furthermore, since film time does not depend on the duration of the event, a new subjective time is introduced—one which is determined by the duration of the shots and the elapsed time implied between them, not by the actual occurrence.

## The Foundations: D. W. Griffith

The American, D. W. Griffith, has been called the father of film because he consolidated and expanded earlier techniques and devised many new ones as well. He was also the first to go beyond gimmickry into the realm of art. One of the medium's creative geniuses, Griffith established more than any other filmmaker the language of film art. Within a brief period, he explored the three basic types of editing styles: (1) cutting to continuity, (2) classical cutting, also known as *découpage classique* (from the French, *découper,* to cut up), and (3) thematic cutting, or *montage,* as it's commonly called in Europe. In his earliest movies, Griffith perfected the technique of cutting to continuity—the most basic and literal kind of editing. Classical cutting—a technique favored by most American fiction directors—was perfected in Griffith's masterpiece *The Birth of a Nation.* In *Intolerance* (1916), he was to explore the technique of thematic montage. However, this style of editing wasn't refined until the 1920s by the filmmakers of the Soviet Union.

Griffith seized upon the principle of the association of ideas in the concept of editing and expanded it in a variety of ways. *Cutting to continuity* is a technique used in most fiction films, if only for exposition sequences. Essentially, this style of editing is a kind of shorthand, consisting of time-honored conventions. Continuity cutting tries to preserve the fluidity of an action without literally showing all of it. For example, a woman leaving work and going home might be condensed into five or six brief shots, each of which leads by association to the next: (1) she enters a corridor as she closes the door to her office, (2) she leaves the office building, (3) she enters and starts her car, (4) she drives her car along a highway, (5) her car turns into her driveway at home. In order to keep the action logical and continuous, there must be no confusing breaks in an edited sequence of this sort. Often all the movement is carried in the same direction on the screen, for if the woman should move from right to left in one shot and the movements are from left to right in the other shots, the viewer might think that she is returning to her office. Cause-effect relationships must be clearly set forth: if the woman slams on her brakes, for example, the director is generally obliged to offer us a shot of what prompted the driver to stop so suddenly.

The continuity of actual space and time is fragmented as unobtrusively as possible in this type of editing. Unless the audience has a clear sense of a continuous action, an edited sequence can be disorienting. (Hence, the term jump-cut means an editing transition that's confusing in terms of space and

**4-2. *The Birth of a Nation* (U.S.A., 1915).**
*Directed by D. W. Griffith.*
Famous for his last-minute rescue finales, Griffith cross-cut between four different groups in the climactic sequence of this film. Despite the sense of speed suggested by the brevity of the shots, the sequence actually expands time. Griffith used 255 separate shots for about 20 minutes of screen action.

time.) In order to make his transitions smooth and continuous, Griffith carefully established his scenes in long shot at the beginning of a sequence. Gradually he cut to medium shots, then to closeups. During the scene, he would often cut to re-establishing shots (a return to the initial long shot) in order to remind the audience of the spatial context of the closer shots. "Between" these various shots, time and space could be expanded or contracted with considerable subtlety.

In exploring the technique now called *classical cutting,* Griffith took the principles of cutting to continuity several steps further. Classical cutting involves editing for dramatic intensity and emotional emphasis rather than for purely physical reasons. Through the use of the closeup within the scene, Griffith managed to achieve a dramatic impact unprecedented in its time. Closeups had been used earlier, but Griffith was the first to use them for psychological rather than physical reasons alone. Audiences were now permitted to see the smallest details of an actor's face. No longer were performers required to flail their arms and tear their hair. The slightest arch of an eyebrow could convey a multitude of subtleties. By splitting the action into a series of fragmentary shots, Griffith achieved not only a greater sense of detail, but a far greater degree of control over his audience's reactions. In carefully selecting and juxtaposing long, medium, and close shots, he constantly shifted the audience's point of view within a scene—excluding here, emphasizing there, consolidating, connecting, contrasting, paralleling, and so on. The possibilities were enormously far ranging. The spatial and temporal continuum of the real scene was radically altered. It was replaced by a subjective continuity—the association of ideas implicit in the connected shots.

In its most refined form, classical cutting presents a series of psychologically connected shots—shots which aren't necessarily separated by real time and space (4-3). For example, if four characters are seated in a room, a director might cut from one speaker to a second with a dialogue exchange, then cut to a reaction shot of one of the listeners, then to a two-shot of the original speakers, and finally to a closeup of the fourth person. The sequence of shots represents a kind of psychological cause–effect pattern. In other words, the breakup of shots is justified on the basis of dramatic rather than literal necessity. The scene could be photographed just as functionally in a single shot, with the camera at long-shot range. (This type of setup is known as a master shot.) Classical cutting is more nuanced. It deconstructs the unity of space, analyzes its components, and refocuses our attention to a *sequence* of details. The action is mental and emotional rather than literal.

During the golden years of the American studio system—roughly the 1930s and 1940s—directors were often urged (or forced) to adopt the *master shot* technique of shooting. What this method involved was shooting an entire scene in long shot without cuts. This take contained all the dramatic variables, and hence served as the basic or "master" shot for the scene. The action was then repeated a number of times with the camera photographing medium shots and closeups of the principals in the scene. When all this footage was gathered together, the editor had a number of choices in constructing a story continuity. Often disagreements arose over the proper sequence of shots. Usually the studio director was permitted a first cut—that is, the sequence of shots representing his interpretation of the materials. Under this system, the studios usually had the right to a final cut. Many directors disliked master shot

(RKO)

**4-3. *It's a Wonderful Life* (U.S.A., 1946).**
*With James Stewart; Directed by Frank Capra.*
Capra was a master of classical editing. His cutting style is fast, light, seamless. But he never displayed his editing virtuosity for its own sake. Like every other technique, editing is subordinated to the needs of the characters in action—the cardinal commandment of classical cutting. In this and other scenes, Capra included a "reactive character" who guides the viewer's response to the action. This character represents a kind of norm, the way an average person would respond to a given situation. In this scene, for example, Capra's charming fantasy takes a whimsical turn. The forlorn hero (Stewart) listens to his guardian angel (Henry Travers, left) explain why he isn't a very *distinguished* angel (he has yet to earn his wings). A casual bystander (Tom Fadden, center) happens to overhear and is totally spooked by their conversation. Capra is able to punctuate the comedy of the scene by cutting to this character's response whenever the angel says something weird.

techniques precisely because with so much footage available, a producer could construct a radically different continuity.

Master shots are still used by many directors. Without a master, editors often complain of inadequate footage—that the available shots won't cut smoothly. Even an experienced director like Arthur Penn apparently undershot in *Little Big Man.* Edited by Dede Allen (who was also responsible for the brilliant cutting in Penn's *Bonnie and Clyde*), the final military sequence of Penn's western—the Battle of the Little Big Horn—is muddled and confused, probably because of inadequate footage. The viewer is unable to tell where General Custer and his men are positioned, or where the Indians are coming from or going to. In complex battle scenes like this, most directors are likely to shoot many cover shots—that is, general shots which can be used to re-establish a sequence if the other shots won't cut. In *Birth of a Nation,* Griffith used multiple cameras to photograph many of the battle scenes, a technique also used by Kurosawa in some of the sequences of *The Seven Samurai.*

Griffith became famous for his chase and rescue sequences which often ended his films. Most of these sequences feature parallel editing—the alterna-

**4-4. *Fat City* (U.S.A., 1972).**

*Directed by John Huston.*

Classical cutting involves editing for dramatic emphasis. In Huston's fight scene, for example, the entire boxing match could have been presented in a single setup (a), although such a presentation would probably strike us as unexciting. Instead, Huston breaks up his shots according to the psychological action within the fighter protagonist (Stacy Keach), his manager, and two friends (Jeff Bridges and Candy Clark) in the auditorium. See also Gerald Pratley, *The Cinema of John Huston* (New York: A. S. Barnes, 1977).

**(a)**

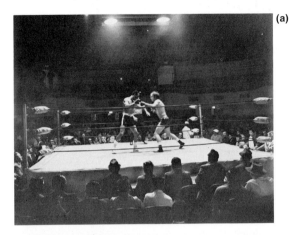

**(b)**

**(c)**

**(d)**

**(e)**

**(f)**

(Columbia Pictures)

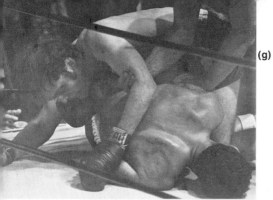

(g)

(h)

(i)

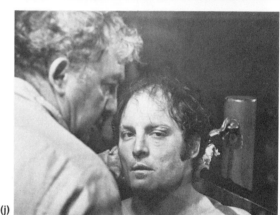

(j)

(k)

(l)

(m)

(n)

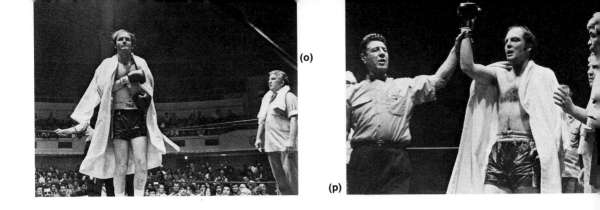

(o)

(p)

tion of shots of one scene with another at a different location. By cross-cutting back and forth between the two (or three or four) scenes, Griffith conveyed the idea of simultaneous time. For example, near the end of *Birth of a Nation*, Griffith cross-cuts between four groups: (1) a besieged group of white people trapped in a cabin, (2) a group of white vigilantes racing to their rescue, (3) rioting Negroes on the rampage, and (4) the heroine being forced into an undesired marriage. Despite its disgusting racism, the sequence is still powerful. In juxtaposing shots from these four scenes, Griffith managed to intensify the suspense by reducing the duration of the shots as the sequence peaked to its climax. The sequence itself lasts 20 minutes of film time, but the psychological effect of the cross-cutting (the shots average about 5 seconds each) suggests speed and tension. Generally speaking, the greater the number of cuts within a scene, the greater its sense of speed. To avoid the risk of monotony during this sequence, Griffith changed his setups many times: there are extreme long, long, medium, and close shots, varied angles, lighting contrasts, even a moving camera. (It was mounted on a truck.)

If the continuity of a sequence is reasonably logical, the fragmentation of space presents no great difficulties. The problem of time is more difficult to solve since its treatment in film is more subjective than the treatment of space. Movies can compress years into two hours of projection time. They can also stretch a split second into many minutes. Most films condense time. There are only a handful that attempt to make screen time conform to real time: Agnès Varda's *Cleo from Five to Seven* and Zinnemann's *High Noon* are perhaps the best known examples. Even these movies cheat by compressing time in the expository opening sequences and expanding it in the climactic scenes. In actual practice, time exists in a kind of limbo: so long as the audience is absorbed by the screen action, time is what the film says it is. The problem, then, is to absorb the viewer.

On the most mechanical level, screen time is determined by the physical length of the filmstrip containing the shot. This length is governed generally by the complexity of the image subject matter. Usually, longer shots are more densely saturated with visual information than closeups and need to be held longer on the screen. Raymond Spottiswoode, an early film theorist, claimed that a cut must be made at the peak of the "content curve"—that is, the point in a shot at which the audience has been able to assimilate most of its information. Cutting after the peak of the content curve produces boredom and a sense of dragging time. Cutting before the peak doesn't give the audience time to assimilate the visual action. An image with a complex mise-en-scène requires more time to assimilate than a simple one. Once an image has been established, however, a return to it during the sequence can be considerably shorter, since it works, in effect, as a reminder.

But the sensitive treatment of time in editing is largely an instinctive matter, one that defies mechanical rules. Most great directors have edited their own films, or at least worked in close collaboration with their editors, so crucial is this art to the success of films. Griffith had an almost unfailing sense of rhythm, and rhythm, or pace, is what makes cinematic time convincing. The best edited sequences are determined by mood as well as subject matter. Griffith, for example, generally edited love scenes in long lyrical takes, with relatively few setups. His chase and battle scenes were composed of brief shots, jammed together. Paradoxically, the love scenes actually compress real time, whereas the rapidly cut sequences elongate it.

**4-5.** *The Last Picture Show* **(U.S.A., 1971).**
*With Ellen Burstyn and Cybill Shepherd; Directed by Peter Bogdanovich.*
In its subtlest form, classical cutting can break up even a confined action into smaller units of meaning. François Truffaut once observed that movies in which people tell lies require more shots than those in which they tell the truth. For example, if a young daughter tells her mother that she thinks she is in love with a boy, and the mother responds by warning the girl of some of the emotional dangers involved, there is no reason why the scene shouldn't be photographed in a single setup with both females in the same frame. Essentially, this is how Bogdanovich presents a similar scene (a). However, if the mother were a lying hypocrite, and the daughter suspected that the older woman might be in love with the boy herself, a director would be forced to break the scene down into five or six shots (b–g) in order to give viewers emotional information they wouldn't receive from the characters themselves.

**(a)**

**(b)**

**(c)**

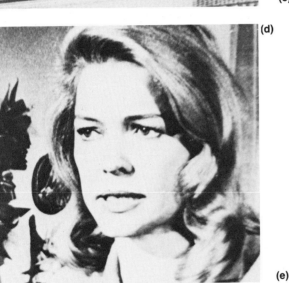

**(d)**

**(e)**

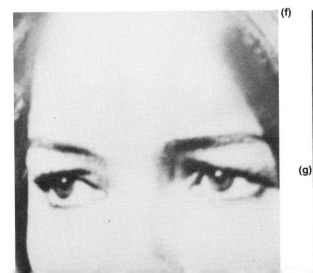

**(f)**

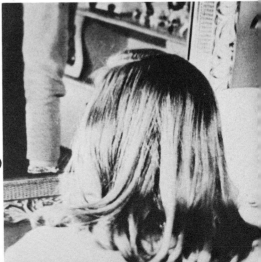

**(g)**

There are no fixed rules concerning rhythm in films. Some editors cut according to musical rhythms. The march of soldiers, for example, could be edited to the beat of a military tune, as can be seen in several marching sequences in King Vidor's *The Big Parade*. This technique is also common with American avant-garde filmmakers who feature rock music soundtracks or cut according to a mathematical or structural formula. In some cases, a director will cut before the peak of the content curve, especially in highly suspenseful sequences. In a number of movies, Hitchcock teases the audience by not providing enough time to assimilate all the meanings of a shot. On the other hand, Antonioni usually cuts long after the content curve has peaked (3-6). In *La Notte,* for example, the rhythm is languorous and even monotonous: the director attempts to create a sense of weariness in the audience, paralleling that of the characters. Antonioni's characters are usually pretty tired people—in every sense of the term. Violent scenes are conventionally cut in a highly fragmented manner. In *Bonnie and Clyde,* however, the exciting shoot-out sequence of the motel escape is photographed in long shot, with only a few cuts. This combination is what produces the scene's weird blend of comedy and danger.

Tact is another editing principle that's difficult to generalize about since it too depends on context. None of us likes to have the obvious pointed out to us, whether in real life or while watching a movie. Like personal tact, directorial tact is a matter of restraint, taste, and respect for the intelligence and sensitivity of others. Hack directors often present us with emotionally gratuitous shots, falling over themselves to make sure we haven't missed the point. In many TV dramatic series, for example, the main characters gather together at the conclusion, at which time they revel in an orgy of self-congratulation. The smugness of these scenes is offensive in long shot, insufferable when individualized in a series of cloying closeups. Such edited sequences lack tact. They're pushy.

In *Intolerance,* Griffith developed the art of editing to its most radical extreme. *Thematic montage* stresses the association of ideas, irrespective of the continuity of real time and space. *Intolerance* is unified by the theme of man's inhumanity to man. Rather than tell one story, Griffith intercut four. One takes place in ancient Babylon; the second deals with the crucifixion of Jesus; the third with the massacre of the Huguenots in sixteenth century France; and the last takes place in America in 1916, the year of the film's release. The stories are not developed separately, but in parallel fashion—with scenes of one time period intercut with scenes of another. At the conclusion, Griffith features hair-breadth chase sequences in the first and last stories, a suspenseful and brutal scene of slaughter in the third, and a slow tragic climax in the story of Jesus. The concluding sequence contains literally hundreds of shots, juxtaposing images that are separated by thousands of years, and by as many miles. All these different time periods and locations are unified by the central theme of intolerance. The continuity is no longer physical, or even psychological, but conceptual—that is, thematic.

*Intolerance* was not a commercial success, but its influence was immense. The filmmakers of the Soviet Union were dazzled by Griffith's movie and based their own theories of montage on his practices in this film. A great many directors have profited from Griffith's experiments in the subjective treatment of time. In *The Pawnbroker,* for example, Lumet exploits the art of editing to produce a series of parallels that are thematically rather than chronologically related. He uses a kind of subliminal editing where some shots are held on the screen for only a fraction of a second. The central character is a middle-aged Jew who survived a Nazi concentration camp twenty-five years earlier. But all his loved ones were killed there. He tries to repress the memories of these earlier experiences, but they insistently force their way into his consciousness. Lumet suggests this psychological process by intercutting a few frames of the memory shots during a scene which is occurring in the present. A present-tense event detonates the protagonist's memory of something similar from his past. As past contends with present, the flickering memory shots endure longer, until a flashback sequence eventually becomes dominant, and the present is momentarily suspended (4-6). With only a few exceptions, however, it was not until the early 1960s that such unorthodox editing practices became widespread. Griffith seldom cut before the peak of the content curve, and most of his successors patterned themselves on his model.

**4-6. *The Pawnbroker* (U.S.A., 1965).**
*With Rod Steiger (right) and Jaime Sanchez; Directed by Sidney Lumet.*
The subliminal cutting and elaborate flashback structure of this movie are Lumet's attempt to suggest the subjective nature of time. In this scene, the protagonist (Steiger) examines some mounted butterflies in a display case which a customer wants to pawn. The butterflies trigger the protagonist's memory, and eventually a sequence from his repressed past—also involving butterflies—displaces the present-tense scene.

*(Allied Artists)*

Filmmakers can interrupt the present with shots not only of the past, but of the future as well. In Dennis Hopper's *Easy Rider,* for example, the protagonist (Peter Fonda) has a prophetic vision of his own death. In Sydney Pollack's *They Shoot Horses Don't They?*, short flash-forwards of a courtroom scene are interspersed throughout the present-tense story. The flash-forwards suggest predestination: like the dance contest of the story proper, the future is rigged, and personal effort is equated with self-deception. Flash-forwards are also used in Alain Resnais' *La Guerre Est Finie* and Joseph Losey's *The Go-Between.*

Griffith also restructured time and place through the use of fantasy inserts. In *Intolerance,* for example, a young woman on the verge of murdering her unfaithful boyfriend imagines a scene where she is apprehended by the police. Flashbacks, flash-forwards, and cutaways to fantasies allow filmmakers to develop ideas thematically rather than chronologically, freeing them to explore the subjective nature of time. The very flexibility of time in movies makes the theme of temporality an ideal subject for the medium.

Like Faulkner, Proust, and other novelists, filmmakers have succeeded in cracking the tyranny of mechanically measured time. One of the most complex instances of the restructuring of time is found in Stanley Donen's *Two for the Road.* The story deals with the development and gradual disintegration of a love relationship. It unfolds in a series of mixed flashbacks. That is, the flashbacks are not in chronological sequence, nor are they completed in any one scene. Rather, they are jumbled and fragmented, somewhat in the manner of a Faulkner novel. To complicate matters, most of the flashbacks take place on the road, during various trips the couple has taken in the past. If each of the time periods of the film were designated with the letters A, B, C, D, and E, its temporal structure might be charted as follows: E (present), A (most distant past), B, C, D, B, A, E, C, D, B . . . ending with E. The audience gradually learns to identify each time period through various continuity clues: the heroine's hair styles, the modes of transporation, the particular crisis during each trip, and so on.

From its crude beginnings, Griffith expanded the art of editing to include a wide variety of functions: locale changes, time lapses, shot variety, emphasis of psychological and physical details, overviews, symbolic inserts, parallels and contrasts, associations, point-of-view shifts, simultaneity, and repetition of motifs. Griffith's method of editing was also more economical. Related shots could be bunched together in the shooting schedule, regardless of their positions (or "time" and "place") in the finished film. Especially in later years, in the era of high-salaried stars, directors could shoot all the star sequences in a brief period and out of cinematic continuity. Less expensive details (extreme long shots, minor actors, closeups of objects, etc.) could be shot at a more convenient time. Later, the shots would be arranged in their proper sequence on the editor's cutting bench. All film directors owe Griffith a debt of gratitude for establishing the basic conventions of cutting to continuity, and the more complex psychological techniques of classical cutting. In *Intolerance,* Griffith was years ahead of his time, for without its audacious thematic cutting, which virtually destroyed literal time and place, the important experiments of the Soviet directors of the next decade would probably not have developed as they did.

## Soviet Montage: V. I. Pudovkin and S. M. Eisenstein

Griffith was a practical artist, concerned with communicating ideas and emotions in the most effective manner possible. In the 1920s, the Russian filmmakers expanded his associational principles and established the theoretical premises for thematic editing, or *montage* as they called it (from the French, *monter,* to assemble). V. I. Pudovkin wrote the first important theoretical treatises on what he called constructive editing. Most of his statements are explanations of Griffith's practices, but he differed with the American (whom he praises lavishly) on several points. Griffith's use of the closeup, Pudovkin claimed, is too limited. It's used simply as a clarification of the long shot, which carries most of the meaning. The closeup, in effect, is merely an interruption, offering no meanings of its own. Pudovkin insisted that each shot should

*(Twentieth Century-Fox)*

**4-7. *Lifeboat* (U.S.A., 1943).**
*With Tullulah Bankhead (center); Directed by Alfred Hitchcock.*
Hitchcock was one of Pudovkin's most articulate champions. "Cinema is form," Hitchcock insisted. "The screen ought to speak its own language, freshly coined, and it can't do that unless it treats an acted scene as a piece of raw material which must be broken up, taken to bits, before it can be woven into an expressive visual pattern." He referred to the piecing together of fragmentary shots as "pure cinema," like individual notes of music that combine to produce a melody. In this movie, he confined himself entirely to nine characters adrift at sea in a small boat. In other words, this photo contains the raw material for every shot in the film. Formalists insist that the artistry lies not in the materials per se, but in the way they are taken apart and reconstructed expressively.

make a new point. Through the juxtaposition of shots, new meanings can be created. The meanings, then, are in the juxtapositions, not in one shot alone (see also 4-7).

To illustrate his point, Pudovkin quotes from the experiments of his mentor, Lev Kuleshov, one of the first filmmakers in the Soviet Union. Kuleshov's experiments are now considered classic. The most impressive, and the most widely known, consists of a series of juxtapositions. First, he shot a closeup of an actor with a neutral expression. He juxtaposed this with a closeup of a bowl of soup. Then he joined the closeup of the actor with a shot of a coffin containing a woman's corpse. Finally, he linked the actor's neutral expression with a shot of a little girl playing. When these combinations were shown to audiences, they exclaimed at the actor's expressiveness in portraying hunger, deep sorrow, and paternal pride. Pudovkin's point carried. In each case, the meaning was conveyed by juxtaposing two shots, not by one alone. Kuleshov's experiments also help to explain why film actors need not necessarily be skillful performers. In large part, they can be used as objects, juxtaposed with other objects. The dramatic emotion is produced by the associations of the juxtaposition, not by the actor's performance. In a sense, the *viewer* creates the emotional meanings, once the appropriate objects have been linked together by the director/editor.

For Pudovkin, a sequence was not filmed, it was constructed. Using far more closeups than Griffith, Pudovkin built a scene from many separate shots, all juxtaposed for a unified effect. The environment of the scene is the source of the images. Long shots are rare. Instead, a barrage of closeups (often of objects) provides the audience with the necessary associations to link together the meaning. These juxtapositions can suggest emotional and psychological states, even abstract ideas.

Pudovkin and other Soviet theorists of his generation were later challenged on several counts. Some critics feel that the extensive use of closeups clogs the pace of a film. (Pudovkin's movies move notoriously slowly, despite the many cuts.) This technique also detracts from a scene's sense of realism, critics have complained, for the continuity of actual time and space is totally restructured. But Pudovkin would claim that realism which is captured in long shot is *too* near reality; it's theatrical rather than cinematic. His main criticism of Griffith was directed at his "slavish" adherence to real time and space. According to Pudovkin, film artists must capture the essence, not merely the surface of reality, which is filled with irrelevancies. They can do so only by conveying *expressively*—through juxtaposed closeups of objects, textures, symbols—what is an undifferentiated jumble in real life.

Some critics also believe that Pudovkin's editing style guides the spectator too much—the choices are already made. The audience must sit back passively and accept the inevitable linking of associations presented to them on the screen. Political considerations are involved here, for the Soviets tended to link film with propaganda. Propaganda, no matter how artistic, doesn't usually involve free and balanced evaluations. Antimontage theorists, on the other hand, believe that the audience should not be passive. They should actively select and evaluate the details for themselves.

Sergei Eisenstein is one of the towering figures of the cinema. A theorist as well as a director, he was also a professor at the Higher Institute of Cinema in Moscow. He was a man of encyclopedic erudition, and his stated aim in life was not only to make movies, but to explore the nature of all kinds of artistic creation. In his teaching and theoretical writings, he constantly alluded to the other arts (especially painting, literature, and drama), in addition to science, history, and philosophy. His contributions to the art of film editing—for which he is best known—can be fully understood only within this broad philosophical context.

Like many theorists, Eisenstein was interested in exploring general principles which could be applied to a variety of apparently different forms of creative activity. He believed that these artistic principles were organically related to the basic nature of all human activity, and ultimately to the nature of the universe itself. Needless to say, only the barest outline of his complex theories can be offered here. Like the ancient Greek philosopher, Heraclites, Eisenstein believed that the essence of existence is constant change. He believed that nature's eternal fluctuation is dialectical—the result of the conflict and synthesis of opposites. What appears to be stationary or unified in nature is only temporary, for all phenomena are in various states of becoming. Only energy is permanent, and energy is constantly in a state of transition to other forms. Every opposite contains the seed of its own destruction in time, Eisenstein believed, and this conflict of opposites is the mother of motion and change.

The function of all artists is to capture this dynamic collision of opposites, to incorporate dialectical conflicts not only in the subject matter of art, but in its techniques and forms as well. The function of the artist is to sensitize the spectator to the eternal fluctuations of the macrocosm. Conflict is universal in all the arts, according to Eisenstein, and therefore all art aspires to motion. Potentially at least, the cinema is the most comprehensive of the arts because it can incorporate the visual conflicts of painting, the kinetic conflicts of dance, the tonal conflicts of music, the verbal conflicts of language, and the character and action conflicts of fiction and drama.

Eisenstein placed particular emphasis on the art of editing. Like Pudovkin, he believed that montage was the foundation of film art. He agreed with Pudovkin that each shot of a sequence ought to be incomplete, contributory rather than self-contained. However, he criticized Pudovkin's concept of linked shots for being mechanical and inorganic. Eisenstein thought that editing ought to be dialectical: the conflict of two shots (thesis and antithesis) produces a wholly new idea (synthesis). Thus, in film terms, the conflict between shot A and shot B is not AB (Pudovkin), but a qualitatively new factor—C (Eisenstein). Transitions between shots should not be flowing, as Pudovkin suggested, but sharp, jolting, even violent. For Eisenstein, editing produces harsh collisions, not subtle linkages. A smooth transition, he claimed, was an opportunity lost.

Editing for Eisenstein was an almost mystical process. He likened it to the growth of organic cells. If each shot represents a developing cell, the cinematic cut is like the rupturing of the cell when it splits in two. Editing is done at the point that a shot "bursts"—that is, when its tensions have reached their maximum expansion. The rhythm of editing in a movie should be like the explosions of an internal combustion engine, Eisenstein claimed. A master of dynamic rhythms, his films are almost mesmerizing in this respect: shots of contrasting volumes, durations, shapes, designs, and lighting intensities collide against each other like objects in a torrential river plunging toward their inevitable destination (4-8).

**4-8. A portion of the Odessa Steps sequence from *Potemkin* (U.S.S.R., 1925).**
*Directed by Sergei Eisenstein.*
Perhaps the most celebrated instance of editing virtuosity in the silent cinema, the Odessa Steps sequence is an illustration of Eisenstein's theory of collision montage in practice. The director juxtaposed lights with darks, vertical lines with horizontals, lengthy shots with brief ones, closeups with long shots, static setups with traveling shots, and so on. See also *Eisenstein's Potemkin: A Shot-by-Shot Presentation,* by David Mayer (New York: Grossman, 1972).

**(a)**

*(Audio-Brandon Films)*

**(b)**

(c)

(d)

(e)

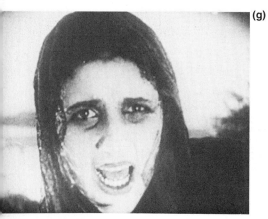

(f)

(g)

(h)

(i)

(j)

 (k)

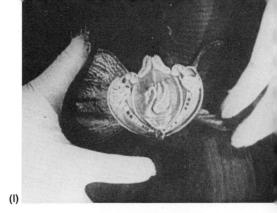 (l)

 (m)

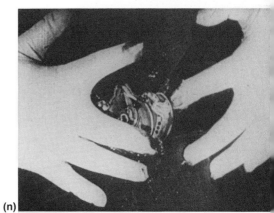 (n)

(o)

 (p)

(q)

 (r)

(s)

(t)

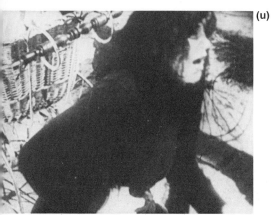

(u)

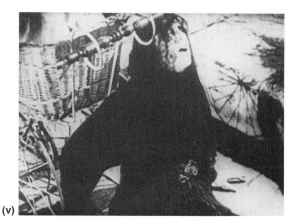

(v)

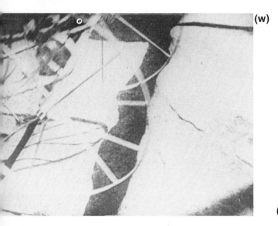

(w)

(x)

(y)

(z)

(aa)

(bb)

(cc)

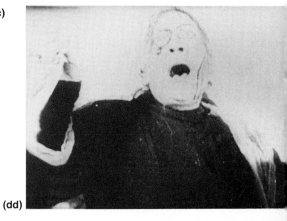

(dd)

(ee)

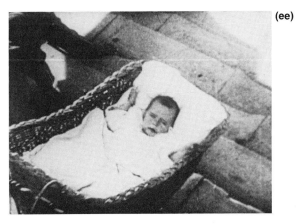

(ff)

(gg)

(hh)

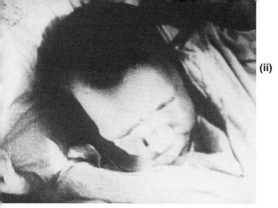
(ii)

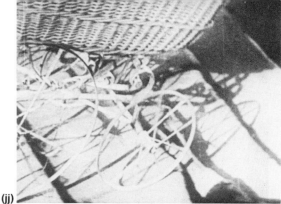
(jj)

(kk)
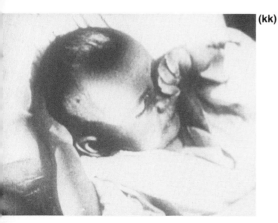

(ll)

(mm)

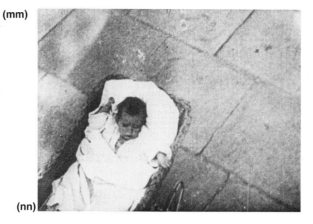
(nn)

(oo)
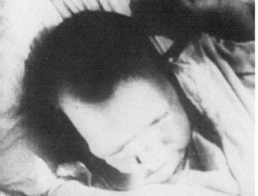

(pp)

(qq)

(rr)

(ss)

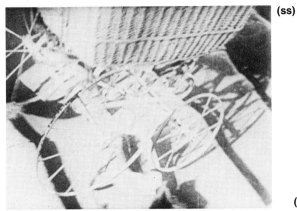

(tt)

(uu)

(vv)

(ww)

(xx)

(yy)

(zz)

(aaa)

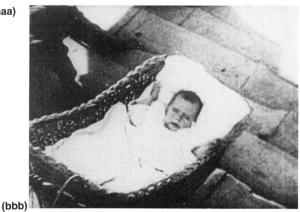

(bbb)

(ccc)

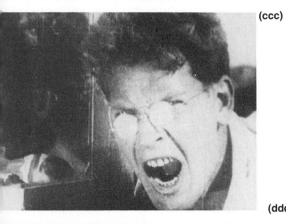

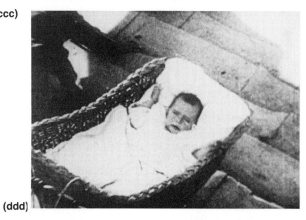

(ddd)

(eee)

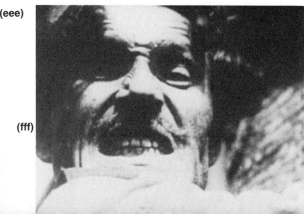

(fff)

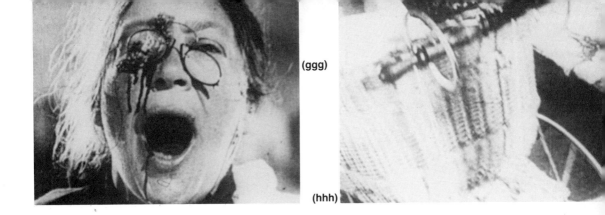

(ggg)

(hhh)

The differences between Pudovkin and Eisenstein may seem academic. In actual practice, however, the two approaches produced sharply contrasting results. Pudovkin's movies are essentially in the classical mold. The shots tend to be additive and are directed toward an overall emotional effect, which is guided by the story. In Eisenstein's movies, the jolting images represent a

**4-9. 8½ (Italy, 1963).**
*Directed by Federico Fellini.*
Fellini's autobiographical movie is an audacious experiment in thematic montage—so audacious, in fact, that even some intelligent critics pronounced the film incoherent. Its principle of unity is not based on the narrative line, but on the romantic ego of its creator. The title is virtually an opus number. The events center on an indecisive film director, Guido Anselmi (Marcello Mastroianni) whose personal life is as complicated as the movie he wants to make. He and his long-suffering wife (Anouk Aimée) are constantly at odds, mostly because of his sexual infidelities (a). He can't be faithful to a single plotline either. His projected movie is constantly being revised because he wants to include several tender childhood memories (b), and they just won't fit his chosen format—a rather improbable sci-fi film. He would also like to include his dreams and sexual fantasies (c) which involve his mistress (Sandra Milo), his wife, his mother, and various other women he finds irresistible. At first, the viewer is able to differentiate these various levels of consciousness, but eventually they begin to merge. Guido's movie is never finished because he's unable to integrate everything he wants to include—which is everything. Although Guido is stymied, Fellini is not. The final circus ring episode (d), which takes place in Guido's imagination, is a triumphant fusion of reality, memory, dreams, and fantasies. The mortar that cements these autobiographical fragments together is thematic montage. See also Dwight Macdonald, "8½: Fellini's Obvious Masterpiece," in *On Movies* (New York: Berkley Medallion Books, 1969).

(a)

*(Embassy Pictures)*

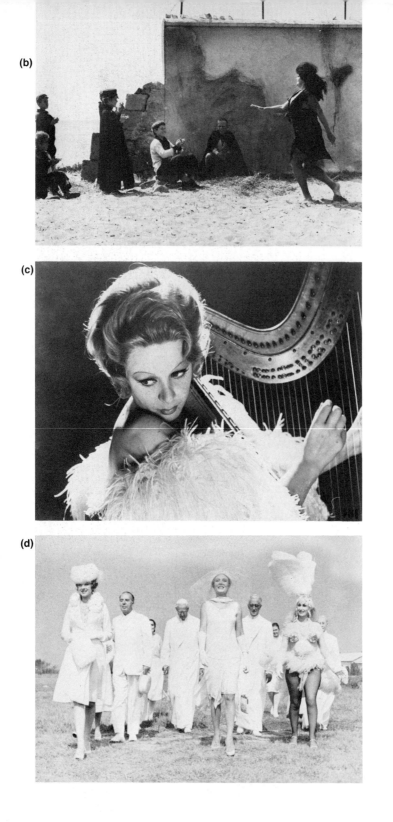

series of essentially intellectual thrusts and parries, directed toward an ideological argument. The directors' choice of narrative structures also differed. Although both artists were Marxist propagandists, Pudovkin's stories didn't differ radically from the kind Griffith used. On the other hand, Eisenstein's stories were much more loosely structured, usually a series of documentary episodes which are used as convenient vehicles for exploring ideas.

When Pudovkin wanted to express an emotion, he conveyed it in terms of physical images—objective correlatives—taken from the actual locale. Thus, the sense of anguished drudgery is conveyed through a series of shots showing details of a cart mired in the mud: closeups of the wheel, the mud, hands coaxing the wheel, straining faces, the muscles of an arm pulling the wheel, and so on. Eisenstein, on the other hand, wanted film to be totally free of literal continuity. Pudovkin's correlatives, he felt, were too restricted by realism. Eisenstein wanted film to be as flexible as literature, especially in its freedom to make figurative comparisions without respect to time and place. Movies should include images that are thematically or metaphorically relevant, Eisenstein claimed, regardless of whether they can be found in the locale or not.

Even in his first feature, *Strike* (1925), Eisenstein intercut shots of workmen being machine-gunned with images of oxen being slaughtered. The oxen are not literally on location, but are intercut purely for metaphorical purposes. A famous sequence from *Potemkin* links three shots of stone lions: one asleep, a second aroused and on the verge of rising, and a third on its feet and ready to spring. Eisenstein considered the sequence an embodiment of a metaphor: "The very stones roar." His most audacious experiments are found in *October,* also known as *Ten Days That Shook the World.* A loose documentary dealing with the earliest phases of the 1917 Revolution, the film is the most radical illustration of Eisenstein's theories in practice. An early sequence shows a statue of the czar being destroyed. Later, when the compromiser Kerensky takes control, Eisenstein metaphorically comments on this setback by running the statue sequence in reverse motion: the statue is reconstructed before our eyes, representing the temporary return of czarism. Many shots of Kerensky in the Winter Palace are satiric: shots of him are juxtaposed with jeweled toy peacocks, with statues of Napoleon, and so on.

Ingenious as these metaphorical comparisons can be, the major problem

*(United Artists)*

**4-10. *West Side Story* (U.S.A., 1961).** *Choreography by Jerome Robbins; Directed by Robert Wise and Robbins.* The editing continuity of a musical number can be highly abstract. The story doesn't necessarily dictate the sequence of shots. Nor are they linked by some principle of thematic association. Rather, the shots are juxtaposed primarily for their visual and kinetic beauty.

**(a)**

**(b)**

**4-11.** *Sisters* **(U.S.A., 1973).**
*Directed by Brian De Palma.*
Multiple images were used as early as 1927 by the great French director Abel Gance in *Napoleon*. The technique employs the aesthetic of fragmentation even more radically than Eisensteinian montage, for individual images from the past, future, or the imagination can be combined within the same frame. This technique can also show two or more points of view at the same time. De Palma's double image presents us simultaneously with a shot and a reverse angle shot (a); a shot and a reaction shot (b), thus reinforcing his doubles theme.

with this kind of editing is its tendency to be obvious, or impenetrably obscure. Eisenstein saw no difficulty in overcoming the spatial and temporal differences between film and literature. But the two mediums employ metaphors in different ways. We have no difficulty in understanding what is meant by the comparison "he's timid as a sheep." Or even the more abstract metaphor, "whorish time undoes us all." Both statements exist outside of time and place. The simile isn't set in a pasture, nor is the metaphor set in a brothel. Such comparisons are not intended to be understood literally, of course. In film, figurative devices of this kind are more difficult. Editing can produce a number of figurative comparisons, but they don't work in quite the same way that they do in literature. Eisenstein's theories of collision montage have been explored primarily in the avant-garde cinema (4-12). Most fiction filmmakers have found them too intrusive and manipulative.

**4-12. *T,O,U,C,H,I,N,G* (U.S.A., 1968).**
*By Paul Sharits.*
In the avant-garde cinema, subject matter is often suppressed or exploited primarily as abstract data. The continuity between shots can be determined by purely subjective or formal considerations (see Chapter 10). In the "flicker films" of Sharits, for example, each frame is a different shot, and when edited together and projected at the standard speed of 24 frames per second, the images flicker by almost subliminally.

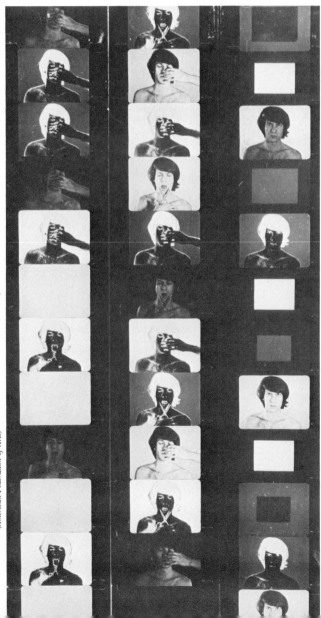

(*American Federation of Arts*)

Soviet montage was enormously influential in the following decades—in theory, if not always in practice. For the most part, film theorists tended to accept the conventional wisdom that editing was *the* cornerstone of the cinema, despite the fact that in the United States, Germany, and elsewhere, filmmakers like Chaplin, Robert Flaherty, Erich von Stroheim, and F. W. Murnau were making movies that owed relatively little to the art of montage—or even to classical cutting. These and other Realist directors found their champion eventually in the Frenchman André Bazin, who established an aesthetic countertradition based on the *preservation* of real time and space.

## André Bazin and the Realist Alternatives

Unlike Griffith, Pudovkin, and Eisenstein, Bazin was not a film director, but solely a critic and theorist. For a number of years, he was the editor of the highly influential journal *Cahiers du Cinéma,* in which he set forth an aesthetic of film that was in sharp opposition to such expressionists as Pudovkin and Eisenstein. Bazin was untainted by dogmatism. While he emphasized the realistic nature of the cinema, he was generous in his praise of movies which exploited the art of editing effectively. Throughout his writings, however, Bazin maintained that montage was merely one of many techniques a director could employ in making movies. Furthermore, he believed that in many instances, editing could actually destroy the effectiveness of a scene (4-13).

**4-13.** *Law and Order* **(U.S.A., 1969).**
*Directed by Frederick Wiseman.*
Like most *cinéma-vérité* documentarists, Wiseman keeps editing to an absolute minimum (see Chapter 9). Implicit in the art of editing is artifice—that is, the manipulation of formal elements to produce a seductive aesthetic effect. Many documentarists believe that an edited analysis of a scene shapes and aestheticizes it—compromising its authenticity. A selected sequence of shots, however factually based, extrapolates one person's truth from an event, and in so doing, infuses it with an ideology. An unedited presentation, on the other hand, preserves a multiplicity of truths. Realists in fiction and the avant-garde also tend to prefer minimal cutting.

*(Zipporah Films)*

Bazin's realist aesthetic is based on his belief that photography and cinema, unlike the other arts, produce images of reality automatically, with a minimum of human interference. This technological objectivity makes the cinema more immediate and credible, linking it directly with the observable physical world. A novelist or a painter must represent reality by *re*-presenting it in another medium—through language and color pigments. The filmmaker's image, on the other hand, is essentially an objective recording of what actually exists. No other art, Bazin felt, can be as literal and comprehensive in the presentation of the physical world. No other art can be as realistic, in the most elementary sense of that word. In film, even the fantastic can be real (3-30).

Bazin's aesthetic has a moral as well as technological bias. He was influenced by the philosophical movement called Personalism which emphasized the individualistic and pluralistic nature of truth. Just as most Personalists agreed that there are many truths, Bazin felt that in the cinema there are many ways of portraying the real. The essence of reality, he believed, lies in its ambiguity. Reality can even be interpreted in opposing, and equally valid, ways, depending on the sensitivities of the artist. To capture this ambiguity, the filmmaker must be modest and self-effacing, a patient observer willing to follow where reality leads. The film artists that Bazin admired most—Flaherty, Renoir, and De Sica, for example—are those whose movies reflect a sense of wonder before the ambiguous mysteries of reality.

Bazin believed that the distortions involved in using expressionist techniques—especially thematic editing—often violate the complexities of reality. Montage superimposes a simplistic ideology over the infinite variability of actual life. Expressionists tend to be too egocentric and manipulative, he felt. They are concerned with imposing their neat scheme of reality, rather than allowing it to exist in its awesome complexity. He was one of the first to point out that such great directors as Chaplin, Mizoguchi, and Murnau preserved the ambiguities of reality by minimizing editing.

Bazin even viewed classical cutting as potentially corrupting. One of his favorite directors, the American William Wyler, reduced editing to a minimum, substituting the use of deep-focus photography and lengthy takes. According to Bazin, classical cutting breaks down a unified scene into a certain number of closer shots that correspond implicitly to a mental process. But the technique encourages us to follow the shot sequence without our being conscious of its arbitrariness. "The editor who cuts for us makes in our stead the choice which we would make in real life," Bazin pointed out. "Without thinking, we accept his analysis because it conforms to the laws of attention, but we are deprived of a privilege." He believed that classical cutting subjectivizes an event because each shot represents what the filmmaker thinks is important, not necessarily what we would think. Bazin admired Wyler's preference for lengthy takes and mise-en-scène rather than editing. "His perfect clarity contributes enormously to the spectator's reassurance and leaves to him the means to observe, to choose, and form an opinion." He believed that Wyler achieved an unparalleled neutrality and transparancy. It would be naive to confuse this neutrality with an absence of art, Bazin insisted, for all of the director's effort tends to hide itself.

Unlike some of his followers, Bazin did not advocate a naive theory of realism. He was perfectly aware, for example, that the cinema—like all art—

involves a certain amount of selectivity, organization, and interpretation: in short, a certain amount of distortion. He also recognized that the values of the filmmaker will inevitably influence the manner in which reality is perceived. These distortions are not only inevitable, but in most cases desirable. For Bazin, the best films were those in which the artist's personal vision is held in delicate balance with the objective nature of the medium. Certain aspects of reality must be sacrificed for the sake of artistic coherence, then, but Bazin felt that abstraction and artifice ought to be kept to a minimum. The materials should be allowed to speak for themselves. Bazinian realism is not mere news-reel objectivity—even if there were such a thing. He believed that reality must be heightened somewhat in the cinema, that the director must reveal the poetic implications of ordinary people, events, and places. By poeticizing the commonplace, the cinema is neither a totally objective recording of the physical world nor a symbolic abstraction of it. Rather, the cinema occupies a unique middle position between the sprawl of raw life and the artificially recreated worlds of the traditional arts.

Bazin wrote many articles overtly or implicitly criticizing the art of editing, or at least pointing out its limitations. If the essence of a scene is based on the idea of division, separation, or isolation, montage can be an effective technique in conveying these ideas. But if the essence of a scene demands the

(Museum of Modern Art)

**4-14. Safety Last (U.S.A., 1923).**
*With Harold Lloyd; Directed by Fred Newmeyer and Sam Taylor.*
In direct opposition to Pudovkin, Bazin believed that when the essence of a scene lies in the simultaneous presence of two or more elements, editing is ruled out. Such scenes gain their emotional impact through the unity of space, not through the juxtaposition of separate shots. In this famous sequence, for example, Lloyd's comedy of thrills is made more comic and more thrilling by the scene's realistic presentation: the dangling hero and the street below are kept in the same frame. Actually, the distance between the two is exaggerated by the cunning placement of the camera, and there was always at least a platform about three stories below him—"but who wants to fall three stories?" Lloyd asked. See also Adam Reilly et al., *Harold Lloyd: The King of Daredevil Comedy* (New York: Collier Books, 1977).

simultaneous presence of two or more related elements, the filmmaker ought to preserve the continuity of real time and space (4-14). He or she can do this by including all the dramatic variables within the same frame—that is, by exploiting the resources of the long shot, the lengthy take, deep focus, and

**4-15.** *The Gold Rush* **(U.S.A., 1925).**
*With Charles Chaplin and Georgia Hale; Directed by Chaplin.*
Bazin admired the tact of Chaplin's deep-focus long shots and lengthy takes. Chaplin's mise-en-scène emphasizes layers and depths of meaning, Bazin pointed out, whereas editing tends to thrust visual information beneath our noses through the use of closeups. Mise-en-scène encourages audience participation, whereas editing preselects materials for us. Philosophically, mise-en-scène emphasizes freedom and the multiplicity of choices, whereas editing tends to suggest coercion and inevitability.

widescreen. The filmmaker can also preserve actual time and space by panning, craning, tilting, or tracking rather than cutting to individual shots.

John Huston's *The African Queen* contains a shot illustrating Bazin's principle. In attempting to take their boat down river to a large lake, the two protagonists (Humphrey Bogart and Katharine Hepburn) get sidetracked on a tributary of the main river. The tributary dwindles into a stream and finally trickles into a tangle of reeds and mud, where the dilapidated boat gets hopelessly mired. The exhausted travelers resign themselves to a slow death in the suffocating reeds, and eventually fall asleep on the floor of the boat. The camera then moves upward, over the reeds, where—just a few hundred yards away—is the lake. The bitter irony of the scene is conveyed by the continuous movement of the camera which preserves the physical proximity of the boat, the intervening reeds, and the lake. If Huston had cut to three separate shots, we wouldn't understand these spatial interrelationships, and therefore the irony would be sacrificed.

Bazin pointed out that in the evolution of the cinema, virtually every technical innovation pushed the medium closer to a realistic ideal: in the late 1920s, the invention of sound; in the 1930s and 1940s, color and deep-focus; in the 1950s, the widescreen. Although Bazin wrote little about the introduction of 3-D in the 1950s, he certainly didn't dismiss it—as virtually every other critic and theorist did. Like previous technological innovations, 3-D represented another leap toward bridging the gap between reality and the artificiality of the screen image.

Bazin pointed out that expressionistic techniques of editing were altered by technology, not by critics or theorists. In 1927, when *The Jazz Singer* was released, sound eclipsed virtually all the advances made in the art of editing since Porter's day. With the coming of sound, films *had* to be more realistic, whether their directors wished them so or not. Microphones were placed on the set itself, and sound had to be recorded while the scene was being photographed. Usually the microphones were hidden—in a vase of flowers, a wall sconce, etc. Thus, in the earliest sound movies, not only was the camera restricted, but the actors as well, for if they strayed too far from the microphone, the dialogue couldn't be recorded properly (4-16).

(*Universal Pictures*)

**4-16. *All Quiet on the Western Front* (U.S.A., 1930).**
*With Lew Ayres (standing); Directed by Lewis Milestone.*
During the early sound period, dialogue sequences were generally photographed in full shots, so that the source of the sound would be visually apparent. Though many expressionists of this era were dismayed by the unedited continuity required by synchronous sound, later theorists like Bazin believed that sound represented a giant leap in the evolution toward a totally realistic medium.

The effects on editing of these early talkies were disastrous. Synchronized sound anchored the images, so whole scenes were played with no cuts. Most of the dramatic values were aural. Even commonplace sequences held a fascination for audiences: if someone entered a room, the camera recorded the fact, whether it was dramatically important or not, and millions of viewers thrilled to the sound of the door opening and slamming shut. Critics and directors despaired: the days of the recorded stage play had apparently returned. Later these problems were solved by the invention of the blimp, a soundproof camera housing which permits the camera to move with relative ease, and by the practice of dubbing sound after the shooting is completed (see Chapter 5). But sound also provided some distinct advantages. Especially in realistic movies, spoken dialogue and sound effects heightened the sense of reality.

Acting styles became more sophisticated. No longer did performers have to exaggerate visually to compensate for the absence of sound. Talkies also permitted directors to tell their stories more economically, without the intrusive titles that interspersed the visuals of silent movies. Tedious expository scenes could also be dispensed with: a few lines of dialogue easily conveyed what an audience needed to know about the premise of the story.

The use of deep-focus photography, reintroduced by Renoir in the 1930s, also exerted a modifying influence on editing practices. Prior to this time, most cameras photographed only one focal plane clearly. These cameras could capture a sharp image of an object from virtually any distance, but unless an enormous number of extra lights were set up, other elements of the picture that weren't at the same distance from the camera remained blurred, out of focus. One justification for editing, then, was purely technical: clarity of image. If all shots—long, medium, and close—were to be equally clear, different lens adjustments were required for each.

Deep-focus photography became popular after it was used in 1941 in *Citizen Kane*. Welles and Wyler are especially associated with this technique, and it's not coincidental perhaps that both these directors had connections with the live theatre. The aesthetic qualities of this process permitted composition in depth: whole scenes could be shot in one setup with no sacrifice of detail, for every distance appeared with equal clarity on the screen (1-9). Deep-focus tended to be most effective when it adhered to the real time–space continuum. For this reason, the technique was thought to be more theatrical than cinematic: the dramatic effects are achieved primarily through a spatially unified mise-en-scène, rather than a fragmented juxtaposition of shots. Bazin was lavish in his praise of Wyler's "invisible" or "styleless" style in which editing was minimized. Some of the most effective movies to use deep focus were Wyler's adaptations of plays, especially *The Little Foxes, The Heiress*, and *The Children's Hour*.

Bazin also liked the objectivity and tact of deep focus. Disregarding for the moment the emphatic elements of composition and movement, details within a shot could be presented more democratically, as it were, without the special attention that a closeup inevitably confers. Thus, Realist critics like Bazin felt that audiences would be more creative—less passive—in understanding the relationships between people and things. Unified space also preserved the ambiguity of life. Audiences aren't led to an inevitable conclusion—à la Eisenstein—but are forced to evaluate, sort out, and eliminate "irrelevancies" on their own.

In 1945, immediately following World War II, a movement called neorealism sprang up in Italy, and gradually influenced directors all over the world (see Chapter 11). Spearheaded by Rossellini and De Sica, two of Bazin's favorite directors, neorealism de-emphasized editing. These filmmakers favored deep-focus photography, long shots, lengthy takes, and an austere restraint in the use of closeups. Rossellini's *Paisan* features a single-take scene which was much admired by Realist critics. An American G.I. talks to a shy Sicilian girl about his family, his life, and his dreams. Neither character understands the other's language, but they try to communicate in spite of this considerable obstacle. By refusing to condense time through the use of separate shots, Rossellini emphasizes the awkward pauses and hesitations between the two characters. Through its preservation of real time, the long take forces us to experience the increasing then relaxing tension that exists between

**4-17.** ***Open City*** **(Italy, 1945).**
*With Anna Magnani; Directed by Roberto Rossellini.*
When asked why he de-emphasized editing, the neorealist Rossellini replied: "Things are there, why manipulate them?" This statement might well serve as Bazin's theoretical credo. He deeply admired Rossellini's openness to multiple interpretations, his refusal to diminish reality by making it serve an *a priori* thesis. "Neorealism by definition rejects analysis, whether political, moral, psychological, logical, or social, of the characters and their actions," Bazin pointed out. "It looks on reality as a whole, not incomprehensible, certainly, but inescapably one." See also José Luis Guarner, *Roberto Rossellini* (New York: Praeger, 1970).

them. An interruption of time through the use of a cut would have dissipated these tensions.

Single-take scenes tend to produce (often unconsciously) a sense of mounting anxiety in the viewer. We expect setups to change during a scene. When they don't, we often get restless, hardly conscious of what's producing our uneasiness. This type of temporal anxiety is exploited effectively in a famous single-take sequence from Joseph H. Lewis' *Gun Crazy*. The camera is mounted in the rear of a getaway vehicle while we wait—along with the robber's accomplice—for the rather sympathetic thief to make his escape. Like the impatient accomplice, we're forced to endure what seems like an eternity of waiting, for we never actually witness the robbery, we experience only its agonizing duration. Long takes are also used with exquisite delicacy in the films of the Japanese director Kenji Mizoguchi (4-18).

Like many technological innovations, widescreen provoked a wail of protest from most critics and directors. The new screen shape would destroy the closeup, many feared, especially of the human face. There simply was too much space to fill, even in long shots, others complained. Audiences would never be able to assimilate all the action, for they wouldn't know where to look. It was suitable only for horizontal compositions, some argued, useful for epic films, but too spacious for interior scenes and small subjects. One wag (Fritz Lang) claimed it was suitable only for photographing funeral pro-

**4-18.** *Utamaro and His Five Women* **(Japan, 1955).**
*Directed by Kenji Mizoguchi.*
Bazin and his disciples were enthusiastic champions of the films of Mizoguchi. The Japanese master favored the use of lengthy takes rather than editing. He generally cut within a continuous take only when there was a sharp psychological shift within the scene. Used sparingly in this way, the cut acquires a greater dramatic impact than can be found in most conventionally edited movies.

(New Yorker Films)

cessions and snakes. Editing would be further minimized, the Expressionists complained, for there would be no need to cut to something if everything was already there, arranged in a long horizontal series.

At first, the most effective widescreen films were, in fact, westerns and historical extravaganzas. But before long, directors began to use the new screen with more sensitivity. Like deep-focus photography, scope meant that

**4-19.** *The Wild Bunch* **(U.S.A., 1969).**
*Directed by Sam Peckinpah.*
Most filmmakers bemoaned the advent of widescreen in the 1950s almost as much as they did sound in the late 1920s. Bazin and other realists embraced the innovation as yet another step away from the distorting effects of montage. Widescreen tends to de-emphasize depth in favor of breadth, but Bazin believed that a horizontal presentation of the visual materials could be more democratic—less distorting even than deep focus, which tends to emphasize visual importance in terms of an object's closeness to the camera's lens.

(Warner Brothers)

**4-20. Z (France, 1969).**
*Directed by Costa-Gavras.*
Almost from the inception of the motion picture, chase scenes have been regarded as intrinsically cinematic, allowing the filmmaker to cut back and forth between pursuer and the pursued. The sense of urgency can be increased considerably by showing the pursuer invading the personal space of the pursued, as in this shot in which a sympathetic character is almost murdered by a speeding auto.

(Cinema V)

they had to be more conscious of their mise-en-scène. More relevant details had to be included within the frame, even at its edges. Films could be more densely saturated, and—potentially at least—more artistically effective. Filmmakers discovered that the most expressive parts of a person's face were the eyes and mouth, and consequently, closeups that chopped off the tops and bottoms of actors' faces weren't as disastrous as had been predicted.

Not surprisingly, the realist critics were the first to reconsider the advantages of widescreen. Bazin liked its authenticity and objectivity. Here was yet another step away from the distorting effects of editing, he pointed out. As with deep focus, widescreen helped to preserve spatial and temporal continuity. Closeups containing two or more people could now be photographed in one setup without suggesting inequality, as deep focus often did in its variety of depth planes. Nor were the relations between people and things fragmented as they were with edited sequences. Scope was also more realistic because the widescreen enveloped the viewer in a sense of an experience, even with its edges—a cinematic counterpart to the eye's peripheral vision. All the same advantages that had been applied to sound and deep-focus were now applied to widescreen: its greater fidelity to real time and space; its detail, complexity, and density; its more objective presentation; its more coherent continuity; its greater ambiguity; and its encouragement of creative audience participation.

## The New Wave and After

Interestingly, several of Bazin's protégés were responsible for a return to more expressionistic editing techniques in the following decades, although they also shared many of Bazin's enthusiasms, particularly for the films of Renoir. Throughout the 1950s, Godard, Truffaut, and Chabrol wrote criticism for *Cahiers du Cinéma*. By the end of the decade, they turned to making their own movies. The *nouvelle vague,* or New Wave as this movement was called in English, was eclectic in its theory and practice. The members of this group, who were not very tightly-knit, were unified by an almost obsessional enthusiasm for film culture, especially American film culture. Unlike most previous movements, the range of enthusiasms of these critic/filmmakers was extraordinarily broad: Hitchcock, Renoir, Eisenstein, Hawks, Bergman, Ford, and many more. While rather dogmatic in their personal tastes, the New Wave critics tended to avoid theoretical dogmatism. They could admire the long takes of a Mizoguchi movie as well as the highly fragmented sequences from the works of Eisenstein. For most of them, technique was meaningful only in terms of subject matter. Discussions of form were usually placed within the context of content, and vice-versa. In fact, it was the New Wave that popularized the principle that *what* a film says is inextricably bound up with *how* it's said.

The New Wave favored no official editing style. The movies of Agnès Varda, for example, tend to follow the Bazinian ideal of long shots and relatively lengthy takes. One of her finest works, *Le Bonheur,* is strongly indebted to the lyrical masterpieces of Renoir. The films of Resnais, on the other hand, tend to emphasize fragmentation. The theme of subjective time is explored through montage in such works as *Hiroshima Mon Amour* and *La Guerre Est Finie.* Chabrol combined the influence of Hitchcock, especially his use of the thriller genre, with the more objective techniques of presentation advocated by Bazin (4-21).

Truffaut and Godard, the most prominent filmmakers of the New Wave,

**4-21. *Wedding in Blood* (France, 1974).**
*With Stephane Audran and Michel Piccoli; Directed by Claude Chabrol.*
James Monaco has pointed out that the New Wave filmmakers were profoundly dialectical: they were constantly trying to fuse opposites. They were fascinated by the aesthetic interplay between the conventions of a genre and the personality of the filmmaker. Like his idol, Hitchcock, Chabrol has worked almost exclusively within one genre—the psychological thriller. Yet Chabrol's editing techniques are predominantly realistic—his debt to Renoir. See James Monaco, *The New Wave* (New York: Oxford, 1976), the best critical study of the movement.

(New World Cinema)

were the most encyclopedic in their techniques. Even within a single movie, there is often a wide variety of editing practices. Truffaut's first feature, *The 400 Blows,* tends to use realistic techniques, with an emphasis on long shots, mise-en-scène, the moving camera, and lengthy takes. *Shoot the Piano Player,* on the other hand, is more expressionistic in its editing style. Truffaut's first movie is indebted to the works of Renoir and the theories of Bazin. His second is more indebted to American gangster films, with their stress on violence, speed, and suspenseful editing. Throughout his career, Truffaut has alternated styles. Films like *Stolen Kisses* reflect his love for the works of Renoir (4-22); movies like *The Bride Wore Black* are indebted to the films of his other

**4-22. *Stolen Kisses* (France, 1968).**
*With Jean-Pierre Léaud and Claude Jade; Directed by François Truffaut.*
Truffaut is a master of what has been called the cinema of the privileged moment—that is, an intimate revelation of the human heart, sincere, sweet, tender. In this scene, for example, the tremulous lovers pledge their troth in an impromptu wedding ceremony at the breakfast table, a heart-shaped bottle opener serving as a wedding ring.

(United Artists)

idol, Hitchcock. But these are generalizations only. Many of these artists combined styles within the same movie. Truffaut's *Jules and Jim,* for example, contains scenes of tender lyricism that only a handful of directors could equal. Yet the same film has scenes of quick sophisticated wit in which montage plays a prominent role.

Godard was the boldest innovator of the New Wave. For over a decade, he turned out nearly two movies a year. His first feature, *Breathless* (1959) was meant to be a homage to *Scarface,* a classic gangster film by Howard Hawks, one of Godard's heroes at the time. *Breathless* popularized the deliberate jump-cuts that were to become so fashionable in the 1960s. In fact, Godard's title seemed to refer as much to the jumpy editing as to the story itself. His nervous cutting was particularly suited to capturing the style of restless and rebellious youth, the subject of many of his movies of the 1960s.

Godard experimented with realistic alternatives to editing as well. *Pierrot le Fou* was his homage to Fritz Lang's *You Only Live Once,* although its style is more indebted to the romantic films of Renoir. *Masculine-Feminine,* one of Godard's finest works, is a typical hybrid of styles and influences. Many shots last only a split second. On the other hand, one scene consists of a single take with a stationary camera and lasts 7 minutes—an incredibly lengthy shot.

What makes so many of the New Wave films attractive is this very stylistic eclecticism. Realistic and expressionistic techniques are exploited according to the dramatic needs of the scene. Within a few years, directors from other nations absorbed the lessons of the *nouvelle vague*—often indiscriminately. Throughout the 1960s, even the trashiest movies employed the editing techniques originally popularized by Truffaut, Godard, and their associates. The films of this manic, youth-obsessed era zoomed in and out, cross-cut, flash-cut, and jump-cut—even if there was nothing in particular to cut *to*. By the mid-1970s, no single editing style prevailed in the international cinema, and audiences had developed a remarkable tolerance for a wide range of cutting styles. The legacy of the New Wave is indispensible. The movement popularized the view that editing styles ought to be determined not by fashion, the limitations of technology, or by dogmatic pronouncements, but by the essence of the subject matter itself.

**4-23. *La Chinoise* (France, 1967).**
*With Anne Wiazemsky (left) and Jean-Pierre Léaud (second from right); Directed by Jean-Luc Godard.*
Like Eisenstein, Godard believed that montage and mise-en-scène are not necessarily in conflict. One implies the other; each is a highly flexible language. In this shot, for example, Godard uses the dividing wall rather than montage to foreshadow a split which will soon develop among the young people in a Maoist cell. Whereas Godard was one of the least political of the New Wave filmmakers at the beginning of his career, by the late 1960s he had become the most stridently Marxist. His influence on political filmmakers in Europe, the Third World, and even America has been enormous.

(*Leacock-Pennebaker, Inc.*)

## Further Reading

BARR, CHARLES, "CinemaScope: Before and After," in *Film Theory and Criticism,* Gerald Mast and Marshall Cohen, eds. (New York: Oxford, 1979). An attack on Eisenstein's editing theories in favor of Bazin, with emphasis on mise-en-scène and the widescreen.

BAZIN, ANDRÉ, *What is Cinema?* Hugh Gray, ed. and trans. (Berkeley: University of California Press, vol. I, 1967, vol. II, 1971). A collection of essays emphasizing the realistic nature of the film medium.

EISENSTEIN, SERGEI, *Film Form* (New York: Harcourt, Brace, 1949). One of the classic studies of montage, written in Eisenstein's typically eliptical, difficult style.

————, *Film Sense* (New York: Harcourt, Brace, 1942). Theoretical essays on sound, color, and editing.

GRAHAM, PETER, ed., *The New Wave* (London: Secker & Warburg, 1968). A collection of essays by and about Bazin, Truffaut, Godard, and others.

JACOBS, LEWIS, "Art: Edwin S. Porter and the Editing Principle," "D. W. Griffith: *The Birth of a Nation* and *Intolerance,*" in *The Rise of the American Film* (New York: Teachers College Press, 1968). An historical account of the evolution of editing in its early years.

NIZHNY, VLADIMIR, *Lessons with Eisenstein,* Ivor Montagu and Jay Leyda, eds. and trans. (New York: Hill and Wang, 1962). A personal account of some of Eisenstein's teaching methods.

PUDOVKIN, V. I., *Film Technique and Film Acting,* Ivor Montagu, ed. and trans. (New York: Grove Press, 1960). See also *Kuleshov on Film,* Ronald Levaco, ed. and trans. (Berkeley: University of California Press, 1974).

REISZ, KAREL, *The Technique of Film Editing* (New York: Hastings House, 1968). The standard text on the history, practice, and theory of editing.

ROSENBLUM, RALPH, AND ROBERT KAREN, *When the Shooting Stops . . . The Cutting Begins* (New York: Viking, 1979). An insider's account of the art and craft of editing, by the editor of *The Pawnbroker, Annie Hall,* and many other films.

## 5

*"Cinematic sound is that which does not simply add to, but multiplies, two or three times, the effect of the image."*
AKIRA KUROSAWA

# SOUND

There are three types of sound in film: sound effects, music, and language. These can be employed independently or in any combination. They can be used expressionistically or realistically. Realistic sounds tend to be synchronous: that is, they derive their source from the images, and are often recorded simultaneously with them. Many exposition sequences, for example, use synchronized sound (dialogue) with corresponding images (two-shots). Even long and extreme long shots are sometimes shot synchronously: to capture the actual noise of traffic in an urban location, for example. Expressionistic sounds tend to be nonsynchronous: that is, they are detached from their sources, often acting in contrast with the image, or existing as totally separate sources of meaning.

## Historical Background

In 1927, when *The Jazz Singer* ushered in the talkie era, many critics felt that sound would deal a deathblow to the art of movies. But the setbacks were temporary, and today sound is one of the richest sources of meaning in film art. Actually, there never was a silent period, for virtually all movies prior to 1927 were accompanied by some kind of music (5-1). In the large city theatres, full orchestras provided atmospheric background to the visuals. In small towns, a piano was often used for the same purpose. In many theatres, the

**5-1. *The Birth of a Nation* (U.S.A., 1915).**
*Musical score by Joseph Carl Breil; Directed by D. W. Griffith.*
There never really was a silent period in movies, only a nontalking period. Griffith took great care in his selection of music, but today his films are usually shown silent, drained of much of their excitement. Viewers who have seen the battle scenes of this movie accompanied by a soundtrack of appropriate music have testified to the brilliance of these sequences—as fine as anything that has been done in the medium. Projected without music, these same scenes can seem remote, academic, uninvolving. Breil's score, which was created with Griffith's aid, was highly praised by contemporary critics. It consisted of symphonic, operatic, and folk music, as well as some original material composed by Breil. Most of the leading characters were assigned musical motifs, and individual melodies were also used to suggest different times and locations. The battle and rescue sequences were accompanied by such powerful pieces as Tchaikovsky's *1812 Overture* and Wagner's *Ride of the Valkyries*. See also Fred Silva, ed., *Focus on The Birth of a Nation*, (Englewood Cliffs, N.J.: Prentice-Hall, 1971).

"Mighty Wurlitzer" organ, with its bellowing pipes, was the standard musical accompaniment. Music was played for practical as well as artistic reasons, for these sounds muffled the noises of the patrons who were occasionally rowdy, particularly when entering the theatre.

Most of the early "100 percent talkies" were visually dull. The equipment of the time required the simultaneous recording of sound and image: the camera was restricted to one position, the actors couldn't move far from the microphone, and editing was restricted to its most minimal function—primarily scene changes. The major source of meaning was in the sound, especially dialogue. The images tended merely to illustrate the soundtrack. Before long, adventurous directors began experimenting. The camera was housed in a soundproof blimp, thus permitting the camera to move in and out of a scene silently. Soon, several microphones, all on separate channels, were placed on the set. Overhead sound booms were devised to follow an actor on a set, so that his voice was always within range, even when he moved around.

Despite these technical advances, Expressionist directors remained hostile to the use of realistic (synchronous) sound recording. Eisenstein was especially wary of dialogue, and he predicted an onslaught of "highly cultured dramas" which would force the cinema back to its stagey beginnings. Synchronous sound, he believed, would destroy the flexibility of editing and thus kill the very soul of film art. Synchronous sound did, in fact, require a more literal continuity, especially in dialogue sequences. Eisenstein's metaphoric cutting, with its leaps in time and space, wouldn't make much sense if realistic sound had to be provided with each image. Indeed, Hitchcock pointed out that the most cinematic sequences are essentially silent. Chase scenes, for example, require only some general sound effects to preserve their continuity.

Most of the talented directors of the early sound era favored expressionistic sound. Eisenstein and Pudovkin issued a manifesto, reasserting their faith in the primacy of editing, but they saw great possibilities in the use of sound if it weren't used synchronously. They advocated a contrastive use of sound and image, with each conveying different—not duplicating— meanings. Sound, especially music, should be used as an aural counterpoint to the images. The proper use of language in film, Eisenstein claimed, was in the

**5-2. *The Jazz Singer* (U.S.A., 1927).**
*With Al Jolson; Directed by Alan Crosland.*
There had been a number of experiments in synchronous sound prior to this film, but they failed to create much of a stir with the public. Significantly, Warner Brothers managed to break the sound barrier with a new genre, the musical. Actually, even this movie was mostly silent. Only Jolson's musical numbers and a few snatches of dialogue were in synch sound. See John Springer, *All Talking, All Singing, All Dancing!* (New York: Citadel, 1966).

(Warner Brothers)

narrated monologue, not dramatic dialogue. The monologue would replace the expository titles of the silent film, giving the images uninterrupted dominance. This preference for the monologue reflected the Soviet bias toward documentary film, whereas dialogue tended to be associated with the live theatre.

Even directors of theatrical biases, however, were opposed to strictly realistic uses of sound. The Frenchman, René Clair, came to the same conclusions as the Soviets. Sound should be used selectively, not indiscriminately. The ear, he believed, is just as selective as the eye, and sound can be edited in the same way images can. As early as 1929, he praised the American musical, *Broadway Melody,* for its imaginative experiments in sound. He observed that the film let us *hear* a door slam; so the director, Harry Beaumont, wisely chose not to show us the action as well. In this, and in other instances, sound could be used to replace the shot. Even dialogue sequences needn't be totally synchronous, Clair believed. Conversation can act as a continuity device, freeing the camera to explore contrasting information—a technique especially favored by ironists, like Hitchcock and Ernst Lubitsch.

Clair made several musicals illustrating his theories. In *Le Million* (1931), for example, music and song often replace dialogue. Language is juxtaposed ironically with nonsynchronous images. Many of the scenes were photographed without sound and later dubbed when the montage sequences were

(MGM)

**5-3. Singin' in the Rain (U.S.A., 1952).** *With Gene Kelly and Donald O'Connor (left); Directed by Kelly and Stanley Donen.*
Regarded by many as the greatest of all musicals, Singin' in the Rain is a witty spoof on the complications which accompanied the coming of sound to the cinema. This sequence satirizes the attempts of a fretful voice coach to teach a silent movie star (Kelly) how to speak with a phony British accent, which was considered *de rigeur* in the early talkie era. Kelly choreographed, codirected, and starred in this milestone work, which, like many of the great MGM musicals, was produced by Arthur Freed. See also Hugh Fordin, *The World of Entertainment* (New York: Avon Books, 1975), a study of the Freed unit at MGM.

completed. These charming musicals are never immobilized by the stagey confinement that ruined most sound films of this era. The dubbing technique of Clair, though ahead of its time, eventually became a major approach in sound film production.

Several American directors also experimented with sound in these early years. Like Clair, Lubitsch used sound and image nonsynchronously to produce a number of witty and often cynical juxtapositions. The celebrated "Beyond the Blue Horizon" sequence from his musical, *Monte Carlo* is a good example of his mastery of the new mixed medium. While the spunky heroine (Jeanette MacDonald) sings cheerily of her optimistic expectations, Lubitsch provides us with a display of technical bravura. Shots of the speeding train which carries the heroine to her destiny are intercut with closeups of the whirring locomotive wheels in rhythmical syncopation with the huffing and the chugging and the tooting of the train. Unable to resist a malicious fillip, Lubitsch even has a chorus of suitably obsequious peasants chime in with the heroine in a triumphant reprise as the train plunges past their fields in the countryside. The sequence is both exhilarating and outrageously funny. Critic Gerald Mast observed: "This visual-aural symphony of music, natural sound, composition, and cutting is as complex and perfect an example of montage-in-sound as Eisenstein's editing devices in *Potemkin* were of montage in silents."

Unfortunately, sound also cut off the careers of many film artists, especially actors. Some historians believe that the great silent clowns, like Keaton, Lloyd, and Harry Langdon, were rendered *passé* by the advent of talkies. Chaplin survived the new medium, though not without a fight. In *Modern Times* (1936) he put up a gallant but ultimately futile battle against spoken language. This was the last movie in which his tramp character was to appear. Although *Modern Times* contains sound effects and a musical score (composed by Chaplin himself), the only spoken dialogue is recited by a Big Brother figure on a TV monitor.

But by 1936, 9 years after *The Jazz Singer*, Chaplin's rejection of spoken dialogue was regarded as a quixotic battle in an already lost war. The advantages of sound had been recognized by all except the most die-hard reac-

**5-4.** *Monsieur Verdoux* **(U.S.A., 1947).**
*With (right to left) Charles Chaplin and Martha Raye; Directed by Chaplin.*
The arrival of sound wiped out the careers of many silent film artists. Chaplin was one of the last to capitulate to the talkies, and in doing so, he was forced to abandon his tramp character. Although his biggest commercial hits—*The Great Dictator* (1940) and *Limelight* (1952)—were both sound movies, perhaps only the sardonic *Monsieur Verdoux* can be ranked with his silent masterpieces.

(rbc Films)

tionaries. The increased realism brought on by sound inevitably forced acting styles to become more natural, for performers no longer needed to compensate visually for the lack of dialogue. Like stage actors, film players realized that the subtlest nuances of meaning could be conveyed through the voice. The movable camera is a further advantage for the screen actor. If he is required to mutter under his breath, for example, he can do so naturally, photographed in closeup. He need not, like the stage actor, mutter in stage whisper—a necessary convention in the live theatre.

In the silent cinema, directors had to use titles to communicate nonvisual information: dialogue, exposition, abstract ideas, and so on. In some films, these interruptions nearly ruined the delicate rhythm of the visuals. Dreyer's *Passion of Joan of Arc*, for example, has frequent interjections of irritating explanatory titles and dialogue. Other directors avoided titles by dramatizing visually as much as possible. This practice led to many visual clichés. Early in the story, for example, the villain might be identified by showing him kicking a dog; or a heroine could be recognized by the halo effect lighting around her head, and so forth.

In some respects, 1941 was a watershed in the history of the sound film, for this was the release year of *Citizen Kane*. Here was the *Birth of a Nation* of its era—bursting with visual brilliance in nearly every shot, the movie also featured a soundtrack so complex that the film world seemed to gasp in astonishment. Welles is often credited with inventing many sound effects when in fact he was primarily a consolidator. Like Griffith, Welles' genius is demonstrated by his ability to combine and expand the piecemeal accom-

**5-5.** *Under the Roofs of Paris* **(France, 1930).**
*Directed by René Clair.*
Because Clair preferred to dub his sound after the visuals had been photographed, and sometimes even after they had been edited together, his early talkies have the same kinetic fluidity of his presound movies. Like most ironists, Clair's stock-in-trade is contrast: not only between what's expected and what actually is, but also between what we see and what we hear. See also Celia McGerr, *René Clair* (Boston: G. K. Hall, 1980).

(Audio Brandon Films)

plishments of his predecessors. Despite his youth—he was only 25 when he made *Citizen Kane*—Welles had spent a number of years acting, writing, producing, and directing radio plays. The lessons he learned in this aural medium were to serve him well in the cinema.

In radio, sounds have to evoke images: an actor speaking through an echo chamber suggests a visual context—a huge auditorium, for example. A distant train whistle suggests a vast landscape, and so on. Welles applied this aural principle to his movie soundtrack, and the results were—and still are—dazzling. With the help of his sound technician, James G. Stewart, Welles discovered that almost every visual technique has its sound equivalent. Each of the shots, for example, has an appropriate sound quality involving volume, degree of definition, and texture. Long and extreme long shot sounds are fuzzy and remote, closeup sounds are crisp, clear, and generally loud. High angle shots are often accompanied by high pitched music and sound effects; low angles by brooding and low pitched sounds. Abrupt cuts can be punctuated by equally abrupt sound transitions. In *Kane*, Welles cuts from a quiet low-keyed scene to a violent flashback, which opens with the piercing shriek of a cockatoo in closeup. Sounds can fade in and out like images. Sounds can be dissolved and overlapped like a montage sequence. Sounds can also suggest a graceful crane movement with a glissando passage of music; the bobbing of a hand-held shot can be enhanced by staccato musical phrases. The possibilities are almost limitless.

*Kane* is a monumental work in all areas of sound: language (the script was cowritten by Welles and Herman J. Mankiewicz), music (composed by Bernard Herrmann), and sound effects. The dialogue is literate, subtle, yet flamboyantly theatrical. While the camera leaps over time periods and different locales, the soundtrack forms the continuity for whole scenes. One famous scene shows Kane listening to a song sung by Susan Alexander, whom he has just met, and who will soon become his mistress. The scene is set in her cramped apartment. While the song continues on the soundtrack, the image dissolves to a parallel shot, revealing Kane in an opulent apartment where an elaborately bedecked Susan finishes her song at a grand piano. In a matter of seconds, Welles establishes the relationship between Kane and his mistress, using only the song to bridge the time–space gap. In another episode, Welles employs a dissolve and montage sequence of Susan on her disastrous operatic tour. On the soundtrack, her aria can be heard, distorted into a screeching dismal wail (5-6).

**5-6. *Citizen Kane* (U.S.A., 1941).**
*With Dorothy Comingore; Directed by Orson Welles.*
Welles demonstrated that virtually every kind of visual had its aural counterpart. This montage sequence is reinforced by an aural montage of Susan Alexander's shrieking arias, orchestral music, popping flashbulbs, and the sounds of newspaper presses rolling.

(RKO)

In an opening sequence of the movie, dialogue is spoken through an echo chamber to suggest the sanctimoniousness of Kane's onetime guardian, whose papers are stored in a cathedrallike archive. To demonstrate Kane's gradual estrangement from his first wife, Welles features a series of breakfast scenes. On the soundtrack, Kane and his wife engage in conversation, beginning with some honeymoon sweet talk, and ending with a furious quarrel (7-25). The sequence contains only some thirty or so lines. The film's very structure is based on a series of visual flashbacks, while five informants speak of their present-day opinions of Kane's paradoxical personality. Throughout the movie, Welles juxtaposes words, sound effects, and music with images of such complexity that many meanings are conveyed simultaneously.

*(RKO)*

**5-7. *The Magnificent Ambersons* (U.S.A., 1942).**
*With Tim Holt, Ray Collins, and Richard Bennett; Directed by Orson Welles.*
In this film, Welles perfected his technique of sound montage in which the dialogue of one character overlaps with that of another, or several others. The effect is almost musical, for the language is exploited not necessarily for the literal information it may convey, but as pure sound which is orchestrated in terms of emotional tonalities.

In his next film, *The Magnificent Ambersons,* Welles refined his technique of sound montage in which dialogue between several groups of characters is recorded simultaneously (5-7). One of the most brilliant episodes employing this technique is the leave-taking scene at the final Amberson ball. The scene is shot in deep focus with expressionistic lighting contrasts throwing most of

**5-8. Othello** (Morocco, 1951).
*With Orson Welles and Suzanne Cloutier; Directed by Welles.*
In 1948, Welles, discouraged by a string of box office failures, left for Europe and Africa where he hoped to work as an independent producer–director. His first movie was this adaptation of Shakespeare. The project was a nightmare. It was over three years in the shooting, and Welles had to interrupt production many times to seek additional funding. He lost several players in the process. There were three Desdemonas, four Iagos. Sequences had to be reshot time and again. But finally the movie was finished. On the Continent it was enthusiastically praised and swept the Grand Prix at the Cannes Film Festival. But British and American critics complained of its crude soundtrack. This was to be the pattern of virtually all his subsequent work outside America. See also Pauline Kael, "Orson Welles: There Ain't No Way," in *Kiss Kiss Bang Bang* (New York: Bantam, 1969).

the characters into silhouette. The dialogue of one group of characters gently overlaps with that of another, which in turn overlaps with a third group. The effect is hauntingly poetic, despite the relative simplicity of the words themselves. Each person or couple is characterized by a particular sound texture: the young people speak rapidly in a normal to loud volume, the middle-aged couple whisper intimately and slowly. The shouts of various other family members punctuate these dialogue sequences in sudden outbursts. The entire scene seems choreographed, both visually and aurally: silhouetted figures stream in and out of the frame like graceful phantoms, their words floating and undulating in the shadows. The quarrels among the Amberson family are often recorded in a similar manner. Welles' actors don't wait patiently for cues: accusations and recriminations are hurled simultaneously, as they are in life. The violent words, often irrational and disconnected, spew out in spontaneous eruptions of anger and frustration. As in many family quarrels, everyone shouts, but people only half listen.

Robert Altman used similar sound montage techniques in *M\*A\*S\*H*, *Nashville,* and other movies. Like Welles, Altman often uses language as pure sound, particularly in *McCabe and Mrs. Miller,* in which as many as twenty different soundtracks were mixed. In several scenes, speeches are deliberately thrown away, and we're able to catch only a fleeting phrase here and there;

however, these phrases are sufficient to give us a sense of what's really going on in a scene. More importantly, they give us a sense of how language and sounds are actually heard in reality—in ambiguous, elliptical wisps which are often incongruous and funny.

## Sound Effects

Although the function of sound effects is primarily atmospheric, they can also be precise sources of meaning in film. Directors like Altman, Coppola, and Antonioni spend nearly as much time with their sound effects as with their music and dialogue. The pitch, volume, and tempo of sound effects can strongly affect our responses to any given noise. High pitched sounds are generally strident and produce a sense of tension in the listener. Especially if these types of noises are prolonged, the shrillness can be totally unnerving. For this reason, high pitched sounds (including music) are often employed in suspense sequences, particularly just before and during the climax. Low-frequency sounds, on the other hand, are heavy, full, and less tense. Often they are used to emphasize the dignity or solemnity of a scene, like the male humming chorus in *The Seven Samurai*. Low pitched sounds can also suggest anxiety and mystery: frequently a suspense sequence begins with such sounds, then gradually increases in frequency as the scene peaks to its climax.

**5-9.** *Blow-Up* **(Italy/U.S.A./Great Britain, 1966).**
*With David Hemmings; Directed by Michelangelo Antonioni.*
Antonioni uses sound starkly and often in a symbolic manner. In this famous sequence, for example, the protagonist's reconstruction of a murder he accidentally photographed in a park is accompanied by the faint rustling of trees, recalling the actual event. See also Roy Huss, ed., *Focus on Blow-Up* (Englewood Cliffs, N.J.: Prentice-Hall, 1971); Pierre Leprohon, *Michaelangelo Antonioni* (New York: Simon and Schuster, 1963); and Ian Cameron and Robin Wood, *Antonioni* (New York: Praeger, 1969).

(MGM)

Sound volume works in much the same way. Loud sounds tend to be forceful, intense, and threatening, whereas quiet sounds strike us as delicate, hesitant, and often weak. These same principles apply to tempo. The faster the tempo of sound, the greater the tension produced in the listener. In the chase sequence of Friedkin's *The French Connection,* all these sound principles are employed masterfully. As the chase reaches its climax, the screeching wheels of the auto and the crashing sound of the runaway train grow louder, faster, and higher pitched. The success of the sequence depends as much on its sound effects as its visuals: both are edited brilliantly.

Off-screen sounds bring off-screen space into play: the sound expands the image beyond the confines of the frame. In Kubrick's *Paths of Glory,* for instance, the sounds of guns and cannons are constant reminders to the soldiers in the trenches of the dangers they must face when they enter the battlefield. Sound effects can evoke terror in suspense films and thrillers. Since we tend to fear what we can't see, directors will sometimes use off-screen sound effects to strike a note of anxiety. The sound of a creaking door in a darkened room can be more fearful than an image of someone stealing through the door. In Lang's *M,* the child murderer is identified by a tune he whistles off-screen. During the early portions of the movie, we never see him and only recognize him by his sinister tune.

**5-10. *The Exorcist* (U.S.A., 1973).**
*Directed by William Friedkin.*
Sound in film is generally geared to space. When a severe discrepancy exists, the effect can be disorienting and even frightening. In this movie, the devil has possessed a young girl (Linda Blair, lying on bed). The sounds emanating from her small body echo loudly, thus reinforcing a cavernous effect as if the girl's slight figure had been spiritually expanded thousands of times in order to accommodate the demons that inhabit it.

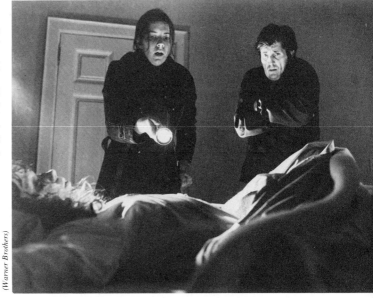

*(Warner Brothers)*

In several scenes of Hitchcock's *Psycho,* Bernard Herrmann's score—consisting entirely of strings—suggests shrill bird noises. This motif is used as a form of characterization. A shy and appealing young man (Anthony Perkins) is associated with birds early in the film. He stuffs birds as a hobby, and his own features are intense and rather hawklike. During a brutal murder sequence, the soundtrack throbs with screeching bird music. The audience assumes the murderer is the boy's mother, but birds have been associated with him, not her. One of Hitchcock's recurrent themes is the transference of guilt. In this film, the transfer is rather complex. The youth has dug up his long-dead mother's body and literally stuffed it. Often he dresses himself up in her clothing. While we think we see the mother killing two victims, we have in fact seen the schizophrenic youth as his other self—his mother. The bird music offers an early clue to this psychological transference (see also 8-19.)

Because images tend to dominate sounds while we're actually experiencing a movie, many sound effects work on a subconscious level. In *Psycho*, the heroine (Janet Leigh) drives her car through a rainstorm. On the soundtrack, we hear her windshield wiper blades slashing furiously against the downpour. Later, when she is taking a shower in a motel, these same sounds are repeated. The source of the water noise is apparent, but the slashing sounds seem to come from nowhere—until a demented killer crashes into the bathroom brandishing a knife. Similarly, throughout Peckinpah's *Straw Dogs*, the sound of broken glass has an unnerving effect on the audience. Not until late in the movie, when the protagonist's eyeglasses are shattered during an assault, do these sound effects become more overtly relevant (2-20).

Sound effects can also serve symbolic functions which are usually determined by the dramatic context. In Luis Buñuel's *Belle de Jour*, for example, the sounds of jingling bells are associated with the heroine's sexual fantasies. Other symbolic sound effects are more universally understood. In Bergman's *Wild Strawberries*, the protagonist, an elderly professor, has a nightmare. The surrealistic sequence is virtually silent except for the insistent sound of a heart beat—a *memento mori* for the professor, a reminder that his life will soon end.

**5-11. *The Conversation* (U.S.A., 1974).**
*With Cindy Williams; Directed by Francis Ford Coppola.*
The quality of sound recording in Coppola's movies is outstanding, thanks in large measure to his regular sound collaborator Walter Murch. This film revolves around the ambiguous recordings of a professional surveillance expert—i.e., a paid eavesdropper. The movie is virtually orchestrated: in addition to mixing the sound, rerecording it, and creating the sound montage, Murch also served as supervising editor. See also Robert K. Johnson, *Francis Ford Coppola* (Boston: G. K. Hall, 1980).

*(Paramount Pictures)*

In reality, there's a considerable difference between hearing and listening. Our minds automatically filter out irrelevant sounds. While talking in a noisy city location, for example, we listen to the speaker, but we barely hear the sounds of traffic. The microphone is not so selective. Most movie soundtracks are cleaned up of such extraneous noises. A sequence might include selected city noises to suggest the urban locale, but once this context is established, outside sounds are diminished and sometimes even eliminated in order to permit us to hear the conversation clearly.

**5-12.** *A Clockwork Orange* **(U.S.A./ Great Britain, 1971).**
*With Malcolm McDowell; Directed by Stanley Kubrick.*
This film is almost consistently in the loud range: noises are magnified and reverberating, dialogue is shouted rather than spoken. Our ears are assaulted by a barrage of relentless sounds. Kubrick uses this technique to attack the audience aurally; the volume never permits us to relax. The noise is as violent in its intensity as the dramatic events of the movie. See also Norman Kagan, *The Cinema of Stanley Kubrick* (New York: Grove Press, 1972); and Alexander Walker, *Stanley Kubrick Directs* (New York: Harcourt, Brace, Jovanovich, 1972), with many frame enlargements.

*(Warner Brothers)*

Since the late 1950s, however, a number of directors have retained these noisy soundtracks in the name of greater realism. Influenced by the documentary school of *cinéma vérité*—which tends to avoid simulated or recreated sounds—directors like Jean-Luc Godard even allowed important dialogue scenes to be partly washed out by on-location sounds. In *Masculine-Feminine,* Godard's use of sound is especially bold. His insistence on natural noises—all of them, as they were recorded on the set—dismayed many critics who complained of the "cacophonous din." The movie deals with violence, the lack of privacy, peace, and quiet. Simply by exploiting his soundtrack, Godard had no need to comment overtly on these themes—they are naggingly persistent in virtually every scene. One of the most effective sound techniques in this movie is the use of gun shots for transitions. Often the abruptness of the editing is punctuated by the shattering blast of these shots which have no visual source. Other scenes are accompanied by the cracking of billiard and bowling balls, the clattering of pinball machines, and the nervous stamping of a typewriter—all of them suggesting gunfire shots. Important dialogue is sometimes drowned out by the noise of street traffic, an adjoining conversation, or the clatter of dishes in a cafe. Because we're accustomed to a clean soundtrack, we are distracted by these extraneous noises. But this is precisely Godard's point: serenity is almost totally absent from contemporary urban life.

Like absolute stasis, absolute silence in a sound film tends to call attention

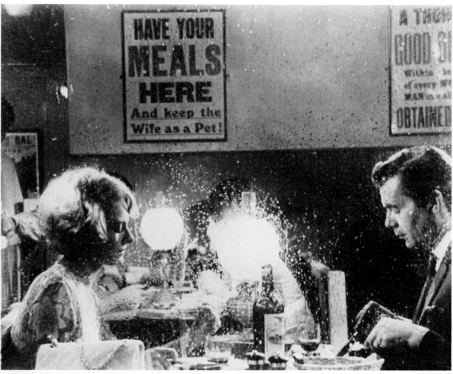

**5-13. *Accident* (Great Britain, 1967).**

*With Dirk Bogarde and Delphine Seyrig; Written by Harold Pinter; Directed by Joseph Losey.*
This nonsynchronous dialogue sequence creates a sense of alienation, deception, and loneliness. A middle-aged college don (Bogarde) decides to look up a former lover when he visits London. Through a rain-streaked window, we see them eating silently in a dingy restaurant. On the soundtrack, we hear a conversation between them, apparently their first social exchange when he entered her apartment. Their dialogue is strained and evasive, filled with awkward pauses and stretches of silence. By juxtaposing this conversation with the nonsynchronous visuals, Losey suggests that the statements of the characters are detached from their actions—the central theme of the movie. See Foster Hirsch, *Joseph Losey* (Boston: G. K. Hall, 1980); and Harold Pinter, *Five Screenplays* (New York: Grove Press, 1973), which includes the scripts to *Accident, The Servant, The Pumpkin Eater, The Quiller Memorandum,* and *The Go-Between.*

to itself. Any significant stretch of silence creates an eerie vacuum—a sense of something impending, about to burst. Arthur Penn exploited this phenomenon in the conclusion of *Bonnie and Clyde.* The lovers stop on a country road to help a friend (actually an informer) with his car which has presumably broken down. Clumsily, he scrambles under the car. There is a long moment of silence while the lovers exchange puzzled, then anxious glances. Suddenly, the soundtrack roars with the noise of machine guns as the lovers are brutally cut down by policemen hiding in the bushes. In some movies—Bergman's *The Silence* is a good example—the empty pauses between lines of dialogue are more significant than the dialogue itself. These pauses suggest anxiety, fear, suspicion, and in other contexts, rage, evasion, or total exhaustion.

Like the freeze frame, silence in a sound film can be used to symbolize death since we tend to associate sound with the presence of an on-going life. Kurosawa uses this technique effectively in *Ikiru*, after the elderly protagonist has been informed by a doctor that he is dying of cancer. Stupified by the specter of death, the old man stumbles out on the street, the soundtrack totally silent. When he's almost run over by a speeding auto, the soundtrack suddenly roars with the noise of city traffic. The protagonist is yanked back into the world of the living.

## Music

Music is a highly abstract art, tending toward pure form. It's impossible to speak of the "subject matter" of a musical phrase. When merged with lyrics, music acquires a more concrete content because words, of course, have specific references. Both words and music convey meanings, but each in a different manner. With or without lyrics, music can be more specific when juxtaposed with film images. In fact, many musicians have complained that images tend to rob music of its ambiguity by anchoring musical tones to specific ideas and emotions. For example, few people today can listen to Strauss' *Thus Spake Zarathustra* without being reminded of Kubrick's *2001: A Space Odyssey*. Some music lovers have lamented that Ponchielli's elegant "Dance of the Hours" conjures images of ridiculous dancing hippos, one of Disney's most brilliant sequences in *Fantasia* (5-14).

**5-14. *Fantasia* (U.S.A., 1940).**
*By Walt Disney.*
Music is the most abstract of the arts. When fused with images, however, it automatically acquires more anecdotal significance—a fact which dismays many musicians. When Disney used Ponchielli's dainty "Dance of the Hours" to accompany a deliciously ludicrous dance between Hyacinth Hippo and Ben Ali Gator in this movie, many music lovers were appalled by the "vulgarization."

(Walt Disney Productions)

Theories about film music are surprisingly varied. Pudovkin and Eisenstein insisted that music must never serve merely as accompaniment: it ought to retain its own integrity. The film critic Paul Rotha claimed that music must even be allowed to dominate the image on occasion. Some filmmakers insist on purely descriptive music—a practice referred to as mickeymousing (so-

**5-15. Audio-visual score from *Alexander Nevsky* (U.S.S.R., 1938).**
*Music by Sergei Prokofiev; Directed by Sergei Eisenstein.*
The composer need not always subordinate his talents to those of the film director. Here, two great Soviet artists aligned their contributions into a totally fused production in which the music corresponds to the movement of the images set in a row. Prokofiev avoided purely "representational" elements (mickey-mousing). Instead, the two concentrated sometimes on the images first, other times on the music. The result was what Eisenstein called "vertical montage," where the notes on the staff, moving from left to right, parallel the movements or major lines of the images which, set side by side, also "move" from left to right. Thus, if the lines in a series of images move from lower left to upper right, the notes of music would move in a similar direction on the musical staff. If the lines of a composition were jagged and uneven, the notes of music would also zigzag in a corresponding manner. See Sergei Eisenstein, "Form and Content: Practice," in *Film Sense* (New York: A Harvest Book, 1947).

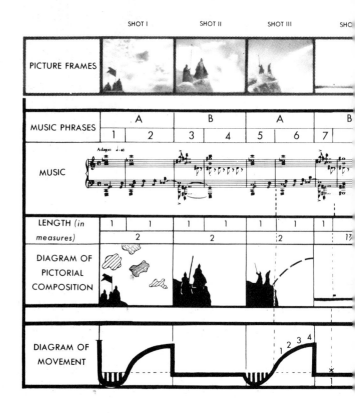

called because of Disney's early experiments with music and animation). This type of score employs music as a literal equivalent to the image. If a character stealthily tiptoes from a room, for example, each step has a musical note to emphasize the suspense. Other directors believe that film music shouldn't be too good, or it will detract from the images. Most imaginative directors reject this notion. For them, the music of even the greatest composers can be used in movies.

In the best movies, music—whether an established work or an original score—is never a careless matter. Nor is film composing a job for hacks, for the list of composers who have worked directly in film is a long and impressive one, including Darius Milhaud, Arthur Honegger, Paul Hindemith, Dimitri Shostakovitch, Arnold Schoenberg, Sergei Prokofiev, William Walton, Benjamin Britten, Aaron Copland, Quincy Jones, Duke Ellington, The Modern Jazz Quartet, Virgil Thompson, Kurt Weill, Bob Dylan, George Gershwin, Ralph Vaughan Williams, Richard Rogers, Cole Porter, Leonard Bernstein, and The Beatles, to mention only a few of the best known.

A filmmaker doesn't need to have technical expertise to use music effectively. As Aaron Copland pointed out, directors must know what they want from music *dramatically:* it's the composer's business to translate these dramatic needs into musical terms. Directors and composers work in a variety of ways. Most composers begin working after they have seen the rough cut of a movie—that is, the major footage before the editor has tightened up the slackness between shots. Some composers don't begin until the film has been

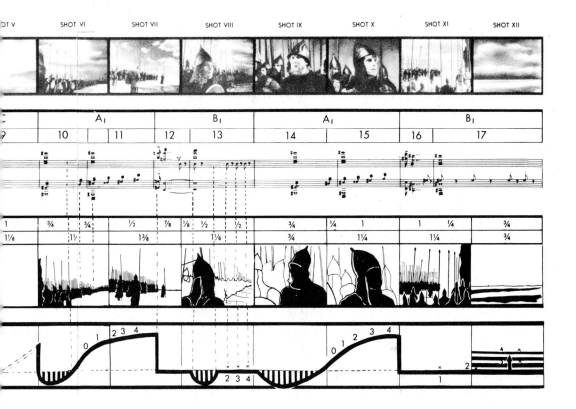

totally completed, except for the music. Directors of musicals, on the other hand, usually work with the composer before shooting begins.

Beginning with the opening credits, music can serve as a kind of overture, to suggest the mood or spirit of the film as a whole. John Addison's opening music in *Tom Jones* is a witty, rapidly executed harpsichord piece. The harpsichord itself is associated with the eighteenth century, the period of the film. The occasionally jazzy phrases in the tune suggest a sly twentieth-century overview—a musical equivalent of the blending of centuries found in the movie itself.

Certain kinds of music can suggest locales, classes, or ethnic groups. For example, John Ford's westerns feature simple folk tunes, like "Red River Valley" or religious hymns like "Shall We Gather At the River," which are associated with the American frontier of the late nineteenth century. Richly nostalgic, these songs are often played on frontier instruments—a plaintive harmonica or a concertina. Similarly, many Italian movies feature lyrical, highly emotional melodies, reflecting the operatic heritage of that country. The greatest composer of this kind of music is Nino Rota who scored virtually all of Fellini's films, as well as such distinguished works as Zeffirelli's *Romeo and Juliet* and Coppola's two *Godfather* movies.

Music can be used as foreshadowing, particularly when the dramatic context doesn't permit a director to prepare an audience for an event. Hitchcock, for example, often accompanied an apparently casual sequence with "anxious" music—a warning to the audience to be prepared. Sometimes these

**5-16.** *Once Upon a Time in the West* **(Italy/U.S.A., 1969).**
*With Charles Bronson and Claudia Cardinale; Music by Ennio Morricone; Directed by Sergio Leone.*
Leone's mythic fable is perhaps the most operatic western ever made, thanks to Morricone's brilliant score which includes a jew's-harp, harmonica, banjo, whistling, and a soprano vocal. The film's principal theme is scored for full orchestra and is almost Verdian in its rapturous lyricism.

musical warnings are false alarms; other times they explode into frightening crescendoes. Similarly, when actors are required to assume restrained or neutral expressions, music can suggest their internal—hidden—emotions. Bernard Herrmann's music functions in both ways in *Psycho* and *Citizen Kane*.

Modern atonal and dissonant music generally evokes a sense of anxiety in listeners. Often such music seems to have no melodic line and can even resemble a series of random noises. Giovanni Fusco's music for several of Antonioni's films (*L'Avventura, Red Desert, Eclipse*) produces precisely this sense of neurosis and paranoia. Fusco's music provides a similar function in the movies of Alain Resnais: *Hiroshima Mon Amour* and *La Guerre Est Finie*.

Music can also control emotional shifts within a scene. In John Huston's *The Red Badge of Courage,* for example, the protagonist (Audie Murphy), in an irrational outburst of daring, snatches the flag from a dying comrade and charges onto a raging battlefield. To emphasize the youth's surge of patriotism, the scene is accompanied by a spirited rendering of Yankee fighting songs. The charging young soldier stumbles by a wounded Confederate standard bearer, writhing in pain on the ground, his flag in tatters. The music shifts to an agonizing dirge and gradually transforms into a grotesque distortion of "Dixie." The kinetic excitement of the protagonist's charge might easily have overshadowed the poignance of the wounded Confederate, but with the aid of the music, the audience as well as the protagonist is suddenly brought to a grim halt.

Music can also provide ironic contrast. In many cases, the predominant mood of a scene can be neutralized or even reversed with contrasting music. In *Bonnie and Clyde,* the robbery scenes are often accompanied by spirited banjo music, giving these sequences a jolly sense of fun. More satirically, a scene from Kenneth Anger's *Scorpio Rising* shows a Hell's Angel motorcyclist putting on his elaborate riding gear. The scene is almost solemnly ritualistic, but the young man's narcissicism is satirized by the banal tune "Blue Velvet" which plays on the soundtrack. The homosexual undertones of his lifestyle are emphasized by the line "she wore blooo vell-vet . . . " Contrasting music needn't always be satiric, however. In Ermanno Olmi's *The Tree of the Wooden Clogs,* for example, the organ music of Johann Sebastian Bach accompanies many of the scenes which are virtually documentary recreations of Italian peasant life around 1900. The music provides these simple episodes with a sense of majesty—celebrating the dignity of labor and the grandeur of the human spirit.

Characterization can be suggested through musical motifs. In Fellini's *La*

**5-17. *The Yellow Submarine* (Great Britain, 1968).**
*By George Dunning and Heinz Edelmann.*
A few movies—very few—were inspired by music. This charming animated fantasy was created around the famous Beatles' album *Sgt. Pepper's Lonely Hearts Club Band.* See also George Melly, *Revolt Into Style* (Garden City: Doubleday, 1971).

(Apple Films)

*Strada,* the pure sad simplicity of the heroine (Giulietta Masina) is captured by a melancholy tune she plays on a trumpet. This theme is varied and elaborated upon in Nino Rota's delicate score, suggesting that even after her death, her spiritual influence is still felt. Herrmann's score for *Citizen Kane* employs motifs flamboyantly and in a more complex manner. Specific musical phrases are used to identify the major characters. These motifs are dropped, picked up again, and woven into elaborate combinations. The Rosebud motif, for example, is introduced early in the movie with Kane's death. The musical phrase is repeated each time the reporter questions several of Kane's former associates about the significance of his final word, "Rosebud." In the concluding scene, the musical phrase swells grandly into dominance as the audience (but not the characters) finally discovers the mystery of Rosebud.

Characterization can be even more precise when lyrics are added to music. In Peter Bogdanovich's *The Last Picture Show,* for instance, pop tunes of the 1950s are used in association with specific characters. The bitchy Jacy (Cybill Shepherd) is linked to "Cold, Cold Heart," while her deceived boy-

**5-18.** *American Graffiti* (U.S.A., 1973).
*With (left to right) Charlie Martin Smith, Richard Dreyfuss, Paul Le Mat, Cindy Williams, and Ron Howard; Directed by George Lucas.*
This movie is a bittersweet exploration of the theme of time and the ironies of history. The action takes place within a 24-hour period, and is appropriately introduced by Jack Haley's "Rock Around the Clock." Other pop tunes of the Kennedy era are used throughout the film to suggest the naiveté of the period.

*(Universal Pictures)*

friend Duane (Jeff Bridges) is characterized by "A Fool Such as I." Lucas' *American Graffiti* uses pop tunes in a similar manner. Two young lovers who have just quarrelled are shown dancing at a sock hop to the tune of "Smoke Gets in Your Eyes." The lyric "yet today my love has flown away" acquires particular poignance for the girl because the boy has just told her that he intends to date others when he goes off to college. The lovers are reconciled at the end of the movie when he decides not to leave after all. On the sound-track, "Only You" is appropriately intuned, its syrupy lyrics emphasing the destiny of love.

Stanley Kubrick is a bold—and controversial—innovator in the use of film music. In *Dr. Strangelove,* he sardonically juxtaposed Vera Lynn's senti-mental World War II tune, "We'll Meet Again" with images of a global nuclear holocaust—a grim reminder that we probably *won't* meet again after World War III. In *2001,* Kubrick juxtaposed images of a twenty-first century rocket ship gliding through the immense blueness of space with the sounds of Strauss' nineteenth century "Blue Danube Waltz"—an aural foreshadowing of man's obsolete technology in the more advanced technological universe beyond Jup-iter. In *A Clockwork Orange,* Kubrick used music as a distancing device, particu-

**5-19. *Bound for Glory* (U.S.A., 1976).**
*With David Carradine; Directed by Hal Ashby.*
Musical biographies might be regarded as a hybrid genre, combining the factual appeal of a musi-cian's life with examples of his art. This movie explores the formative period in the life of the folk singer Woody Guthrie (Carradine), and how his music was politicized by the turbulent events of the Great Depression.

larly in violent scenes. Musical incongruity undercuts the realism of an otherwise vicious gang fight which takes place to the accompaniment of Rossini's urbane and witty overture to *The Thieving Magpie*. A brutal attack and rape scene is accompanied by a grotesque song-and-dance routine set to the tune of "Singin' in the Rain."

Music can also be used to communicate the major theme of a film. Dennis Hopper's *Easy Rider* begins with the two likable protagonists selling some white powder—apparently heroin—in order to stake themselves to a journey they plan to take to New Orleans. The visuals during this sequence are not particularly condemnatory, but on the soundtrack Steppenwolf's sinister tune "The Pusher" has a decided influence on what we think of the transaction. ("But the pusher don't care if you live or die—godamn the pusher.") The lyrics also refer to hard drug pushers as having "tombstones in their eyes."

A frequent function of film music is to underline speech, especially dialogue. A common assumption about this kind of music is that it merely acts to prop up bad dialogue or poor acting. The hundreds of mediocre love scenes performed to quivering violins have perhaps prejudiced many viewers against this kind of musical accompaniment; however, some of the most gifted actors have benefited from it. In Olivier's *Hamlet*, the composer William Walton worked out his score with painstaking precision. In the "To be or not to be" soliloquy, the music provides a counterpoint to Olivier's brilliantly modulated delivery, adding yet another dimension to this complex speech.

One of the most enduring and popular film genres is the musical whose principal *raison d'être* is song and dance. Like opera and ballet, the narrative elements of a musical are usually pretexts for the production numbers, but many musicals are exceptionally sophisticated dramatically. Even musicals can be divided into two types: the realistic and expressionistic. Realistic musicals are generally backstage stories (5-20). Production numbers are presented as

*(Allied Artists)*

**5-20. *Cabaret* (U.S.A., 1972).**
*With Joel Grey; Choreographed and directed by Bob Fosse.*
*Cabaret* is an example of a realistic musical. The story proper is a straight drama about a musical performer (Liza Minnelli) who works in a cheap dive in Germany during the early Nazi era. The dramatic scenes are intercut with musical numbers that comment indirectly on the narrative action—almost like a mocking chorus.

dramatically plausible. Such musicals usually justify a song or dance with a brief bit of dialogue—"Hey kids, let's rehearse the barn number"—and the "barn number" is then presented to the audience. A few realistic musicals are virtually dramas with music. In George Cukor's *A Star is Born,* for example, the narrative events would hold up without the musical numbers, although audiences would thereby be deprived of some of Judy Garland's best scenes—a documentation, as it were, of her character's talent. *New York, New York* and *Cabaret* are also dramas interspersed with music.

Expressionistic musicals make no pretence at verisimilitude. Characters burst out in song and dance in the middle of a scene without easing into the number with a realistic or plausible pretext. This convention must be accepted as an aesthetic premise, otherwise the entire film will strike the viewer as absurd. Everything is heightened and stylized in such works—sets, costumes, acting, etc. Most of Vincente Minnelli's musicals are expressionistic: *Meet Me in St. Louis, The Band Wagon, An American in Paris,* and *Gigi* (5-21).

**5-21. *Gigi* (U.S.A., 1958).**
*With Louis Jourdan, Leslie Caron, and Hermione Gingold; Music by Frederick Loewe; Screenplay and lyrics by Alan Lerner; Directed by Vincente Minnelli.*
The conventions of expressionist musicals are deliberately artificial. Characters launch into song and dance spontaneously, without a "realistic" excuse. This film also employs many authentic Parisian locales, primarily because of their spectacular beauty. Minnelli's love for French culture is reflected in a number of his movies, like *An American in Paris, Lust for Life,* and *Gigi,* the latter based on a story by Colette.

*(MGM)*

**5-22. *The Merry Widow* (U.S.A., 1934).**
*With Maurice Chevalier; Music by Franz Lehár; Directed by Ernst Lubitsch.*
More indebted to the traditions of the Viennese comic operetta than to the jazz and Tin Pan Alley idioms of most American musicals, Lubitsch's works in this genre are light, elegant, and incorrigibly parodic. Even while he's exploiting the artificial conventions of the operetta form, he simultaneously zaps their patent silliness. See also Ethan Mordden, *The Hollywood Musical* (New York: St. Martin's Press, 1982).

Although musicals have been produced in several countries, the genre has been dominated by Americans perhaps because it's so intimately related to the American studio system. In the 1930s, several major studios specialized in a particular type of musical. RKO produced the charming Fred Astaire–Ginger Rogers vehicles such as *Top Hat, Shall We Dance?* and *Carefree,* all directed by Mark Sandrich (see 3-7). Paramount specialized in sophisticated "Continental" musicals like Lubitsch's *The Love Parade, One Hour with You,* and *Monte Carlo.* At Warner Brothers, choreographer–director Busby Berkeley delighted audiences with his proleterian show biz stories like *Gold Diggers of 1933* and *Dames.* Berkeley's stylistic signature is his fondness for abstract geometrical patterns (created with the optical printer) and photography of dancers from unconventional angles (3-3).

In the 1940s and 1950s, the musical was dominated by MGM which had the finest musical directors under contract: Kelly, Donen, and Minnelli. Indeed, this prosperous studio had a virtual monopoly on the musical personalities of the day, including Garland, Kelly, Frank Sinatra, Mickey Rooney, Ann Miller, Vera-Ellen, Leslie Caron, Donald O'Connor, Cyd Charisse, Howard Keel, Kathryn Grayson, and many others. MGM also lured away Astaire, Pan, and Berkeley, who along with Michael Kidd, Bob Fosse, Gower Champion, and the ubiquitous Kelly, created most of the choreographies for the studio. Arthur Freed was the producer of most of Metro's important musicals, including the majority of Minnelli's films, as well as the stylish works of Donen: *On the Town*, *Singin' in the Rain* (both codirected by Kelly), the exquisite *Funny Face*, and *Seven Brides for Seven Brothers* (5-23).

(MGM)

**5-23. Seven Brides for Seven Brothers (U.S.A., 1954).**
*With Jacques d'Amboise (aloft); Choreography by Michael Kidd; Directed by Stanley Donen.*
There are dancing musicals and singing musicals, but usually the genre is so cunningly contrived that both can be included. Donen's robust tour-de-force is based on the ancient Roman legend of the rape of the Sabine women, only transferred to the Oregon Territory in the nineteenth century. In accordance with the genre's predilection for symmetry, here there are seven lusty males paired with seven somewhat reluctant females.

The combining of music with drama is a practice extending back at least to ancient Greece, but no other medium excels the expressive range of the cinema. The stage has no equivalent of the musical documentary, like *Woodstock* (9-30) or *Gimme Shelter* (9-29). Movie musicals can take the form of animated fantasies, such as the Disney features *Bambi* and *Dumbo*. Musical biographies like *Funny Girl* and *The Buddy Holly Story* are commonplace in film. Examples of great musicals created directly for the screen are *Singin' in the Rain* and *The Band Wagon*. Others are loose adaptations of stage musicals,

**5-24. *New York, New York* (U.S.A., 1977).**
*With Liza Minnelli and Robert De Niro; Music by John Kander and Fred Ebb; Directed by Martin Scorsese.*
A number of commentators have pointed out that the most enduring genres tend to evolve toward a revisionist phase— mocking many of the genre's original values by subjecting them to skeptical scrutiny. For example, most musicals of the big studio era were essentially love stories and are concluded with the obligatory boy-wins-girl finale. Such revisionist musicals as *Cabaret* and *New York, New York,* however, end with the lovers going their separate ways, too absorbed by their own careers to submit to love's rituals of self-sacrifice.

*(United Artists)*

**5-25. *The Magic Flute* (Sweden, 1975).**
*With Josef Köstlinger; Music by Wolfgang Amadeus Mozart; Directed by Ingmar Bergman.*
Film is an ideal medium for opera. In fact, in the 19th century the German composer Richard Wagner advocated a theory of a universal artwork (*Gesamtkunstwerk*), combining music, choreography, drama, poetry, architecture, and painting. Wagner's ideal is more fully realized in the expressive possibilities of cinema than any other medium. Oddly enough, only a handful of operatic films approach major stature, perhaps because only a handful of first-rate filmmakers have been attracted to the subgenre. One immense advantage: movie subtitles are far more convenient than theatrical librettos in explaining the action. (Mozart's masterpiece, however, has a loony libretto that's based on fairy tales and the arcane symbolism of eighteenth-century freemasonry, and hence, is not a monument of lucidity in any form). Subtitles permit the spectator to concentrate on the immediacy of the musical moment, rather than trying to place it within a larger narrative context. In adapting this opera, Bergman staged it "realistically"—that is, as a straightforward presentation of a theatrical production, with all the wires and stage fakery in plain sight. It's an enchanting movie.

*(A Surrogate Release)*

like *My Fair Lady* and *Hair* (3-33). The cinema is also an ideal operatic medium, as can be seen in Bergman's *The Magic Flute* (5-25) and Joseph Losey's *Don Giovanni* (Mozart's two greatest operas), which are more flexible spatially than any stage productions could hope to be, without compromising the genius of the music.

## Spoken Language

A common misconception, held even by otherwise sophisticated moviegoers, is that language in film cannot be as complex as it is in literature. The fact that Shakespeare has been successfully brought to the screen—with no significant impoverishment in either language or visual beauty—should stand as an obvious contradiction to this notion. In fact, a number of great films are not particularly literary. But this is not to say that movies are incapable of literary distinction, only that some filmmakers wish to emphasize other aspects of their art. Those who dismiss literary movies as uncinematic find themselves in the shaky position of condemning Welles, Bergman, Huston, Richardson, Losey, Wilder, Truffaut, and Woody Allen, to mention only a few directors with literary sensibilities.

**5-26. *Xala* (Senegal, 1974).**
*Directed by Ousmane Sembene.*
Senegal, a former French colony, has a population of only 4 million, yet it has produced the most important movies of black Africa, most notably those of Sembene, the continent's best-known filmmaker. *Xala* (which roughly translates "the curse of impotence"), is spoken in French and Wolof, the native language of Senegal. The movie is an exposé of the nation's servile ruling class, whose members have eagerly embraced the culture of their white colonial predecessors. (At this lavish wedding reception, for example, several Frenchified Beautiful People wonder what the English translation is for "le weekend.") The cultural commentator Hernandez Arregui has observed: "Culture becomes bilingual not due to the use of two languages but because of the conjuncture of two cultural patterns of thinking. One is national, that of the people, and the other is estranging, that of the classes subordinated to outside forces. The admiration that the upper classes express for the United States or Europe is the highest expression of their subjection." Like many Third World artists, Sembene advocates the creation of a truly indigenous culture. (Not unlike Emerson's call in the nineteenth century for our own artists to stop producing tepid imitations of British models in favor of a truly American idiom.)

(New Yorker Films)

In some respects, language in film can be more complex than in literature. In the first place, the words of a movie, like those of the live theatre, are spoken, not written, and the human voice is capable of far more nuances than the cold printed page. The written word is a crude approximation of the connotative richness of spoken language. Thus, to take a simple example of no literary merit, the meaning of the words "I will see him tomorrow" seem obvious enough in written form. But an actor can emphasize one word over the others and thus change the meanings of the sentence completely. Here are a few possibilities:

I will *see* him tomorrow. (Implying, but that's all I'll do.)
I will see him *tomorrow*. (Implying, not today, or any other time.)
*I* will see him tomorrow. (Implying, not you or anyone else.)
I *will* see him tomorrow. (Implying, and I don't care if you approve.)
I will see *him* tomorrow. (Implying, but not his mother-in-law.)

Of course a novelist or poet could emphasize specific words by italicizing them. But unlike actors, writers don't generally underline words in every sentence. On the other hand, actors routinely go through their speeches to see which words to stress, which to "throw away" and the ways to best achieve these effects—in each and every sentence. To a gifted actor, the written speech is a mere blueprint, an outline, compared to the complexities of spoken speech. A performer with an excellent voice—an Alec Guinness, for example—could wrench ten or twelve meanings from this simple sentence, let alone a Shakespearean soliloquy.

Written punctuation is likewise a simplified approximation of speech rhythms. The pauses, hesitancies, and rapid slurs of speech can only be partially suggested by punctuation:

I will . . . see him—tomorrow.
I will see him—tomorrow!
I . . . will . . . see him—tomorrow?

And so on. But how is one to capture all the meanings that have no punctuation equivalents? Even professional linguists, who have a vast array of diacritical marks to record speech, recognize that these symbols are primitive devices at best, capable of capturing only a fraction of the subtleties of the human voice. An actor like Laurence Olivier built much of his reputation on his genius in capturing little quirks of speech—an irrepressible giggle between words, for example, or a sudden vocal plummeting on one word, a gulp, or an hysterical upsurge in pitch. The gamut of sounds and rhythms in Olivier's delivery suggests the virtuosity of a musical instrument.

By definition, speech patterns deviating radically from the official dialect are generally regarded as substandard—at least by those who take such pat distinctions seriously. Dialects can be a rich source of meaning in movies (and in life too for that matter). Since dialects are usually spoken by people outside the Establishment, they tend to convey a subversive ideology. For example, the comic art of Richard Pryor is steeped in the jivy idiom of America's black ghettos—best illustrated perhaps by his diabolically funny film *Richard Pryor—Live in Concert*. Similarly, such performers as Kris Kristofferson and Sissy Spacek have virtually specialized in "talkin' country." The earthiness of

Cockney and the robust dialects of Britain's northern industrial cities like Liverpool were popularized by such working-class rock groups as The Rolling Stones and The Beatles. A number of Continental filmmakers have also exploited the expressive richness of dialects, most notably Lina Wertmüller (5-27).

**5-27.** *All Screwed Up* **(Italy, 1973).**
*Directed by Lina Wertmüller.*
Spoken language is steeped in ideology: it's an instant revealer of class, education, and cultural bias. In most countries of the world, regional dialects are regarded as substandard—at any rate by those speaking the "official" (i.e., ruling class) dialect. Wertmüller is acutely sensitive to the ideological implications of dialects. Her movies often explore culture clashes, generally between the prosperous bourgeois north, and the impoverished south of Italy. Much of her comedy is mined from the earthy idioms of her working-class southerners in contrast with the standard (Tuscan) dialect spoken in the north. Needless to say, much of this political comedy is lost in translation. Dialects have a way of getting diluted in subtitles. For example, "Piss off!" becomes "Go away" or worse yet, "Please leave me alone." On the other hand, dubbed-in "equivalents" are incongruous. For example, rural Appalachian or black ghetto dialects have different cultural connotations, and would sound weird coming out of the mouths of Italian characters.

*(New Line Cinema)*

Because language is spoken in movies and plays, these two mediums enjoy an advantage over printed language in that the words of a text can be juxtaposed with ideas and emotions of a subtext. Briefly, a subtext refers to those meanings implicit *behind* the language of a film or play script. For example, the following lines of dialogue might be contained in a script:

Woman: May I have a cigarette, please?
    Man: Yes, of course. (Lights her cigarette.)
Woman: Thank you. You're very kind.
    Man: Don't mention it.

As written, these four not very exciting lines seem simple enough and rather neutral emotionally. But, depending on the dramatic context, they can be exploited to suggest other ideas, totally independent of the apparent meaning of the words. If the woman was flirting with the man, for example, she would deliver the lines very differently from an efficient businesswoman. If they

**5-28. *The Nun's Story* (U.S.A., 1958).**
*With Audrey Hepburn and Peter Finch; Directed by Fred Zinnemann.*
Feelings don't have to be articulated to be important, in movies or in life. Often social decorum, shame, or conscience prevent people from discussing their thoughts and emotions openly. In such cases, film performers must act the subtext rather than the text proper; they must convey these inner qualities *despite* the surface neutrality of their dialogue. Zinnemann is a master of subtexts. For example, one of the main themes of this film is how respect and admiration can meld imperceptibly into love. Yet the love that grows between the missionary nun, Sister Luke (Hepburn), and the nonbeliever, Dr. Fortunati (Finch), is never spoken of in the movie.

detested one another, the lines would take on another significance. If the man were flirting with a hostile female, the lines would be delivered in yet another way, suggesting other meanings. In other words, the meaning of the passage is provided by the actors, not the language which is merely camouflage. (For a more detailed discussion of the concept of a subtext, see Chapter 6.)

Any script meant to be spoken has a subtext, even one of great literary distinction. A good example from a classic text can be seen in Zeffirelli's *Romeo and Juliet,* in which Mercutio (John McEnery) is played not as the witty *bon vivant* who's intoxicated with his own talk, but as a neurotic young man with a shaky grasp of reality. This interpretation upset some traditionalists, but in the context of the movie, it reinforces the loving bond between Romeo and his best friend, and helps justify Romeo's impulsive (and self-destructive) act of revenge later in the film when Mercutio is killed by Tybalt.

Some contemporary filmmakers deliberately neutralize their language, claiming that the subtext is what they're really after. Harold Pinter, the dramatist and screenwriter, is perhaps the most famous example of a contemporary writer who stresses the significance of the subtext. In *The Home-coming,* a scene of extraordinary eroticism is conveyed through dialogue involving the request for a glass of water! Pinter claims that language is often a kind of "cross-talk," a way of concealing fears and anxieties. In some respects, this technique can be even more effective in film, where closeups can convey the meanings behind words more subtly than an actor on a stage. Pinter's movie scripts are among the most suggestive subtexts of the contemporary cinema: *The Pumpkin Eater, The Servant, Accident* (5-13), *The Go-Between,* two adaptations of his plays, *The Caretaker* and *The Homecoming,* and *The French Lieutenant's Woman.*

But these are merely some of the advantages of language that film enjoys over literature—advantages shared, in large part, by the live theatre. As an art of juxtapositions, movies can also extend the meanings of language by contrasting spoken words with images. The sentence "I will see him tomorrow" acquires still other meanings when the image shows the speaker smiling, for example, or frowning, or looking determined. All sorts of juxtapositions are possible. The sentence could be delivered with a determined emphasis, but an image of a frightened face (or eye, or a twitching mouth), can modify the

**5-29. *Sunset Boulevard* (U.S.A., 1950).**
*With William Holden and Gloria Swanson; Directed by Billy Wilder.*
Voice-over monologues are often used to produce ironic contrasts between the past and the present. Almost inevitably, such contrasts suggest a sense of destiny and fate. This film is narrated by a dead man (Holden), while the flashback images show us how he managed to get himself killed.

(*Paramount Pictures*)

verbal determination or even cancel it out. The juxtaposed image could be a reaction shot—thus emphasizing the effect of the statement on the listener. Or the camera could photograph an important object, implying a connection between the speaker, the words, and the object. If the speaker is photographed in long shot, his juxtaposition with his environment could also change the meanings of the words. The same line spoken in closeup would emphasize yet different meanings.

This advantage of simultaneity extends to other sounds. Music and sound effects can modify the meanings of words considerably. The same sentence spoken in an echo chamber will have different connotations from the sentence whispered intimately. If a clap of thunder coincided with the utterance of the sentence, the effect would be different from the chirping of birds or the whining of the wind. Since film is also a mechanical medium, the sentence could be modified by a deliberate distortion in the sound recording. In short, depending on the vocal emphasis, the visual emphasis, and the accompanying soundtrack, this simple sentence could have dozens of different meanings in film, some of them impossible to capture in written form.

There are two types of spoken language in movies—the monologue and dialogue. Monologues are often associated with documentaries, in which an off-screen narrator provides the audience with factual information accompanying the visuals. Most documentary theorists are agreed that the cardinal rule in the use of this technique is to avoid duplicating the information in the

**5-30.** *Blume in Love* **(U.S.A., 1973).**
*With George Segal, Kris Kristofferson, and Susan Anspach; Written and directed by Paul Mazursky.*
Interior monologues are especially effective in presenting us with a contrast between what's said socially and what's thought privately. In this movie, for example, Blume (Segal, right) narrates what he was really feeling when he attempted to ingratiate himself with his ex-wife and her lover.

image. The commentary should provide what is not apparent on the screen. The audience, in short, is provided with two types of information, one concrete (visuals), the other abstract (narration). *Cinéma vérité* documentarists have extended this technique to include interviews, a practice pioneered by the French filmmaker Jean Rouch. Thus, instead of an anonymous narrator, the soundtrack conveys the actual words of the subjects of the documentary—slum dwellers, perhaps, or students. The camera can focus on the speaker or can roam elsewhere, with the soundtrack providing the continuity.

Monologues have also been employed in fiction films. This technique is especially useful in condensing events and time. Early in *Citizen Kane* a simulated *News on the March* sequence is presented, recounting the highlights of Kane's public life. The mock Voice-of-God narrator sets up most of the major characters and events which are developed later in the movie. Narrative monologues can also be used omnisciently to provide an ironic contrast with the visuals. In Richardson's *Tom Jones*, John Osborne's script features an off-screen narrator who's nearly as witty and urbane as Fielding's, though necessarily less chatty. This narrator sets up the story, provides us with thumbnail sketches of the characters, connects many of the episodes with necessary transitions, and comments philosophically on the escapades of the incorrigible hero.

**5-31. *Badlands* (U.S.A., 1974).**
*With Sissy Spacek; Written and directed by Terrence Malick.*
Not all voice-over narratives are omniscient. This movie is narrated by a bored and dim-witted teenager (Spacek) who talks in *True Romance* clichés and hasn't a glimmer of insight into what wrecked her life.

(Warner Brothers)

Off-screen narration tends to give a movie a sense of objectivity and often an air of predestination. Many of the works of Billy Wilder are structured in flashbacks, with ironic monologues emphasizing fatality: the main interest is not what happened, but how and why. In *Double Indemnity*, for example, the story is narrated by the fatally wounded hero who admits his guilt at the opening of the film. As Wilder pointed out: "By identifying the criminals right off the bat—and identifying ourselves with them—we can concentrate on what follows: their efforts to escape, the net closing, closing."

The interior monologue is one of the most valuable tools of filmmakers, for with it they can convey what a character is thinking. Originally a dramatic and novelistic device, the interior monologue is in fact frequently used in adaptations of plays and novels. Before Olivier, most film soliloquies were delivered as they are on stage: that is, the camera and microphone record a character literally talking to himself. Olivier's *Hamlet* introduced a more cinematic soliloquy. In the "To be or not to be" speech, several of the lines are not spoken but "thought"—via a voice-over soundtrack. Suddenly, at a crucial line, Olivier spews out the words in exasperation. Through the use of the soundtrack, private ruminations and public speech can be combined in interesting ways, with new and often more subtle emphases. In *Richard III*, the villain Richard (Olivier) brazenly directs his soliloquies to the camera—forcing us to be his confidants, and thereby suggesting that we are, in a sense, his accomplices.

A major difference between stage dialogue and screen dialogue is degree of density. One of the necessary conventions of the live theatre is articulation: if something is bothering a character, we can usually assume that he or she will *talk* about the problem. The theatre is a visual as well as aural medium, but in general the spoken word is dominant: we tend to hear before we see. If information is conveyed visually in the theatre, it must be larger than life, for most of the audience is too far from the stage to perceive visual nuances. The convention of articulation is necessary, therefore, to compensate for this visual loss. Like most artistic conventions, stage dialogue is not usually realistic or natural, even in so-called realistic plays. In real life people don't articulate their ideas and feelings with such precision. In movies, the convention of articulation can be relaxed. Since the closeup can show the minutest detail, verbal comment is often superfluous. This greater spatial flexibility means that film language doesn't have to carry the heavy burden of stage dialogue. In fact, since the image conveys most meanings, dialogue in film can be as spare and realistic as it is in everyday life, as in such starkly dialogued movies as Don Siegel's *Escape from Alcatraz,* and most of the works of Antonioni (5-32).

*(Rizzoli Film)*

**5-32. Red Desert (Italy, 1964).**
*With Monica Vitti, Richard Harris (right), and Carlo Chionetti; Directed by Michelangelo Antonioni.*
Talk is usually kept to a minimum in the films of Antonioni. The neurotic anguish of the heroine of *Red Desert* is literally unspeakable—she can only grope and stammer. Her feelings are more eloquently expressed by the closed form of the mise-en-scène and the woundlike splotches of red paint against the white walls.

But movie dialogue doesn't have to conform to natural speech. If language is stylized, the director has several options to make it believable. Like Olivier, he or she can emphasize an intimate style of delivery—sometimes even whispering the lines. Welles' Shakespearean films are characterized by a visual flamboyance: the expressionistic stylization of the images in *Othello* complements the artificiality of the language. Generally speaking, if dialogue is nonrealistic, the images must be co-expressive: sharp contrasts of style between language and visuals can produce jarring and often comic incongruities.

The advantages of language, then, make it indispensable to the film artist and not only to those of literary tastes. As René Clair forsaw many years ago, language permits a director more visual freedom, not less. Because speech can reveal a person's class, region, occupation, prejudices, etc., the director doesn't need to waste time establishing these facts visually. A few lines of dialogue can convey all that's necessary, thus freeing the camera to go on to other matters. There are many instances where language is the most economical and precise way of conveying information in film.

Foreign language movies are shown either in dubbed versions or in their

**5-33.** *Padre Padrone* **(Italy, 1977).**
*With Omero Antonutti; Directed by Paolo and Vittorio Taviani.*
Also known as *My Father, My Master,* this film is an exploration of two worlds: an objective, documentarylike presentation of peasant life on the primitive island of Sardinia, as conveyed by the visuals; and the private world of subjective fantasies, as conveyed by the soundtrack. The story is narrated in flashbacks by a distinguished dialect scholar on whose life the movie is based. We are also allowed to hear the imagined thoughts of many of the secondary characters—and even the complaints of a goat! Music is used expressionistically, to suggest a variety of psychological states. Sound effects evoke ancient, archetypal experiences. The Taviani brothers also offer a cogent demonstration of the ideological disadvantages of peasant dialects on the technologically sophisticated mainland. Throughout the movie, the images present us with sociological facts, the soundtrack with spiritual truths.

(Cinema V)

original language, with written subtitles. Both methods of translation have obvious limitations. Dubbed movies often have a hollow, tinny sound, and in most cases the dubbing is performed by less gifted actors than the originals. Sound and image are difficult to match in dubbed films, especially in the closer ranges where the movements of the actors' lips aren't synchronized with the sounds. Even bilingual actors who do their own dubbing are less nuanced when they're not speaking their native language. For example, Sophia Loren's performance in the English-language version of *Two Women* is very good, but it lacks the vocal expressiveness of her brilliant line-readings in the original Italian. In English, Loren's classy pear-shaped tones are somewhat at odds with her role as an earthy peasant. In a similar vein, actors with highly distinctive voices, like Mae West or John Wayne, sound preposterous when dubbed in German or Japanese. On the other hand, dubbed movies permit the spectator to concentrate on the visuals rather than the subtitles which are distracting and can absorb much of a viewer's energy.

Most experienced filmgoers still prefer subtitles, however, despite their cumbersomeness. In the first place, some spectators are sufficiently conversant in foreign languages to understand most of the dialogue (especially in Europe where virtually all educated people speak a second language, and in some cases three or four). An actor's tone of voice is often more important than the dialogue per se, and subtitled movies allow us to hear these vocal nuances. In short, particularly when sound is a major source of meaning in a film, subtitles permit the spectator to hear what the original artists said, not what some disinterested technician—however clever—decided we would settle for.

## Further Reading

CLAIR, RENÉ, "The Art of Sound," in *Film: A Montage of Theories*, Richard Dyer MacCann, ed. (New York: Dutton, 1966); and SERGEI EISENSTEIN and V. I. PUDOVKIN, "A Statement on the Sound Film," in *Film Form* (New York: Harcourt, Brace, 1949).

EISLER, HANS, *Composing for the Films* (New York: Oxford University Press, 1947).

HAGEN, EARL, *Scoring for Films* (New York: Wehman, 1972). Technical emphasis.

HUNTLEY, JOHN, AND ROGER MANVELL, *The Technique of Film Music* (London: Focal Press, 1957).

JACOBS, LEWIS, "Refinements in Technique," in *The Rise of the American Film* (New York: Teachers College Press, 1968); and ARTHUR KNIGHT, "The Movies Learn to Talk," in *The Liveliest Art* (New York: Mentor, 1979).

KRACAUER, SIEGFRIED, "Dialogue and Sound" and "Music" in *Theory of Film* (New York: Oxford Univ. Press, 1960).

MCCARTHY, CLIFFORD, *Film Composers in America* (New York: Da Capo, 1972).

PRENDERGAST, ROY M., *Film Music* (New York: Norton, 1977).

THOMAS, TONY, *Music for the Movies* (New York: A. S. Barnes, 1973).

WALKER, ALEXANDER, *The Shattered Silents* (New York: William Morrow, 1979).

## 6

*"In the cinema the actor must think and let his thoughts work upon his face. The objective nature of the medium will do the rest. A theatrical performance requires magnification, a cinema performance requires an inner life."*

CHARLES DULLIN

# PLAYER

In the live theatre, actors are usually classified either as stars or professional players. Film acting is a more complex art. Performers can serve as camera material, like a landscape or a set. Movies can also employ amateur players even in principal roles: they are chosen not because of their acting ability (which can be negligible), but because of their authentic appearance. The star system in movies was developed and has been dominated by the American cinema, though it's hardly unique to film. Virtually all the performing arts—opera, dance, live theatre, television, concert music—have exploited the box office popularity of a charismatic performer. The influential Russian stage director and theorist Constantin Stanislavsky believed that "an actor in the talking films is obliged to be incomparably more skillful and technically expert than an actor on the stage." Many filmmakers—and film lovers—regard acting as the *sine qua non* of fiction movies. "I'm not an actor, I am a poet," Chaplin proudly proclaimed. Most movie players concede, however, that their work is shaped by the person who literally and figuratively calls the shots: "Film acting is unquestionably a director's medium," Chaplin insisted.

## Stage and Screen Acting

The differences between stage and screen acting are largely determined by the differences in space and time in each medium (see also Chapter 7, "Drama"). In general, the live theatre seems to be a more satisfactory medium

**6-1. *Valentino* (U.S.A., 1977).**
*With Rudolf Nureyev and Michelle Phillips; Directed by Ken Russell.*
The beauty of the human form—both male and female—is one of the most persistent attractions of the cinema and can be traced back almost to its inception. Indeed, sexual allure has been a compelling aphrodisiac in most of the performing arts, dating back to ancient times. Even in painting and sculpture, eroticism is fundamental to an appreciation of the nude, as the art scholar Kenneth Clark has pointed out. See also Thomas R. Atkins, ed., *Sexuality in the Movies* (Bloomington, Ind.: Indiana University Press, 1975).

for the player, for once the curtain goes up he or she tends to dominate the proceedings. In movies, this is not necessarily the case. The essential requisites for the stage performer are to be seen and heard clearly. Thus, the ideal theatrical actor must have a flexible, trained voice. Most obviously, his or her voice must be powerful enough to be heard even in a theatre containing thousands of seats. Since language is the major source of meaning in the theatre, the nuances of the dialogue must be conveyed through vocal expressiveness. An actor's voice must be capable of much variety; it is necessary to know which words to stress and how, how to phrase properly for different types of lines, when to pause and for how long, and how fast or slow a line or speech ought to be delivered. Above all, the stage actor must be *believable*, even when reciting dialogue that's highly stylized and unnatural. Most of the credit for an exciting theatrical production is given to the performers, but much of the burden is also theirs, for when we're bored by a production of a play, we tend to assign the responsibility to the actors.

Physical requirements are less exacting in the theatre than in movies. Most obviously, the stage actor must be seen—even from the back of the auditorium. Thus, it helps to be tall, for small actors tend to get lost on a large stage. It also helps to have large and regular features, although makeup can cover a multitude of deficiencies. For this reason, casting a forty-year-old actor as Romeo is not necessarily a disaster in the theatre, for if the actor is in reasonably good physical shape, his age won't show beyond the first few rows of seats. Because of the low visual saturation in the theatre, actors can play roles twenty years beyond their actual age, providing their voices and bodies are flexible enough (see also 6-34A).

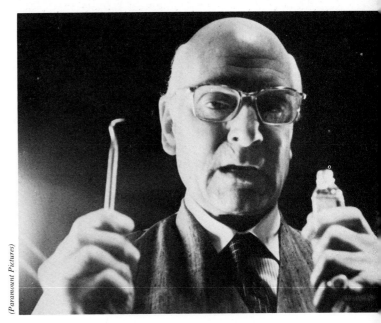

**6-2. *Marathon Man* (U.S.A., 1976).**
*With Laurence Olivier; Directed by John Schlesinger.*
Olivier is regarded as the dean of British actors, and that scepter'd isle is widely conceded to have the finest actors in the world. His range is extraordinary, encompassing most of the Shakespearean repertory as well as many roles of the classical Continental drama. He has played principals, character roles, and cameo parts. He has moved freely from movies to the live theatre, both as an actor and a director, in America as well as England. Lord Olivier is the only actor to have been elevated to the peerage on the basis of his art.

*(Paramount Pictures)*

The stage actor's entire body is always in view, and for this reason he must be able to control it with some degree of precision. Some obvious activities as sitting, walking, and standing are performed differently on the stage than they are in real life. An actor must usually learn how to dance a little, how to fence, and how to move naturally in period costumes. He must know what to do with his hands—when to let them hang and when to use them for expressive gestures. Furthermore, stage actors must know how to adjust their bodies to different characters: a seventeen-year-old girl moves differently from a woman of thirty; an aristocrat moves differently from a clerk of the same age. The body must communicate a wide variety of emotions in pantomime: a happy person even stands differently from one who is dejected, or fearful, or bored.

Theatrical acting preserves real time. The performer must build—scene by scene—toward the climactic scene near the end of the play. Usually the stage actor begins at a relatively low energy level, then increases with each progressive scene, until, in the climax, the energy reaches its bursting point

**6-3. Publicity photo for *Magnum Force* (U.S.A., 1973).**
*With Clint Eastwood and Adele Yoshioka; Directed by Ted Post.*
In the live theatre, actors are selected not only on the basis of their looks and talent, but also on how well they match up with the other actors on stage. Theatrical directors must always conceive of their productions in terms of an ensemble effect. In the cinema, these considerations are secondary. In this movie, Eastwood, who stands 6′ 4″ is romantically paired with Adele Yoshioka, who is 5′ 4″. On stage, this height discrepancy would be a sight gag, but on the screen (or more accurately, off-screen), the problem was easily resolved through the art of exclusion.

(*Warner Brothers*)

and finally tapers off in the resolution of the play. In short, the actor generates in psychic energy the play's own structure. Within this overall structure, the stage performer "builds" within each scene, although not every scene is automatically played at a greater intensity than its predecessor, for different plays build in different ways. What's essential for the stage actor is to sustain an energy level for the duration of a scene. Once the curtain rises, he's alone on the stage. Mistakes aren't easily corrected, nor can a scene be replayed or cut out.

In general, the film player can get along quite well with a minimum of stage technique. The essential requisite for a performer in the movies is what Antonioni calls "expressiveness." That is, he or she must *look* interesting. No amount of technique will compensate for an unphotogenic face (6-4). A

**6-4.** *The Whisperers* **(Great Britain, 1967).**
*With Edith Evans; Directed by Bryan Forbes.*
The Hungarian theoretician, Béla Balázs, believed that the cinematic closeup can isolate the human face from its surroundings and penetrate the soul: "What appears on the face and in facial expression is a spiritual experience," Balázs observed. This experience is impossible to achieve in the live theatre because the spectator is too distant from the player who must rely on the intermediary of words. See Béla Balázs, "The Face of Man," in *Theory of the Film* (New York: Dover, 1970).

(*United Artists*)

number of stage performers have fared badly in the movies because of this deficiency. For example, Kim Stanley and Tallulah Bankhead were among the most admired stage stars in America, but their film work failed to excite much interest. Similarly, Ian Richardson is regarded as one of the most brilliant actors of the British stage—where brilliant actors are commonplace—but his few film performances are lacklustre. Some of the most famous stage actors in history—including Sarah Bernhardt—look preposterous on film: her techniques are mannered and stagey to the point of caricature. In movies, then, too much technique can actually undercut a performance, can make it seem hammy and insincere.

Acting in the cinema is almost totally dependent upon the filmmaker's approach to his or her materials. In general, the more realistic the director's techniques, the more necessary it is to rely on the abilities of the players. Such

(a)

(b)

(c)

(g)

(h)

(i)

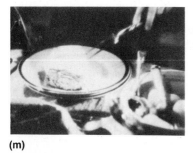

(m)

(n)

(o)

(s)

(t)

(u)

*(Gaumont-British)*

(d)　　　　　　　　　　　　　　(e)　　　　　　　　　　　　　　(f)

 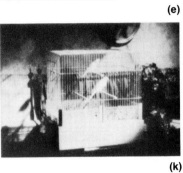 

(j)　　　　　　　　　　　　　　(k)　　　　　　　　　　　　　　(l)

  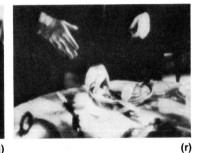

(p)　　　　　　　　　　　　　　(q)　　　　　　　　　　　　　　(r)

(v)　　　　　　　　　　　　　　(w)　　　　　　　　　　　　　　(x)

**6-5. Sequence from *Sabotage* (Great Britain, 1936).**
*With Sylvia Sidney and Oscar Homolka; Directed by Alfred Hitchcock.*
Through the art of editing, a director can construct a highly emotional "performance" by juxtaposing shots of his actors with shots of objects. In scenes such as these, the actor's contribution tends to be minimal: the effect is achieved through the linking of two or more shots. This associational process is the basis of Pudovkin's theory of constructive editing.

directors tend to favor long shots which keep the performer's entire body within the frame. This is the camera distance that corresponds to the proscenium arch of the live theatre. The realist also tends to favor lengthy takes—thus permitting the actors to sustain performances for relatively long periods without interruption. From the audience's point of view, it's easier to evaluate acting in a realistic movie than in an expressionistic film for we are permitted to see sustained scenes without any apparent directorial interference. The camera remains essentially a recording device.

The more expressionistic the director, the less likely he or she is to value the actor's contribution. Although he was by no means an exclusive expressionist, some of Hitchcock's most stunning cinematic effects were achieved by minimizing the contributions of actors. During the production of *Sabotage,* Hitchcock's leading lady, Sylvia Sidney, burst into tears on the set because she wasn't permitted to act a crucial scene. The episode involved a murder in which the sympathetic heroine kills her brutish husband in revenge for his murder of her young brother. On stage, of course, her feelings and thoughts would be communicated by the actress' exaggerated facial expressions. But in real life, Hitchcock observed, people's faces don't necessarily reveal what they think or feel. The director preferred to convey these ideas and emotions through edited juxtapositions (6-5).

The setting for the scene is a dinner table. The heroine looks at her husband who is eating as usual. Then a closeup shows a dish containing meat and vegetables with a knife and fork lying next to it; the wife's hands are seen behind the dish. Hitchcock then cuts to a medium shot of the wife thoughtfully slicing some meat. Next, a medium shot of the brother's empty chair. Closeup of the wife's hands with knife and fork. Closeup of a bird cage with canaries—a reminder to the heroine of her dead brother. Closeup of wife's thoughtful face. Closeup of the knife and plate. Suddenly a closeup of the husband's suspicious face: he notices the connection between the knife and her thoughtful expression, for the camera pans, rather than cuts, back to the knife. He gets up next to her. Hitchcock quickly cuts to a closeup of her hand reaching for the knife. Cut to an extreme closeup of the knife entering his body. Cut to a two-shot of their faces, his convulsed with pain, hers in fear. Cut to a deep-focus long shot, in which his dead body drops out of frame.

One of Hitchcock's recurrent themes is the idea of complicity. By forcing the audience to identify with his protagonists, he involves us in their behavior. In effect, we share the responsibility for certain questionable acts because of this identification. In *Sabotage,* we must somehow excuse the heroine's act of murder by participating in it. He forces this identification by fragmenting the sequence at the dinner table. Like the heroine, we too connect the knife with the dead brother and the guilty husband. The knife gradually seems to acquire a will of its own, a kind of destiny. Before we (or the heroine) realize what's happening, the knife is in the husband's body—almost as though it were predestined to find its home there. The revenge is complete, yet we don't really blame the distraught wife for we have, in a way, helped commit the act. When Sylvia Sidney saw the finished product, she was delighted with the results. The entire scene, of course, required very little acting in the conventional sense of the term.

Antonioni has stated that he uses his actors only as part of the composition—"like a tree, a wall, or a cloud" (see also 6-6). Many of the major themes of his films are conveyed through long shots where the juxtaposition

**6-6. *A Condemned Man Escapes* (France, 1956).**
*With François Leterrier (right); Directed by Robert Bresson.*
Bresson usually prefers nonprofessional players in his movies. (Leterrier was a philosophy student at the Sorbonne when he made this film.) The director believes that a screen actor is not an interpretive artist but merely one of the "raw materials" of the mise-en-scène and the editing. He avoids using professionals because they tend to want to convey emotions and ideas through performance, as in the live theatre. For Bresson, films should be made cinematically rather than theatrically, by "bypassing the will of those who appear in them, using not what they do, but what they *are*."

of people and their settings are used to suggest complex psychological and spiritual states. Perhaps more than any other director, Antonioni is sensitive to how meanings change, depending on the mise-en-scène. Thus, the significance of a line of dialogue can be totally altered when it's uttered by an actor standing before a brick wall or on a deserted street. Antonioni has also pointed out that a line spoken by an actor in profile may have a different meaning from one delivered at full face.

Generalizing about acting in movies is difficult because directors don't approach every film with the same attitudes. In some cases they will use predominantly realistic techniques, and in others, expressionistic. In *Rope*, for example, Hitchcock included virtually no edited sequences, for he was experimenting with 10-minute takes which preserve actual time. In *Psycho*, on the other hand, the most effective scenes are highly fragmented. Directors like Elia Kazan and Ingmar Bergman, distinguished stage directors as well as filmmakers, will vary their techniques considerably, depending on the dra-

(New Yorker Films)

**6-7. *Jonah Who Will be 25 in the Year 2000* (Switzerland, 1976).**
*With Jean-Luc Bideau and Miou-Miou; Directed by Alain Tanner.*
Actors in every medium (except radio) must be conscious of body language and what it reveals about character. In this photo, for example, the giggly spontaneity of two former 1960s radicals is expressed primarily by the actors' bodies. Filmmakers can also create provocative tensions by contrasting the body language of the players with their facial expressions or their dialogue. See Julius Fast, *Body Language* (New York: Pocket Books, 1971).

matic needs of the film. Nor is there any "correct" approach to filming a scene. A director like Chaplin might convey a specific idea through acting, whereas Carl Dreyer might approach the same idea through editing or mise-en-scène. Each version could be effective: whatever *works* is right.

But whether a director is a Realist or Expressionist, the differences between film acting and stage acting remain fundamental. For example, a player in movies is not so restricted by vocal requirements since sound volume is controlled electronically. Marilyn Monroe's small breathy voice wouldn't have projected beyond the first few rows in the theatre, but on film it was perfect for conveying that childlike vulnerability which gave her performances such poetic delicacy. Some film actors are popular precisely because of the off-beat charm of their voices. James Stewart's twangy nasality, for example, is an essential aspect of his country-boy unpretentiousness. Since acting in movies is not so dependent upon vocal flexibility, many performers have succeeded despite their wooden, inexpressive voices: Gary Cooper, John Wayne, Gregory Peck.

Even the quality of a movie actor's voice can be controlled mechanically. Music and sound effects can totally change the meaning of a line of dialogue. Through electronic devices, a voice can be made to sound garbled, or booming, or hollow. Indeed, Antonioni claims that language in film is primarily pure sound, and only secondarily meaningful as dialogue. Since much of the dialogue in a movie is dubbed, a director can rerecord a line until it's perfect. Sometimes he'll select one or two words from one recorded take and blend them with the words of another, or even a third or fourth. This kind of synthesizing can be carried even further—by combining one actor's face with another actor's voice (6-8).

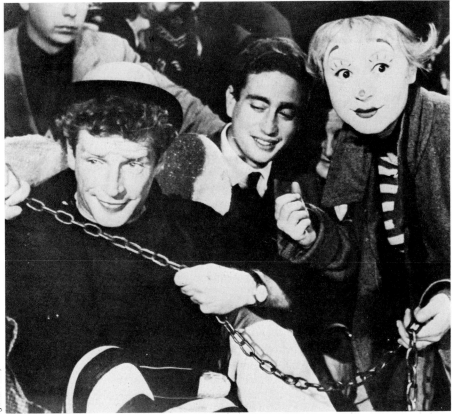

*(Janus Films)*

**6-8. *La Strada* (Italy, 1954).**
*With Giulietta Masina and Richard Basehart; Directed by Federico Fellini.*
In the Italian cinema, live sound recording is rare. Virtually all movies are dubbed after the footage has been photographed and often even after it's been edited. Fellini selects his players according to their face, body type, or personality. Like many Italian film artists, he frequently uses foreign players, even in principal roles. The American Richard Basehart spoke his lines in English during this film's production. Once shooting was completed, Fellini hired an Italian actor with the same vocal quality to dub in the character's voice. See Edward Murray, *Fellini the Artist* (New York: Frederick Ungar Publishing, 1976); and Stuart Rosenthal, *The Cinema of Federico Fellini* (New York: A. S. Barnes, 1976).

Similarly, the physical requirements for a film actor are different from those of a stage performer. The movie player doesn't have to be tall, even if he's a leading man type. Alan Ladd, for example, was quite short. His directors simply avoided showing his body in full unless there was no one else in frame to contrast with his height. He played love scenes standing on a box, his body cut off at the waist. Low-angle shots also tended to make him seem taller. A film actor's features don't have to be large, only expressive—particularly the eyes and mouth. Nor does he have to be handsome. For example, Humphrey Bogart was not a good-looking man, but the camera "liked him." That is, his face was uncannily photogenic, opening up to the camera in a way that often surprised his cinematographers. Sometimes this contrast between reality and its illusion can be tiresome. Complained Jean Arthur: "It's a strenuous job every day of your life to live up to the way you look on the screen."

An actor who moves clumsily is not necessarily at a disadvantage in film. The director can work around the problem by not using many long shots and by photographing the actor *after* he has moved. Complicated movements can be faked by using stuntmen or doubles. Elaborate sword fights, for example, are usually performed by specially trained stuntmen, dressed like the principal players. These shots are intercut with closer shots of the leading actors, and the edited juxtaposition leads the audience to assume that the main performers are involved in all the shots. Even in closeup, the film performer's physical appearance can be changed through the use of special lenses, filters, and lights.

Since the shot is the basic building unit in film, the actor doesn't have to sustain a performance for very long—even in realistic movies in which the takes can run to 2 or 3 minutes. In an expressionistic film—in which shots can last for less than a second—one can scarcely refer to the performer's contribution as acting at all: he or she simply *is.*

Furthermore, the shooting schedule of a movie is determined by economic considerations. Thus, the shooting of various sequences isn't always artistically logical. An actor may be required to perform the climactic scene first, and low-keyed exposition shots later. The screen actor, then, doesn't "build" emotionally as the stage actor must. The film player must be capable of an intense degree of concentration—turning emotions on and off for very short periods of time. Most of the time the player must seem totally natural, as if he or she weren't acting at all. "You do it just like in reality," Henry Fonda explained. Certainly the film player is almost always at the mercy of the director who later constructs the various shots into a coherent performance. Some directors have tricked actors into a performance, asking for one quality in order to get another.

Since acting in the cinema is confined to short segments of time and space, the film player doesn't need a long rehearsal period to establish a sense of ease with other actors, the set, or costumes. Many directors keep rehearsals to a minimum so as not to dissipate the spontaneity of the players, their sense of discovery and surprise. Unlike the stage player, the film actor doesn't have to create an intimate rapport with other performers: sometimes they haven't even met until they arrive on the set or on location. Actors occasionally don't know their lines: this is remedied by having a prompter on the set, or by writing the lines on a blackboard off frame where the actor can read them.

A film actor is expected to play even the most intimate scenes with dozens of technicians on the set, working or observing. He must seem totally at ease,

**6-9. *Dersu Uzala . . . The Hunter* (U.S.S.R./Japan, 1975).**
*With Maxim Munzuk; Directed by Akira Kurosawa.*
Realism in the movies can be far more "real" than stage realism, for a theatrical player's skill and discipline are always apparent to the audience. Film realism is often more convincing precisely because of the player's lack of technical skill. This movie explores the friendship between a Russian naturalist and his Siberian guide, Dersu Uzala, in the early 1900s. Authenticity, not technical skill, was Kurosawa's main concern in casting the nonprofessional player Munzuk in the leading role of the film. The scars and character lines on his face are not the handiwork of a makeup artist, but of nature itself. See also Patricia Erens, *Akira Kurosawa: A Guide to References and Resources* (Boston: G. K. Hall, 1979).

even though the lights are unbearably hot, and his running makeup must be corrected between shots. Since the camera distorts, actors are required to perform some scenes unnaturally. In an embrace, for example, lovers can't really look at each other in the eyes or they will appear cross-eyed on the screen. In point-of-view shots, actors must direct their lines at the camera rather than at another player. Much of the time the performer has no idea what he or she is doing, or where a shot might appear in the finished film, if indeed it appears at all, for many an actor's performance has been left on the cutting room floor. In short, the discontinuity of time and space in the cinema places the performer almost totally in the hands of the director.

## The American Star System

The star system has been the backbone of the American film industry since the mid-teens. Stars are the creations of the public, its reigning favorites. Their influence in the fields of fashion, values, and public behavior has been enormous. "The social history of a nation can be written in terms of its film stars," Raymond Durgnat has observed. Stars confer instant consequence to

**6-10. Publicity photo of John Travolta in *Saturday Night Fever* (U.S.A., 1977).** *With Karen Lynn Gorney; Directed by John Badham.*
Anthropologist Hortense Powdermaker noted that good looks and sex appeal have always been the conspicuous traits of most film stars, and their vehicles are tailored to enhance their particular style of eroticism. "Dance is the activity where the sexual connection is most explicit," Michael Malone has pointed out, "which is why movies use it to symbolize sex and why skillful dancing is an invariable movie clue to erotic sophistication, a prerequisite for the lover." See Michael Malone, *Heroes of Eros: Male Sexuality in the Movies* (New York: E. P. Dutton, 1979) and Hortense Powdermaker, *Hollywood: The Dream Factory* (Boston: Little, Brown, 1950).

*(United Artists)*

any film they appear in. Their fees have staggered the public. In the second decade of this century, Mary Pickford and Charles Chaplin were the two highest paid employees in the world. Contemporary stars like Robert Redford and Marlon Brando command salaries of $3 million and up per film, so popular are these box office giants. Some have reigned five decades: Bette Davis and John Wayne, to name just two. Alexander Walker, among others, has pointed out that stars are the direct or indirect reflection of the needs, drives, and anxieties of American society: they are the food of dreams, allowing us to live out our deepest fantasies and obsessions. Like the ancient gods and goddesses, stars have been adored, envied, and venerated as mythic and psychic icons.

Prior to 1910, actors' names were almost never included in movie credits because producers feared the players would then demand higher salaries. But the public named their favorites anyway. Mary Pickford, for example, was first known by her character's name, "Little Mary." From the beginning, the public often fused a star's artistic persona with his or her private personality, and in Pickford's case, as with many others, the two were radically dissimilar. She specialized in playing waggish juveniles—the bouncy, high-spirited, and sentimental young heroines of such popular hits as *Rebecca of Sunnybrook Farm* (1917) and *Pollyanna* (1920), in which her blonde curls were her trademark. In actuality, Pickford was clever and sophisticated and the most powerful woman in the American film industry of the silent era. "My career was planned," she insisted, "there was never anything accidental about it." By the time she was five, she was performing in the live theatre. She began working with Griffith in 1909 and made seventy-five short films with him at Biograph before leaving the studio in 1912. Soon she was earning $40,000 per picture. By 1914 she was pulling in $150,000. She was neck-to-neck with Chaplin in the star salaries sweepstakes, and collected from $300,000 to $500,000 per film between the years 1917–19. In 1919 she helped form United Artists, with Chaplin, Griffith, and Douglas Fairbanks (her husband) as partners. As an independent producer, she grossed as much as $1.2 million per film. Reputedly she was the business brains behind United Artists. She also directed many of her own films, although never with official credit.

Carl Laemmle, who eventually founded Universal Pictures, is usually credited with introducing the star system. In 1910 he staged one of his flamboyant publicity stunts by announcing that he had hired away "the Biograph Girl" who was identified as Florence Lawrence. Adolph Zukor (later of Paramount Pictures) also contributed to the star craze. In 1911 he secured the distribution rights to the French film *Queen Elizabeth,* featuring the aging Sarah Bernhardt, the most famous stage star of her generation. With the profits from this movie, Zukor established the Famous Players Company in 1912, and he soon was able to hire some of the most prestigious stage stars of that era to perform before his cameras. But most of these players were too old for the movies, and too stagey in their techniques. Film-trained actors were younger, better looking, and more natural in their gestures.

"The fabrication of stars is the fundamental thing in the film industry," Laemmle proclaimed. In 1915, William Fox (later of the Fox Film Corporation which eventually became 20th Century-Fox) took Laemmle at his word and manufactured Theda Bara. To audiences of this era, she was the incarna-

**6-11. Publicity photos of Robert De Niro in *Raging Bull* (U.S.A., 1980).**
*Directed by Martin Scorsese.*
Acting is a demanding art, requiring dedication, discipline, and Spartan endurance. De Niro is famous for his rigorous preparations prior to production. This film is a biography of Jake La Motta, the middle-weight boxing champion of the 1940s. De Niro trained for several months with the real La Motta (who served as technical advisor to the film) in order to capture the fighter's pugilistic style. Amazed by De Niro's skill, La Motta claimed that the actor could be a professional boxer if he wanted. During a shooting hiatus, De Niro even put on fifty pounds so he wouldn't have to resort to padding in order to portray La Motta in later life, when his body was encased in fat. De Niro prefers to bury himself in a role. He rarely exploits his personal charisma, insisting that life should take precedence over art. But De Niro's is an art that conceals art. "Some of the old movie stars were terrific," he explained, "but they romanticized. People chase illusions and these illusions are created by movies. I want to make things concrete and real and to break down the illusion. There's nothing more ironic or strange or contradictory than life itself. I don't want people years from now to say: 'Remember De Niro, he had real style'."

(a)  (b)

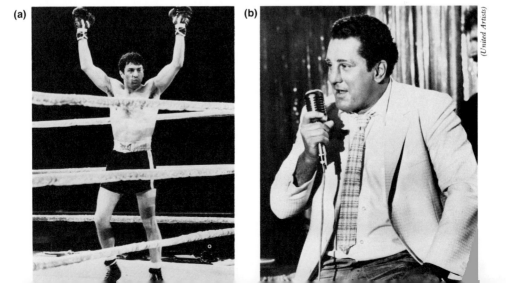

(United Artists)

**6-12. Publicity photo of Marilyn Monroe in *The Seven Year Itch* (U.S.A., 1955).**
*Directed by Billy Wilder.*
Marilyn Monroe has become a symbol of the personal tragedy which can befall a star. She was born (illegitimate) to an emotionally unstable mother who spent most of her life in mental asylums. As a child, Marilyn was raised in a series of orphanages and foster homes. Even then—especially then—she dreamed of becoming a famous Hollywood star. She was raped at the age of eight, married to her first husband at fourteen. She used sex (like many before her) as a means to an end—stardom. In the late 1940s she had a few bit roles, mostly as sexy dumb blondes. Not until John Huston's *The Asphalt Jungle* (1950) did she create much of a stir. In that same year, Joseph Mankiewicz cast her in *All About Eve,* as "a graduate of the Copacabana School of Dramatic Art," as George Sanders drily deadpans in the film. (Sanders claimed he knew Marilyn would one day become a star "because she desperately needed to be one.") After Twentieth Century-Fox signed her to a contract, the studio didn't know what to do with her. She appeared in a series of third-rate studio projects, but despite their mediocrity, the public clamored for more Marilyn. She rightly blamed Fox for mismanaging her career: "Only the public can make a star. It's the studios who try to make a system out of it," she bitterly complained. At the peak of her popularity, she left Hollywood in disgust, to study at the Actors' Studio. When she returned, she demanded more money and better roles—and got both. Joshua Logan, who directed her in *Bus Stop* (1956), said she was "as near genius as any actress I ever knew." Supremely photogenic, she gave herself entirely to the camera,

allowing it to probe her deepest vulnerabilities. Laurence Olivier, her costar and director in *The Prince and the Showgirl* (1957), marvelled at her cunning way of fusing guilelessness with carnality—the mind and soul of a little girl wrapped in the body of a whore. Throughout her years as a top star, her private life was a shambles. "She was an unfortunate doped-up woman most of the time," biographer Maurice Zolotow observed. Her failed marriages and love affairs were constantly in the headlines, and increasingly she turned to drugs and alcohol for solace. She was notorious for her irresponsibility, often not even bothering to show up on the set for days at a time, thus incurring enormous cost overruns. Because of her addiction to drugs and alcohol, even when she did show up she scarcely knew who—much less where—she was. Repeatedly she needed thirty, forty, even fifty takes before she could warm up to a scene. Astonishingly, she usually came out smelling like a rose, for her directors managed to piece together a performance. There was often much bitterness between her and her directors after a production was finally wrapped up. She was found dead in 1962: an overdose of barbituates and alcohol. She is probably the most written-about film personality in history; but even after her death, Billy Wilder—among others—scoffed at the myths of martyrdom promulgated about her: "I have never met anyone as utterly mean as Marilyn Monroe," he said. "Nor as utterly fabulous on the screen, and that includes Garbo." Three interesting biographies are: Maurice Zolotow, *Marilyn Monroe* (New York: Harcourt Brace, 1960); Fred Lawrence Guiles, *Norma Jean* (New York: McGraw-Hill, 1969); and Norman Mailer, *Marilyn* (New York: Warner Paperback, 1973).

tion of forbidden sexuality—insatiable in her lust, indifferent to the misery she inflicted on her adoring slaves. This first in a long line of sex queens was later found to be the former Theodosia Goodman whose father was a tailor in Ohio. Bara's career was intense and brief: she made forty movies at Fox, but by 1920 she was considered ludicrously passé. Most attempts at "fabricating" stars were unsuccessful. Unless the public is receptive to a given screen personality, audiences can be remarkably resistent to someone else's notion of a star. For example, producer Samuel Goldwyn ballyhooed his Russian import, Anna Sten, without stinting on costs. But audiences stayed away from her movies in droves. "God makes the stars," the chastened Goldwyn finally concluded. "It's up to the producers to find them."

Throughout the silent era, the public's love affair with its stars encouraged film producers to plunder each others' stables like bandits. Stars grew giddy with their sudden wealth and power. Intoxicated by the opulence of Hollywood's royalty, the public was eager to learn more of its favorites. Fan (short for fanatic) magazines sprang up by the dozens, and the burgeoning studios churned out a steady stream of publicity—most of it imbecilic—to feed this insatiable curiosity. Throughout the Jazz Age, legends circulated concerning the lavish parties and palaces of such celebrities as Pickford, Harold Lloyd, and a host of others. Paramount's rival queens, Gloria Swanson and Pola Negri, vied with each other in the extravagance of their lifestyles. Both of them married many times, and each managed to snare at least one petty nobleman among their stable of rapt admirers. Swanson's contract stipulated that she could be seen only in the most expensive designer clothes. "I have gone through a long apprenticeship," Swanson said. "I have gone through enough of being nobody. I have decided that when I am a star I will be every inch and every moment the star. Everyone from the studio gateman to the highest executive will know it." The mythology of stardom often incorporated this rags-to-riches motif. The humble origins of many stars encouraged the public to believe that anyone—even ordinary people—could be "discovered" and make it to Hollywood where all their dreams would come true (see 6-12).

Few of the stars of the silent cinema survived the transition to talkies. Most of them had risen to fame on the basis of their good looks, but after 1927 they were regarded, rather unfairly in some cases, as so many pretty faces. A good number of silent stars were foreign-born, but their command of English was so shaky that audiences couldn't understand them when they talked. Even American-born stars often spoke in regional dialects which conflicted with their screen images. Others had voices that were squeaky, croaky, or too high-pitched. The problem wasn't just their voices. Sound made movies startlingly realistic, and the exaggerated gestures which silent players had developed to compensate for their lack of voices now appeared florid and old-fashioned. Audiences laughed at their former deities (6-13).

The so-called golden age of the star system—roughly the 1930s and 1940s—coincided with the supremacy of the Hollywood studio system. Most of the stars during this period were under exclusive contract to the five major production companies: MGM, Warner Brothers, Paramount, 20th Century-Fox, and RKO—known in the trade as the Big Five or the majors. Throughout this period, the majors produced approximately 90 percent of the fiction films in America. They also ruled the international market: between the two World Wars, American movies dominated 80 percent of the world's screens

**6-13. *Mata Hari* (U.S.A., 1932).**
*With Greta Garbo and Ramon Novarro;*
*Directed by George Fitzmaurice.*
The talkie revolution cut short the careers
of many silent stars, especially those with
heavy accents. Garbo was an exception.
Her throaty, world-weary voice enhanced
her allure, and her accent lent her an exotic aura. Like her famous face, her voice
conveyed a sense of exhaustion, concealed suffering, and a noble stoicism.
Sound made most players instantly more
realistic, but Garbo's voice, tinged with
regret and longing, made her more mysterious and inaccessible. She was the
foremost *femme fatale* of the international cinema from the mid-1920s to 1942
when she retired into seclusion at the age
of thirty-seven. See John Bainbridge,
*Garbo* (New York: Galahad Books,
1971); and Kenneth Tynan, "Garbo," in
*Film Theory and Criticism,* Gerald Mast
and Marshall Cohen, eds. (New York:
Oxford University Press, 1979).

(MGM)

and were more popular with foreign mass audiences than all but a few na-
tively produced movies.

After the talkie revolution, the majors turned to the live theatre for its
new stars. Such important newcomers as James Cagney, Bette Davis, Edward
G. Robinson, Cary Grant, Mae West, and Katharine Hepburn became popular in part because of their distinctive manner of speaking—the "personality
voices" as they were known in the trade. In their first years under studio
contract, they were given maximum exposure. For example, Clark Gable
appeared in fourteen movies in 1930, his first year at MGM. Each of his roles
represented a different type, and the studio kept varying them until one
clicked with the public. After a particularly popular performance, a star was
usually locked into the same type of role—often under protest. Since the
demand for stars was the most predictable economic variable in the business
of filmmaking, the studios used their stars as a guarantee of box office success.
In short, stars provided some measure of stability in a traditionally volatile
industry. To this day, stars are referred to as "bankable" commodities—that is,
insurance for large profits to investors.

The majors viewed their stars as valuable investments, and the build-up
techniques developed by the studios involved much time, money, and energy.
Promising neophytes—both foreign and domestic—served an apprenticeship
as "starlets," a term reserved for females, although male newcomers were
subjected to the same treatment. They were often assigned a new name, were
taught how to talk, walk, and wear costumes. Frequently their social schedules
were arranged by the studio's publicity department to insure maximum press
exposure. Suitable "romances" were concocted to fuel the columns of the 400

**6-14.** *Two Women* **(Italy, 1961).**
*With Sophia Loren; Directed by Vittorio De Sica.*
The public's affection for its stars has often been based on personality rather than artistry, although the two aren't necessarily exclusive. Despite the fact that Loren has made very few good films, she has remained a favorite with both critics and audiences for over twenty years. Her life story is in the classic rags-to-riches mold. She was born out of wedlock, and lived most of her first fourteen years in desperate poverty with her mother in a Naples slum. At the age of fourteen she won a beauty contest and became the protegée of film producer Carlo Ponti who eventually became her husband. She appeared in a series of forgettable Italian movies before deciding to try her luck in America in 1957. In Hollywood, her mentors attempted to obliterate her individuality by embalming her in makeup and corseting her voluptuous figure to within an inch of its life. Her American films were mostly potboilers, but she usually emerged triumphant, thanks to her charm and compelling sensuality. The merriment and good humor she brought to her roles were products of her own personality rather than her scripts or directors. Unlike most sex queens, Loren was rarely self-conscious about her eroticism, and often regarded it with ironic amusement. Eventually she returned to her native soil where she found a director more attuned to her talent, her fellow Neopolitan Vittorio De Sica. Her powerful performance as an earthy peasant in *Two Women* was a startling revelation, even to her admirers, and it won her the Best Actress Academy Award of 1961, the New York Film Critics' Award, and the top prize at the Cannes Film Festival.

or more reporters and columnists who covered the Hollywood beat during the studio era. A few zealous souls even agreed to marry a studio-selected spouse if such an alliance would further their careers.

Though stars were often exploited by the studios, there were some compensations. As a player's box office power increased, so did his or her demands. Top stars had their names above the title of the film, and they often had script approval stipulated in their contracts. Some of them also insisted on director, producer, and costar approval. Glamorous stars boasted their own cameramen who knew how to conceal physical defects and enhance virtues. Many of them demanded their own clothes designers, hair stylists, and lavish dressing rooms. The biggest stars had movies especially tailored for them, thus guaranteeing maximum camera exposure, and in some cases even a specified number of closeups—the favored shot of the stars.

And, of course, they were paid enormous sums of money. In 1938, for example, there were over fifty stars who earned more than $100,000 a year. But the studios got much more. Mae West rescued Paramount from bankruptcy in the early 1930s. Later in the decade, Shirley Temple made over $20 million for 20th Century-Fox. Furthermore, although there were a few important exceptions, movies without stars generally failed at the box office. Most serious stars used money and power to further their art, not just to gratify their vanity. Bette Davis was considered "difficult" during her stormy tenure at Warners because she insisted on better scripts, more varied roles, more sensitive directors, and stronger costars (she was often paired with the serviceable George Brent as her leading man).

Top stars attracted the loyalty of both men and women, although as sociologist Leo Handel pointed out, 65 percent of the fans preferred stars of their own sex. The studios received up to 32 million fan letters per year, 85 percent of them from young females. Major stars received about 3000 letters per week, and the volume of their mail was regarded as an accurate barometer of their popularity. The studios spent as much as $2 million a year processing these letters, most of which asked for autographed photos. Box office appeal was also gauged by the number of fan clubs devoted to a star. By 1934 there were already 535 of these clubs, with a total membership of over 750,000. During this period, the stars with the greatest number of fan clubs were Gable, Jean Harlow, and Joan Crawford—all of them under contract to MGM, "The Home of the Stars." Gable alone had 70 clubs which partly accounted for his supremacy as the top male star of the 1930s.

During the big studio era, most of the majors had a characteristic style, determined in part by the stars under contract. In the early 1930s, sophisticated Paramount could boast such polished players as Claudette Colbert, Marlene Dietrich, Carole Lombard, and Frederic March. Paramount was especially receptive to comedy, and also included in its roster Mae West, the Marx Brothers, and Cary Grant, who became the finest light comedian of the big studio period. Warners was a male-dominated studio, with an emphasis on fast-moving urban melodramas. Many of the stars were the famous tough guys: Edward G. Robinson, James Cagney, Paul Muni, and Humphrey Bogart. MGM, "The Tiffany of studios," had the largest number of stars, most of them glamorous females (6-15).

The majors began to decline in power in the late 1940s after their business practices were declared monopolistic by the U.S. Supreme Court. The studios were ordered to divest themselves of their vast chain of theatres where their films had been guaranteed automatic exhibition. Studios no longer molded the careers of stars. Perhaps 20th Century-Fox's Marilyn Monroe was the last to benefit from—or endure—the buildup techniques developed by the majors. After nearly a quarter of a century, Gable left the security of MGM in

**6-15. MGM publicity photo of Jean Harlow, circa 1936.**
Studio publicity photos often presented stars as lofty deities. Critic Parker Tyler observed that glamorous stars fulfill an ancient need, unsatisfied by contemporary religions: "Somehow their wealth, fame, and beauty, their apparently unlimited field of worldly pleasure—these conditions tinge them with the supernatural, render them immune to the bitterness of ordinary frustrations." Harlow's insolent sexuality and wisecracking cheapness were somewhat at variance with MGM's rather genteel image, but she was one of the studio's top stars until 1937, when she died at the age of 26. The fact that many stars have died young—at the height of their physical beauty—only enhances their image of immutable perfection.

1954, but he never regained his former eminence. The great prewar icons were fading, and such new stars as Marlon Brando, James Dean, and Montgomery Clift openly sneered at the Hollywood studio system. Acting in movies was no longer considered second best to the live theatre, and besides, many of the new stars had conquered both. Glamor was increasingly considered old-fashioned and tinselly. During the 1960s even such strikingly attractive stars as Elizabeth Taylor and Paul Newman coarsened their images to demonstrate their considerable talent as actors. After 1970, few of the top stars were conventionally glamorous, and many of them were first-rate actors pursuing distinguished careers. Such stars as Jane Fonda, Dustin Hoffman, and Robert De Niro are among the most respected performers in the world.

From the beginning, stars were commonly classified into character types: virgins, vamps, romantic leading men, swashbucklers, flappers, and so on. At Mack Sennett's Keystone Studio, the leading clowns were classified by physical type—fat, tall, skinny, cross-eyed, and so forth. Over the years, a vast repertory of types evolved: the Latin Lover, the He-man, the Heiress, the Good/

Bad Girl, the Cynical Reporter, the Career Girl, and many others. Of course all great stars are unique even though they might fall under a well-known category. For example, the Cheap Blonde has long been one of America's favorite types, but such important stars as Mae West, Jean Harlow, and Marilyn Monroe are highly distinctive as individuals. A successful type was always imitated. In the mid-1920s, for example, the Swedish import Greta Garbo supplanted such passé vamps as Bara and Negri in favor of a more sophisticated and complex type, the *femme fatale*. Garbo inspired many imitations, including such important stars as Marlene Dietrich and Carole Lombard who were first touted as "Garbo types," only with a sense of humor. In the 1950s Sidney Poitier became the first black star to attract a wide following outside of his own race. In later years a number of other black performers attained stardom in part because Poitier had established the precedent. He was one of the great originals and hence worthy of imitation (6-16).

(Warner Brothers)

**6-16.** *Uptown Saturday Night* **(U.S.A., 1974).**
*With Sidney Poitier and Bill Cosby; Directed by Poitier.*
Poitier is the pre-eminent black star of the American cinema. He was the first Negro player to rise to the top not as a singer, dancer, or comedian, but as a straight leading man. In the 1970s, he turned to producing and directing. In addition to this film, Poitier also produced, directed, and starred in *Let's Do It Again* (1975) and *A Piece of the Action* (1977), which were popular with white and black audiences alike. Studies of blacks in American movies include James Murray, *To Find an Image* (Indianapolis: The Bobbs-Merrill Company, 1973); Donald Bogle, *Toms, Coons, Mulattoes, Mammies & Bucks* (New York: A Bantam Book, 1974); Thomas Cripps, *Slow Fade to Black: The Negro in American Film* (New York: Oxford University Press, 1977); Thomas Cripps, *Black Film as Genre* (Bloomington, Ind.: Indiana University Press, 1977); and Daniel J. Leab, *From Sambo to Superspade* (Boston: Houghton Mifflin, 1975).

At about the turn of the last century, George Bernard Shaw (who was then a theatre critic) wrote a famous essay comparing the two foremost stage stars of the day—Eleonora Duse and Sarah Bernhardt. Shaw's comparison is a useful springboard for a discussion of the different kinds of film stars. Bernhardt, Shaw wrote, was a bravura personality, and she managed to tailor each different role to fit this personality. This is what her fans both expected and desired. Her personal charm was larger-than-life, yet undeniably captivating. Her performances were filled with brilliant effects that had come to be associated with her personality over the years. Duse, on the other hand, possessed a more quiet talent, less dazzling in its initial impact. She was totally different with each role, and her own personality never seemed to intrude on the playwright's character. Hers was in invisible art: her impersonations were so totally believable that the viewer was likely to forget it *was* an impersona-

**6-17. *Red River* (U.S.A., 1948).**
*With John Wayne and Montgomery Clift; Directed by Howard Hawks.*
Wayne was the most popular star in film history. From 1949 to 1976 he was absent from the box office Top Ten only three times. "I play John Wayne in every part regardless of the character, and I've been doing okay, haven't I?" he once asked rhetorically. He began his career in the late 1920s, and throughout the next decade he performed mostly in grade B westerns. When director John Ford cast him in the leading role of *Stagecoach* (1939), Wayne was suddenly a star. Most of his best work was done under three directors: Ford, Hawks, and Henry Hathaway. In the public mind, Wayne is the archetypal Westerner, a man of action—and violence—rather than words. His iconography is steeped in a distrust of sophistication and intellectuality. Confident of his identity, the Wayne character is chary of his honor and can intimidate by his sheer massive presence. Beneath his brusqueness, however, is a sense of loneliness and isolation, especially in Ford's *The Searchers* (1956), which many critics regard as Wayne's finest performance. His name is virtually synonymous with masculinity—although his persona suggests more of the warrior than the lover. As he grew older, he played more paternalistic figures, chivalrous to the ladies, though generally ill-at-ease in their presence. He also grew more human, developing his considerable talents as a comedian by mocking his own macho image, as in his Academy Award winning performance in Hathaway's *True Grit* (1969). An outspoken advocate of conservative values, Wayne was admired even by many liberals as an icon of Americanism. He was strongly pro-military in his sympathies, and publicly applauded patriotism, guts, and self-sacrifice.

*(United Artists)*

tion. In effect, Shaw was pointing out the major distinctions between a personality/star and an actor/star.

Personality stars commonly refuse all parts that go against their type, especially if they're leading men or leading ladies (6-17). Performers like Barbra Streisand would never play cruel or psychopathic roles, for example, because such parts would conflict with her sympathetic image. If a star is locked into his or her type, any significant departure can result in box office disaster. For example, when Pickford tried to abandon her little girl roles in the 1920s, her public stayed at home: they wanted to see Little Mary or nothing. In desperation, she defiantly cut off her curls in 1929—at the age of thirty-seven. Her new flapper's bobb was her emancipation proclamation, but she appeared in only a few more films after that, and none of them was popular with the public. She retired in disgust at the age of forty, just when most players are at the peak of their powers.

The top box office attractions tend to be personality stars. They stay on top by being themselves, by not trying to impersonate anyone. Gable insisted that all he did in front of the camera was to "act natural." Gary Cooper's sincerity and homespun decency attracted audiences for over three decades, and the persona he projected on the screen was virtually identical with his actual personality. Similarly, Marilyn Monroe was always at her best when she played roles that exploited her indecisiveness, her vulnerability, and her pathetic eagerness to please. Such contemporary charmers as Woody Allen and Burt Reynolds are never so attractive as when they play variations of their own personalities.

On the other hand, there have been many stars who refuse to be typecast and attempt the widest array of roles possible. Such actor/stars as Davis, Hepburn, Brando, and De Niro have sometimes undertaken unpleasant character roles rather than conventional leads in order to expand their range, for variety and breadth have traditionally been the yardsticks by which great acting

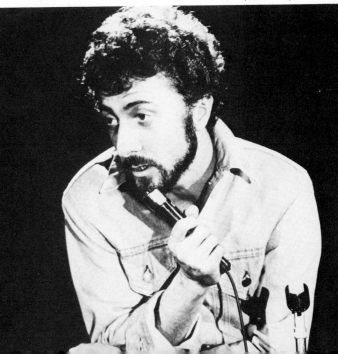

*(United Artists)*

**6-18. *Lenny* (U.S.A., 1974).**
*With Dustin Hoffman; Directed by Bob Fosse.*
Hoffman is one of the most admired actor-stars of his generation, changing radically from role to role. His range is exceptionally broad, encompassing such disparate roles as the klutzy college grad in Mike Nichols' *The Graduate* (1967); the sleazy urban vagrant Ratso Rizzo in John Schlesinger's *Midnight Cowboy* (1969); and the tragi-comic frontiersman Jack Crabb in Arthur Penn's *Little Big Man* (1970), in which Hoffman was required to age over a hundred years! In Sam Peckinpah's *Straw Dogs* (1972), Hoffman played a self-deluded, overintellectual mathematician; in Franklin Schaffner's *Papillon* (1973), a grizzled inmate of a penal colony. His performance as the persecuted and self-destructive comedian Lenny Bruce (pictured) was authentic to the point of mimicry. Even in leading man roles, like those in Alan J. Pakula's *All the President's Men* (1976) and Robert Benton's *Kramer vs. Kramer* (1979), Hoffman rarely relies on his actual personality unless a given trait is appropriate to the character he is playing.

is measured (6-18). For example, just as Brando was being typed as the sexy young working-class stud (*A Streetcar Named Desire, On the Waterfront*), he completely reversed his image with a Shakespearean role (*Julius Caesar*) and a stint at musical comedy (*Guys and Dolls*). In *The Teahouse of the August Moon,* he played an oriental houseboy, in *The Young Lions,* an effete German aristocrat. His Fletcher Christian in *Mutiny on the Bounty* was not the standard star vehicle that Clark Gable had made of the role in the earlier version of this film, but a performance which stressed the character's fastidious and rather effeminate snobbishness. In *The Godfather,* Brando astonished his public by playing an elderly Mafia don (6-32), and in his brilliant performance in *Last Tango in Paris,* he played a neurotic middle-aged romantic, totally obsessed with sexuality.

Many stars fall somewhere between the two extremes, veering toward personality in some films, toward impersonation in others. Such gifted performers as James Stewart, Cary Grant, and Audrey Hepburn have played wider variations of certain types of roles. Nonetheless, we can't imagine a star like Miss Hepburn playing a woman of weak character or a coarse or stupid woman, so firmly entrenched is her image as an elegant and rather aristocratic female. Similarly, most people know what's meant by "the Clint Eastwood type."

The distinction between a professional actor and a star is not based on technical skill, but on mass popularity. By definition, a star must have enormous personal magnetism, a riveting quality which commands our attention. Few public personalities have inspired such deep and widespread affection as the great movie stars. Some are loved because they embody such traditional American values as plain speaking, integrity, and idealism: Gary Cooper and Henry Fonda are examples of this type. Others are identified with antiestablishment images, and include such celebrated loners as Bogie, Clint Eastwood, and Jack Nicholson. Players like Cary Grant and Carole Lombard are so captivating in their charm that they're fun to watch in almost anything. And of course many of them are spectacularly good-looking: names like Garbo and Redford are virtually synonymous with godlike beauty.

Sophisticated filmmakers exploit the public's affection for its stars by creating ambiguous tensions between a role as written, as acted, and directed. "Whenever the hero isn't portrayed by a star the whole picture suffers," Hitchcock observed. "Audiences are far less concerned about the predicament of a character who's played by someone they don't know." When a star rather than a conventional actor plays a role, much of the characterization is automatically fixed by the casting; but what the director and star then choose to add to the written role is what constitutes its *full* dramatic meaning. Some directors have capitalized on the star system with great artistic effectiveness, particularly studio-era filmmakers like Frank Capra, Howard Hawks, and George Cukor. The most perceptive film critics and commentators on the American cinema have also been exceptionally sensitive to the complexities of the star system (see 6-19).

Perhaps the ultimate glory for a star is to become an icon in American popular mythology. Like the gods and goddesses of ancient times, some stars are so universally known that one name alone is enough to evoke an entire complex of symbolic associations—"Marilyn" for example. Unlike the conventional actor (however gifted) the star automatically suggests ideas and emotions that are deeply embedded in his or her persona. These undertones are

*(United Artists)*

**6-19. *Coming Home* (U.S.A., 1978).**
*With Jane Fonda and Jon Voight; Directed by Hal Ashby.*
As Richard Dyer has pointed out, stars are signifying entities: any sensitive analysis of a film with a star in its cast must take into account that star's iconographical significance. Stars like Jane Fonda embody complex political associations simply by demonstrating the lifestyle of her politics and displaying those political beliefs as an aspect of her personality/characterization. Like John Wayne—like most stars—she conveys an ideology, implying ideal ways of behaving. As such, stars can have tremendous impact in transmitting values. Dyer also demonstrates how a star's iconography is always developing. For example, he divides Fonda's career into four phases: (1) *The Father:* Her entry into the film industry in 1960 was facilitated by Henry Fonda's prestige. Physically, she clearly resembled him, and he too was a well-known liberal, with an all-American iconography. Jane's roles during this period emphasized a rambunctious sexiness, with more of the tomboy than the siren. This phase culminated with Elliott Silverstein's *Cat Ballou* (1965). (2) *Sex:* This period is dominated by Fonda's French film-director husband, Roger Vadim, who exploited her good looks and sensational figure in a series of erotic films, most notably *Barbarella* (France, 1968). Although the marriage ended in divorce, Fonda claimed that Vadim liberated her from her sexual hangups and all-American innocence. (3) *Acting:* She returned to America where she studied with Lee Strasberg at the Actors' Studio in New York. Her depth and range as an actress expanded considerably during this period, and she was nominated for an Academy Award for her work in Sydney Pollack's *They Shoot Horses, Don't They?* (1969). She won one for her performance as a prostitute in Alan J. Pakula's *Klute* (1971). (4) *Politics:* Fonda was radicalized by Vietnam and the Women's Movement. She spoke out frequently against the war, racism, and sexism. She also politicized her work, joining forces with her fellow Marxist Jean-Luc Godard in *Tout va bien* (France, 1973). She starred in Joseph Losey's movie version of Ibsen's feminist play, *A Doll's House* (Great Britain, 1974). She was eager to play one of her idols, Lillian Hellman, in Fred Zinnemann's *Julia* (1977). Hellman, the author of *The Little Foxes,* was an outspoken Marxist, even during the McCarthy era of political repression. *Coming Home* is virtually a spiritual autobiography of Fonda's evolution, and won the actress-star her second Academy Award. See Richard Dyer, *Stars* (London: British Film Institute, 1979).

determined not only by the star's previous roles, but often by his or her actual personality as well. Naturally, over the course of many years this symbolic information can begin to drain from public consciousness, but the iconography of a great star like Gary Cooper becomes part of a shared experience. As the French critic Edgar Morin has pointed out, when Cooper played a character, he automatically "garycooperized" it, infusing himself into the role and the role into himself. Since audiences felt a deep sense of identification with Coop and the values he symbolized, in a sense they were celebrating themselves—or at least their spiritual selves. The great originals are cultural archetypes, and their box office popularity is an index of their success in synthesizing the aspirations of an era. As a number of cultural studies have shown, the iconography of a star can involve communal myths and symbols of considerable complexity and emotional richness.

## Styles of Acting

Acting styles differ radically, depending on period, genre, tone, national origins, and directorial emphasis. Such considerations are the principal means by which acting styles are classified. Even within a given category, however, generalizations are, at best, a loose set of expectations, not Holy Writ. For example, the Realism–Expressionism dialectic which has been used as a classification aid throughout this book can also be applied to the art of acting. But there are many variations and subdivisions of realistic and expressionistic acting. These terms are also subject to different interpretations from period to period. Lillian Gish was regarded as a great realistic actress in the silent era, but by today's standards, her performances look rather ethereal. In a parallel vein, the playing style of Klaus Kinski in such movies as *Aguirre, the Wrath of God* is stylized, but compared to an extreme form of expressionistic acting, such as that of Conrad Veidt in *The Cabinet of Dr. Caligari,* Kinski is relatively realistic (6-20). It's a matter of degree.

*(New Yorker Films)*

**6-20. *Aguirre, the Wrath of God* (West Germany, 1973).**
*With Klaus Kinski; Directed by Werner Herzog.*
Expressionistic acting is generally associated with the German cinema—a cinema of directors, rarely actors. Stripped of individualizing details, this style of acting stresses a symbolic concept rather than a believable three-dimensional character. It is presentational rather than representational, a style of extremes rather than norms. Psychological complexity is replaced by a stylized thematic essence. For example, Kinski's portrayal of a Spanish conquistador is conceived in terms of a treacherous serpent. His Dantean features a frozen mask of ferocity, Aguirre can suddenly twist and coil like a cobra poised for a strike.

Classifying acting styles according to national origins is also likely to be misleading, at least for those countries which have evolved a wide spectrum of styles, like Japan, the U.S.A., and Italy. For example, the Italians (and other Mediterranean peoples) are said to be theatrical by national temperament, acting out their feelings with animation, as opposed to the reserved deportment of the Swedes and other Northern Europeans. But within the Italian cinema alone, these generalizations are subject to considerable modification. Southern Italian characters tend to be acted in a manner that conforms to the volatile Latin stereotype, as can be seen in the movies of such directors as Pietro Germi and Lina Wertmüller (6-21). Northern Italians, on the other hand, are usually played with more restraint and far less spontaneity, as the works of Antonioni demonstrate.

*(New Line Cinema)*

**6-21. The Seduction of Mimi (Italy, 1971).**
*With Giancarlo Giannini and Elena Fiore; Directed by Lina Wertmüller.*
Farcical acting is one of the most difficult and misunderstood styles of performance. It requires an intense comic exaggeration, and can easily become tiresome and mechanical if the farceur is not able to preserve the humanity of the character. Here, Giannini plays a typical ethnic stereotype—a sleazy, heavy-lidded lothario who, in an act of sexual revenge, embarks on a campaign to seduce the unlovely wife of the man who has cuckolded him. Giannini is Wertmüller's favorite actor, and has appeared in many of her movies. Other famous actor–director teams include Dietrich and Sternberg, Audran and Chabrol, Wayne and Ford, Ullmann and Bergman, Bogart and Huston, Mifune and Kurosawa, Léaud and Truffaut, and many more.

Genre and directorial emphasis also influence acting styles significantly. For example, in stylized genres like the samurai film, Toshiro Mifune is bold, strutting, and larger-than-life, as in Kurosawa's *Yojimbo.* In a realistic contemporary story like *High and Low* (also directed by Kurosawa), Mifune's performance is all nuance and sobriety. For the most part, the individual differences within a given style of acting are aesthetically more significant than the general characteristics which typify the style.

The *art* of silent acting encompasses a period of only some 15 years or so, for though movies were being produced as early as 1895, most historians regard Griffith's *The Birth of a Nation* (1915) as the first indisputable masterpiece of the silent cinema. The changeover to sound was virtually universal by 1930. Within this brief span, however, a wide variety of playing styles evolved, ranging from the detailed, underplayed realism of Gibson Gowland in Erich von Stroheim's *Greed,* to the grand, ponderous style of such tragedians as Emil

Jannings in Josef von Sternberg's *The Last Command.* The great silent clowns like Chaplin, Keaton, Harold Lloyd, Harry Langdon, and Laurel & Hardy also developed highly personal styles which bear only a superficial resemblance to each other.

A popular misconception about the silent cinema is that all movies were photographed and projected at "silent speed"—16 frames per second. In fact, silent speed was highly variable, subject to easy manipulation because cameras were hand cranked. Even within a single film, not every scene was necessarily photographed at the same speed. Generally speaking, comic scenes were undercranked to emphasize speed, while dramatic scenes were overcranked to slow down the action, usually at 20 or 22 fps. Since most present day projectors feature only two speeds—16 silent and 24 sound—the original rhythms of the performances are violated. This is why players in silent dramas can appear jerky and slightly ludicrous. In comedies, this distortion can enhance the humor which is why the performances of the silent clowns have retained

**6-22. *Metropolis* (Germany, 1926).**
*Directed by Fritz Lang.*
Lang's early movie career coincided with the German Expressionist movement, which was deeply pessimistic in its view of the human condition. People are architecturalized into elaborate geometrical patterns, presented as swarms or mechanized zombies, soulless in their lemminglike behavior. Actors playing in this style are seldom permitted to express their humanity. They are used as camera material, as a formal component of the *visual* statement. The German cinema has a long tradition of subordinating the player to the *mise-en-scène*. See also Lotte H. Eisner, *Fritz Lang* (New York: Oxford University Press, 1977); and Roger Manvell and Heinrich Fraenkel, *The German Cinema* (New York: Praeger, 1971).

(Janus Films)

**6-23. *The Gold Rush* (U.S.A., 1925).**
*With Charles Chaplin and Mack Swain; Directed by Chaplin.*
Since silent players were deprived of their voices, they externalized their feelings and thoughts through gesture, movement, body language, and facial expression—all of which had to be heightened to compensate for their lack of speech. In this shot, for example, Big Jim McKay is puzzled by the weird rumbling of their cabin, while the hung-over Charlie explains—through pantomime—that his queasy stomach is the culprit.

much of their original charm. Outside the comic repertory, however, due allowances must be made for the distortions of technology.

The most popular and most critically admired player of the silent cinema was Chaplin (6-23). The wide variety of comic skills he developed in his early years of vaudeville made him the most versatile of the clowns. In the area of pantomime, no one approached his inventiveness. Critics waxed eloquently on his balletic grace, and even the brilliant dancer Nijinsky proclaimed Chaplin his equal. His ability to blend comedy with pathos was unique. George Bernard Shaw, the greatest living playwright of this era, described Chaplin as "the only genius developed in motion pictures." After viewing Chaplin's powerful—and very funny—performance in *City Lights*, the fastidious critic Alexander Woolcott, who otherwise loathed movies, said: "I would be prepared to defend the proposition that this darling of the mob is the foremost living artist."

Chaplin's body was as finely tuned as any instrument, and he was able to control it with precision. His expressive hands, small and delicate, had a life of their own; in *A Dog's Life* he uses them to carry on an elaborate conversation while the remainder of his body is totally hidden from view. Over the years he developed a number of specialties, like hopping and "skidding" too far on one leg while rounding a corner trying to escape a pursuer. The boxing matches in such movies as *The Knockout, The Champion,* and *City Lights* are exquisitely timed and choreographed. In addition, he was an expert skater, juggler, acrobat, and aerialist, and used these skills in many of his films.

Greta Garbo perfected a romantic style of acting which had its roots in the silent cinema, and held sway throughout the 1930s. Critics have sometimes referred to this mode of performance as star acting. "What, when drunk, one sees in other women, one sees in Garbo sober," said the British critic Kenneth Tynan. Almost invariably, MGM cast her as a woman with a mysterious past: mistress, courtesan, the "other woman"—the essence of the Eternal Female. Her face, in addition to being stunningly beautiful, could unite conflicting emotions, withholding and yielding simultaneously, like a succession of waves rippling across her features. Tall and slender, she moved gracefully, her collapsed shoulders suggesting the exhaustion of a wounded butterfly. She could also project a provocative bisexuality, as in Rouben Mamoulian's *Queen*

*(New Line Cinema)*

**6-24. *Get Out Your Handkerchiefs* (France, 1978).**
*With (left to right) Gerard Depardieu, Carol Laure, and Patrick Dewaere; Directed by Bertrand Blier.*
A film's tone dictates its acting style. Tone is determined primarily by genre, dialogue, and the director's attitude toward the dramatic materials. In this film, for example, Depardieu and Dewaere play characters who are both in love with the same woman, an impenetrable cipher who finds their exuberant charm eminently resistable. Like its American cousin, screwball comedy, Blier's movie is a *jeu d'esprit,* bubbling over with whimsical improbabilities, loony twists and turns in the plot, and spritely dialogue which is delivered in a throwaway style.

**6-25a. *Public Enemy* (U.S.A., 1931).** With James Cagney and Mae Clark; Directed by William Wellman.

**6-25b. *The Last Metro* (France, 1980).** With Catherine Deneuve and Gerard Depardieu; Directed by François Truffaut.

Acting styles are determined in part by a player's energy level. High-voltage performers like Cagney usually project *out* to the audience, commanding our attention with a larger-than-life bravura style. Much of our pleasure in a Cagney performance is watching him "struttin' his stuff." He was a highly kinetic actor, expressing his character's emotions through movement, like the famous scene in which the gangster hero silences his nagging mistress by smashing a grapefruit in her face. Other high-energy performers include Harold Lloyd, John Barrymore, Katharine Hepburn, Bette Davis, Gene Kelly, George C. Scott, and Barbra Streisand. Low-keyed performers like Deneuve are sometimes said to work "small" or "close to the lens." Rather than projecting out to the audience, these performers allow the camera to tune *in* on their behavior, which is seldom exaggerated for dramatic effect. Eye-witness accounts of Deneuve's acting usually stress how little she seems to be working: the subtleties are apparent only at very close ranges. Other players in this mode include Harry Langdon, Spencer Tracy, Henry Fonda, Marilyn Monroe, Montgomery Clift, Robert DeNiro, and Jack Nicholson. Of course dramatic context is all-important in determining an actor's energy level.

*(Warner Brothers)*

*(United Artists)*

*Christina,* where her resolute strides and masculine attire provide a foil to her exquisite femininity.

The love goddess *par excellence,* Garbo was most famous for her love scenes which epitomized her romantic style. "The man she loves is of less importance than love itself," Molly Haskell has noted, for Garbo's is a love that "asks nothing in return except an occasional glimpse of its own noble reflection." She is often self-absorbed in her love scenes, musing on a private irony which can even exclude the lover. Frequently she looks away from him, allowing the camera—and us—to savor the poignance of her conflict. She rarely expresses her feelings in words, for her art thrives on silence, on the unspeakable. Charles Affron and others have noted that her love scenes are sometimes played in literal solitude with objects serving as erotic fetishes. The way she touches a bouquet of flowers, a bed post, a telephone—these allude to the missing lover, recalling a multitude of painful pleasures. She is often enraptured by her surroundings, "like Eve on the morning of creation," to use Tynan's memorable phrase. But she is also oppressed by the knowledge that such ecstasy cannot last; she arms herself against her fate with irony and stoicism.

Garbo's performances are striking examples of how great acting can salvage bad scripts, and even bad direction. "Subtract Garbo from most of her movies and you are left with nothing," one critic noted. She disliked most of her films which she thought were trivial and overromanticized. Virtually every eyewitness account of her work (and there are few, for she insisted on a closed set) emphasized the sudden change which came over her when the camera began to roll. In reality, she was sober, businesslike, and austere, with a strong need for privacy. She was at her best playing characters with a genuine tragic dimension such as the title roles in *Anna Karenina* (directed by Clarence Brown) and *Camille* (directed by George Cukor). Garbo regarded her performance in Ernst Lubitsch's *Ninotchka* as her best. It's also one of her least typical, although the love scene (see 8-5) is played with characteristic rapture.

The most important British film actors are also the most prominent in the live theatre (but see 6-26). The British repertory system is the envy of the

**6-26. Publicity photos of Peter Sellers in *Dr. Strangelove, Or How I Learned to Stop Worrying and Love the Bomb* (U.S.A./Great Britain, 1964).**
*Directed by Stanley Kubrick.*
Unlike most British actors, Sellers (a) worked very little on stage. His apprenticeship was served primarily on TV, especially the long-running BBC series *The Goon Show,* where he developed his gift for comic improvising. His idol was Alec Guinness who also enjoyed the challenge of playing multiple roles in a single movie. Like Guinness, Sellers was a brilliant mimic and a master of face and voice disguises. In Kubrick's Cold War satire, he played three roles: a stiff-upper-lipped British military aide (b); the ineffectual liberal American President Merkin Muffley (c); and the German-born evil genius Dr. Strangelove who is confined to a wheelchair and has a mechanical arm which seems to want to strangle him (d). At the end of the movie, Strangelove is so intoxicated by the possibility of outwitting the Soviets and escaping a nuclear holocaust that he struggles to his feet, screaming to President Muffley, "*Mein Führer,* I can walk!" while his metal arm snaps wildly into a Nazi salute. "Peter has the most responsive attitude of all the actors I've worked with to the things I think are funny," said Kubrick. "He is always at his best in dealing with grotesque and horrifying ideas."

(a)　　　　　　(b)

**(c)**  **(d)**

civilized world. Virtually every medium-sized city has a resident drama company where actors can learn their craft by playing a variety of roles from the classic repertory, especially the works of Shakespeare. As players improve, they rise through the ranks, attempting more complex roles. The best of them migrate to the larger cities where the most prestigious theatre companies are found. The discipline that most British actors have acquired in this repertory system has made them the most versatile of players. The finest of them are regularly employed in the theatres of London which is also adjacent to the center of film production of Great Britain. This centralization allows them to move from the live theatre to film to TV with a minimum of inconvenience.

British players have been favorites with the American public ever since the introduction of talkies. Many of them have made significant contributions to the cinema of the United States: Laurence Olivier, Ronald Coleman, John Gielgud, Vivien Leigh, Deborah Kerr, Jean Simmons, James Mason, Vanessa Redgrave, Peter O'Toole, David Niven, Alan Bates, Julie Christie, Richard Burton, Angela Lansbury, Glenda Jackson, Peter Finch, Audrey Hepburn, Rex Harrison, Alec Guinness, Richard Harris, Albert Finney, Tom Courtenay, Edith Evans, Peter Sellers, Dirk Bogarde, Claire Bloom, Sean Connery—the list is a long and distinguished one. British traditions of acting tend to favor a mastery of externals, based on close observation. Virtually all players are trained in diction, movement, makeup, dialects, fencing, dancing, body control, and ensemble playing. Above all, British players have perfected the art of reciting highly stylized dialogue—the language of Shakespeare, Shaw, Wilde, and Pinter—without violating the believability of their characters.

The post–World War II era tended to emphasize realistic styles of acting (6-27). Filmmakers from many countries were encouraged by the example of the Italian neorealists (see Chapter 11, "Theory"). Coming from a background of documentary movies, Roberto Rossellini established the viability of using nonprofessionals in secondary roles with his fiction film *Open City* (1945). The early works of Luchino Visconti and Vittorio De Sica also employed amateur actors, even in principal parts (see 6-33). They were chosen precisely because they hadn't been seen in repetitive and familiar roles. In a

**6-27. *The End of Summer* (Japan, 1961).**
*Directed by Yasujiro Ozu.*
A master of psychological nuances, Ozu believed that in the art of acting, less is more. He detested melodramatic excesses and demanded the utmost realism from his players, who frequently chafed at his criticism that they were "acting" too much. He avoided using stars and often cast against type so that audiences would view the characters with no preconceptions. He usually chose his players according to their personality rather than their acting ability. Above all, Ozu explored the conflict between individual wishes and social necessity. His scenes are often staged in public settings, where politeness and social decorum require the stifling of personal disappointment. Ozu often instructed his players not to move, to express their feelings only with their eyes. Note how the two characters on the left are privately miles away, while still conforming superficially to the decorum of the occasion.

**6-28. *Black Girl* (Senegal, 1965).**
*With Mbissine Therese Diop; Directed by Ousmane Sembene.*
Unlike stars, or even little-known actors, nonprofessional players convey a sense of anonymity—itself an ideological statement. Sembene's movie explores the hoax of decolonization—a frequent theme of the Third World cinema. The story deals with a young Senegalese woman who works as a maid on the French Riviera. Only when she leaves Africa does she realize what it means to be an African in the so-called Western democracies: she is virtually stripped of her personal identity and is referred to as "the black girl," like a possession.

sense, such performers are neutral in the eyes of the public. The filmmaker can exploit only those aspects of their personality—usually their authentic appearance—which are relevant to the character in the film. This practice is still employed by such important directors as Ermanno Olmi in movies like *Il Posto* and *The Tree of the Wooden Clogs*. Nor is this technique limited only to Italian filmmakers (see 6-28).

In the early 1950s, a new interior style of acting, known as *the Method,* or *the System,* was introduced to American movie audiences. It was commonly associated with the former stage director Elia Kazan. Kazan's *On the Waterfront* was a huge success and a virtual showcase for this style of performance. It has since become the dominant style of acting in the American cinema as well as the live theatre. Throughout the 1950s, Kazan was said to have "invented" the Method, although he repeatedly pointed out that it was not new and was not his. It was an off-shoot of a system of training actors and rehearsing which had been developed by Constantin Stanislavsky at the Moscow Art Theatre. Stanislavsky's ideas were widely adopted in New York theatre circles in the 1930s, especially by the acting teacher Stella Adler and by the Group Theatre (which was headed by Lee Strasberg and Harold Clurman). Kazan had been a member of the Group Theatre. In 1947, he and several associates founded the Actors Studio in New York which received much publicity during the 1950s because it had developed such well-known graduates as Marlon Brando, James Dean, Julie Harris, Rod Steiger, and many others (6-29).

**6-29. On the Waterfront (U.S.A., 1954).**
*With Marlon Brando and Eva Marie Saint; Directed by Elia Kazan.*
Kazan considers Brando as close to a genius that he has ever encountered among actors—a view that's widely shared by others, especially other actors. Many regard his performance in this movie as his best—emotionally powerful, tender, poetic. It won him his first Best Actor Academy Award, as well as the New York Film Critics Award and the British Oscar as Best Foreign Actor—his third year in a row. Kazan was often surprised by his gifted protegé because he came up with ideas so fresh and arrived at in so underground a fashion that they seemed virtually discovered on the spot. See Joe Morella and Edward Z. Epstein, *Brando: The Unauthorized Biography* (New York: Crown, 1973); and Bob Thomas, *Marlon: Portrait of the Rebel as an Artist* (New York: Ballantine, 1973).

Kazan continued there as a teacher until 1954, when he asked his former mentor Strasberg to take over the organization. Within a short period, Strasberg became the most celebrated acting teacher in America, and his former students were—and still are—among the most famous performers in the world.

The central credo of Stanislavsky's system was: "You must live the part every moment you are playing it." He rejected the tradition of acting which emphasized externals. He believed that truth in acting can only be achieved by exploring a character's inner spirit which must be fused with the actor's own emotions. One of the most important techniques he developed is emotional recall, in which an actor delves into his or her own past to discover feelings which are analogous to those of the character. "In every part you do," Julie Harris explained, "there is some connection you can make with your own background or with some feeling you've had at one time or another." Stanislavsky's techniques were strongly psychoanalytical: by exploring their own subconscious, actors could trigger *real* emotions, which are recalled in every performance and transferred to the characters they are playing. He also devised techniques for helping actors to focus their concentration on the "world" of the play—its concrete details and textures. In some form or another, these techniques are probably as old as the acting profession itself, but Stanislavsky was the first to systemize them with exercises and methods of analysis (hence the terms the System and the Method). Nor did he claim that inner truth and emotional sincerity are sufficient unto themselves. He insisted that actors need to master the externals as well, particularly for classic plays which require a somewhat stylized manner of speaking, moving, and wearing costumes.

Stanislavsky was famous for his lengthy rehearsal periods, in which players were encouraged to improvise with their roles in order to discover the resonances of the text—the subtext, which is analogous to Freud's concept of the subconscious. Kazan and other Method-oriented directors used this concept in directing movies: "The film director knows that beneath the surface of his screenplay there is a subtext, a calendar of intentions and feelings and inner events. What appears to be happening, he soon learns, is rarely what is happening. The subtext is one of the film director's most valuable tools. It is what he directs." Spoken dialogue is secondary for Method players. In order to capture a character's "inner events," actors sometimes throw away their lines, choke on them, or even mumble. Throughout the 1950s, Method actors like Brando and Dean were ridiculed by some critics for mumbling their lines.

Stanislavsky disapproved of the star system and individual virtuosity. In his own productions, he insisted on ensemble playing, with genuine interactions among the actor/characters. Players were encouraged to analyse all the specifics of a scene: What does the character really *want*? What has happened prior to the immediate moment? What time of day is it? And so on. When presented with a role utterly foreign to their experience, actors were urged to research the part so that it would be understood in their guts as well as their minds. Method actors are famous for their ability to bring out the emotional intensity of their characters. Method-oriented directors generally believe that a player must have a character's experience within him or her, and they go to considerable lengths to learn about the personal lives of their players in order to use such details for characterization.

**6-30. *Antonio Das Mortes* (Brazil, 1969).**
*Directed by Glauber Rocha.*
Acting styles are strongly influenced by genre. Traditionally, the epic has favored an heroic style of presentation, whether in the form of an American western, a Japanese samurai film, or a Germanic saga. Like most examples of its genre, Glauber Rocha's folk epic is based on mythic materials. It deals with the legends of the *cangaceiros,* the rebel guerrilla bandits of Brazil who joined forces with the peasants of the countryside to fight their common oppressors—the rich landlords. The film combines a number of acting styles, ranging from the heroic to the realistic to the satiric. This mixture is in keeping with the polymorphous cultural makeup of Brazil itself. Rocha also includes indigenous music from Africa and Portugal, in addition to native Brazilian dances and folk ballads. See also "Cinema Novo vs. Cultural Colonialism: An Interview with Glauber Rocha," in *Cineaste* (Summer, 1970); and Hans Proppe and Susan Tarr, "Cinema Novo: Pitfalls of Cultural Nationalism," in *Jump Cut* (June, 1976).

In the 1960s, the French New Wave directors—especially Godard and Truffaut—popularized the technique of improvisation while their players were on-camera. The resultant increase in realism was highly praised by critics. Of course there was nothing new in the technique itself. Actors often improvised in the silent cinema, and it was the foundation of silent comedy. For example, Chaplin, Keaton, and Laurel & Hardy needed to know only the premise of a given scene: the comic details were improvised and later refined in the editing stage. The cumbersome technology of sound put an end to most of these practices. Method-trained actors use improvisation primarily as an exploratory rehearsal technique, but their performances are usually set when the camera begins to roll.

Godard and Truffaut, in order to capture a greater sense of discovery and surprise, would occasionally instruct their players to make up their dialogue while a scene was actually being photographed. The flexible technology introduced by *cinéma vérité* (see Chapter 9, "Documentary") allowed these directors to capture an unprecedented degree of spontaneity. (However, also see 6-31.) In Truffaut's *The 400 Blows,* for example, the youthful protagonist

**6-31. *La Chinoise* (France, 1967).**
*With Juliet Berto; Directed by Jean-Luc Godard.*
Though Godard was a pioneer in exploring the possibilities of realistic acting, after his conversion to Marxism in the late 1960s he came to repudiate this style of performance, dismissing it as "a bourgeois concept of representation." He was strongly influenced by the German dramatist Bertolt Brecht. Like Brecht, Godard believed that performers should act as *intermediaries* between the fictional characters they are playing and the spectators watching the movie. Instead of lulling the viewer with an illusion of reality which pretends to be objective (a view steeped in bourgeois ideology), the actor should confront the spectator directly, acknowledging his presence, and presenting him not with a vicarious emotional thrill, but an analysis of how capitalist ideology works. In short, through the rejection of a realistic style of acting, the Marxist ideal of demystification is embodied on an aesthetic level within the movie itself. Instead of pretending that his images and actors are a "reflection of reality," the filmmaker frankly demonstrates how they can be manipulated, thus allowing the viewer to accept or reject the ideas in a more objective manner. See James Roy MacBean, *Film and Revolution* (Bloomington, Ind.: Indiana University Press, 1975).

(Jean-Pierre Léaud) is interviewed by a prison psychologist about his family life and sexual habits. Drawing heavily on his own experience, Léaud (who wasn't informed of the questions in advance) answers them with disarming frankness. Truffaut's camera is able to capture the boy's hesitations, his embarrassment, and his charming macho bravado.

In one form or another, improvisation has become a valuable technique in the contemporary cinema. Such filmmakers as John Cassavetes, Rainer Werner Fassbinder, and Martin Scorsese have employed it with brilliant results. One of the most admired of contemporary directors is Robert Altman, who allows his players an unprecedented degree of creative autonomy. "What I'm looking for instead of actors is behaviors, " Altman has said—that is, people who can *be* instead of *act*. Improvisation is a term he uses to describe several techniques. Sometimes the players are given scenes written by Altman or his screenwriter, then urged to rewrite their parts to suit their own personalities. Some of the improvising takes place during rehearsal periods, although nothing is set until shooting. His usual method is to provide each player with a descriptive sketch of their characters, and then allow them to reconstruct their histories and write their dialogue which is later edited by Altman or the writer. In *Nashville,* the actors even composed their own songs. Altman is fascinated by the artistic chemistry of chance combinations, and he has often compared his method of improvisation to the way jazz musicians interrelate instinctively during a jam session. The artistry is found not in a preordained form, but in a process of discovery: "You're not planning any of this that you film. You're capturing. You can't even hope to see it, you just turn on the camera and hope to capture it."

When different acting styles are mixed in the same film, the results can be disorienting, even unintentionally comical. For example, Joseph L. Mankiewicz's 1953 adaptation of Shakespeare's *Julius Caesar* combines an assortment of styles, all individually valid in their own right, but sometimes jarring in combination. At one extreme is the performance of John Gielgud, lyrical and voicey in the most stylized British tradition. At another extreme is Greer Garson—pure MGM gloss. Sticking out like the proverbial sore thumb is Marlon Brando—realistic, prosey, intense. The performers who fare best in this film are those who avoid these extremes: James Mason and Deborah Kerr. There are some instances where mixing styles of acting is a valid aesthetic device (see 6-30). In Victor Fleming's *The Wizard of Oz,* for example, the people of Kansas behave very differently from the fanciful creatures of Oz. Similarly, Nicholas Meyer's *Time After Time* is a sci-fi fantasy which thrusts the English Victorian hero H. G. Wells (Malcolm McDowell) into the world of present-day San Francisco, and much of the charm of the film derives from this incongruous clash of cultures.

## Casting

Casting a movie is almost an art in itself. It requires an acute sensitivity to a player's type, a convention inherited from the live theatre. Most stage and screen performers are classified according to role categories: leading men, leading ladies, character actors (6-32), juveniles, villains, light comedians, tragedians, ingenues, singing actors, dancing actors, and so on. Typing conventions are rarely violated. For example, even though homely people obviously fall in love, romantic roles are almost always performed by attractive players. Similarly, audiences are not likely to be persuaded by a player with an all-American iconography (like Doris Day) cast in European roles. Nor is one likely to accept a performer like Klaus Kinski as the boy-next-door, unless one lives in a very weird neighborhood. Of course a player's range is all-important

(Paramount Pictures)

**6-32.** *The Godfather* **(U.S.A., 1972).**

*With Marlon Brando and Robert Duvall (left, in soft focus); Directed by Francis Ford Coppola.* Character actors are the unsung heroes of the profession. By definition, they are kept at the fringes of the action—in soft focus, as it were—lending support to the principal players. Duvall is one of the finest actors of the contemporary cinema—so fine, in fact, that audiences often don't recognize him from role to role, so different is each performance. He is a master of dialects, scrupulous in researching authentic details, and can almost literally transform his body into the form of the character he is impersonating. He has played such diverse roles as the inarticulate Southern sharecropper in *Tomorrow,* a slightly demented Jesse James in *The Great Northfield, Minnesota Raid,* the retarded recluse in *To Kill a Mockingbird,* a timid banker in *The Chase,* the pious hypocrite Frank Burns in *M\*A\*S\*H,* a cowboy in *True Grit,* and the gung-ho paterfamilias in *The Great Santini.* He is one of Coppola's favorite players and has appeared in five of his movies: as a neurotic cop in *The Rain People,* as the adopted son Tom Hagen in both *Godfather* films, a millionaire businessman in *The Conversation,* and the supermacho Colonel Kilgore in *Apocalypse Now.*

in determining his or her type. Some, like Gene Hackman, have extremely broad ranges, while others, like Woody Allen, are confined to variations of the same type.

Typecasting was almost invariable in the silent cinema. In part, this was because characters tended toward allegorical types rather than unique individuals, and often were even identified with a label: "The Man," "The Wife," "The Mother," "The Vamp," and so on. Blonde players were usually cast in parts emphasizing purity, earthy brunettes in erotic roles. Eisenstein insisted that players ought to be cast strictly to type and was inclined to favor non-professionals because of their greater authenticity. Why use an actor to imper-

**6-33. _The Bicycle Thief._ (Italy, 1948).**
_With Lamberto Maggiorani and Enzo Staiola; Directed by Vittorio De Sica._
One of the most famous casting coups in film history is De Sica's selection of Maggiorani and Staiola as an impoverished laborer and his idolizing son. Both were nonprofessionals. Maggiorani actually was a laborer, and had difficulty finding a factory job after this movie. When De Sica was trying to finance the film, one producer agreed to put up the money provided the leading role was played by Cary Grant! Needless to say, De Sica couldn't imagine an elegant and graceful actor like Grant in the role, and the director wisely went elsewhere for his financing.

sonate a factory worker, he asked, when a filmmaker can use a _real_ factory worker instead (see 6-33)?

But trained actors tend to resent being typed and often attempt to broaden their range. Sometimes it works, sometimes it doesn't. Humphrey Bogart is a good example. For years he was stereotyped as a tough, cynical gangster, until he joined forces with director John Huston who cast him as the hard-boiled detective Sam Spade in _The Maltese Falcon._ Huston weaned him even further from his type in _The Treasure of the Sierra Madre_ in which Bogart played a crafty paranoid, the prospector Fred C. Dobbs. The actor totally reversed his image in _The African Queen_ in which he played Charlie Allnut, a lovable and funny drunk whose vulnerability endeared him to audiences and won Bogart a Best Actor Academy Award. But in _Beat the Devil_, Huston's celebrated casting instincts deserted him when he used Bogart in a role beyond his powers—as a sophisticated adventurer stranded with a shabby assortment of rogues and loons. The witty tongue-in-cheek dialogue fell flat in

Bogart's self-conscious performance. A polished player like Cary Grant could have acted the part with much greater believability and grace.

"Casting is characterization," Hitchcock pointed out. Once a role has been cast, especially with a personality-star, the essence of the fictional character is already established. In a sense, stars are more "real" than other characters, which is why many people refer to a character by the actor's name, rather than

**(a)** *(MGM)*

**6-34a. *Romeo and Juliet* (U.S.A., 1936).**
*With Leslie Howard and Norma Shearer; Directed by George Cukor.*

**6-34b. *Romeo and Juliet* (Great Britain/Italy, 1968).**
*With Leonard Whiting and Olivia Hussey; Directed by Franco Zeffirelli.*

Cukor's version of Shakespeare's play is an example of the disasters that can befall a movie when a director casts against type. The lovers are a far cry from the youngsters called for in the original. Shearer was 37 when she played the 13-year-old Juliet, Howard as Romeo was 44. At 55, John Barrymore was preposterous as Mercutio, Romeo's firebrand friend. The spectacle of middle-aged adults behaving so childishly makes the whole dramatic action seem ludicrous.

Zeffirelli's version of the play is much more successful because he cast to type and awarded the roles to two teenagers. To be sure, Cukor's actors speak the lines better, but Zeffirelli's *look* truer. The differences between the ages of an actor and character are far more important on screen than on stage, for the cinematic close shot can be merciless in revealing age.

**(b)** *(Paramount Pictures)*

**6-35. Publicity photo of Robert Redford and Mia Farrow in *The Great Gatsby* (U.S.A., 1974).**
*Directed by Jack Clayton.*

*Gatsby* is a sad instance of how miscasting can throw off the entire meaning of a movie. The production had all the makings of a first-rate film, which is what everyone involved wanted to make. The opulent production values are in keeping with F. Scott Fitzgerald's classic novel. Francis Ford Coppola's script is a model of intelligent adaptation. Clayton's direction is lush and romantic without being sentimental. Technically, the leading roles were within the ranges of Redford and Farrow, who are both accomplished actors. But their iconography conflicted with their parts. What was needed in the role of Daisy Buchanan was a player who brought with her an air of glamor, mystery, and inaccessibility, a compelling radiance which would make Gatsby's extraordinary romanticism plausible. Perhaps a major star would have been more suitable than a straight actress like Farrow. Thirty years earlier, Vivien Leigh would have been right for the role; fifteen years earlier, the exquisite Elizabeth Taylor could probably have carried it off. With Redford, the problem was just the opposite. Jay Gatsby is a man of shady origins, awkward and somewhat vulgar, the kind of man few would notice if he weren't a millionaire. This is hardly a role suited to Redford, whose iconography is steeped in glamor. What was needed in the part was an "ordinary" actor, a mere mortal, not a WASP Adonis. Audiences might have been willing to believe that Farrow would pine for Redford for eight years, but few were inclined to accept the opposite. See Louis D. Giannetti, "The Gatsby Flap," in *Literature/Film Quarterly* (Winter 1975).

*(Paramount Pictures)*

that of the person in the story. After working with Hitchcock on the script of *Strangers on a Train*, the novelist Raymond Chandler ridiculed the director's method of characterization. "His idea of character is rather primitive," Chandler complained: "Nice Young Man," "Society Girl," "Frightened Woman," and so on. Like many literary types, Chandler believed that characterization must be created through language. He was insensitive to the other options available to a filmmaker. For example, Hitchcock was a cunning exploiter of the star system—a technique that has nothing to do with language. For his leading ladies, for instance, he favored elegant blondes with an understated sexuality and rather aristocratic, ladylike manners—in short, the Society Girl type. But there are great individual differences between such heroines as Joan Fontaine, Ingrid Bergman, and Grace Kelly, to mention only three of Hitchcock's famous blondes.

**6-36. *The Gospel According to Saint Matthew* (Italy, 1964).**
*With Enrique Irazoqui (extreme right); Directed by Pier Paolo Pasolini.*
The casting of historical personages is always a ticklish matter, especially with revered figures like Jesus. Perhaps the most successful portrayal is that of Irazoqui, a nonprofessional player whose quiet simplicity and Semitic appearance at least suggest an historical accuracy. In George Stevens' *The Greatest Story Ever Told* (1965), Jesus is played by Max Von Sydow, an actor of dignity and commanding presence. Other directors have been less fortunate. For example, in Nicholas Ray's *King of Kings* (1962), the part was essayed by Jeffrey Hunter who specialized in heart-throb roles and good-hearted oafs. (One wag referred to the film as *I Was a Teenage Jesus*.)

Hitchcock's casting is often meant to deceive. His villains were usually actors of enormous personal charm—like James Mason in *North by Northwest*. Hitchcock counted on the audience's good will toward an established star, permitting his "heroes" to behave in ways that can only be described as morally dubious. In *Rear Window,* for example, James Stewart is literally a voyeur, yet we can't bring ourselves to condemn such a wholesome type as Jimmy Stewart, the all-American boy. Audiences also assume that a star will remain in the movie until the final reel, at which point it's permissible—though seldom advisable—to kill him or her off. But in *Psycho*, the Janet Leigh character is brutally murdered in the first third of the film—a shocking violation of convention which jolts audiences out of their complacency. Sometimes Hitchcock cast awkward, self-conscious actors in roles requiring a note of evasive anxiety, like Farley Granger in *Rope* and *Strangers on a Train*. In cases such as these, bad acting is precisely what's called for—it's part of the characterization.

Many filmmakers believe that casting is so integral to character, they don't even begin work on a script until they know who's playing the major

*(Continental)*

roles. Yasujiro Ozu confessed: "I could no more write, not knowing who the actor was going to be, than an artist could paint, not knowing what color he was using." Billy Wilder always tailored his dialogue to fit the personality of his players. When Montgomery Clift backed out of playing the lead in *Sunset Boulevard,* Wilder rewrote the part to fit William Holden who brought totally different character nuances to the role. Similarly, when Paul Douglas died two weeks before production was to begin on *The Apartment,* Wilder asked Fred MacMurray to take over the part which was completely revised to exploit his iconography.

**6-37. *From Here to Eternity* (U.S.A., 1953).**
*With Deborah Kerr and Burt Lancaster; Directed by Fred Zinnemann.*
Casting against type can have its rewards as well as its pitfalls. Prior to this movie, Kerr had been stereotyped by MGM as a young well-bred British matron, in parts she ironically referred to as her "tiara roles." Zinnemann cast her in this film because he thought her ladylike gentility would provide a provocative contrast to the character's sordid past. After receiving almost universal acclaim for her performance, Kerr's roles became far more diversified.

*(Columbia Pictures)*

    Some filmmakers are almost unerring in their casting instincts, whether working with nonprofessionals, trained actors, or stars. Fred Zinnemann is a good example. In movies like *The Search* and *The Men,* he used mostly nonprofessional and unfamiliar players, thus forcing the audience to suspend immediate judgment and evaluate the characters as their situations unfold. Even with established stars, Zinnemann has often cast against type. In such cases he discouraged his players from using familiar mannerisms, thus creating surprising tensions between what we expect and what we actually see the players do (6-37). In other cases, he simply asked his stars to behave as naturally as possible—like Gary Cooper in *High Noon.* Cooper's Best Actor Academy Award in this movie was viewed as something of a joke by critics, for his range was among the most narrow of all the great stars. Yet there's not a false note in his performance as the sheriff of a scared frontier town, largely because Zinnemann asked him to be himself: "Cooper is first of all a tremendous personality," the director observed. "He is best when he doesn't act. His just being on the screen exerts something that is very powerful."

## Further Reading

AFFRON, CHARLES, *Star Acting: Gish, Garbo, Davis* (New York: Dutton, 1977). Critical analysis, copiously illustrated.

BRAUDY, LEO, "Acting and Characterization," in *The World in a Frame* (Garden City, N.Y.: Doubleday, 1976).

HASKELL, MOLLY, *From Reverence to Rape* (Baltimore: Penguin, 1974); and MARJORIE ROSEN, *Popcorn Venus* (New York: Coward, McCann & Geoghegan, 1973). Two feminist studies of images of women in the American cinema.

MORIN, EDGAR, *The Stars* (New York: Grove Press, 1960); and RICHARD GRIFFITH, *The Movie Stars* (Garden City, N.Y.: Doubleday, 1970).

MUNK, ERIKA, ed., *Stanislavsky in America* (New York: Hill and Wang, 1966). A collection of essays.

SCHICKEL, RICHARD, *The Stars* (New York: Dial Press, 1962).

SHIPMAN, DAVID, *The Great Movie Stars,* vol. I, *The Golden Years* (New York: Bonanza Books, 1970); vol. II, *The International Years* (New York: St. Martin's Press, 1972).

THOMPSON, DAVID, *A Biographical Dictionary of Film* (New York: Morrow, 1976). Also includes entries on international directors.

WALKER, ALEXANDER, *Sex in the Movies* (London: Penguin, 1968); and ALEXANDER WALKER, *Stardom, The Hollywood Phenomenon* (London: Penguin, 1974).

# 7

"The function of the cinema is to reveal, to bring to light certain details that the stage would have left untreated."

ANDRÉ BAZIN

# DRAMA

Many people cling to the naive belief that theatre and film are two aspects of the same art, the only major difference being that drama is "live" while movies are "recorded." Certainly there are undeniable similarities between the two arts. Most obvious perhaps is that both employ action as a principal mode: what people *do* is a major source of meaning. The theatre and movies are also collaborative enterprises, involving the coordination of writers, directors, actors, and technicians. Drama and film are both social arts, exhibited before groups of people, and experienced publicly as well as individually. But films are not mere recordings of plays. The materials of the two mediums are fundamentally different.

## Time, Space, and Language

In the live theatre, time is generally less flexible than in movies. The basic unit of construction in the theatre is the scene, and the amount of dramatic time that elapses during a scene is roughly equal to the length of time it takes to perform. True, some plays traverse many years, but usually these years transpire "between curtains." We're informed that it is "7 years later," either by a stage direction or by the dialogue. The basic unit of construction in movies is the shot, which can lengthen or shorten time more subtly since the average shot lasts only 10 or 15 seconds. Drama has to chop out huge blocks of time between the relatively few scenes and acts; films can expand or contract time between the many hundreds of shots.

Theatrical time is usually continuous. It moves forward. Temporal dislocations like the flashback are rare in the theatre but commonplace in movies. On the stage, time is usually in the present tense, and events from the past and present are seldom presented simultaneously. Cinematic time is often more complex. Throughout Bergman's *Wild Strawberries,* for example, an elderly professor (Victor Sjöström) witnesses scenes from his youthful past, sometimes even participating in them. The other characters in these scenes are in period, but the professor remains an elderly man, a captive of the present (see also 7-1).

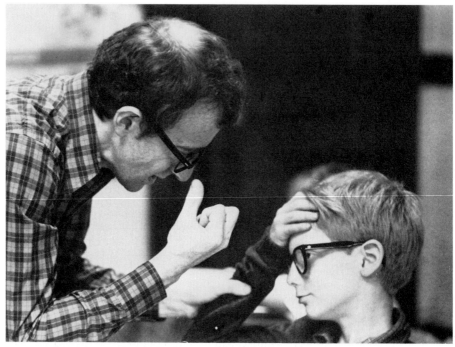

*(United Artists)*

**7-1. *Annie Hall* (U.S.A., 1977).**
*With Woody Allen and Jonathan Munk; Directed by Allen.*
In the cinema, different time periods can be presented simultaneously. In this scene, for example, the neurotic writer Alvie Singer (Allen) drifts through some scenes of his past and encounters himself as a nine-year-old neurotic, deeply immersed in gloom. See Eric Lax, *On Being Funny: Woody Allen & Comedy* (New York: Manor Books, 1977); and Maurice Yacowar, *Loser Take All: The Comic Art of Woody Allen* (New York: Ungar, 1979).

Space in the theatre is also dependent upon the basic unit of the scene. Theatrical space is continuous: the action takes place in a unified area which has specific limits, usually defined by the proscenium arch. A synthetic art, theatre confines all the relevant meanings within this given area. Drama, then, almost always deals with closed forms: we don't imagine that the action is being continued in the wings and dressing rooms of the theatre. The "proscenium arch" in film is the frame—a masking device that isolates objects and people only temporarily. As an analytical art, movies deal with a series of space fragments. Though shots can be in either open or closed form, a closed form image is still only a temporary piece of a larger whole. Beyond the frame of a given shot, another aspect of the action waits to be photographed. A closeup of an object, for example, is generally a detail of a subsequent long shot which will give us the context of the closeup. In the theatre, it's more difficult to withhold information in this manner.

The relationship between the audience and the work of art is also different in these two mediums. In the theatre, the viewer remains in a stationary position: the distance between the audience and the stage is constant. To be sure, an actor can move close to an audience; but compared to the fluid space in the cinema, distance variation in the live theatre is negligible. The film

**7-2. Fantastic Voyage (U.S.A., 1966).**
*Art direction by Jack Martin Smith and Dale Hennesy; Special effects by Art Cruickshank; Directed by Richard Fleischer.*
Screen space can explore even microscopic areas: literally, through microcinematography, or figuratively, through special effects. The principal setting of this film—the interior of a human body—couldn't possibly be duplicated on stage. In order to perform a delicate brain operation, several scientists are reduced to the size of bacteria. They travel through the patient's blood stream in a miniaturized submarine. This photo shows the crew's only survivors floating in the area of the optic nerve, as they frantically search for the patient's eye in order to escape his body before they return to normal size. See also John Baxter, *Science Fiction in the Cinema* (New York: A. S. Barnes, 1970); and William Johnson, ed., *Focus on the Science Fiction Film* (Englewood Cliffs, N.J.: Prentice-Hall, 1972).

*(Twentieth Century-Fox)*

viewer, on the other hand, identifies with the camera's lens which permits him or her to "move" in any direction and from any distance. An extreme closeup allows us to count the lashes of an eye; the extreme long shot permits us to see miles in each direction. In short, the cinema has the advantages of editing and the moving camera. Most theatrical equivalents to these techniques have been crude at best.

These spatial differences don't necessarily favor one medium over the other. In the theatre, space is three dimensional, occupied by tangible people and objects, and therefore is more realistic: our perception of space and volume is essentially the same as in real life. The living presence of actors, with their subtle interactions—both with other actors and the audience—is impossible to duplicate in film. Movies provide us with a two-dimensional *image* of space and objects, and no interaction exists between the screen actors and the audience. For this reason, nudity is not so controversial an issue on the screen as in the theatre, for on stage the naked people are real, whereas on film they're "only pictures." The stage player interacts with viewers: he or she must establish a delicate rapport with each different audience. The screen player, on the other hand, is inexorably fixed on celluloid: he or she can't readjust to each audience for the worlds of the screen and the viewer aren't connected

(United Artists)

**7-3.** *A Bridge Too Far* **(Great Britain/U.S.A., 1977).**
*Directed by Richard Attenborough.*
Epic stories can be treated on the stage, but they are always stylized. Theatrical space is too constricted for a realistic presentation. In movies, even a complex World War II military invasion can be reconstructed in a realistic manner. See also Lawrence H. Suid, *Guts & Glory* (Reading, Mass.: Addison-Wesley Publishing, 1978).

and continuous as they are in the theatre. Movies often seem dated because acting styles can't be adjusted to newer audiences. Stage actors, on the other hand, can make even a four-hundred-year-old play seem fresh and relevant, for while the words remain the same, their interpretation and delivery can always be changed to conform with contemporary acting styles.

Because of these spatial differences, the viewer's participation is different in each medium. In the theatre, the audience generally must be more active. Since all of the visual elements are provided within a given space, the viewer must sort out what's essential from what's incidental. Disregarding for the moment the importance of language in the theatre, drama is a medium of low visual saturation. That is, the audience must fill in certain meanings in the absence of visual detail. A movie audience, on the other hand, is generally more passive. All the necessary details are provided by closeups and by edited juxtapositions. Film, then, is a medium of high visual saturation—that is, the pictures are densely detailed with information, requiring little or no filling in. These generalizations are relative, of course. Realist film directors tend to be more theatrical in their handling of space, forcing their audiences to participate more than they would in viewing an expressionist or highly fragmented film.

Although both drama and film are eclectic arts, the theatre is a narrower medium, one specializing in spoken language. Most of the meanings in the theatre are found in words which are densely saturated with information. For this reason, drama is generally considered a writer's medium. The primacy of the text makes it a kind of special branch of literature. In the live theatre, we tend to hear before we see. The film director René Clair once noted that a blind man could still grasp the essentials of most stage plays. Movies, on the other hand, are generally regarded as a visual art and a director's medium, for it is the director who creates the images. Clair observed that a deaf man could

**7-4. *Pickpocket* (France, 1959).**
*Directed by Robert Bresson.*
In the live drama, if a small prop (like a wallet) is important, it must be highlighted conspicuously or the audience will fail to notice its existence, much less its importance. In the cinema, small articles can be isolated from their context. In this photo, Bresson captures a pickpocket's swift stroke as he lifts a wallet from a pedestrian on a busy walkway. This snapshot quality is difficult to produce on stage: the conventions of the medium are at odds with the essence of the subject matter. See also *The Films of Robert Bresson* (New York: Praeger, 1969).

still grasp most of the essentials of a film. But these generalizations are also relative, for some movies—many of the works of Welles, for example—are densely saturated, both visually and aurally.

Since plays stress the primacy of language, one of the major problems in adapting them for the screen is determining how much of the language is necessary in a predominantly visual art like movies. George Cukor's version of Shakespeare's *Romeo and Juliet* (6-34a) was a conservative film adaptation. Virtually all the dialogue was retained, even the exposition and purely functional speeches of no particular poetic merit. The result was a respectful but often tedious film in which the visuals tended merely to illustrate the language. Often images and dialogue contained the same information, producing an overblown, static quality that actually contradicted the swift sense of action in the stage play.

Zeffirelli's film version of this play was much more successful (7-5). Verbal exposition was cut almost completely and replaced (just as effectively) by

*(Paramount Pictures)*

**7-5. *Romeo and Juliet* (Great Britain/Italy, 1968).**
*With Michael York (aloft); Directed by Franco Zeffirelli.*
In most respects, the cinema is a more kinetic medium than the stage, for the camera can move as well as the players. The essence of Shakespeare's play is found in the impulsive haste of its youthful protagonists, the dominolike swiftness of the chain of events, and the violence of much of the action. Zeffirelli heightened these characteristics by kineticizing many of the scenes, and by avoiding visual–verbal redundancies. This fight scene is photographed with a hand-held camera that lurches and swirls with the combatants as they spill onto the streets of Verona.

visual exposition. Single lines were pruned meticulously from some of the speeches where the same information could be conveyed by images. Most of the great poetry was preserved but often with nonsynchronous visuals to expand—not duplicate—the language. The closeups looked like a series of exquisite Renaissance portraits. The camera recorded the most intimate details of the lives of the lovers, and the sound track picked up the most delicate sighs. Zeffirelli's movie, though technically less faithful to the stage script, was actually more Shakespearean in spirit than the scrupulously literal version of Cukor.

Both theatre and cinema are audio-visual mediums, then, but they differ in their stress of certain conventions. The two major sources of information in drama are action and dialogue. We observe what people do and what they say. The action of a play is no mere illustration of the words. Hedda Gabler's burning of Lovbörg's manuscript, for example, embodies emotional and intellectual information that can't be adequately paraphrased in language. The contrast between what people say and do is a common source of irony on the stage. Chekhov, for instance, built several of his plays around this ironic contrast. Even in a talky play like Shaw's *Man and Superman*, the audience delights in watching Ann Whitefield vamping John Tanner while he talks on and on.

Action in the theatre is restricted primarily to objective long shots, to use a cinematic metaphor. Only fairly large actions are effective: the duel between

**7-6. *Macbeth* (U.S.A./Great Britain, 1971).**
*Production design by Wilfred Shingleton; Art direction by Fred Carter; Directed by Roman Polanski.*
Film is a medium of high visual saturation. Certain types of information—like Macbeth's prowess as a warrior—can be presented in visual as well as verbal detail. See also Charles W. Eckert, ed., *Focus on Shakespearean Films* (Englewood Cliffs, N.J.: Prentice-Hall, 1972).

(Columbia Pictures)

Hamlet and Laertes; Amanda helping Laura to dress in *The Glass Menagerie*, and so on. Extreme long-shot ranges—to continue the cinematic metaphor—must be stylized in the theatre. The epic battles of Shakespeare's history plays, for example, would appear ridiculous if staged realistically. Likewise, closeup actions would be missed by all but those in the front rows unless the actions were exaggerated and stylized by the actors. Hamlet's distaste for Claudius must be expressed visually either by exaggerated facial expressions, or by the prince's larger-than-life gestures and movements. Except in the most intimate theatres, closeup actions in the drama have to be verbalized—that is, the subtlest actions and reactions of stage characters are usually conveyed by language rather than by visual means. We know of Hamlet's attitude toward Claudius primarily through Hamlet's soliloquies and dialogue. On the closeup level of action, then, what we see on stage is often not what people do, but what people *talk* about doing, or what's been done.

Because of these visual problems, most plays avoid actions requiring vast or minute spaces. Theatrical action is usually confined to the full- and long-shot range. If vast or minute spaces are required, the theatre tends to resort to

**7-7. *The Golden Voyage of Sinbad* (U.S.A., 1973).**
*With John Phillip Law; Special effects by Ray Harryhausen; Directed by Gordon Hessler.*
"A film is a ribbon of dreams," Orson Welles has observed. "The camera is much more than a recording apparatus, it is a medium via which messages reach us from another world that is not ours and that brings us to the heart of a great secret. Here magic begins." Since ancient times, artists have attempted to create a magical world where the real and the fantastic are fused. Perhaps no medium is so suited to the realistic presentation of fantasy materials as film, thanks to such special effects wizards as Harryhausen. See also John Brosnan, *Movie Magic: The Story of Special Effects in the Cinema* (New York: New American Library, 1974).

*(Columbia Pictures)*

unrealistic conventions: to ballets and stylized tableaux for extreme long-shot actions, and to the convention of verbal articulation for closeup actions. Movies, on the other hand, can move easily among all these ranges. For this reason, the cinema often dramatizes the action that takes place on stage only "between the curtains." This is not to say that the cinema doesn't have its own set of conventions. The movable camera, expressionistic sound, and editing

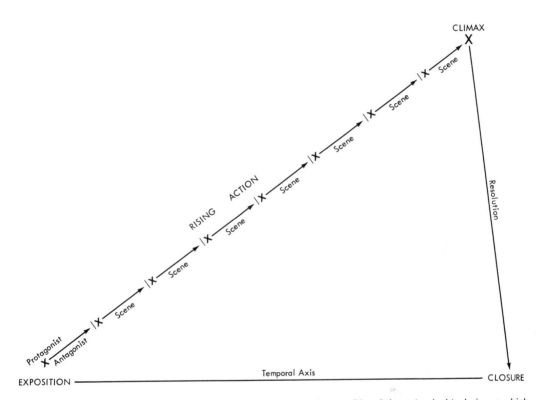

**7-8.** The conventions of classical cinema are based on traditional dramaturgical techniques which can be traced back to the theatre of ancient times. Like most aesthetic conventions, they are a loose set of expectations, not Divine Law. Classical cinema is story-oriented, posited on a heightened conflict between a protagonist who initiates the action, and an antagonist who resists it. Most films in this form begin with an implied dramatic question: we want to know how the protagonist will get what he or she wants in the face of considerable opposition. The subsequent scenes intensify this conflict in a rising pattern of action. This escalation is treated in terms of cause–effect, with each scene implying a link to the next. Dramatic details that don't intensify the central conflict are suppressed or subordinated to an ancillary function. The conflict swells to its maximum tension in the climax, at which point the protagonist and antagonist clash overtly. After their confrontation, the dramatic intensity subsides in the resolution. The story ends with some kind of formal closure—traditionally a wedding or a dance in comedies, a death in tragedies, a return to normalcy in domestic dramas. The final shot—because of its privileged position—is often meant to be a philosophical overview of some kind, a summing up of the significance of the previous material. Classical cinema emphasizes unity, plausibility, and coherence of its constituent parts. Each shot is seamlessly elided to the next in an effort to produce a smooth flow of action, and often a sense of inevitability. To add urgency to the situation, filmmakers sometimes include some kind of deadline which intensifies the emotion. Narrative structures are linear and often take the form of a journey, a chase, or a search.

are just as artificial as the conventions of the live theatre. In both cases, the audience accepts these conventions as the rules of the game.

There's a certain obviousness in the theatre precisely because of some of these problems. Most dramatic plots, for example, involve a clear-cut conflict between a protagonist and an antagonist: between Antigone and Creon, Lear and his daughters, Stanley Kowalski and Blanche Dubois. This dramatic conflict is presented in the opening exposition and intensifies progressively over the course of the ensuing scenes, resulting finally in a climactic confrontation where either protagonist or antagonist triumphs. Not all plays conform to this classical paradigm, but a surprising number of them do, even a delicate "detheatricalized" play like Chekhov's *The Cherry Orchard*.

"Classical cinema" is a vague but convenient term that film critics and scholars use to describe the kind of movie that adheres to this type of structure (7-8). It's by far the most popular type of organization used by fiction filmmakers, especially in the United States. Classical cinema is a descriptive term meant to suggest a norm of actual practice, not necessarily an aesthetic value judgment which connotes a high degree of excellence, as when one refers to a "classic work" of art—that is, one that has withstood the test of time and is still regarded as a masterpiece. In short, there are just as many bad movies as good in this form. Most American fiction films produced from the time of Griffith's mature style to the present conform to this classical paradigm. It was also the dominant type of cinematic structure in Europe until the advent of the New Wave. The classical mode is only one of several that can be employed in movies. Because of its greater spatial and temporal flexibility, film can employ a number of other modes and structures as well: the documentary, the stream-of-consciousness, the essay (like Godard's *Masculine-Feminine*), even the purely formal (like the abstract films of the Whitney brothers). In short, movies can dispense with overt conflicts,

*(Audio-Brandon Films)*

**7-9. *Eclipse* (Italy, 1962).**
*Directed by Michelangelo Antonioni.*
Virtually all plays are social in emphasis—that is, they deal with the interrelationships between people. The cinema can also deal with the relationship of people with things. Antonioni is especially interested in the way that environment—both natural and man-made—can affect humans, and vice-versa. Such themes are difficult to convey in the theatre, for the environment must be created on the artificial world of the stage which usually bears only a symbolic resemblance to outside environments.

climaxes, and even plots. Cinematic action can be theatrical or nontheatrical with equal ease.

The human being is central to the aesthetic of the theatre: words must be recited by people, conflicts must be embodied by actors. The cinema is not so dependent on humans. The aesthetic of film is based on photography, and anything that can be photographed can be the subject matter of a movie (7-9). For this reason, adapting a play to the screen, while difficult, is hardly impossible, for much of what the stage can do can be duplicated on the screen. To adapt most movies to the stage, however, would be much more difficult. Movies with exterior locations would be almost automatically ruled out, of course: how would one go about adapting John Ford's epic westerns like *The Searchers*? But even films with interior locations would probably be impossible to translate into theatrical terms. True, the words would present no problem, and some actions would be transferable. But how would one deal with the time and space dislocations of Resnais' *Hiroshima, Mon Amour* (7-10)? Or the kaleidoscopic dislocations of space in Richard Lester's Beatles film, *A Hard Day's Night*? Theme and characterization in Joseph Losey's *The Servant* are communicated primarily through the use of camera angles—impossible to duplicate in the theatre (11-13). The theme of Bergman's *The Silence* is con-

**7-10. *Hiroshima, Mon Amour* (France, 1959).**
*With Emmanuèle Riva (left), Bernard Fresson (center rear), and Eiji Okada (right); Directed by Alain Resnais.*
There is no theatrical equivalent for the cinematic dissolve which Resnais uses as a major aesthetic device throughout this film. It deals with an affair between a French actress and a Japanese architect, some years after the atom-bombing of Hiroshima. Their relationship is doomed, in part because she is unable to escape the memory of her traumatic love affair with a German soldier during the Nazi occupation of her country. (Note how the shadowy German youth of her past seems to come between the lovers of the present.) The film opens with shots of nude torsos covered with an eerie atomic dust—producing an effect that's both erotic and chilling. The movie is at once a love story, a political statement, a treatise on time and memory, and a stylistic tour-de-force. See also James Monaco, *Alain Resnais* (New York: Oxford University Press, 1979); and John Francis Kreidl, *Alain Resnais* (Boston: G. K. Hall, 1979).

veyed primarily through images of empty corridors, doors, and windows. How could one transfer this technique to the stage?

One should not assume from this that the best method of adapting a play for the screen is to "open it up"—to substitute exterior locations for interiors. Cinema doesn't always mean extreme long shots, sweeping pans, and flashy editing. Hitchcock once observed that many filmed versions of plays fail precisely because the tight, compact structure of the original is lost when the film director "loosens it up" with inappropriate cinematic techniques. Particularly when a play emphasizes a sense of confinement—and a great many of them do, either physical or psychological—the best adaptors respect the spirit of the original by finding filmic equivalents (7-11).

*(Columbia Pictures)*

**7-11. *The Member of the Wedding* (U.S.A., 1953).**
*With Ethel Waters and Julie Harris; Directed by Fred Zinnemann.*
Because of its spatial limitations, the live theatre is an ideal medium for dealing with the theme of confinement. One of the problems facing the film director who wishes to adapt a play is whether to "open it up"—that is, whether to dramatize off-stage actions on the screen. To do so would run the risk of releasing the spatial tensions of the original, which the dramatist exploits as part of the artistic form. Zinnemann's adaptation of Carson McCuller's play (itself based on her novel) confined most of the action to a single location. The theme of the novel, play, and movie are the same: the sense of entrapment of a girl (Harris) about to enter young womanhood. In the novel, her isolation is conveyed primarily by a limited point-of-view narration. In the play, the theme is spatially symbolized by the narrow confines of a single set. In the film, this idea is communicated principally by the close, tightly framed shots which seem to imprison both the young heroine and her closest friend, the family maid (Waters). Much of the language of the novel is sacrificed in the play, and even more is cut out of the movie version which uses spatial equivalents for many of the verbal ideas. See Louis D. Giannetti, *"The Member of the Wedding,"* in *Literature/Film Quarterly* (Winter 1976).

In the mid-1950s, the French periodical *Cahiers du Cinéma* popularized the *auteur* theory, a view which stressed the dominance of the director in film art (see Chapter 11, "Theory"). According to this view, whoever controls the mise-en-scène—the medium of the story—is the true "author" of a movie. The other collaborators (writers, cinematographer, actors, editor, etc.) are merely the director's technical assistants. No doubt the *auteur* critics exaggerated the primacy of the director, particularly in America, where many film directors were at the mercy of the Hollywood studio system which tended to emphasize group work rather than individual expression and publicized stars rather than directors. Nevertheless, despite the anonymous artisans who merely directed traffic on the sound stages of the studios, the *auteur* critics were essentially correct about the most artistically significant films.

Even today, the most admired movies—from whatever country—tend to be director's films. To refer to a movie as "good except for its direction" is as contradictory as referring to a play as "good except for its script." Of course we can enjoy a poorly directed movie or a badly written play, but what we enjoy are usually the secondary aspects of the art—a touching performance, a

**7-12.** *The Little Foxes* **(U.S.A., 1941).**
*With Dan Duryea and Carl Benton Reid; Directed by William Wyler.*
André Bazin believed that in adapting a play, a filmmaker's greatest challenge is translating the artificial space of the theatre into the realistic space of the cinema without losing the essence of the original. For example, in Lillian Hellman's stage play, this scene between a devious father and his creepy son takes place in the same living room set as most of the other scenes. Wyler's presentation is at once more effective and realistic. The two characters are shaving in the family bathroom while they haltingly probe the possibility of swindling a relative. Neither wants to reveal himself, neither looks at the other directly. Instead, they address each other by looking in their respective mirrors, their backs turned. "There is a hundred times more cinema, and of a better kind, in a shot in *The Little Foxes*," Bazin claimed, "than in all the outdoor dolly shots, natural locations, exotic geography, and flipsides of sets with which the screen so far has tried to make up for stagey origins." See André Bazin, "Theatre and Cinema," in *What is Cinema?*, Hugh Gray, ed. and trans. (Berkeley: University of California Press, 1967), in two volumes. See also Michael A. Anderegg, *William Wyler* (Boston: G. K. Hall, 1979).

(RKO)

striking set, or some amusing costumes. Good acting and stylish camerawork have often redeemed rubbish material. Such enjoyable elements generally represent the individual triumph of a gifted interpretive artist (actors, set designers, costumers, cinematographers, etc.) over the mediocrity of the dominant artist—the director in film, the writer in the theatre.

On the stage, then, the director is essentially an interpretive artist. If we see a rotten production of *King Lear,* we don't dismiss Shakespeare's play, but only a specific interpretation of the play. True, the stage director creates certain patterns of movement, appropriate gestures for his actors, and spatial relationships, but all of these visual elements take second place to the language of the script which is created by the playwright. The theatrical director's relation to the text is similar to the stage actor's relation to a role; he can add much to what's written down, but what he contributes is usually secondary to the text itself—an improvisation, as it were, which is circumscribed by the limits set down by the author.

The stage director is a kind of go-between for the author and the production staff. That is, the director is responsible for the general interpretation of the script and usually defines the limits for the other interpretive artists: actors, designers, technicians. The director must see to it that all the production elements are harmonized and subordinated to an overall interpretation. His or her influence tends to be stronger during rehearsals than in the actual performance. Once the curtain opens before an audience, the director is powerless to control what then takes place.

On the other hand, screen directors have a good deal more control over the final product. They too dominate the preproduction activities, but unlike the stage director the filmmaker controls virtually every aspect of the finished work as well. The degree of precision a film director can achieve is impossible on the stage, for movie directors can rephotograph people and objects until they get exactly what they want. As we have seen, films communicate *primarily* through moving images, and it's the director who determines most of the visual elements: the choice of shots, angles, lighting effects, filters, optical effects, framing, composition, camera movements, and editing. Furthermore, the director usually authorizes the costume and set designs and the choice of locales.

The differences in control and precision can be best illustrated perhaps by examining their handling of the mise-en-scène. Stage directors are much more restricted: they must work within one stationary set per scene. All patterns of movement and spatial relationships take place within this given area. Since this is a three-dimensional space, they have the advantage of depth as well as breadth to work with. Through the use of platforms, they can also exploit height on the stage. The theatrical director must use certain space conventions to assure maximum clarity. Thus, with a proscenium stage, the audience pretends it's peeping into a room where one wall has been removed. Naturally no furniture is placed against this "wall," nor do players turn their backs against it for very long periods for their dialogue would not be audible. If a thrust stage is used, the audience surrounds the acting area on three sides, forcing the performers to rotate their movements and speeches so that no side is neglected. Again, this convention is necessary to assure maximum clarity.

In the cinema, the director converts three-dimensional space into a two-dimensional image of space. Even with deep-focus photography, "depth" is not literal (7-13). But the flat image has certain advantages. Since a camera

**7-13.** *Ikiru,* **also known as** *To Live* **(Japan, 1952).**
*Directed by Akira Kurosawa.*
On the stage, the size of objects is constant, in movies relative. In this deep-focus shot, for example, the materials of three depth planes are precisely aligned to produce an ironic contrast. The protagonist (Takashi Shimura, whose picture adorns the Buddhist altar) was a lowly bureaucrat who did something really significant with his existence only in the final months of his life, when he realized he was dying of cancer. In the flashback portions of the movie, his battered hat is a symbol of his humility and dogged perseverance. His funeral wake (pictured) is a rigid, dismal affair, attended primarily by the deceased's fellow bureaucrats. The placement of the camera in this photo implicitly contrasts the unpretentious hat with the chagrined faces of the office workers with the formal photograph and altar. Since each viewer in the live theatre has a unique perspective of the stage, contrasts of this type are rare. In the cinema they are common, for the camera determines one perspective for all. For a brilliant study of Kurosawa's art, see Donald Richie, *The Films of Akira Kurosawa* (Berkeley, Cal.: University of California Press, 1970).

can be placed virtually anywhere; the film director is not confined to a stationary set with a given number of "walls." The eye-level long shot more or less corresponds to the theatrical proscenium arch. But in movies, the closeup also constitutes a given space—in effect, a cinematic "roomlet" with its own "walls" (the frame). Each shot, then, represents a new given space with different (and temporary) confines. Eisenstein referred to this kind of volume arrangement as the "mise-en-shot." Furthermore, the moveable camera permits the director to rearrange the "walls" many times for maximum expressiveness with no sacrifice of clarity. Thus, in film, a character can enter the frame from below, from above, from any side, and from any angle. By dollying or craning, a camera can also take us "into" a set, permitting objects to pass by us. Because of the audience's identification with the camera's lens, the viewer in the cinema is, in a sense, mobile.

Since the stage director's mise-en-scène is confined to the unit of the scene, a certain amount of compromise is inevitable. He or she must combine a maximum of expressiveness with a maximum of clarity—not always an easy task, especially in realistic productions. Film directors have to make fewer compromises of this sort, for they have a greater number of "scene-lets" at their disposal: most movies average well over a thousand shots. The film

**7-14. Publicity photo of *The Scarlet Empress* (U.S.A., 1934).**
*Art direction by Hans Dreier; Décor by Peter Ballbusch and Richard Killorsz; Costumes by Travis Banton; Directed by Josef von Sternberg.*
Expressionist filmmakers like Sternberg were concerned with presenting a subjective, personal vision of reality, one that had no counterpart in the actual world. When asked why he preferred to work with studio sets rather than authentic historical locations, Sternberg replied, "Because I am a poet." This film deals with the life of Catherine the Great, but the costumes, décor, and even the statuary (all closely supervised by the director) owe little to what literally existed in eighteenth-century Russia. Sternberg claimed that he was responsible for the visual style of all his films, regardless of what the credits stated. See also Andrew Sarris, *The Films of Josef von Sternberg* (New York: Museum of Modern Art, 1966); Herman C. Weinberg, *Josef von Sternberg* (New York: Dutton, 1967); and John Baxter, *The Cinema of Josef von Sternberg* (New York: A. S. Barnes, 1971).

*(Paramount Pictures)*

director can give us a half dozen shots of the same object—some emphasizing clarity, others emphasizing expressiveness. Some shots can show a character with his back to the camera: the sound track guarantees the clarity of his speech. A character can be photographed through an obstruction of some kind—a pane of glass, or the dense foliage of a forest. Eisenstein occasionally had one actor block out another by having the first stand before the camera. Such "impediments" are usually employed for symbolic reasons, but since the cinematic shot need not be lengthy, clarity can be suspended temporarily in favor of expressiveness.

These generalizations are postulated upon the assumption that the stage is essentially realistic in its handling of time and space, whereas the cinema is basically expressionistic. But the differences are relative, of course. Indeed, a good argument could be made that Strindberg's expressionistic plays—*The Dream Play*, for example—are more fragmented and subjective than a realistic movie like Keaton's *Steamboat Bill, Jr.* which emphasizes the continuity of time and space. Certainly it's true that most realistic film directors (like the Italian neorealists, for example) treat time and space theatrically, while some expressionistic dramatists (the Absurdists, for example) handle time and space cinematically. In each case, however, we use the terms "theatrical" and "cinematic" as metaphors: when all is said, the differences in time and space remain fundamental.

In adapting a stage play, the filmmaker is confronted with thousands of choices, petty and monumental, which can alter the original in ways never dreamed of by the original dramatist. Even with classic texts, a filmmaker can

*(Janus Films)*

**7-15. *Richard III* (Great Britain, 1955).**
*With Laurence Olivier; Directed by Olivier.*
In adapting a play to the screen, the filmmaker places the camera according to the proxemic implications of the dialogue. When the action is essentially private and intimate, the camera moves closer to exclude any visual distractions. Since the character is vulnerable, he's photographed from a high angle. On the stage these ideas are generally communicated with lights and through the actors' voices. See also John Cottrell, *Laurence Olivier* (Englewood Cliffs, N.J.: Prentice-Hall, 1975); and Foster Hirsch, *Laurence Olivier* (Boston: G. K. Hall, 1979).

*(Cinerama Releasing)*

**7-16. *The Trojan Women* (Greece, 1971).**
*With Vanessa Redgrave; Directed by Michael Cacoyannis.*
Too often Greek tragedies are presented on stage as bloodless academic exercises, drained of their savage power. By transferring the action of Euripides' play to authentic locations, Cacoyannis was able to recapture much of the raw energy of the original. In ancient Greece, dramas were enacted in outdoor amphitheatres, though of course they lacked the expansiveness and realism of an entire countryside. Cacoyannis is the foremost filmmaker of Greece, much admired for his adaptations of ancient and modern Greek authors. This film is the second of his Euripides Trilogy, which began with *Electra* (1962) and concluded with *Iphigenia* (1977).

**7-17. *King Lear* (Great Britain, 1971).**
*Art design by Georges Wakhevitch; Directed by Peter Brook.*
In adapting plays to movies, the filmmaker can expand on an idea only hinted at in the text, and thus enrich the work. Shakespeare's tragedy is characteristically laden with nature imagery—nature most violent. By placing the action of the play in a harsh northern climate, Brook synthesized and transformed these literary images into a powerful visual statement. When old Lear is buffeted by a tempest in this film, his howl is all but drowned out by the sleet and raging winds. See also Roger Manvell, *Shakespeare and the Film* (New York: Praeger, 1971); and "Shakespeare on Film," a special issue of *Literature/Film Quarterly* (Fall 1973).

*(Athena-Laterna Films)*

emphasize the psychological (7-15), the social (7-16), or the epic (7-17), since these are determined in large measure by the way space is used in movies. A filmmaker can stage the action on studio sets or in a natural setting, but the choice will significantly alter the meaning of the work. In short, the filmmaker enjoys an awesome freedom. D. W. Griffith was among the first to extol the medium's extraordinary range of expression: "The motion picture, although a growth of only a few years, is boundless in its scope and endless in its possibilities. The whole world is its stage, and time without end its limitations."

## Settings and Décor

In the best movies and stage productions, settings are not merely backdrops for the action, but symbolic extensions of the theme and characterization. Settings can convey an immense amount of information, especially in the cinema. Stage sets are generally less detailed than film sets, for the audience is too distant from the stage to perceive many small details. The director in this medium must generally work with fewer sets, usually one per act. Inevitably the stage director must settle for less precision and variety than most screen directors who have virtually no limits of this kind, especially when shooting on location.

Spatial considerations force the stage director to make constant compromises with his sets. If he uses too much of the upstage (rear) area, the audience wouldn't be able to see or hear well. If he uses high platforms to give an actor dominance, the director then has the problem of getting the actor back on the main level quickly and plausibly. The stage director must also use a constant-sized space; settings, therefore, are confined to "long shots." If he wants to suggest a vast field, for example, he must resort to certain conventions. He can stage an action in such a way as to suggest that the playing area is only a small corner of the field. Or he can stylize his set with the aid of a cyclorama which gives the illusion of a vast sky in the background. If he wants to suggest a confined area, he can do so only for short periods, for an audience grows restless when actors are restricted to a small playing area for long periods. Stage directors can use vertical, horizontal, and oblique lines in a set to suggest psychological states; but unlike the film director, these lines (or colors or objects) cannot be cut out in scenes or speeches where they are inappropriate.

The film director has far more freedom in his use of settings. Most importantly, of course, the cinema permits a director to shoot out-of-doors—an enormous advantage. The major works of a number of great directors would have been impossible without this freedom: Griffith, Eisenstein, Keaton, Kurosawa, Antonioni, Huston, De Sica, Renoir (7-18). Antonioni often structures his films around a location. In *Red Desert*, for example, the main "character" of the film is really the polluted industrial wastelands of Ravenna, a northern Italian city. The middle portion of Antonioni's *Zabriskie*

(Janus Films)

**7-18. *The Rules of the Game* (France, 1939).**
*Directed by Jean Renoir.*
The cinema is particularly suited to dealing with man's relationship with nature—a rare theme in the drama. Renoir's famous movie is technically a comedy of manners, a theatrical genre traditionally associated with sophisticated urban life. Nature is used as a gauge for measuring the degree of artificiality of the characters. But like his celebrated father, the painter Auguste Renoir, Jean Renoir rarely condemned artifice out of hand—it has many captivating charms. See Gerald Mast, *Filmguide to The Rules of the Game* (Bloomington, Ind.: Indiana University Press, 1973); André Bazin, *Jean Renoir* (New York: Delta, 1974); and Leo Braudy, *Jean Renoir: The World of His Films* (Garden City, N.Y.: Doubleday, 1972).

*Point* takes place in Death Valley, which is intended as a symbol of the sterility of contemporary America. Epic films would be virtually impossible without the extreme long shots of vast expanses of land. The poetry in the westerns of John Ford, for example, is largely found in the exquisite photography of the American plains, mountains, and deserts. Other genres, particularly those requiring a degree of stylization or deliberate unreality, have been associated with the studio: musicals, horror films, and many period films. Such genres often stress a kind of magical, sealed-off universe, and images taken from real life tend to clash with these essentially claustrophobic qualities.

However, these are merely generalizations. There are some westerns that have been shot mostly indoors, and some musicals which have been photographed in actual locations. If a location is extravagantly beautiful, there's no reason why a romantic musical can't exploit such a setting. The Paris locations of Minnelli's *Gigi* are a good example of how actual locations can enhance a stylized genre. Similarly, a period film like *Tom Jones* uses a number of London locations. *Rosemary's Baby* is a realistic horror film—that is, the movie attempts to show supernatural elements in everyday life, and director Polanski wisely chose to use real locations whenever possible. In short, it all depends on how it's done. As the French historian Georges Sadoul pointed out: "The dichotomy between the studio and the street, the antithesis between Lumière and Méliès, are false oppositions when one attempts to find in them the solution to the problems of realism and art. Films completely outside time have been shot out of doors; completely realistic films have been shot in the studio."

In set design, as in other aspects of movies, the terms Realism and Expressionism are simply convenient critical labels. Most sets *tend* toward one style or the other, but few are pure examples. For instance, in *Birth of a Nation*, Griffith proudly proclaims that a number of his scenes are historical facsimiles of real places and events—like Ford's Theatre where Lincoln was assassinated, or the signing of the Emancipation Proclamation. These scenes were modeled on actual photographs of the period. Yet Griffith's facsimiles were created in a studio. On the other hand, real locations can be exploited to create a somewhat artificial—expressionistic—effect. For example, in shooting *Ten Days That Shook the World*, Eisenstein had the Winter Palace at his disposal for several months. Yet the images in the movie are baroque: richly textured and formally complex. Although Eisenstein chose actual locations for their authenticity, they are never just picturesque accompaniments to the action. Each shot is carefully *designed*. Each exploits the inherent *form* of the setting, contributing significantly to the emotional impact of the sequence. Realistic or expressionistic?

Realism is never a simple term. In movies it's used to describe a variety of styles. Some critics employ modifiers like "poetic realism," "documentary realism," and "studio realism" to make finer distinctions. The nature of beauty in realism is also a complex issue. Beauty of form is an important component of poetic realism. Movies like *The Children of Paradise* (7-21) and the early works of Fellini, such as *The Nights of Cabiria* (1-15), are handsomely mounted and slightly aestheticized to appeal to our visual sense. Similarly, John Ford shot eight of his westerns in Monument Valley (2-33) because of its spectacular beauty. Among other things, Ford was a great landscape artist. Many realistic films shot in the studio are also slightly stylized to exploit this "incidental" visual beauty.

(a)

**7-19. Production photo of *The Sands of Iwo Jima* (U.S.A., 1949).**
*With John Wayne (front and center); Directed by Allan Dwan.*

Because a studio allows a director more control and precision than an actual location, some filmmakers use the so-called process shot in scenes requiring exterior locations. What this technique involves is the rear projection of a moving image on a translucent screen. Live actors and a portion of a set are placed in front of this screen, and the entire action and background are then photographed by a camera which is synchronized with the rear projector. The finished product (b) looks reasonably authentic, although backgrounds tend to look suspiciously washed out and flat in comparison to foreground elements.

(b)

269

In other realistic films, beauty—in this conventional sense—plays a lesser role. A major criterion of aesthetic value in a movie like Pontecorvo's *Battle of Algiers* (9-4) is its deliberate roughness. The story deals with the struggle for liberation of the Algerian people from their French colonial masters. It was shot entirely in the streets and houses of Algiers. The setting is rarely exploited for its aesthetic beauty. In fact, Pontecorvo's lack of formal organization, his refusal to yield an inch in matters of "style," is his principal virtue as an artist. The moral power of the materials takes precedence over formal considerations. The setting's beauty is in its truth. In films such as these, style (i.e., distortion) is regarded as prettification, a form of insincerity and therefore ugly. Even outright ugliness can be a criterion of aesthetic beauty. The gaudy sets and décor in *Touch of Evil* are organic to the nature of the materials (7-20).

Few directors have been so unrelenting in their mania for realism as John Huston. He insists on staging his films on authentic locations, even if that means a nineteenth-century whaling vessel, as in *Moby Dick*. The project took 35 weeks to shoot—mostly on the open seas. During the production of this movie, actor Richard Basehart broke three bones, Leo Genn slipped a disk in

*(Universal-International)*

**7-20. *Touch of Evil* (U.S.A., 1958).**
*Art direction by Alexander Golitzen and Robert Clatworthy; Directed by Orson Welles.*
Like a filmmaker's other collaborators, art directors gear their style to suit the spirit of the story. The sleazy bordertown setting of this movie required the utmost vulgarity in the art design. But Welles was able to transcend this deliberate bad taste by aestheticizing it—through his masterful control of the camera, the lighting, and the editing. Paradoxically, *Touch of Evil* is a bravura masterpiece of style, yet its materials consist almost exclusively of ugliness. See also Ronald Gottesman, ed., *Focus on Orson Welles* (Englewood Cliffs, N.J.: Prentice-Hall, 1976).

his back and got pneumonia, Gregory Peck damaged his kneecap, and dozens of others were injured at sea. The enormous rubberized whale was lost several times, and the ship's mast snapped three times during turbulent weather. A crucial scene required Peck to be lashed to the back of the huge artificial whale and repeatedly plunged underwater—an extremely dangerous stunt, especially if the crew failed to bring the whale back to the surface in time for Peck to regain his breath. "I could have *really* come up dead," Peck recalled with a shudder, "which I think would have secretly pleased John—providing the last touch of realism he was after."

To the unsympathetic, the cult of realism verges on madness. But there's a method to it. For example, Huston shot *The African Queen* in the tropics because he knew he wouldn't have to worry about a thousand little details, such as how to get the actors to sweat a lot, or how to get their clothes to stick to their bodies. Perhaps the most famous, if not infamous, example of this passion of authenticity is Erich von Stroheim, who detested studio sets. In *Greed,* he insisted that his actors actually live in a seedy boarding house to get the "feel" of the film's low-life setting. He forced them to wear shabby clothing and deprived them of all the amenities that their characters would lack in actuality. Perhaps because of the severe hardships his cast and crew suffered, the movie's authenticity is incontestable.

Not all realists are so fanatical. For example, Billy Wilder has generally preferred the studio to shooting on location because controlled environments produce fewer headaches. He has been brilliantly served by his regular art director Alexandre Trauner. Wilder is concerned only with an effect of realism—it doesn't matter how it's achieved. For instance, in *The Apartment,* Trauner used the principle of a diminishing scale for a vast office set which consists of an endless succession of desks receding into the horizon. At the rear of the set, he placed small-scale desks, with dwarfs as extras. In *Witness for the Prosecution,* Trauner recreated London's Old Bailey Court for Wilder; in *Love in the Afternoon,* an entire floor of Paris' Ritz hotel. Trauner built an exact duplicate of Berlin's Brandenburg Gate (at a cost of $200,000) for *One, Two, Three.* His most elaborate set was the recreation of the Les Halles section of Paris for Wilder's *Irma La Douce,* which included forty-eight buildings and cost $350,000 (see also 7-21).

Spectacle films usually require the most elaborate sets. Historical reconstructions of ancient Rome or Egypt are enormously expensive to build, and they can make or break a film in this genre because spectacle is the major attraction. Perhaps the most famous sets of this type are found in the Babylonian story of Griffith's *Intolerance* (1-7). The unprecedented monumentality of these sets is what skyrocketed Griffith's budget to an all-time high of $1.9 million—an astronomical figure by 1916 standards, hefty even by today's. The banquet scene for Belshazzar's feast alone cost a reputed $250,000 and employed over 4000 extras. The story required the construction of a walled city, so vast that for years it remained a standing monument—called "Griffith's Folly" by cynics in the trade. The set extended nearly three-quarters of a mile in length. The court was flanked by enormous colonnades supporting pillars 50 feet high, each one supporting a huge statue of an erect elephant-god. Behind the court were towers and ramparts, their tops planted with cascading flowers and exotic trees representing Belshazzar's famous hanging gardens. The outer walls of the city were 200 feet high, yet were wide enough so that

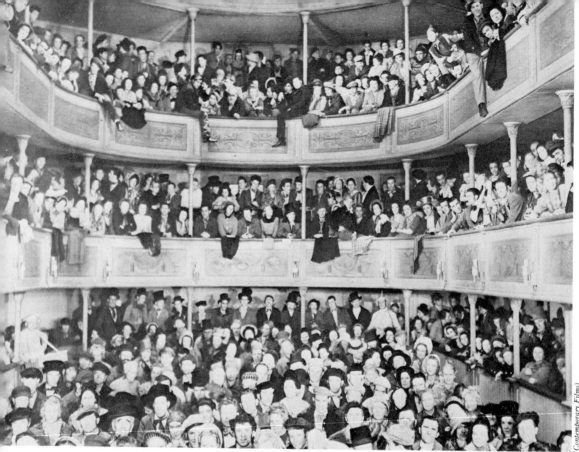

**7-21. *The Children of Paradise* (France, 1945).**
*Art direction by Alexandre Trauner; Directed by Marcel Carné.*
Trauner is France's greatest designer and one of the most versatile. He has been equally at home with such realistic films as Zinnemann's *The Nun's Story* and Huston's fanciful Kipling adaptation *The Man Who Would Be King*. His baroque sets for Welles' *Othello* are stunning. In his early years, he designed for such important French directors as René Clair (*Le Million*) and Jacques Feyder (*Carnival in Flanders*). Trauner was the art director for nine of the movies of Carné (most of them written by Jacques Prévert), including *Port of Shadows*, *Le Jour se Lève*, and *Les Visiteurs du Soir*—all of them, like *The Children of Paradise*, emphasizing a poetic realism. The visual style of this film was inspired by the prints of Daumier. Trauner's sets are often enormous, like the interior of a nineteenth-century theatre (pictured), and the sprawling Boulevard du Crime, with its teaming masses of humanity. Since the 1950s, Trauner has worked mostly for American filmmakers, especially Billy Wilder.

two chariots were able to roar past each other on the road that perched on top. Astonishingly, this and other sets in the film were built without architectural plans. As Griffith kept making additional suggestions, his art director, Frank "Huck" Wortman, and his crew kept expanding the set from day to day.

Expressionistic sets are usually created in the studio where the contaminations of reality cannot penetrate. (7-22) Magic, not realism, is the aim. Méliès is the prototypical example (10-1). He was called "the Jules Verne of films" because his feats of prestidigitation astonished the public. The first in a long line of special effects wizards, Méliès usually painted his sets, often with

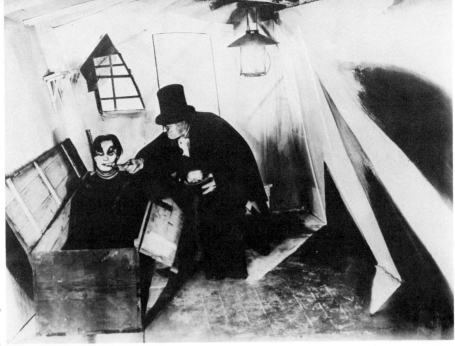

**7-22. *The Cabinet of Dr. Caligari* (Germany, 1919).**
*With Conrad Veidt and Werner Krauss (wearing hat); Production design by Hermann Warm, Walter Röhrig, and Walter Reimann; Directed by Robert Wiene.*
The German Expressionist movement of the post-World War I era emphasized visual design above all. The movement's main contributions were in the live theatre, the graphic arts, and the cinema. The great stage director Max Reinhardt was a seminal influence. In his theory of design, Reinhardt advocated an ideal of "landscapes imbued with soul." The declared aim of most German Expressionists was to eliminate nature for a state of absolute abstraction. It is a style steeped in anxiety and terror. The sets are deliberately artificial: flat, obviously painted, with no attempt to preserve the conventions of perspective and scale. They are meant to represent a state of mind, not a place. The lighting and set designs are carefully coordinated, with one shading off into the other. A tortured hallucinatory atmosphere is evoked by the twisted shapes that violate the surface of the image. Horizontal and vertical lines are avoided in favor of diagonals which produce a sense of instability and visual anguish. The jerky, machinelike acting is meant to convey the essence of depersonalization. In the cinema, the German Expressionist movement lasted only from 1919 to 1923, but its influence has been enormous, especially in the United States. See Lotte H. Eisner, *The Haunted Screen: Expressionism in the German Cinema and the Influence of Max Reinhardt* (Berkeley, Cal.: University of California Press, 1973), a copiously illustrated critical study.

*trompe-l'oeil* perspectives to suggest depth. He combined live actors with fanciful settings to produce a dreamlike atmosphere. He used animation, miniatures, and a wide range of optical tricks, charming his audiences with vistas of imaginary realms. He was the artistic godfather of the German Expressionists and the French Surrealists, not to speak of such contemporary sorcerers as Stanley Kubrick (*2001*) and George Lucas (*Star Wars*).

Expressionistic sets appeal to our sense of the marvellous. The work of Danilo Donati, Italy's best-known designer, is a good example. The extravagance and exquisite artificiality of the sets and costumes in such movies as Fellini's *Satyricon, Amarcord,* and *Casanova* are pure products of the imagination—Fellini's as well as Donati's. The director often provides his designer with preliminary sketches, and the two artists work closely in determining the visual design of each film. Their conjurations can be moving, as well as witty and beautiful. For example, *Amarcord* is a stylized reminiscence of Fellini's youth in his home town of Rimini. (The title, from the Romagnan dialect, means "I remember.") But Fellini shot the movie in a studio, not on location. He wanted to capture feelings, not facts (7-23). Throughout the film, the townspeople feel stifled by the provincial isolation of their community. They are filled with loneliness, and long for something extraordinary to transform their lives. When they hear that a mammoth luxury liner, the "Rex," will pass through the ocean waters a few miles beyond the town's shore,

*(New World Pictures)*

**7-23. *Amarcord* (Italy, 1973).**
*Art direction and costumes by Danilo Donati; Cinematography by Giuseppe Rotunno; Directed by Federico Fellini.*
For Fellini, who began his career as a realist, the studio has become a place to create magic—along with his fellow magicians Donati and Rotunno. "To me and other directors like me," Fellini has said, "the cinema is a way of interpreting and remaking reality through fantasy and imagination. The use of the studio is an indispensable part of what we are doing." Donati is perhaps the foremost expressionist designer of the contemporary cinema. His style is so intimately associated with Fellini that it's difficult to know where one sensibility leaves off and the other begins. Rotunno is also a major contributor to this unique vision which combines elements from comic strips, adolescent sexual fantasies, the circus, old 1930s movies, and a Catholic High Mass. See also Louis D. Giannetti, "*Amarcord:* The Impure Art of Federico Fellini," in *The Western Humanities Review* (Spring 1976).

many of these wistful souls decide to row out to sea to greet the ship. Hundreds of them crowd into every available boat and stream away from the beach like fervent pilgrims on a quest. Then they wait. Evening settles, bringing with it a thick fog. Still they wait. In one boat, Gradisca, the charming town sexpot, confides to some sympathetic friends of her dissatisfaction with her life. At thirty she is still single, childless, and unfulfilled. Her "heart overflows with love," yet she has never found a "truly dedicated man." In the dark silence, she weeps softly over the prospect of a barren future. Midnight passes, and still the townspeople wait faithfully. Then, when most of the characters are sleeping in their fragile boats, they're awakened by a boy's shout: "It's here!" Like a graceful apparition, the light-bedecked "Rex" glides past in all its regal grandeur. Nino Rota's rapturous music swells to a crescendo as the townspeople wave and shout joyously. Gradisca's eyes stream with tears of exhilaration and yearning while a blind accordionist asks excitedly, "Tell me what it looks like!" Then, as mysteriously as it appeared, the phantom ship is swallowed by the fog, and slips silently off into the night.

During the golden age of the Hollywood studio system, each of the majors had a characteristic visual style, determined in large part by the designers at each studio. Some were called production designers, others art directors, a few simply set designers. Their job was to determine the "look" of each film, and they worked closely with producers and directors to assure that the sets, décor, costumes, and photographic style were coordinated to produce a unified effect. For example, MGM specialized in glamor, luxury, and opulent production values, and their art director Cedric Gibbons virtually stamped each film with "the Metro look" (7-24). Since all of the studios attempted to diversify their products as much as possible, however, their art directors had to be versatile. For instance, RKO's Van Nest Polglase super-

(MGM)

**7-24. Grand Hotel (U.S.A., 1932).**
*With Greta Garbo; Art direction by Cedric Gibbons; Gowns by Adrian; Directed by Edmund Goulding.*
MGM, "the Tiffany of studios," prided itself on its opulent and glossy production values. It was the most prosperous studio in Hollywood in the 1930s, boasting twenty-three sound stages and 117 acres of standing backlots, which included a small lake, a harbor, a park, a miniature jungle, and many streets of houses in different periods and styles. The "Metro look" was largely determined by Gibbons who was the studio's art director from 1924 to 1956. See John Douglas Eames, *The MGM Story* (New York: Crown, 1976); and Bosley Crowther, *The Lion's Share* (New York: Dutton, 1957).

(RKO)

**7-25. *Citizen Kane* (U.S.A., 1941).**
*With Orson Welles and Ruth Warrick; Art direction by Van Nest Polglase and Perry Ferguson; Directed by Welles.*
Polglase was RKO's supervising art director from 1932 to 1942 and was highly admired for his inventiveness and style. Like most studio art directors, his job was essentially advisory and administrative. The actual designing was executed primarily by a unit art director, like Ferguson. RKO was famous for its big white sets and its use of Art Deco designs, as in the Astaire–Rogers musicals. Polglase, who established the studio's "look" in the 1930s, was strongly influenced by the UFA style, especially in his fondness for monumentality, unusual sources of light, and tense juxtapositions between curved and straight lines. See also Pauline Kael, *The Citizen Kane Book* (Boston: Little, Brown, 1971).

**7-26. Production photo of *Monte Carlo* (U.S.A., 1930).**
*Set design by Hans Dreier; Directed by Ernst Lubitsch.*
The lights for movies are generally mounted from above, and must be carefully coordinated with the sets and camera. If the camera must travel through a set, the designer often uses "wild walls"—that is, walls which can be removed while the camera is in motion. If only a portion of a setting is required, as in this shot, the designer concerns himself only with what will be in view of the camera. (Note how this set consists primarily of a back wall and gambling tables.) Of course this economy presupposes that the director knows exactly what he wants, which is not always the case. Many like to improvise with their sets and don't decide on their camera setups until they see the actors in rehearsal. Lubitsch worked from very detailed scripts and knew every shot in advance. His sets were famous for their elegance and polish, thanks largely to Paramount's gifted art director Dreier. Paramount was a sister studio of Germany's famous UFA, and Dreier, like many Paramount regulars, was German-trained. See also Neil D. Isaacs, "Lubitsch and the Filmed-Play Syndrome," in *Literature/Film Quarterly* (Fall 1975); and Robert L. Carringer and Barry Sabath, *Ernst Lubitsch: A Guide to References and Resources* (Boston: G. K. Hall, 1978).

vised the design of such diverse movies as *King Kong, Top Hat, The Informer,* and *Citizen Kane* (7-25). Paramount's Hans Dreier began his career at Germany's famous UFA studio (7-26). He was usually at his best in creating a sense of mystery and romantic fantasy, as in the films of Josef von Sternberg. Dreier also designed the superb Art Deco sets for Lubitsch's *Trouble in Paradise,* as well as the atrocious (deliberate) Hollywood "villa" in Wilder's *Sunset Boulevard.* Warner Brothers' art director, Anton Grot, was a specialist in grubby, realistic locales (7-27). The studio claimed that its films were "Torn from Today's Headlines!" to quote from its publicity blurbs. Warners favored

**7-27. *Little Caesar* (U.S.A., 1930).**
*With Edward G. Robinson (standing); Art direction by Anton Grot; Directed by Mervyn LeRoy.*
Grot was art director at Warners from 1927 to 1948. Unlike his counterparts Gibbons, Dreier, and Polglase, however, Grot often took an active hand in designing the studio's major films. His earliest work is somewhat in the German Expressionist tradition, but he soon became one of the most versatile of artists. He designed films like the gritty and realistic *Little Caesar,* as well as the Busby Berkeley musical *Gold Diggers of 1933,* with its surrealistic, dreamlike sets (10-14). See also Donald Deschner, "Anton Grot, Warners Art Director," in *The Velvet Light Trap* (Fall, 1975); Charles Higham, *Warner Brothers* (New York: Scribners, 1975); and James R. Silke, *Here's Looking at You, Kid* (Boston: Little, Brown, 1976).

*(Warner Brothers)*

topical genres with an emphasis on working-class life: gangster films, urban melodramas, and proletarian musicals. Like his counterparts at other studios, however, Grot could work in a variety of styles and genres. For example, he designed the enchanting sets for *A Midsummer Night's Dream.* Unfortunately, there's not much else in this movie that's enchanting.

Certain types of locales were in such constant demand that the studios constructed permanent backlot sets which were used in film after film: a turn-of-the-century street, a European square, an urban slum, and so on. Of course these were suitably altered with new furnishings to make them look different each time they were used. The studio with the largest number of backlots was MGM, although Warners, Paramount, and Twentieth Century-Fox also boasted a considerable number of them. Not all standing sets were located close to the studio. It was cheaper to construct some outside the environs of Los Angeles where real estate values weren't at a premium. If a movie called for a huge realistic set—like the Welsh mining village for *How Green Was My Valley*—it was often built miles away from the studio, although

**7-28. How Green Was My Valley (U.S.A., 1941).**
*Art direction by Nathan Juran and Richard Day; Directed by John Ford.*
The art directors at Twentieth Century-Fox specialized in realistic sets, like this turn-of-the-century Welsh mining village which covered over eighty-six acres and was built in a California valley. Elaborate sets like these were not always dismantled after production, for with suitable alterations, they could be converted into other locations. For example, two years after Ford's film, this set was transformed into a Nazi-occupied Norwegian village for *The Moon is Down*.

not so far as the real thing (7-28). Similarly, most of the studios owned western frontier towns, ranches, and midwestern type farms which were located outside the Los Angeles area.

What matters most in a setting is how it embodies the essence of the story materials and the artistic vision of the filmmaker. As the British designer Robert Mallet-Stevens noted: "A film set, in order to be a good set, must act. Whether realistic or expressionistic, modern or ancient, it must play its part. The set must present the character before he has even appeared. It must indicate his social position, his tastes, his habits, his life style, his personality. The sets must be intimately linked with the action." Settings can also be used to suggest a sense of progression in the characters. For example, in Fellini's *La Strada*, one of his most realistic movies, the protagonist and his simple-minded assistant are shown as reasonably happy, travelling together from town to town with their tacky theatrical act. After he abandons her, he heads for the mountains. Gradually, the landscape changes: trees are stripped of their foliage, snow and dirty slush cover the ground, the sky is a murky gray. The

(Museum of Modern Art)

**7-29.** *Stairway to Heaven* [British title: *A Matter of Life and Death*] (Great Britain, 1947).
*Set design by Alfred Junge; Directed by Michael Powell and Emeric Pressburger.*
The German-born and trained Junge did more for the reputation of British set design than any Englishman of his generation. From 1923 to 1928 he worked in his native land. He moved to London in 1932, where he remained until the end of his career in 1957. The influence of surrealism is strong in his work. His sets are economical, highlighting a few carefully chosen elements, and suppressing all irrelevant details.

changing setting is a gauge of the protagonist's spiritual condition: nature itself seems to grieve after the helpless assistant is left alone to die.

On the stage, a setting is generally admired with the opening of the curtain, then forgotten as the actors take over the center of interest. In the movies, a director can keep cutting back to the setting to remind the audience of its significance. A setting can even be likened to a character—like Kane's opulent palace, Xanadu, in *Citizen Kane.* The lavish estate is used to externalize Kane's fantastic wealth and growing dominance over others. During the course of his life, he keeps adding more and more clutter to the palace. Even his second wife is essentially an object to be stored in his vast warehouse. The castle is a bizarre mixture of styles and periods—just as Kane's personality is an inconsistent blend of psychological contradictions. Finally, the mansion becomes a grotesque prison, for Kane discovers too late that a man can become possessed by his possessions.

A film can fragment a set into a series of shots, now emphasizing one aspect of a room, later another, depending upon the needs of the director in

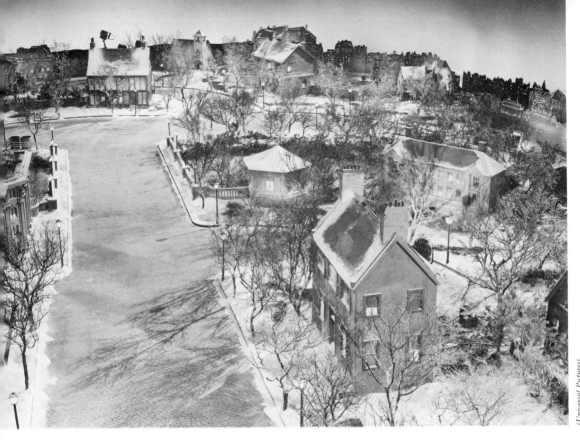

**7-30. Miniature set for *Letter From an Unknown Woman* (U.S.A., 1948).**
*Directed by Max Ophüls.*
Period films often benefit from the slight sense of unreality of studio sets. If a set is needed only for establishing purposes, miniatures are often constructed. These scaled-down sets can be as tall as 6 or 8 feet, depending on the amount of detail and realism needed. Note the two studio flood lights behind the houses of this miniature, and the flat, two-dimensional apartment dwellings on the horizon in the upper right.

finding appropriate visual analogues for thematic and psychological ideas. In Losey's *The Servant*, a stairway is used as a major thematic symbol. The film deals with a servant's gradual control over his master. Losey uses the stairway as a kind of psychological battlefield where the relative positions of the two men on the stairs give the audience a sense of who's winning the battle. Losey also uses the rails on the stairway to suggest prison bars: the master of the house is often photographed from behind these bars. In John Frankenheimer's *All Fall Down*, the separate rooms and corridors of a house are used to suggest the emotional fragmentation of a family. The father is usually seen in the cellar, the mother on the ground floor, the two sons in the upper bedrooms.

Even the furniture of a room can be exploited for psychological and thematic reasons. In one of his classes, Eisenstein once discussed at length the significance of a table for a set. The class exercise centered on an adaptation of Balzac's novel *Père Goriot*. The scene is set at a dinner table which Balzac described as circular. But Eisenstein convincingly argued that a round table is wrong cinematically, for it implies equality, with each person linked in a circle. To convey the stratified class structure of the boarding house, Eisenstein suggested the use of a long rectangular table, with the haughty mistress of the house at the head, the favored tenants close to her sides, and the lowly Goriot alone, near the base of the table.

Such attention to the details of a set often distinguishes a master of film from a mere technician who settles for only a general effect. In fact, some directors feel that the set is so important they will even construct different versions for a separate shot. In *The Graduate*, Mike Nichols wanted to emphasize the sudden sense of humiliation of Anne Bancroft when she is betrayed by Dustin Hoffman. To convey the effect more forcefully, a separate set was constructed with an oversized doorway towering above her. With the camera at a high angle, a vast expanse of white wall to one side, and a huge empty doorway at the other side, Bancroft was literally reduced to insignificance.

The setting of a movie—far more than any play—can even take over as the central interest. In Kubrick's *2001*, the director spends most of his time lovingly photographing the instruments of a spaceship, various space stations, and the enormous expanses of outer space itself. The few people in the movie

**7-31. Ugetsu (Japan, 1953).**
*With Masayuki Mori (left) and Machiko Kyo; Set design by Itoh Kisaku and Kosabura Kakajima; Directed by Kenji Mizoguchi.*
In the Japanese cinema, eroticism is usually aestheticized rather than presented explicitly. The ravishing sets and Kazuo Miyagawa's evocative cinematography combine to produce a haunting, diaphanous atmosphere in Mizoguchi's fable of erring manhood. See also Joan Mellen, *Voices from the Japanese Cinema* (New York: Liveright, 1975).

(Janus Films)

seem almost incidental and certainly far less interesting than the real center of concern—the setting. It would be impossible to produce *2001* on stage: the materials of the film are not theatrically convertible. Kubrick's film, like many others, is a vivid embodiment of Bazin's observation, quoted at the head of this chapter.

## Costumes and Makeup

In the most sensitive films and plays, costumes and makeup aren't merely frills added to enhance an illusion, but aspects of character and theme (7-32). Their style can reveal class, self-image, even psychological states. In Jack Clayton's *The Pumpkin Eater,* the hair styles and costumes of the heroine (Anne Bancroft) are used to convey her sense of freedom or confinement.

**7-32. *The Leopard* (Italy, 1963).**
*With Rina Morelli (center); Art direction by Mario Garbuglia; Costumes by Piero Tosi; Directed by Luchino Visconti.*
Visconti had the unusual distinction of being both a Marxist and an aristocrat (he was the Duke of Modrone). A master of the period film, he was exceptionally sensitive to the symbolic significance of costumes and décor. They are part of Visconti's political statement. For example, the clutter, texture, and florid patterns of the Victorian furnishings in this movie suggest a stifling, hot-house artificiality, sealed off from nature. The costumes, impeccably accurate to period, are elegant, constricting, and totally without utility. They were meant to be. Idle people of independent income—that is, income derived from the labor of others—rarely concern themselves with utility in clothing.

**7-33.** *Juliet of the Spirits* **(Italy, 1965).**
*Art direction and costumes by Piero Gherardi; Directed by Federico Fellini.*
"A costume is a state of mind," Gherardi has said. His designs for Fellini represent his most delerious state, for they are filled with whimsy and malicious wit. Throughout the film, Fellini contrasts a bevy of gaudy females with his protagonist (Giulietta Masina, extreme right). She is a woman of simplicity and directness, qualities emphasized by her more conventional mode of dress.

Whenever she's happy—usually when she is pregnant or with her young children—her costumes are casual and a bit sloppy, her hair loose and wild. When she feels unhappy and useless, her costumes are neat, fashionable, yet oddly sterile. One especially effective outfit of this sort is a smart tailored suit and a severe Garbo-type hat which conceals her hair. The effect is somewhat like a chic straitjacket.

Depending upon their cut, texture, and bulk, certain costumes can suggest agitation, fastidiousness, delicacy, dignity, and so on. A costume, then, is a medium, especially in the cinema where a closeup of a fabric can suggest information that's independent even of the wearer. One of the directors most sensitive to the meanings of costumes was Sergei Eisenstein. In his *Alexander Nevsky*, the invading German hordes are made terrifying primarily through their costumes. The soldiers' helmets, for example, don't reveal the eyes: two sinister slits are cut into the fronts of the metal helmets. Their inhumanity is

**7-34. *Frankenstein* (U.S.A., 1931).**
*With Boris Karloff and Dwight Frye; Makeup by Jack Pierce; Directed by James Whale.*
The horror film was one of Universal Pictures' specialties. The genre often entails elaborate makeup problems. Pierce's monster makeup for Karloff took hours to prepare and apply. Note the distortion of the set and lights in this shot. (The horror film has its stylistic roots in German Expressionism.) See also Roy Huss and T. J. Ross, eds., *Focus on the Horror Film* (Englewood Cliffs, N.J.: Prentice-Hall, 1972).

further emphasized by the animal claws and horns the officers have at the top of their helmets as insignia. The highly ornate armor they wear suggests their decadence and machinelike impersonality. An evil churchman is costumed in a black monk's habit: the sinister hood throws most of his hawklike features into darkness. In contrast, Nevsky and the Russian peasants are costumed in loose and flowing garments. Even their war armor reflects a warm, humane quality. Their helmets are shaped like Russian church onion domes and permit most of the features of the face to be seen. Their chain mail reminds the viewer of the fishing nets of the earlier portions of the movie where the peasants are shown happiest at their work repairing their fishing apparatus. In Eisenstein's *Ivan the Terrible*, the evil boyars are portrayed as animallike, especially the boyar princess whose bulky black headdress, cape, and dress suggest a huge, sinister vulture. Ivan, on the other hand, is Christ-like (at least

(RKO)

**7-35. Publicity photo of Bette Davis in *The Little Foxes* (U.S.A., 1941).**
*Costumes by Orry-Kelly; Makeup by Perc Westmore; Directed by William Wyler.*
Although Davis prided herself on the diversity of her roles, she was most famous for playing bitches—women who refuse to allow their wills to be thwarted. Her bravura style was intensely physical, punctuated with abrupt, restless movements. Her gestures were almost always decisive, razor-sharp. For example, she didn't just smoke a cigarette, she attacked it, inhaling deeply while her nervous darting eyes sized up her opponent. Even when she was still, her hands often clenched and unclenched at the sides of her tense body. Her speech was fast, brittle, the words spewed out in a precise, clipped, diction. She was one of the few stars of her era who enjoyed playing villainess roles. The character of Regina Giddens in *The Little Foxes* is essentially in this same mold, but the setting of the story—the American South in 1900—precluded the possibility of her using such mannerisms. Regina's fury had to be internalized. Her exterior conforms to the bourgeois ideal of womanhood in the Gibson era, but her exterior conceals a spirit smoldering in resentment. Her body is imprisoned in tightly corseted gowns, restricting her freedom. Her face is powdered to a ghostly pallor, her mouth a cruel slash of red. It is a masklike face, with only the hooded eyes betraying her contempt for weakness, especially in men. See also Bette Davis, *The Lonely Life* (New York: Putnam's, 1962); and Frank Westmore and Murial Davidson, *The Westmores of Hollywood* (New York: Berkley Medallion, 1976).

in the first half of this two-part film), with his simple flowing hair, beard, and unpretentious white robes.

Color symbolism is used by Zeffirelli in *Romeo and Juliet.* Juliet's family, the Capulets, are characterized as aggressive parvenues: their colors are appropriately rich reds, yellows, and oranges. Romeo's family, on the other hand, is older and perhaps more established, but in obvious decline. They are costumed in blues, deep greens, and purples. These two color schemes are echoed in the liveries of the servants of each house, which helps the audience identify the combatants in the brawling scenes. The color of the costumes can also be used to suggest change and transition. The first view of Juliet, for example, shows her in a vibrant red dress. After she marries Romeo, her colors are in the blue spectrum. Line as well as color can be used to suggest psychological qualities. Verticals, for example, tend to emphasize stateliness and dignity (Lady Montague); horizontal lines tend to emphasize earthiness and comicality (Juliet's nurse).

Perhaps the most famous costume in film history is Chaplin's Charlie the tramp outfit. The costume is an indication of both class and character, conveying the complex mixture of vanity and dash that makes Charlie so appealing. The moustache, derby hat, and cane all suggest the fastidious dandy. The cane is used to give the impression of self-importance as Charlie swaggers confidently before a hostile world. But the baggy trousers several sizes too large, the oversized shoes, the too-tight coat—all these suggest Charlie's insignificance and poverty. Chaplin's view of mankind is symbolized by that costume: self-deceived, vain, absurd, and—finally—poignantly vulnerable.

Makeup in the cinema is generally more subtle than on stage. The theatrical actor uses makeup primarily to enlarge his features so that they'll be visible from long distances. On the screen, makeup tends to be more understated, although Chaplin used stage makeup for the tramp character since he was generally photographed in long shot. Even the most delicate changes in

(*United Artists*)

**7-36.** *Apocalypse Now* **(U.S.A., 1979).**
*With Martin Sheen; Art direction by Dean Tavoularis; Directed by Francis Ford Coppola.*
This film might almost be viewed as Coppola's *Inferno,* a descent into the hell of Vietnam. It draws heavily on primitive rites and myths. The décor, costumes, and makeup suggest a degeneration into savagery. Yet for all its horror, the eerie visual style is seductive in its primordial beauty.

makeup can be perceived in the cinema. Mia Farrow's pale green face in Polanski's *Rosemary's Baby,* for example, was used to suggest the progressive corruption of her body while she is pregnant with the devil's child. Similarly, the ghoulish makeup of the actors in Fellini's *Satyricon* suggests the degeneracy and death-in-life aspect of the Roman population of the period. In *The Graduate,* Anne Bancroft is almost chalk white in the scene where she is betrayed by her lover.

In *Tom Jones,* Richardson used elaborate, artificial makeup on the city characters like Lady Bellaston to suggest their deceitfulness and decadence. (In the eighteenth-century comedy of manners, cosmetics are a favorite source of imagery to suggest falseness and hypocrisy.) The country characters, on the other hand, especially Sophy Weston, are more naturally made up with no wigs, powder, and patches. In Richardson's *Joseph Andrews* (also based on a novel by Henry Fielding), the makeup is much more whorish. If *Tom Jones* suggests Boucher and Sir Joshua Reynolds, *Joseph Andrews* recalls Hogarth.

Cinematic makeup is closely associated with the type of performer wearing it. In general, stars prefer makeup that tends to glamorize them. Monroe, Garbo, and Harlow usually had an ethereal quality (see 6-12, 6-13, 6-15). Marlene Dietrich probably knew more about makeup than any star of her generation—glamor makeup that is (7-37). Straight actors and actor/stars are

*(Paramount Pictures)*

**7-37. Publicity photo of Marlene Dietrich in *Blonde Venus* (U.S.A., 1932).**
*Directed by Josef von Sternberg.*
Dietrich and Sternberg were amused by the Trilby-Svengali publicity put out by Paramount Pictures where they made a number of films together in the 1930s. The publicity had some basis in fact, for the director used her as a virtual medium, like a musician and his instrument. But no matter how preposterously she was wigged and costumed, he usually preserved her shimmering, ethereal beauty. Hers is an example of star makeup at its most glamorous. The exquisite Dietrich face, with its perfect bone structure, was heightened by Sternberg's painstaking calculation. See also John Kobal, *Marlene Dietrich* (London: Studio Vista, 1968); and Charles Higham, *Marlene* (New York: Pocket Books, 1977).

less concerned with glamor unless the characters they're playing are in fact glamorous. In an effort to submerge their own personalities, such performers often use makeup to disfigure the familiarity of their features. Brando and Olivier are particularly likely to wear false noses, wigs, and distorting cosmetics. Because Orson Welles is known primarily for playing strong domineering roles, he has resorted to such tricks in makeup to maximize the differences between his roles. Nonprofessional players probably wear the least amount of makeup, since they're chosen precisely because of their interesting and authentic physical appearance (6-28).

## Further Reading

BARSACQ, LÉON, *Caligari's Cabinets and Other Grand Illusions: A History of Film Design* (New York: New American Library, 1978). Copiously illustrated, written by a distinguished French Designer.

CARRICK, EDWARD, *Designing for Moving Pictures* (London: Studio, 1947). Sensible, somewhat outdated.

CHIERICHETTI, DAVID, *Hollywood Costume Design* (New York: Harmony Books, 1976). Copiously illustrated.

FIELDING, RAYMOND, *The Technique of Special Effects Cinematography* (New York: Hastings House, 1972). A standard scholarly source.

HURT, JAMES, ed., *Focus on Film and Theatre* (Englewood Cliffs, N.J.: Prentice-Hall, 1975). A collection of articles.

LEESE, ELIZABETH, *Costume Design in the Movies* (New York: Ungar, 1978).

McCONATHY, DALE, and DIANA VREELAND, *Hollywood Costume* (Englewood Cliffs, N.J.: Prentice-Hall, 1977). Lavishly illustrated.

NICOLL, ALLARDYCE, *Film and Theatre* (New York: Crowell, 1936). An early standard work.

PANOVSKY, ERWIN, "Style and Medium in the Moving Pictures" in *Film: An Anthology,* Daniel Talbot, ed. (Berkeley: University of California Press, 1966). A classic essay.

ROACH, MARY ELLEN, and JOANNE BUBOLZ EICHER, *Dress, Adornment, and the Social Order* (New York: John Wiley and Sons, 1965). A collection of articles.

## 8

*"The filmmaker/author writes with his camera as a writer writes with his pen."*

ALEXANDRE ASTRUC

# LITERATURE

It's been variously estimated that from one-fourth to one-fifth of all feature films have been literary adaptations. Nor has the relationship between movies and literature been one way; many commentators have remarked upon the cinematic qualities of much modern fiction and poetry, including Joyce's *Ulysses* and Eliot's "The Love Song of J. Alfred Prufrock." The relationship between these two mediums can be traced back almost to film's infancy. At the turn of the century, George Méliès was using literary sources as a basis for several of his movies. Griffith claimed that many of his cinematic innovations were in fact taken directly from the pages of Dickens. In his essay, "Dickens, Griffith, and the Film Today," Eisenstein shows how Dickens' novels provided Griffith with a number of techniques, including equivalents to fades, dissolves, frame compositions, the breakdown into shots, special modifying lenses, and—most importantly—the concept of parallel editing.

## The Writer

Perhaps more than any of the director's other collaborators, the script writer has been brought forward from time to time as the main "author" of a film. After all, writers are generally responsible for the dialogue, they outline most of the action (sometimes in great detail), and they often set forth the main theme of a movie. Particularly after the advent of sound when film scripts

**8-1. *Modern Times* (U.S.A., 1936).**
*With Charles Chaplin; Directed by Chaplin.*
Some movies are centered on character and theme rather than story. Chaplin's silent features are episodic, unified by the nearly continual presence of the Tramp—a vagabond and wanderer. Like the protagonist of a picaresque novel, the Tramp is constantly in search of novelty. This characteristic necessarily precludes the likelihood of a single locale or occupation, an overriding goal, or a permanent relationship. The only constant in his life is the open road. Many movies employ a journey structure. Road films often take the form of a quest, a search, or a chase. Most of Chaplin's Tramp features are also unified by a central symbolic concept: in *Modern Times,* the governing symbol is machinery. In this sequence, Charlie goes berserk while toiling on an assembly line. In a demented ballet, he whirls and twirls like a loon around the gears and levers of an enormous factory generator, only to be injested by the infernal machine.

became more elaborate, precise, and—most of all—verbal, many established literary figures were attracted to the new audio-visual medium.

Generalizing about the writer's contribution in the movie-making process is an exercise in futility because the writer's role varies immensely from film to film, and from director to director. In the first place, some filmmakers have hardly bothered with scripts. Especially in the silent era, improvisation was the rule rather than the exception. Others used only the barest outlines. Even in more recent times, filmmakers like Jean-Luc Godard have rarely used scripts. Most of his movies were begun with only a few ideas jotted down on a scrap of paper.

Many of the greatest directors have written their own scripts: Cocteau, Eisenstein, Bergman, and Herzog, to name only a few. In the American cinema, there are also many writer–directors: Griffith, Chaplin, Stroheim, Huston, Welles, Mankiewicz, Wilder, Sturges, Woody Allen, and Coppola are among the most famous. The majority of important directors have taken a major hand in writing their scripts, but they bring in other writers to expand on their ideas. Fellini, Truffaut, and Kurosawa have all worked in this manner. Surprisingly few major directors depend on others for their scripts. Joseph Losey and Harold Pinter, Marcel Carné and Jacques Prévert, and Vittorio De Sica and Cesare Zavattini (8-6) are perhaps the most famous director–writer teams.

The American studio system tended to encourage multiple authorship of scripts. Often writers had a certain specialty such as dialogue, comedy, construction, atmosphere, and so on. Some writers were best at doctoring weak scripts, others were good idea people but lacked the skill to execute their ideas. In such collaborative enterprises, the screen credits are not always an accurate reflection of who contributed what to a movie. Furthermore, although many directors such as Hitchcock, Capra, and Lubitsch, contributed a

**8-2. _Masculine–Feminine_ (France, 1966).**
_With Jean-Pierre Léaud and Chantal Goya; Directed by Jean-Luc Godard._
"I consider myself an essayist," Godard said, "producing essays in novel form or novels in essay form: only instead of writing, I film them." Godard's cinematic essays are a frontal attack on the hegemony of classical cinema (see 7-8). "The Americans are good at storytelling," he noted, "the French are not. Flaubert and Proust can't tell stories. They do something else. So does the cinema. I prefer to use a kind of tapestry, a background on which I can embroider on my own ideas." Instead of scripts, Godard set up dramatic situations, then asked his actors to improvise their dialogue, as in this interview scene—a technique he derived from the documentary movement called _cinéma vérité_. He intersperses these scenes with digressions, opinions, and jokes. Above all, he wanted to capture the spontaneity of the moment which he believed was more authentic when he and his actors had to fend for themselves, without the security of a script. "If you know in advance everything you are going to do, it isn't worth doing," Godard insisted. "If a show is all written down, what is the point of filming it? What use is cinema if it trails after literature." See also Louis D. Giannetti, "Godard's _Masculine-Feminine_: The Cinematic Essay," in _Godard and Others: Essays in Film Form_ (Cranbury, N.J.: Fairleigh Dickinson Univ. Press, 1975).

(Columbia Pictures)

great deal to the final shape of their scripts, they rarely bothered to include their names in the credits, allowing the official writer to take it all.

For many years, American critics were inclined to believe that art must be solemn—if not actually dull—to be respectable. Indeed, even in the heyday of the Hollywood studio system, such intellectual writers as Dalton Trumbo, Carl Foreman, and Dore Schary enjoyed tremendous prestige because their scripts were filled with fine speeches dealing with Justice, Brotherhood, and Democracy. Today these purple patches of dialogue seem clumsy, schoolmarmish, and ultimately dishonest, for often even rough, unlettered characters burst forth with eloquent speeches that are totally out of character.

Not that these themes aren't important, but to be effective artistically ideas must be dramatized with tact and honesty, not parcelled out to the characters like high-sounding speeches on a patriotic holiday. Generally speaking, only students, artists, and intellectuals discuss ideas and abstractions

(MGM)

**8-3. *The Band Wagon* (U.S.A., 1953).**
*With Fred Astaire and Cyd Charisse; Dances and musical numbers staged by Michael Kidd; Story and screenplay by Betty Comden and Adolph Green; Directed by Vincente Minnelli.*
No one could surpass the wit and snap of the writing team of Comden and Green. In addition to this great work, they also scripted such nifty musicals as *On the Town, Singin' in the Rain, It's Always Fair Weather,* and *Bells Are Ringing.* They enjoyed incorporating literary jokes into their scripts, like this amusing spoof on the "hard-boiled" fiction of such novelists as Dashiell Hammett, Raymond Chandler, and Mickey Spillane.

without a sense of self-consciousness. Many of Bergman's movies, for example, feature highly articulate people as protagonists. In order to be convincing, then, eloquent language must be dramatically probable: we must believe that the words belong to the *character,* and are not merely the writer's preachments dressed up as dialogue.

It's difficult to generalize about what constitutes good screen writing: much depends on the genre. For example, John Ford was at his best with laconic and even inarticulate characters. The scripts to his best films—especially his westerns—are spare and poetic precisely because the writing is so understated. Other filmmakers are at their best with talky scripts—providing it's scintillating talk, as in the best movies of Wertmüller, Lubitsch, and Woody Allen. The French and British cinemas are also exceptionally literate. Among the important writers who have written for the screen in Great Britain are George Bernard Shaw, Graham Green (1-14), Alan Sillitoe (1-12), John Osborne, Harold Pinter (5-13), and David Storey (8-4).

**8-4. *This Sporting Life* (Great Britain, 1963).**
*With Richard Harris and Rachel Roberts; Screenplay by David Storey; Directed by Lindsay Anderson.*
The British cinema has traditionally drawn much of its strength from literature. Many of their landmark films are dramatic or literary adaptations of classic works. Distinguished novelists and dramatists like David Storey have also written directly for the screen.

Good writing in the movies or elsewhere is not a matter of following the rules: it all depends on how it's done. In Arthur Penn's *Little Big Man*, for example, the protagonist's Indian grandfather (Chief Dan George) discusses abstract ideas and moral issues with complete believability. Much of the humor of his speeches results from the contrast between the sophistication of his ideas and the naive racism of most viewers who expect Indians to grunt in monosyllables. Calder Willingham's script (based on the novel by Thomas Berger) avoids sentimental clichés. Just as the Indian chief seems to be slipping into a "noble soul" stereotype, the writing wittily undercuts the potential bathos. In a scene late in the movie, the elderly chief climbs a high hill where he plans to die. He performs solemn death rituals, then lies down on the ground, his sorrowful grandson (Dustin Hoffman) watching helplessly. Inexplicably, the chief doesn't die. Shrugging philosophically, he rises and remarks to his grandson, "Sometimes the magic works, sometimes it doesn't." Undaunted, the chief returns with his grandson to the Indian village in the valley, to the land of the living.

Despite the enormous importance that the script can play in a sound film, some directors scoff at the notion that a writer could be the dominant artist in the cinema. When asked what value he placed on narrative, for example, Josef von Sternberg replied that the story elements of his works were of "no importance whatsoever" to him. Antonioni once remarked that Dostoyevsky's *Crime and Punishment* was a rather ordinary crime thriller—the genius of the novel lies in *how* it's told, not in the subject matter per se. Certainly the large number of excellent movies based on routine or even mediocre books seems to bear out such a view.

Movie scripts seldom make for interesting reading precisely because they are like blueprints of the finished product. Unlike a play script, which usually can be read with pleasure, too much is missing in a screenplay. Even highly detailed scripts seldom offer us a sense of a film's mise-en-scène, one of the principal methods of expression at the director's disposal. With characteristic wit, Andrew Sarris has pointed out how the director's choice of shot—or the way in which the action is photographed—is the crucial element in most films:

> The choice between a close-up and a long-shot, for example, may quite often transcend the plot. If the story of Little Red Riding Hood is told with the Wolf in close-up and Little Red Riding Hood in long-shot, the director is concerned primarily with the emotional problems of a wolf with a compulsion to eat little girls. If Little Red Riding Hood is in close-up and the Wolf in long-shot, the emphasis is shifted to the emotional problems of vestigial virginity in a wicked world. Thus, two different stories are being told with the same basic anecdotal material. What is at stake in the two versions of Little Red Riding Hood are two contrasting directorial attitudes toward life. One director identifies more with the Wolf—the male, the compulsive, the corrupted, even evil itself. The second director identifies with the little girl—the innocence, the illusion, the ideal and hope of the race. Needless to say, few critics bother to make any distinction, proving perhaps that direction as creation is still only dimly understood. (Quoted from "The Fall and Rise of the Film Director," in *Interviews with Film Directors* [New York: Avon Books, 1967].)

A film script is rarely an autonomous literary product, otherwise screenplays would be published with greater frequency. The scenarios of a few prestigious filmmakers, like Bergman, Fellini, and Truffaut, have reached print, but even these are merely linguistic approximations of the films themselves. Even a casual perusal of the two script versions of *North by Northwest* (see Appendix) reveals the enormous differences between the art of writing for movies, and the infinitely more complex art of directing them.

## Story and Genre

Beginning around 1900, fiction movies were structured around a story of some kind. These early narratives were pretty crude until Griffith refined the art of storytelling about 15 years later. The narrative structure he perfected, derived in large part from the live theatre, has been called the classical paradigm (7-8). This and terms like classical cinema are labels of convenience, but essentially vague and imprecise, encompassing such disparate filmmakers as Keaton, Capra, Ford, and a multitude of others both in the United States and abroad.

In fact, until the advent of the French New Wave in the late 1950s, virtually all fiction films conformed to the narrative conventions of classical cinema. Of course, practices varied from country to country. In Japan and

**8-5. *Ninotchka* (U.S.A., 1939).**
*With Greta Garbo and Melvyn Douglas; Screenplay by Billy Wilder, Charles Brackett, and Walter Reisch; Directed by Ernst Lubitsch.*
Like most of the major directors of the American cinema, Lubitsch shaped the screenplays of all his movies, though rarely with official credit. He wanted every detail worked out in advance, down to the last raised eyebrow. See also Richard J. Anobile, ed., *Ernst Lubitsch's Ninotchka* (New York: Darien House, 1975), a copiously illustrated text of the film.

Europe, for example, narratives are usually very loose compared to the tight, compact structures of the average American movie. In the 1960s, the supremacy of classical narrative was challenged by such radical innovators as Fellini (4-9), Resnais (7-10), Godard (8-2), and Bergman (8-21). Their movies overlapped considerably with the traditional purview of the avant-garde. In general, however, these experiments remained isolated achievements, unique to the artists who created them. The hegemony of classical cinema has been loosened somewhat, but it's still the most popular narrative structure for fiction features—especially in the United States where it remains virtually unchallenged.

Since the publication in 1835 of Alexis de Tocqueville's *Democracy in America*, the French have been among the most perceptive commentators on American culture, perhaps because it's so radically different from their own. Especially after World War II, French enthusiasm for American films verged on idolatry. The New Wave directors, who began as critics, were awed by the

*(Audio-Brandon Films)*

**8-6.** *Umberto D* **(Italy, 1951).**
*With Carlo Battisti (right); Written by Cesare Zavattini; Directed by Vittorio De Sica.*
Zavattini is the most famous scenarist of the Italian cinema, and one of its most important theorists. (See the section on neorealism in Chapter 11.) His best work was done in collaboration with De Sica, including such important works as *Shoeshine, Bicycle Thief, Miracle in Milan, Umberto D, Two Women, The Garden of the Finzi-Continis,* and *A Brief Vacation.* De Sica worked in close collaboration with his scenarists. For example, the protagonist of this film, a retired government employee (Battisti), is a veiled portrait of the director's father Umberto De Sica, to whom the film is dedicated. See also Cesare Zavattini, *Sequences From a Cinematic Life* (Englewood Cliffs, N.J.: Prentice-Hall, 1970); Roy Armes, *Patterns of Realism: A Study of Italian Neo-Realist Cinema* (New York: A. S. Barnes, 1971); and Pierre Leprohon, *The Italian Cinema* (New York: Praeger, 1972).

narrative vitality of the American cinema. When Truffaut, Godard, Chabrol and the others became filmmakers themselves, they imitated American models. Interestingly (and perhaps inevitably) they drifted away from action in favor of character delineation, atmosphere, and the exploration of ideas—essentially static elements. "If you want to say something," Godard once remarked of his movies, "there is only one solution: say it." An American filmmaker would have said "show it."

With surprisingly few exceptions, the best American movie artists have been excellent storytellers. In fact, even modestly talented filmmakers have at least mastered the craft—if not the art—of narrative action. Stories are seductive, and many viewers have known the experience of getting hooked on an otherwise banal picture because they want to see how it turns out. Elements such as character, theme, and mood are all subsumed within the story line—the structural spine of virtually all American fiction films. Seldom does the narrative drift or the pace of the action slacken. Dull stretches are edited out. Characters are almost invariably doers rather than thinkers or dreamers, and what they do constitutes the story. American movies *move*. Within the first few minutes, we are presented with a clear-cut conflict that's intensified according to conventions traceable to ancient times.

Narrative structures can be classified according to a variety of criteria. For example, they can be broadly differentiated by the stylistic terms that have been used throughout this book: realistic and expressionistic. Generally

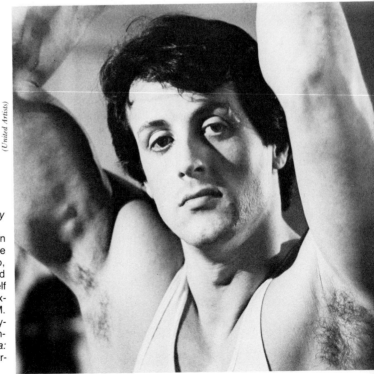

(United Artists)

**8-7. Rocky (U.S.A., 1976).**
*With Sylvester Stallone; Directed by John Avildsen.*
One of the most popular story patterns in America is the Horatio Alger myth—the inspiring tale of a social nobody who, through hard work, perseverence, and against all odds, manages to pull himself up by his bootstraps and achieve extraordinary success. See also Stuart M. Kaminsky, *American Film Genres* (Dayton: Pflaum Publishing, 1974); and Stanley J. Soloman, *Beyond Formula: American Film Genres* (New York: Harcourt, Brace, Jovanovich, 1976).

(New Yorker Films)

**8-8.** *Late Spring* **(Japan, 1959).**
*With (left to right) Chishu Ryu and Setsuko Hara; Directed by Yasujiro Ozu.*
One of the most common genres in Japan is the home drama. It was the only genre Ozu worked in, and he was one of its most popular practitioners. This type of film deals with the day-to-day routines of domestic life. Although Ozu is a profoundly philosophical artist, his movies consist almost entirely of "little things"—the bitter pills of self-denial that ultimately render life disappointing. Many of Ozu's films have seasonal titles that symbolically evoke appropriate human analogues. *Late Spring,* for example, deals with the attempts of a decent widower (Ryu) to marry off his only daughter (Hara) before she wilts into spinsterhood.

speaking, realistic narratives tend to appear unmanipulated. They are usually somewhat random in their development. Conflicts emerge unobtrusively, they aren't presented as *donnés*—as premises to the story. Details don't always "mean" anything, but are offered for their own sake to heighten the sense of authenticity. The key plot scenes are interspersed with incidental vignettes suggesting the casual clutter of everyday reality. Virtually all storytelling artists must resort to some kind of abstraction, of course, otherwise their tales would be filled with the same dull stretches that typify real life. The realist eliminates many—but not all—of these undramatic elements as unobtrusively as possible. Realists also tend to favor stories with ambiguous, and inconclusive endings, as if more could be shown of the story.

The expressionist not only makes no pretence at realistic narration, he actually heightens the artificiality of the story line in order to convey his vision more forcefully—without irrelevancies, as it were. Expressionist narratives allow a high degree of abstraction, of restructuring. The pattern of the narrative is often an important formal achievement, like the exquisitely symmetrical narrative structures of Buster Keaton. Such stylized genres as musicals also emphasize pattern as an aesthetically desirable element in the narrative. Like other expressionist traits, manipulation of the story line is viewed as a legitimate method of revealing the truths and beauties that lie concealed beneath the surface sprawl of reality (11-15).

A more precise method of classifying narrative structures is by genre, or story type. Most fiction films fall into some recognizable narrative category, especially in Japan and the United States where genre films are extremely popular. Genres are distinguished by a characteristic set of conventions in style, values, and subject matter. Genre is also a method of organizing and focusing the story materials. Virtually all westerns, for instance, deal with a specific era of American history—the western frontier of the late nineteenth century. A genre is a loose set of expectations, then, not a Divine Injunction. That is, each example of a given story type is related to its predecessors, but not in iron-clad bondage. André Bazin once referred to the western as "a form in search of a content." The same could be said of other genres.

(Cinema 5)

**8-9.** *A Slave of Love* **(U.S.S.R., 1976).**
*With Elena Solovei; Directed by Nikita Mikhalkov.*
A popular genre in the Soviet Union and other Communist countries is the brigade film. A work crew of some sort—in this case a movie crew—is divided in its sentiments concerning the best method to proceed with a project. Eventually the conflict is resolved in favor of the greatest good for the greatest number. Brigade films usually stress the need for individuals to make sacrifices for a higher cause. They often revolve around love versus duty conflicts, with the former usually yielding to the latter. See also Barry K. Grant, ed., *Film Genre: Theory and Criticism* (Metuchen: Scarecrow Press, 1977).

The major shortcoming of genre pictures of course is that they're easy to imitate and have been debased by stale mechanical repetition. Genre conventions are mere clichés unless they're united with significant innovations in style or subject matter. But this is true of all the arts, not just movies. As Aristotle notes in *The Poetics,* genres are qualitatively neutral: the conventions of classical tragedy are basically the same whether they're employed by a genius or a forgotten hack. Certain genres enjoy more cultural prestige because they have attracted the most gifted artists. Genres that haven't are widely regarded as innately inartistic, but in many cases their *déclassé* status is due to neglect rather than intrinsic hopelessness (8-10). For example, the

**8-10. *In the Realm of the Senses* (Japan, 1976).**
*With Eiko Matsuda (above) and Tatsuda Fuji; Directed by Nagisa Oshima.*
Serious artists like Oshima are often attracted to *déclassé* genres precisely because they offer opportunities for exploring taboo themes which are only superficially treated in conventional films. By almost any definition, this movie qualifies as pornography since it presents many scenes of explicit sexuality. But it is also an attempt to explore the ideology of sex and its underlying motivations—especially the death wish, which Oshima associates with the experience of orgasm. According to Carl Jung: "The cinema makes it possible to experience without danger all the excitement, passion, and desirousness which must be suppressed in a humanitarian ordering of society." See *Man and His Symbols,* edited, with an introduction by Carl Jung (New York: Dell, 1968).

earliest film critics considered slapstick comedy an infantile genre—until such important comic artists as Chaplin and Keaton entered the field. Today, no critic would malign the genre for it boasts a considerable number of masterpieces.

The most critically admired genre films strike a balance between the form's pre-established conventions and the artist's unique contributions. The artists of ancient Greece drew upon a common body of mythology, and no one thought it strange when dramatists and poets returned to these tales again and again. Incompetent artists merely repeat. Serious artists reinterpret. By exploiting the broad outlines of a well-known tale or story type, the storyteller can play off its main features, creating provocative tensions between the genre's conventions and the artist's inventions, between the familiar and the original, the general and the particular. Myths embody the common ideals and aspirations of a civilization, and by returning to these communal tales the artist becomes, in a sense, a psychic explorer, bridging the chasm between the known and the unknown. The stylized conventions and archetypal story patterns of genres encourage viewers to participate ritualistically in the basic beliefs, fears, and anxieties of their time.

Filmmakers are attracted to genres because they automatically synthesize a vast amount of cultural information, freeing them to explore more personal concerns. A nongeneric movie must be more self-contained. The artist is forced to communicate virtually all the major ideas and emotions within the

**8-11. *Walkabout* (Australia/Great Britain, 1971).**
*With Gulpilil (holding spear); Photographed and directed by Nicholas Roeg.*
Rite-of-passage stories usually emphasize a series of prescribed rituals which demonstrate a youth's fitness for adult life. In this film, the symbolic rites are drawn from the culture of Australian aborigines and test the physical endurance as well as the mental readiness of the postulants.

work itself—a task that preempts much of his screen time. On the other hand, the genre artist never starts from scratch. He can build upon the accomplishments of his predecessors, enriching their ideas or calling them into question, depending on his inclinations.

The most enduring genres tend to adapt to changing social conditions. Most of them begin as naive allegories of Good versus Evil. Over the years they become more complex in both form and thematic range. Finally they veer into an ironic mode, mocking many of the genre's original values and conventions. Some critics claim that this evolution is inevitable and doesn't necessarily represent an aesthetic improvement. Genres at the beginning of their development tend to be simple, direct, and powerful in their emotional impact. A genre in its intermediate stage is often said to embody such classical ideals as balance, richness, and poise. In its ironic phase, the same genre is often self-conscious, stylistically nuanced, and more intellectual in its appeal. For example, the western's naive phase is exemplified by Edwin S. Porter's *The Great Train Robbery* (1903). Its classical phase could be typified by Ford's *Stagecoach* (1939). A transitional western like Zinnemann's *High Noon* (1952) features many ironic elements, although it's still essentially in the heroic mold. Altman's *McCabe and Mrs. Miller* (1971) is virtually a parody of the genre

**8-12. *McCabe and Mrs. Miller* (U.S.A., 1971).**
*Directed by Robert Altman.*
Most of Altman's genre films are revisionist—they ironically undercut an implied classical ideal. This western contains such standard generic elements as the establishment of a frontier community, a love story, and a shootout. But unlike most classical westerns, Altman's movie concludes on a note of loss, disintegration, and defeat. The characters are left with their dreams dispersed, the fragile strands of love and affection blasted by a ritualized death—not of the villains, but the hero. See also Gary Engle, "*McCabe and Mrs. Miller:* Robert Altman's Anti-western," in *The Journal of Popular Film* (Fall, 1972).

(8-12). A number of cultural theorists insist that questions of individual value in a genre's evolution are largely matters of taste and fashion.

Some of the most suggestive critical studies have explored the relationship of a genre to the society that nurtured it. This sociopsychic approach was pioneered by the French literary critic Hippolyte Taine in the nineteenth century. Taine claimed that the social and intellectual anxieties of a given era and nation will find expression in its art. The implicit function of an artist is to harmonize and reconcile cultural clashes of value. He believed that art must be analyzed both for its overt and its covert meaning, that beneath its explicit content there exists a vast resevoir of latent social and psychic information. In the cinema, for example, genre critics have pointed out how crime films are often vehicles for exploring rebellion myths and are especially popular during periods of social breakdown.

There are a number of dangers in this approach. In the first place, no one can tell for certain what an artist "really meant" if the ideas are not presented in the work of art itself. Nor can one say for certain why audiences respond to a given work, otherwise it would be easy to imitate. Indeed, this is how most genres are born. But some genre films succeed, while others of the same mold fail. Another problem with this approach involves documentation and method which are sometimes suspect in sociopsychic studies of this sort. Siegfried Kracauer's *From Caligari to Hitler: A Psychological History of the German Film* is a good example. The thesis of this book is that German movies of the 1920s were filled with premonitions of Nazi totalitarianism of the 1930s. Unfortunately, many of the films Kracauer offers in evidence were popular only with foreign critics and intellectuals, not with the German public whose consciousness these movies presumably reflected.

This approach tends to work best with popular genres which reflect the shared values and fears of a large audience. Such genres might be regarded as

**8-13.** *Black God, White Devil* **(Brazil, 1963).**
*Directed by Glauber Rocha.*
As the title of this film suggests, Third World movies often reverse the thematic polarities of imperialist myths. Revolutionary filmmakers like Rocha have called for a "cinema of subversion," in which racist clichés are turned upside down and demystified.

*(New Yorker Films)*

contemporary myths, lending philosophical meaning to the facts of everyday life. As social conditions change, genres often change with them, challenging some traditional customs and beliefs, reaffirming others. Gangster films, for example, are often covert critiques of American capitalism. The protagonists—usually played by small men—are likened to ruthless businessmen, their climb to power a sardonic parody of the Horatio Alger myth. During the Jazz Age, gangster films like *Underworld* (1927) dealt with the violence and glamor of the Prohibition era in an essentially apolitical manner. During the harshest years of the Depression in the early 1930s, the genre became subversively ideological. Movies like *Little Caesar* (1930) reflected the country's shaken confidence in authority and traditional social institutions. In the final years of the Depression, gangster films like *Dead End* (1937) were pleas for liberal reform, arguing that crime is the result of broken homes, lack of opportunity, and slum living. Gangsters of all periods tend to suffer from an inability to relate to women, but during the 1940s, movies like *White Heat* (1949) featured protagonists who were outright sexual neurotics. In the 1950s, partly as a result of the highly publicized Kefauver Senate Crime Investigations, gangster movies like *The Phoenix City Story* (1955) took the form of confidential exposés of syndicate crime. Francis Ford Coppola's *The Godfather* (1972) and *The Godfather, Part II* (1974) are a virtual recapitulation of the history of the genre, spanning three generations of characters and reflecting the weary cynicism of a nation still numbed by the hearts-and-minds hoax of Vietnam and the Watergate conspiracy.

The ideas of Sigmund Freud and Carl Jung have also influenced many genre theorists. Like Taine, both psychiatrists believed that art is a reflection of underlying structures of meaning, that it satisfies certain subconscious

*(New Yorker Films)*

**8-14. *In the Name of the Father* (Italy, 1971).**
*Directed by Marco Bellocchio.*
Almost all civilizations have myths dealing with the rebellion of son against father, but this narrative motif is often submerged beneath the surface details of a story. Parker Tyler defined myth as "a free, unharnessed fiction, a basic, prototypic pattern capable of many variations and distortions, many betrayals and disguises, even though it remains *imaginative* truth." An underlying structure in Bellocchio's film is the Oedipus complex, which Freud believed was the paradigm of prepubescent human sexuality. Its feminine form is known as the Electra complex, also derived from Greek myth. See also Frank McConnell, *Storytelling and Mythmaking* (New York: Oxford Univ. Press, 1979); and Parker Tyler, *Magic and Myth of the Movies* (New York: Simon and Schuster, 1944).

needs in both the artist and audience. For Freud, art was a form of daydreaming and wish-fulfillment, vicariously resolving urgent impulses and desires that can't be satisfied in reality. Pornographic films are perhaps the most obvious example of how anxieties can be assuaged in this surrogate manner, and in fact Freud believed that most neuroses were sexually based. He thought that art was a byproduct of neurosis, although essentially a socially beneficial one. Like neurosis, art is characterized by a repetition compulsion, the need to go over the same stories and rituals in order to reinact and temporarily resolve certain psychic conflicts (8-14).

Jung began his career as a disciple of Freud, but eventually broke away, believing that Freud's theories lacked a communal dimension. Jung was fascinated by myths, fairy tales, and folklore which he believed contained symbols and story patterns that were universal to all individuals in all cultures and

**8-15.** *Bringing Up Baby* **(U.S.A., 1938).**
*With Cary Grant and Katharine Hepburn; Directed by Howard Hawks.*
Genres can be classified according to subject matter, style, period, national origin, and a variety of other criteria. In the 1930s, a new American genre was born: screwball comedy. Its heyday was roughly 1934–45. Essentially love stories, these films featured zany but glamorous lovers, often from different social classes. More realistic than the slapstick of the silent era, screwball comedy is also more collaborative, requiring the sophisticated blending of talents of writers, actors, and directors. (This film was scripted by Hawks, Dudley Nichols, and Hagar Wilde.) The snappy dialogue crackles with wit and speed. Sappy, sentimental speeches are often meant to deceive. The narrative premises are absurdly improbable, and the plots, which are intricate and filled with preposterous twists and turns, tend to snowball out of control. The movies center on a comic/romantic couple rather than a solitary protagonist. Often they are initially antagonistic, with one trying to outwit or outmaneuver the other. Much of the comedy results from the utter seriousness of the characters who are usually unaware that they're funny, even though they engage in the most loony masquerades and deceptions. Sometimes one of them is engaged to a sexless prude or a humorless bore: this lends an urgency to the attraction between the coprotagonists, who are clearly made for each other. The genre usually includes a menagerie of secondary characters who are as wacky as the lovers.

(RKO)

periods. According to Jung, unconscious complexes consist of archetypal symbols that are as deeply rooted and as inexplicable as instincts. He called this submerged reservoir of symbols the collective unconscious, which he thought had a primordial foundation, traceable to primitive times. Many of these archetypal patterns are bipolar and embody the basic concepts of religion, art, and society: god–devil, light–dark, active–passive, male–female, static–dynamic, and so on. Jung believed that the artist consciously or unconsciously draws on these archetypes as raw material which must then be rendered into the generic forms favored by a given culture. For Jung, every work of art (and especially generic art) is an infinitesimal exploration of a universal experience—an instinctive groping toward an ancient wisdom. He also believed that popular culture offers the most unobstructed view of archetypes and myths, while elite culture tends to submerge them beneath a complex surface detail (8-16).

A story can be many things. To a producer it's a property that has a box office value. To a writer it's a script. To a film star it's a vehicle. To a director

**8-16. *Snow White and the Seven Dwarfs* (U.S.A., 1937).**
*By Walt Disney.*
The French cultural anthropologist Claude Levi-Strauss noted that myths have no author, no origin, no core axis—they allow "free play" in a variety of artistic forms. Disney's work draws heavily from fairy tales, myths, and folklore which are profuse in archetypal elements. *Snow White*, based on a complex of tales collected by the Grimm brothers, features many scenes derived from the Sleeping Beauty myth: storms, magical transformations, a poisoned apple, a forbidden garden, enchanted palaces, a wicked stepmother, and so on.

it's an artistic medium. To a genre critic it's an objective, classifiable narrative form. To a sociologist it's an index of public sentiment. To a psychiatrist it's an instinctive exploration of hidden fears or communal ideals. To a moviegoer it can be all of these, and more.

## Motifs, Symbols, Metaphors, and Allusions

In his essay "*La Caméra-Stylo*" Alexandre Astruc observed that one of the traditional problems of film has been its difficulty in expressing thought and ideas. The invention of sound, of course, was an enormous advantage to the filmmaker, for with spoken language he or she could express virtually any kind of abstract thought. But film directors also wanted to explore the possibilities of the image as a conveyor of abstract ideas. Indeed, even before the sound era, filmmakers had devised a number of nonverbal figurative techniques.

A figurative technique can be defined as an artistic device which suggests abstract ideas over and beyond the literalness of the medium that conveys them. There are a number of these techniques in both literature and cinema, but perhaps the most common are motifs, symbols, and metaphors. In actual practice, there's a considerable amount of overlapping between these terms. All of them are "symbolic" in the sense that an object or event means something beyond its literal significance. But perhaps the most pragmatic method of differentiating these techniques is their degree of obtrusiveness. Instead of

**8-17.** *Day for Night* (France, 1973).
*With François Truffaut (leather jacket) Directed by Truffaut.*
Film titles are chosen with great deliberation because they are meant to embody the central concept behind a movie. Film titles, in short, are symbolic. The original-language title of this film is *La Nuit Américaine*, The American Night. It reflects Truffaut's great love for American culture, especially its cinema, and deals with the making of an "old-fashioned" kind of movie—the kind they made in Hollywood in the 1940s. (Truffaut even includes a tender homage to *Citizen Kane*.) "La nuit américaine" is also what the French call the day-for-night filter (1-27) which converts sunlit scenes into nighttime scenes. The filter transforms reality—makes it magical. For Truffaut, cinema is magic.

(Warner Brothers)

locking each of these terms into an airtight compartment, however, we ought to view them as general demarcations, with motifs representing the least obtrusive extreme, metaphors representing the most conspicuous, and each category overlapping somewhat with its neighbor.

*Motifs* are so totally integrated within the realistic texture of a film that we can almost refer to them as submerged or invisible symbols. A motif can be a technique, an object, or anything that's systematically repeated in a movie yet doesn't call attention to itself. Even after repeated viewings a motif is not always apparent, for its symbolic significance is never permitted to emerge or detach itself from its context. The circular shape from *The Seven Samurai* is a good instance of a visual motif, but motifs can also be musical, kinetic (like the travelling shots in *8 ½*), verbal (like the term "Rosebud" in *Citizen Kane*), and aural (like the pounding of the waves in *L'Avventura*).

*Symbols* can also be palpable things, but they imply additional meanings which are relatively apparent to the sensitive observer. Furthermore, the symbolic meanings of these things can shift with the dramatic context. A good example of the shifting implications of a symbol can be seen in Kurosawa's *The Seven Samurai* (8-18). In this movie, a young samurai and a peasant girl are attracted to each other, but their class differences present insurmountable

**8-18.** *The Seven Samurai* **(Japan, 1954).**
*Directed by Akira Kurosawa.*
Realistic films tend to employ symbols less densely than expressionist movies, and the symbolism is almost always contextually probable. For example, in addition to being a symbol, the fire in this scene is also a fire.

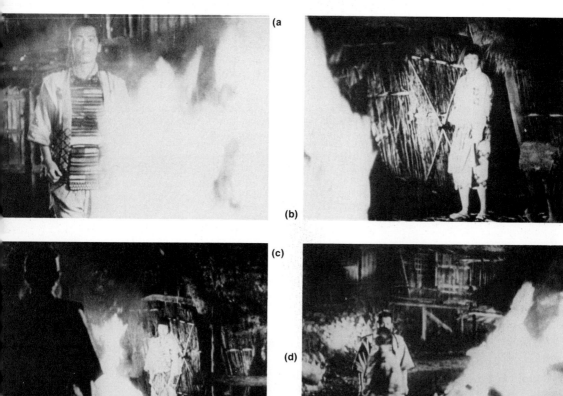

(a

(b)

(c)

(d)

*(Toho International)*

barriers. In a scene that takes place late at night, the two accidentally meet. Kurosawa emphasizes their separation by keeping them in separate frames, a raging outdoor fire acting as a kind of barrier (a and b). But their attraction is too strong, and they then appear in the same shot, the fire between them now suggesting the only obstacle, yet paradoxically, also suggesting the sexual passion they both feel (c). They draw toward each other, and the fire is now to one side, its sexual symbolism dominating (d). They go inside a hut, and the light from the fire outside emphasizes the eroticism of the scene (e). As they begin to make love in a dark corner of the hut, the shadows cast by the fire's light on the reeds of the hut seem to streak across their bodies (f). Suddenly, the girl's father discovers the lovers, and now the billowing flames of the fire suggest his moral outrage (g). He is so incensed that he must be restrained by the samurai chief, both of them almost washed out visually by the intensity of the fire's light (h). It begins to rain, and the sorrowing young samurai walks away despondently (i). At the end of the sequence, Kurosawa offers a closeup of the fire as the rain extinguishes its flames (j).

A *metaphor* is usually defined as a comparison of some kind that cannot be literally true. Two terms not ordinarily associated are yoked together, producing a certain sense of literal incongruity. "Poisonous time," "torn with grief," "devoured by love" are all verbal metaphors involving symbolic rather than literal descriptions. Editing is a frequent source of metaphors in film, for two shots can be linked together to produce a third, and symbolic idea. This is the basis of Eisenstein's theory of montage. In *October*, for example, he satirized the fears and anxieties of an antirevolutionary politician by intercutting shots of a "heavenly choir" of harpists with shots of the politician delivering his cowardly speech. The row of pretty blonde harp players is brought in "from nowhere": that is, they are certainly not found in the locale (a meeting hall), but are introduced solely for metaphoric purposes. Special-effects cinematography is also used to create metaphoric ideas. For example, through the use of the optical printer, two or more objects can be yoked together in the same frame to create ideas that have no literal existence in reality (8-19). Cinematic

**8-19.** *Psycho* (U.S.A., 1960).
*Directed by Alfred Hitchcock.*
Cinematic metaphors can be created through the use of special effects, as in this dissolve which yields the final shot of the film—the dredging up of a car from a swamp. Three images are dissolved: (1) a shot of a catatonic youth (Anthony Perkins) looking directly at us; (2) a duplicate shot of his mother's skeleton, whose skull flickers briefly beneath her son's features and whose personality he has now assumed; and (3) a heavy chain which seems anchored to his/her heart, hauling up the murder victim's car which contains her corpse. See also Louis D. Giannetti, "Cinematic Metaphors," in *The Journal of Aesthetic Education* (October, 1972).

metaphors are always somewhat obtrusive; unlike motifs and most symbols, metaphors are less integrated contextually, less "realistic" in terms of our ordinary perceptions.

There are two other kinds of figurative techniques in film and literature: *allegory* and *allusions*. The first is seldom employed in movies since it tends toward simplemindedness. What's usually involved in this techinque is a total avoidance of realism and probability. A one-to-one correspondence exists between a character or situation and a specific symbolic idea. One of the most famous examples of allegory is the character of Death in Bergman's *The Seventh Seal* (1-5). Needless to say, there's not much ambiguity involved in what the character is supposed to symbolize. Allegorical narratives are especially popular in the German cinema. For example, virtually all the works of Werner Herzog deal with the idea of life in general, the nature of the human condition in broadly symbolic terms (8-20).

An allusion is a common type of literary analogy. It's an implied reference, usually to a well-known event, person, or work of art. The protagonist of

**8-20. *Stroszek: A Ballad* (West Germany, 1977).**
*With Bruno S. (playing accordian); Written and directed by Werner Herzog.*
Like a number of German artists, Herzog is a master of the allegorical form. Most of his movies are structured around a mythical quest. Interspersing these mock-heroic journeys are stark poetic images and occasional outbursts of black humor. In this film, for example, three endearing if none-too-bright pilgrims abandon the harshness of Berlin to seek their El Dorado in the Promised Land of America—northern Wisconsin, to be exact. The weirdest of them, Stroszek (Bruno S.) is a sweet innocent buried in a hulking body that doesn't seem to connect to his brain. They begin their odyssey in the dead of winter, with practically no money and even less English. Herzog lacks technical polish, but he is capable of creating images of forlorn desolation. They're like metaphysical home movies.

Hawks's *Scarface* was modeled on the gangster Al Capone (who had a well-publicized scar in the shape of a cross on his cheek), an allusion that wasn't lost on audiences of the time. One of Buñuel's most famous shots is the blasphemous allusion to Leonardo's *Last Supper* in *Viridiana* (3-34). Filmmakers often draw on religious mythology for their allusions. For example, the Christian myth of the Garden of Eden is used in such disparate works as *The Garden of the Finzi Continis* (1-25), *Days of Heaven* (1-36), *How Green Was My Valley* (7-28), and *The Tree of the Wooden Clogs* (11-11). The films of Ingmar Bergman are also rich in Christian allusions.

In the cinema, an overt reference or allusion to another movie, director, or memorable shot is sometimes called a *homage*. The cinematic homage is a kind of quote, the director's graceful tribute to a colleague or established master. Homages were popularized by Godard and Truffaut whose movies are profuse in such tributes. In Godard's *A Woman Is a Woman*, for example, two decidedly nonmusical characters burst out in spontaneous song and dance while expressing their desire to appear in an MGM musical by Gene Kelly, choreographed by Bob Fosse. Fosse's *All That Jazz* contains many homages to his idol Fellini, and especially to *8 1/2* (3-12). Similarly, Bruno Bozzetto's *Allegro Non Troppo* is a playful tribute to his idol Walt Disney, especially to *Fantasia* (3-32).

Perhaps the most practical method of seeing how motifs, symbols,

**8-21. *Persona* (Sweden, 1966).**
Written and directed by Ingmar Bergman.

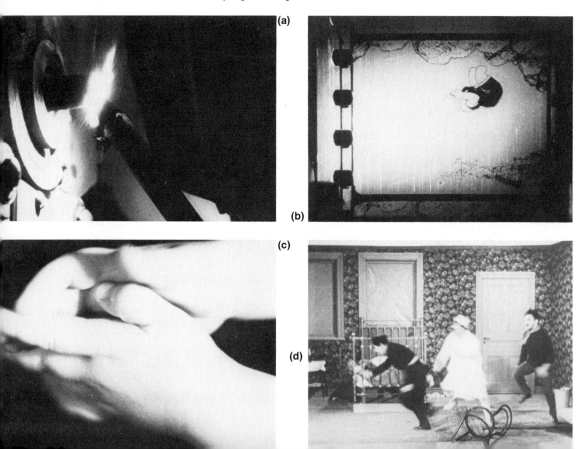

(a)

(b)

(c)

(d)

metaphors, and allusions actually function in motion pictures is to explore in detail their use in a single movie. Bergman's *Persona* is one of the most complex films ever created (8-21). The director uses virtually every kind of cinematic metaphor: editing juxtapositions, as well as kinetic, aural, and optical metaphors. There are also many allusions and motifs in *Persona*. Two motifs in particular stand out: the doubles theme (implying the splitting and merging of personalities), and motifs of paralysis and immobility (suggesting catatonia and perhaps even death). There are also motifs of blood, hands, and eyes.

The basic narrative deals with the theme of schizophrenia which Bergman exploits as a symbolic basis for more philosophical and metaphysical concerns. A well-known actress, Elisabeth Vogler (Liv Ullmann), suddenly stops speaking while performing on stage in the title role of *Electra*. After many days of total silence, during which she refuses to talk even to her husband and young son, she is referred to a psychiatric hospital. Alma, an impressionable young nurse (Bibi Andersson), is asked to take charge of the actress at the summer cottage of the psychiatrist, where the doctor hopes that the young nurse might induce the actress to speak. Alone on the barren rocky island, the two women are drawn together emotionally, although Elisabeth continues to remain silent. Encouraged by Elisabeth's flattering attention, Alma painfully recounts a story of an orgy she once took part in. As a result, the nurse got pregnant and eventually decided to have an abortion. In telling the story, Alma only now begins to feel the anguish and guilt of her past acts. After this shared confidence, the nurse is drawn to Elisabeth more than ever, even to the point of imagining that the two are very much alike, both physically and temperamentally.

All the while, the mysterious Elisabeth listens attentively, sometimes with apparent compassion, at other times with a certain affectionate amusement. Alma's life seems so trivial in comparison with the horrors that Elisabeth has apparently experienced. When Alma offers to mail her patient's letter, the nurse is unable to resist the temptation to read it, for Elisabeth has neglected (deliberately?) to seal the envelope. In her letter, the actress writes with detached curiosity of Alma's sexual experiences. Elisabeth can't resist "studying" her friend (possibly for a future role?). This casual betrayal has a traumatic effect on Alma. From this point on in the movie, we are never sure whether we are watching real events or imagined ones. Nor are we certain whether the fantasist is Alma or Elisabeth—although most likely it is Alma. The two women quarrel violently. Their identities begin to merge, subtly at first, then dramatically, uncontrollably. Alma even makes love with Mr. Vogler while his wife watches with detachment, sorrow, and hopelessness. Bergman includes a number of other fantasy sequences between the two women which take place in a kind of timeless void. Alma tries desperately to resist merging personalities with Elisabeth but is unsuccessful. Suddenly, Elisabeth mysteriously disappears. Soon after, we see Alma packing her clothes, shutting up the cottage, and departing alone on an empty bus. The psychiatric story ends here—with an unresolved, ambiguous conclusion.

Despite its tremendous dramatic power, this is only the narrative scaffolding of Bergman's movie, for the film is also an elaborate philosophical exploration of the problems and responsibilities of the artist in relationship to others. The story of the two women is enclosed by a kind of frame which consists of a series of brief, almost subliminal shots. Many of these shots are not contextually related to the story proper, but serve as metaphors for Bergman's philosophical themes. These editing metaphors are found not only at the beginning and ending of the movie, but also at the midpoint where they erupt violently as Alma's love for Elisabeth turns to hatred.

The elaborate precredit sequence functions almost like a musical overture, briefly introducing most of the important ideas that will be developed in the story proper. Some of the shots in this sequence defy precise analysis, and even Bergman is unsure of what a few of them mean. At this point in viewing the film, of course, we aren't expected to know the significance of most of these shots. They function mostly on a visceral level: they're intended to jolt us out of our passivity. The opening shot of the movie shows us the carbon arc lamps of a film projector lighting up (a). Then, in quick succession, we see a film strip unfurling off the sprockets of a projector and some movie images whirling out of control on a screen. Bergman then cuts to a shot of an upside-down cartoon figure washing her face in the water of a rocky harbor (b). The sprocket holes of this animated film can be seen plainly. All of these images suggest that *Persona* will deal at least in part with the problems of making movies, perhaps that the figures of Alma and Elisabeth are themselves personas or masks for Bergman's own experiences. The mechanical breakdown of the projector certainly suggests a metaphorical foreshadowing of the breakdown of the emotional mechanisms of the two women. The animated shot of the woman washing is followed by a closeup of two real hands washing (c). Perhaps this juxtaposition is a comment on the pitiful ineffectuality of art in capturing real experiences in all their complexity. No matter how complex, art appears to be an inadequate caricature of the real thing to the artist who is trying to externalize his or her feelings and ideas. The juxtaposition might also be an indication of the various levels of reality that Bergman will be using throughout the film.

The director then cuts to a fast-motion sequence which seems to be an old silent movie farce, with a man being pursued by the devil and a skeleton (d). Again, one is tempted to view this scene as a tacit comment on the inadequacies of film art in dealing with such complex themes as evil and death. Bergman then intercuts three shots which suggest religious allusions. First, there's a shot of a black spider, which is apparently an allusion to Bergman's earlier *Through a Glass Darkly*. (In that movie, an artist—in this case a novelist— is fascinated by his daughter's descent into madness, and uses her experiences as a basis for his creativity. At the end of the film, the girl imagines that she sees God—a terrifying black spider.)

The second shot is an overexposed image of a dead lamb being slashed open. A hand reaches into its belly and dredges out its guts. The camera pans slightly, and we see the lamb's glassy eye staring dumbly (e). The third shot shows a spike being driven into a hand, an obvious crucifixion allusion (f). It's difficult to know whether Bergman is suggesting the Christ-like agony of the artist in creating, or the agony of his "victims," his subject matter from real life. Perhaps both ideas are implied, for in the story proper, both Elisabeth (the artist figure) and Alma (the "raw material" of art) undergo terrible anguish.

Bergman then offers a shot of a blank concrete wall, the first motif of immobility. This dissolves to a shot of some trees stripped of their foliage in a bleak winter setting. Next, we see an image of a spiked iron fence with a pile of snow in front of it. This in turn leads to a series of close shots of an old woman lying silently in what seems to be a hospital, or perhaps a morgue, for one shot is a closeup of her hand dangling lifelessly off the edge of the bed (g). On the soundtrack, we hear some eerie dripping sounds, metaphors perhaps for the passage of time, or dripping drops of blood, life's basic substance.

Bergman then begins one of the most ambiguous series of shots in this precredit sequence. We see a pubescent boy lying naked under a white sheet. Unable to sleep, the boy sits up on his bed, puts on his glasses and tries to read, but he is too restless (h). He then looks at the camera—at us—and his hand gropes slowly toward the lens (i). The movement seems to suggest a reaching out, but also a kind of conjuring effect. Bergman then gives us a reverse-angle shot, and we see that the boy is reaching toward an out-of-focus image of a woman's face—the face of Bibi Andersson, who plays Alma (j). This sequence has been interpreted in various ways, but Bergman deliberately keeps its symbolism ambiguous. The boy could represent Elisabeth's son whom she has guiltily rejected. He could also be an embodiment of Alma's aborted child: his groping for her face could represent Alma's subjective projection of guilt. But the boy is also a kind of conjurer of images, and as such he could represent Bergman himself, childlike before his own creations which seem to overpower him.

At this point, Bergman begins his credits, but interspersed with them are various shots that are actually a continuation of the precredit sequence. Included in these shots is an image of Liv Ullmann as Elisabeth playing Electra. There is also a shot of a barren rocky seacoast which will be the major setting

(e)

(f)

(g)

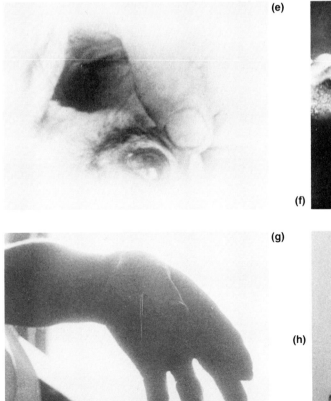

(h)

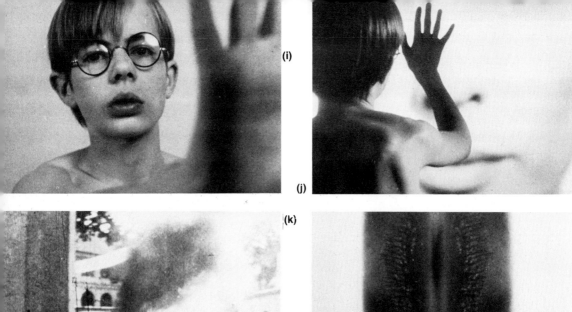

of the story proper, and a television image of a Buddhist monk immolating himself (k). There is also an extreme closeup of a pair of lips, only photographed vertically, so that the lips seem to resemble a vagina (l). Possibly the shot is meant to suggest the idea of giving birth: George Bernard Shaw, as well as Freud, believed that the artist is essentially a neurotic who, in creating a work of art, is subconsciously trying to mimic a woman's giving birth normally. The fact that this image appears at the "birth" of the film tends to confirm this interpretation. Bergman then intercuts three closeups with his concluding titles. The boy's closeup is repeated a number of times. We then are offered a shot of Alma (m) and one of Elisabeth (n), both of them, like the boy, staring directly into the camera. The two women are photographed in such a way that their striking physical resemblance is emphasized. The fact that these shots are conspicuously parallel seems to suggest that they all represent aspects of the same single consciousness.

All of these shots take no longer than a few minutes of screen time. The story proper begins with the psychiatrist's recounting Elisabeth's breakdown to Alma. The fact that the actress began to giggle while playing Electra is significant. *Electra* deals with the theme of matricide, of a child's revenge for a mother's betrayal (o). We later learn that Elisabeth hated being a mother because it interfered with her artistic career. The complex pattern of guilt this hatred produced in Elisabeth is apparently what precipitated her giggles and later silent withdrawal. Art seems so *simple* in comparison with life, with all its messy ambiguities and contradictions. Later, in the hospital room, Elisabeth

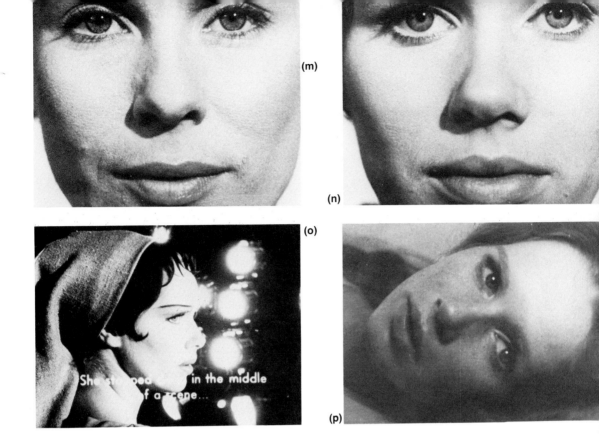

(m)

(n)

(o)

She stopped in the middle of a scene...

(p)

again begins to giggle when she hears a radio melodrama which strikes her as a ludicrous caricature of real life. Bergman never offers us an explicit explanation for Elisabeth's withdrawal, but by permitting us to watch Alma's step-by-step deterioration, we can infer the causes underlying both women's condition, for they are virtually the same: the betrayals, compromises, deceptions, and self-deceptions of everyday life.

In a powerful scene which is photographed in a very long take, Bergman gives us a closeup of Elisabeth lying in bed in the hospital. Slowly, very slowly, her face is gradually submerged into total darkness (p). Another hospital scene tends to confirm this interpretation of Elisabeth as a despairing artist figure. The actress is watching TV, where she sees a newsreel of the war in Vietnam (q). Suddenly the television screen is filled with a shot of a Buddhist monk setting fire to himself in protest. Elisabeth recoils in horror, withdrawing to a corner of the room and the very edge of Bergman's frame (r). In a series of shots that cut closer and closer to Elisabeth's face, in which the symbolic effects of the proxemic ranges are brilliantly exploited, we see all the anguish and despair that has precipitated her revolt of silence (s,t). But no matter how much she withdraws, the horrors of reality are always there—even if at second hand, on a TV screen.

Once the scene shifts to the island retreat, Elisabeth's condition seems to improve, although Bergman often cuts to shots of the barren immobile rocks which act as constant reminders of the essential sterility of such an isolated existence (u). As the women draw closer, Bergman photographs them in

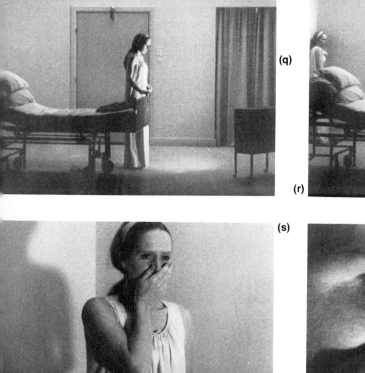

(q)

(r)

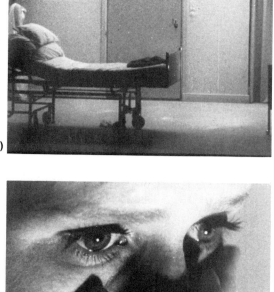

(s)

(t)

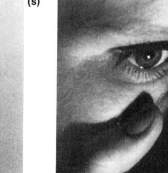

(u)

(v)

My sufferings were real enough.

(w)

(x)

(y)

(z)

(aa)

(bb)

complementary costumes, parallel setups, and he even blocks their movements so that their bodies seem to merge (v). This doubles motif is carried over into a dream sequence (probably Alma's) where Elisabeth enters the nurse's room through one door (w) and leaves through another adjacent to it (x). Photographed mostly in slow motion through a gauzy lens, this graceful sequence is one of the first overt dramatizations of the merging of personalities. Both women stand before a dark mirror, where Elisabeth pulls back Alma's hair to reveal their extraordinary physical resemblance (y).

Bergman even brings the reality of the audience into the film. Lest we become too complacent in viewing this "freak show," the director begins one sequence with a shot of the rocky shore. Suddenly, from beneath the frame, Elisabeth emerges with a still camera and clicks our picture (z). *Persona* is as much a portrait of ourselves as it is a study of the "neurotic" characters of the film.

Roughly at the midpoint of the movie, Alma learns of Elisabeth's betrayal. After reading the letter, the nurse stands thoughtfully at the edge of a pool of water in a shot which emphasizes the doubles theme by including her full reflection (aa). Seething with anger, Alma leaves a jagged piece of glass on the walkway, hoping Elisabeth will step on it. When she does, Bergman cuts to a shot of Alma looking at the scene from behind a window and curtain (bb). Suddenly the soundtrack reverberates with a cracking noise, and a literal crack tears the film image down the middle (cc). Half the image drops from sight, literally splitting Alma's face in two (dd).

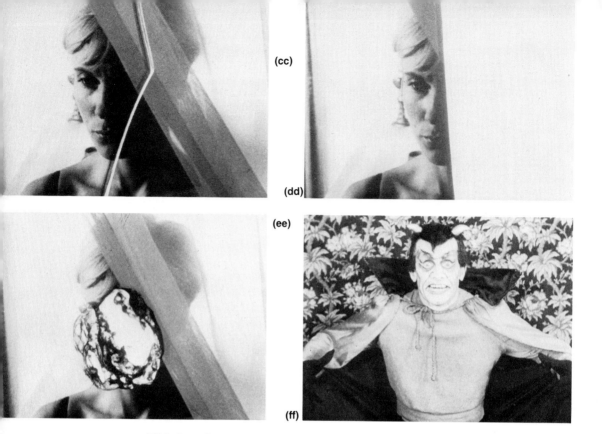

(cc)

(dd)

(ee)

(ff)

This "crack-up" of course is a metaphor of Alma's emotional collapse. A burning hole then penetrates Alma's face and consumes the image surface (ee). Beneath the burn hole, incongruous images of the silent movie devil (ff) and the skeleton (gg) emerge—Bergman's reminders of the primitiveness and inadequacies of his medium in conveying intense passions. After the two women quarrel, Alma withdraws to the rocks where she remains for hours (hh), silently huddled in a kind of immobile trance (ii).

In her bedroom, Elisabeth finds a photograph of a Nazi concentration camp and its victims (jj). Again, she is struck by the horrors of the real world, particularly by a small Jewish boy who is among those being herded (kk). The boy recalls her own son, perhaps, whom we saw earlier in a photograph. The fact that Elisabeth is jolted back to reality by several "documentary" images possibly reflects Bergman's own despair in trying to capture honest and uncompromised emotions in a "fictional" image. After this, the boundaries of fantasy and reality seem to merge.

In one particularly dreamlike sequence, Elisabeth's husband (who is apparently blind) visits the cottage. Mr. Vogler speaks to Alma as though she were his wife. At first Alma resists (ll), but prodded by the mysterious Elisabeth, Alma pretends to be his wife, even going so far as to make love with him (mm). All the while, the silent Elisabeth seems to recall her marital relationship with tender sorrowful futility, her face half in darkness, or cut off by the frame (nn).

In another sequence, Alma sees Elisabeth guiltily covering with her hands the torn photograph of her boy. The nurse prods the mother to speak of her

(gg)

(hh)

(ii)

(jj)

(kk)

Mr. Vogler, I am not your wife.

(ll)

(mm)

(nn)

(oo)

(pp)

(qq)

Tell me about it, Elisabeth.

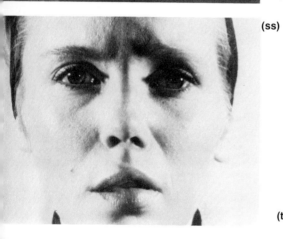

Tell me about it, Elisabeth.

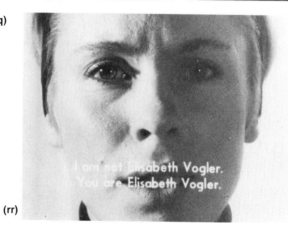

I am not Elisabeth Vogler.
You are Elisabeth Vogler.

(rr)

(ss)

(tt)

(uu)

(vv)

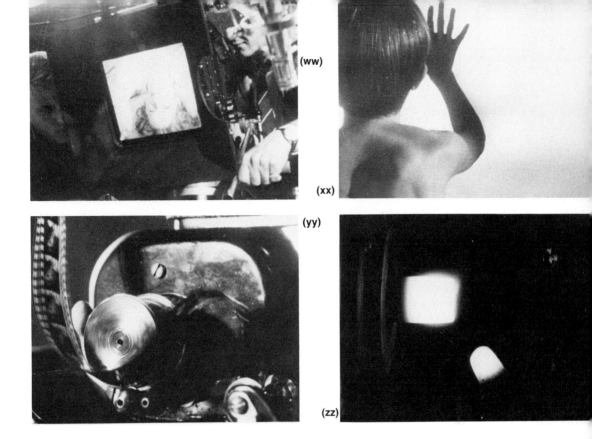

(ww)

(xx)

(yy)

(zz)

son, but Elisabeth refuses (oo). Instead, Alma tells the story, almost as though it were her own. As she recounts Elisabeth's horror at being pregnant and in giving birth to an unwanted child, the camera moves from an over-the-shoulder two-shot to a closeup of Elisabeth—half her face plunged in symbolic darkness (pp). Then Bergman repeats the same story of guilt and anguish, only this time he moves the camera toward Alma, the opposite side of her face likewise in darkness (qq). The repetition of the story with the two separate shots suggests the merging of personalities. Alma denies this identity fusion (rr), but suddenly, through the use of special-effects photography, Bergman literally fuses the faces of the two women into one (ss).

Near the end of the film, we see Elisabeth packing her clothes. Later, we see Alma doing the same. She looks into a mirror, and again we see an image of fused identities, dreamily shot in double exposure (tt). As Alma leaves the cottage with her suitcase, Bergman crowds her figure with the face of a wooden ship's masthead (uu). He then cuts to a closeup of Elisabeth's frozen features as Electra, another striking motif of immobility (vv). This in turn is intercut with a shot of Bergman and his cinematographer Sven Nykvist behind a camera, which is descending slowly on a crane (ww). The juxtaposition of these three shots once again suggests their parallelism, implying that Alma and Elisabeth are two sides of Bergman's own personality.

The film concludes with a reversal of some of the opening shots. We see the boy reaching for a totally out-of-focus image of the fused Bibi Andersson–Liv Ullmann face (xx). The soundtrack seems to whirl out of control as we see an image of a film strip uncoiling wildly off its sprocket (yy). Finally, the carbon arc lamps of the projector sputter out (zz), and there is only darkness.

## Point-of-View and Literary Adaptations

Point-of-view in fiction generally concerns the narrator, through whose eyes the events of a story are viewed. The ideas and incidents are sifted through the consciousness and language of the story teller, who may or may not be a participant in the action, and who may or may not be a reliable guide for the reader to follow. There are four basic types of point-of-view in fiction: the first person, the omniscient, the third person, and the objective. In the movies, point-of-view tends to be less rigorous than in fiction, for while there are cinematic equivalents of the four basic types of narration, feature films tend to fall naturally into the omniscient form.

The *first-person narrator* tells his own story. In some cases, he is an objective observer who can be relied upon to relate the events accurately. Nick Carraway in Fitzgerald's *The Great Gatsby* is a good example of this kind of narrator. Other first person narrators are subjectively involved in the main action, and can't be totally relied upon. In *Huckleberry Finn,* the immature Huck relates all the events as he experienced them. Huck obviously can't supply his readers with all the necessary information when he himself does not possess it. In employing this type of first-person narrator, the novelist must somehow permit the reader to see the truth without stretching the plausibility of the narrator. Generally, a novelist solves this problem by providing the reader with clues which permit him to see more clearly than the narrator himself. For example, when Huck enthusiastically recounts the glamor of a circus and the "amazing feats" of its performers, the more sophisticated reader sees beyond Huck's words and infers that the performers are in fact a rather shabby crew, and their theatrical acts merely cheap deceptions.

Many films employ first-person narrative techniques, but only sporadically. The cinematic equivalent to the "voice" of the literary narrator is the "eye" of the camera, and this difference is an important one. In literature, the distinction between the narrator and the reader is clear: it's as if the reader were listening to a friend tell a story. In film, however, the viewer identifies with the lens, and thus tends to fuse with the narrator. To produce first-person narration in film, the camera would have to record all the action through the eyes of the character, which, in effect, would also make the viewer the protagonist.

In *The Lady of the Lake,* Robert Montgomery attempted to use the first-person camera throughout the film. It was an interesting experiment, but a failure, for several reasons. In the first place, the director was forced into a number of absurdities. Having the characters address the camera was not too much of a problem, for point-of-view shots are common in most movies. However, there were several actions where the device simply broke down. When a woman walked up to the hero and kissed him, for example, she had to slink toward the camera and begin to embrace it while her face came closer to the lens. Similarly, when the hero was involved in a fist fight, the antagonist literally had to attack the camera, which jarred appropriately whenever the "narrator" was dealt a blow. The problem with the exclusive use of the first-person camera, then, is its literalness. Furthermore, it tends to create a sense of frustration in the viewer, who wants to *see* the hero. In fiction, we get to know the first person through his words, through his judgments and values, which are reflected in his language. But in movies, we get to know a character by seeing how he reacts to people and events. Unless the director breaks the first-person camera convention, we can never see the hero, we can only see what he sees.

A useful first-person technique in film is to have a narrator tell his story in words on the soundtrack while the camera records the events, usually through a variety of narrative shots. An interesting variation of this sound technique is multiple first-person narration. In *Citizen Kane*, five different people offer their ideas on what kind of person Kane was. Each sound narra-

**8-22. *War and Peace* (U.S.S.R., 1968).**

*With Sergei Bondarchuk (black coat); Directed by Bondarchuk.*
Except for mysteries and suspense films, in which the audience is deliberately kept in ignorance of certain facts, the cinema tends to fall into omniscient narration automatically. As in omnisciently narrated novels like Tolstoy's *War in Peace*, the film director provides us with all the necessary information we need to know in order to comprehend the characters and events of a story. Much is usually eliminated from a novel of this length, but much is also added, as Leo Braudy has pointed out: "The muted emphasis on gesture, makeup, intonation, and bodily movement possible in film can enrich a character with details that would intrude blatantly if they were separately verbalized in a novel." See Leo Braudy, *The World in a Frame* (Garden City, N.Y.: Doubleday, 1976).

*(A Continental Release)*

**8-23. *Gulliver's Travels* (Great Britain, 1939).**
*Based on the tale by Jonathan Swift; Animation by Max Fleischer.*
In literature, fantastic elements have to be imagined; but because of the cinema's virtually unlimited range of expression, fantasy materials can be presented concretely and in great detail.

tion is accompanied by a flashback sequence, although not in the first-person camera. The flashbacks present Kane in somewhat contradictory terms, each reflecting the prejudices of the storyteller. Where one narrator leaves off, another who knew Kane in a different period of his life picks up the narrative line and develops it further, until the final storyteller concludes with a tale of Kane's last days.

The *omniscient narrator* is often associated with the nineteenth-century novel. Generally, such narrators are not participants in a story, but are all-knowing observers who supply the reader with all the facts he or she needs to know in order to appreciate the story. Such narrators can span many locations and time periods, and can enter the consciousness of a number of different characters, telling us what they think and feel. Omniscient narrators can be relatively detached from the story, as in *War and Peace,* or they can take on a distinct personality of their own, as in *Tom Jones* where the amiable storyteller amuses us with his wry observations and judgments.

Omniscient narration is almost inevitable in film. In literature, the first person and the omniscient voice are mutually exclusive, for if a person tells us his own thoughts directly, he can't also tell us, with certainty, the thoughts of others. But in movies, the combination of first-person and omniscient narration is common. Each time the director moves his camera—either within a shot or between shots—we are offered a new point-of-view from which to evaluate the scene. The filmmaker can cut easily from a subjective point-of-view shot (first person) to a variety of objective shots. He can concentrate on a single reaction (closeup) or the simultaneous reactions of several characters (long shot). Within a matter of seconds, the film director can show us a cause and an effect, an action and a reaction. He can connect various time periods and locations almost instantaneously (parallel editing), or literally superimpose different times periods (dissolve or multiple exposure). The omniscient camera can be a dispassionate observer, as it is in many of Chaplin's films, or it can be a witty commentator—an evaluater of events—as it often is in Hitchcock's films or those of Lubitsch.

**8-24. *Cabaret* (U.S.A., 1972).**
*With Liza Minnelli; Choreographed and directed by Bob Fosse.*
Some stories have been adapted in so many mediums the artistic permutations seem almost incestuous. Christopher Isherwood first created the main characters and corrupt milieu of the early Nazi period in his collection of short stories, *Goodbye to Berlin.* Some of the materials of these stories were adapted by John Van Druten in a play *I am a Camera,* which itself was adapted into a nonmusical film of the same title. Some years later, these materials were adapted into a stage musical entitled *Cabaret.* Fosse's musical film, adapted by Jay Allen and Hugh Wheeler, used much of the stage music, but also incorporated a good deal of the original Isherwood material.

*(Allied Artists)*

The *third-person point-of-view* is essentially a variation of the omniscient. In the third person, a nonparticipating narrator tells a story from the consciousness of a single character. In some novels, this narrator completely penetrates the mind of a character; in others, there is virtually no penetration. In Jane Austen's *Pride and Prejudice,* for example, we learn what Elizabeth Bennett thinks and feels about events, but we're never permitted to enter the consciousness of the other characters. We can only guess what they feel through Elizabeth's interpretations—which are often inaccurate. Her interpretations are not offered directly to the reader as in the first person, but through the intermediacy of the narrator who tells us her responses.

In movies, there is a rough equivalent to the third person, but it's not so rigorous as in literature. Usually, third-person narration is found in documentaries where an anonymous commentator tells us about the background of a central character. In Sidney Meyer's *The Quiet One,* for example,

**8-25. Lolita (U.S.A./Great Britain, 1962).**
*With Peter Sellers and James Mason; Based on the novel by Vladimir Nabokov; Directed by Stanley Kubrick.*
Novelists and dramatists are not always dismayed when filmmakers drastically alter an original property. Nabokov wrote the first draft of this screenplay, but it was much too long. Kubrick and his producer James B. Harris rewrote it extensively, preserving about 20 percent of the original. Nonetheless, Nabokov considered it a first-rate film, with magnificent actors, and he called Kubrick "a great director." See Vladimir Nabokov, *Lolita: A Screenplay* (New York: McGraw-Hill, 1974), which includes many scenes that were cut from the film version; and Alfred Appel, Jr., *Nabokov's Dark Cinema* (New York: Oxford, 1974).

the visuals dramatize certain traumatic events in the life of an impoverished youngster, Donald. On the soundtrack, James Agee's commentary tells us some of the reasons why Donald behaves as he does, how he feels about his parents, his peers, and his teachers.

The *objective point-of-view* is also a variation of the omniscient. Objective narration is the most detached of all: it doesn't enter the consciousness of any character, but merely reports events from the outside. Indeed, this voice has been likened to a camera which records events impartially and without bias. It presents facts and allows readers to interpret for themselves. The objective voice is more congenial to film than to literature, for movies literally employ a recording camera. The cinematic objective point-of-view is generally used by realistic directors who keep their camera at long shot and avoid all distortions or "commentary" such as angles, lenses, and filters.

A great many movies are adaptations of literary sources (8-24). In some respects, adapting a novel or play requires more skill and originality than an original screenplay. Furthermore, the better the literary work, the more difficult the adaptation. For this reason, many film adaptations are based on mediocre sources, for few people will get upset at the modifications required in film if the source itself isn't of the highest caliber. There are many adaptations that are superior to their originals: *Birth of a Nation*, for instance, was based on Thomas Dixon's trashy novel *The Klansman* which is more blatantly racist than the film. Some commentators believe that if a work of art has reached its fullest artistic expression in one form, an adaptation will inevitably be inferior. According to this argument, no film adaptation of *Pride and Prejudice* could equal the original, nor could any novel hope to capture the richness of *Persona*, or even *Citizen Kane* which is a rather literary movie. There's a good deal of sense in this view, for we've seen how literature and film tend to solve problems differently, how the true content of each medium is organically governed by its forms.

The real problem of the adapter is not how to reproduce the *content* of a literary work (an impossibility), but how close he or she should remain to the raw data of the *subject matter,* in the sense that these terms have been used throughout this book. This degree of fidelity is what determines the three types of adaptations: the loose, the faithful, and the literal. Of course these classifications are for convenience only, for in actual practice most movies fall somewhere in between.

The *loose adaptation* is barely that. Generally, only an idea, a situation, or a character is taken from a literary source, then developed independently. Loose film adaptations can be likened to Shakespeare's treatment of a story from Plutarch or Bandello, or to the ancient Greek dramatists who often drew upon a common mythology. A film that falls into this class is Kurosawa's *Throne of Blood,* which transforms Shakespeare's *Macbeth* into a quite different tale, set in medieval Japan, though the filmmaker retains several plot elements from Shakespeare's original (8-26).

**8-26. *Throne of Blood* (Japan, 1957).**
*With Toshiro Mifune; Based on Shakespeare's* Macbeth; *Directed by Akira Kurosawa.*
The loose adaptation takes a few general ideas from an original source, then develops them independently. Many commentators consider Kurosawa's film the greatest of all Shakespearean adaptations precisely because the filmmaker doesn't attempt to compete with the dramatist. Kurosawa's samurai movie is a *cinematic* masterpiece, these commentators claim, owing relatively little to language for its power. Its similarities to Shakespeare's literary masterpiece are superficial, just as the play's similarities to Holingshed's *Chronicles* (Shakespeare's primary source) are of no great artistic significance.

**8-27. *The Man Who Would Be King* (U.S.A., 1976).**
*With (right to left) Sean Connery and Michael Caine; Written by John Huston and Gladys Hill; Based on a story by Rudyard Kipling; Directed by Huston.*
Virtually all of Huston's works are based on novels, plays, and short stories. James Agee noted that the better the original material, the better Huston functions as an artist. His adaptations have encompassed such disparate authors as Dashiell Hammett, B. Traven, Stephen Crane, Herman Melville, Arthur Miller, Tennessee Williams, Carson McCullers, Flannery O'Conner, and the writers of the Book of Genesis. "I don't seek to interpret, to put my own stamp on the material," Huston has pointed out. "I try to be as faithful to the original material as I can." See James Agee, "Undirectable Director," in *Agee on Film: Reviews and Comments* (Boston: Beacon Press, 1958).

*Faithful adaptations,* as the phrase implies, attempt to recreate the literary source in filmic terms, keeping as close to the spirit of the original as possible (8-27). André Bazin likened the faithful adapter to a translator who tries to find equivalents to the original. Of course, Bazin realized that fundamental differences exist between the two mediums: the translator's problem in converting the word "road" to "*strada*" or "*strasse*" is not so acute as a filmmaker's problem in transforming the word into a picture. An example of a faithful adaptation is Richardson's *Tom Jones.* John Osborne's screenplay preserves much of the novel's plot structure, its major events, and most of the important characters. Even the witty omniscient narrator is retained. But the film is not merely an illustration of the novel. In the first place, Fielding's book is too packed with incidents for a film adaptation. The many inn scenes, for example, are reduced to a central episode: the Upton Inn sequence. Two minor aspects of the novel are enlarged in the movie: the famous eating scene between Tom and Mrs. Waters, and the fox-hunting eposide. These sequences are included because two of Fielding's favorite sources of metaphors throughout the novel are drawn from eating and hunting. In effect, Osborne uses these scattered metaphors as raw material, or filmic "equivalents," in Bazin's sense.

*Literal adaptations* are pretty much restricted to plays. As we have seen, the two basic modes of drama—action and dialogue—are also found in films. The major problem with stage adaptations is in the handling of space and time rather than language. If the film adapter were to leave his camera at long shot and restrict his editing to scene shifts only, the result would be similar to the original. But we've seen that few filmmakers would be willing merely to record a play, nor indeed should they, for in doing so they would lose much of the excitement of the original and contribute none of the advantages of the adapting medium, particularly its greater freedom in treating space and time.

Movies can add many dimensions to a play, especially through the use of closeups and edited juxtapositions. Since these techniques aren't found in the theatre, even "literal" adaptations are not strictly literal, they're simply more subtle in their modifications. Stage dialogue is often retained in film adaptations, but its effect is different on the audience. In the live theatre, the meaning of the language is determined by the fact that the characters are on the same stage at the same time, reacting to the same words (8-28). In a movie, time and space are fragmented by the individual shots. Furthermore, since even a literary film is primarily visual and only secondarily verbal, nearly all the dialogue is modified by the images. The differences between loose, faithful, and literal adaptations, then, are essentially matters of degree. In each case, the cinematic form inevitably alters the content of the literary original.

(American Film Theatre)

**8-28.** *The Iceman Cometh* **(U.S.A., 1973).**
*With Frederic March and Lee Marvin; Based on the play by Eugene O'Neill; Directed by John Frankenheimer.*
Virtually all literal adaptations were originally stage plays, for the language and actions of the live theatre are cinematically convertible. The most significant changes in a literal adaptation of a play are more likely to involve differences in time and space rather than language.

## Further Readings

ASTRUC, ALEXANDRE, "The Birth of a New Avant-Garde: La Caméra-Stylo," in *The New Wave,* Peter Graham, ed. (London: Secker & Warburg, 1968).

BEJA, MORRIS, *Film and Literature* (New York: Longman, Inc., 1979).

BLUESTONE, GEORGE, *Novels into Film* (Baltimore: Johns Hopkins Press, 1957).

CHATMAN, SEYMOUR BENJAMIN, *Story and Discourse: Narrative Structure in Fiction and Film* (Ithaca, N.Y.: Cornell Univ. Press, 1978).

CORLISS, RICHARD, *The Hollywood Screenwriters* (New York: Avon Books, 1972).

FELL, JOHN L., *Film and the Narrative Tradition* (Norman, Okla.: University of Oklahoma Press, 1974).

LUHR, WILLIAM, and PETER LEHMAN, *Authorship and Narrative in the Cinema* (New York: Oxford Univ. Press, 1977).

RICHARDSON, ROBERT, *Literature and Film* (Bloomington, Ind.: Indiana Univ. Press, 1969).

SCHATZ, THOMAS, *Hollywood Genres: Formulas, Filmmaking, and the Studio System* (Philadelphia: Temple University Press, 1981).

SIMON, JOHN, *"Persona,"* in *Ingmar Bergman Directs* (New York: Harcourt, Brace, Jovanovich, 1972).

*"Documentary and newsreel are the noblest of genres. They do not seek the instantaneous for its own sake, but for what it secretes of eternity."*

JEAN-LUC GODARD

# DOCUMENTARY

Documentarists—both practitioners and theorists—are by no means agreed on the definition of a documentary movie. The very term "documentary" has been disputed. Some commentators prefer the more general "nonfiction film," while others argue for "the factual film." According to a few of these critics, "documentary" should be used to describe only those movies in which a creative interpretation is involved. A mere presentation of facts (such as industrial films, travelogues, training movies) ought to be designated by some less prestigious term. For some, then, the term "documentary" is qualitative, suggesting at least a degree of artistic excellence. But these distinctions are more trouble than they're worth. Most fiction films (or for that matter, plays, novels, and paintings) are artistically negligible, but no one would think of differentiating them by assigning another term. As in the other arts, there are good and bad documentaries, and in the following pages the term will be used in the generic rather than qualitative sense.

We also tend to be rather jaded about the "mere" recording properties of the movie camera—as if this were a contemptible achievement. The original audiences of *The Arrival of a Train* were enchanted precisely by the medium's ability to capture reality "alive," as it were (9-1). Similarly, present-day audiences aren't disappointed by such objectively photographed works as *Richard Pryor—Live in Concert* which is really a *recording* of an artistic presentation in another medium. In cases such as these, film functions as a kind of xerography: we don't *want* the camera to deform the original materials. Pryor is the sole attraction; the rest is just hardware.

(Museum of Modern Art)

**9-1. *The Arrival of a Train* (France, 1895).**
*Directed by Louis and Auguste Lumière.*
The Lumière brothers might be regarded as the godfathers of the documentary movement. Their brief *actualités* (as they referred to them) are primitive documentaries, stressing the charm of ordinary events as they can be seen in everyday life. Audiences of this era were astonished by the new medium's ability to present a mirror image of reality-in-motion.

## Fact and Fiction

The distinction between fiction films and documentaries is blurred in some instances. No sooner does one begin to describe the main features of the documentary than a number of prominent exceptions come to mind. Despite individual exceptions, however, there are certain general characteristics that are found in most examples of this type of film.

The most obvious, of course, is that documentaries deal with facts rather than fiction, with real people, places, and events rather than imagined ones. Authenticity is at once the greatest glory and the greatest potential source of controversy in a documentary. In fiction movies, "authenticity" is defined internally, in terms of the "world" of the film. But no matter how convincing the "reality" of the fiction film might be, in the back of our minds we're always aware that "it's only a movie," that the events are simulated. Therefore, we are able to watch scenes of gruesome violence—as in Peckinpah's *Straw Dogs*—without losing our sense of external reality. We willingly suspend our disbelief in order to respond fully to a fiction film; at the same time, we have enough aesthetic distance to realize that the screen events have been staged for us. Fiction movies are faked—at least on this literal level. The desire of the fiction filmmaker—or any artist who creates an imaginary world—is for the audience to accept the *symbolic* truth of the situations and characters. Aristotle valued art over history precisely because he believed in the greater universality of art. History, on the other hand, deals with authentic events and people, and therefore may be too idiosyncratic to have universal significance.

**9-2.** *Paisan* **(Italy, 1946).**
*Directed by Roberto Rossellini.*
Rossellini began his career as a documentarist, and in movies like *Paisan* he used nonprofessional players to re-create scenes that were based on actual events which took place in Italy during World War II. Because these events were dramatically heightened and synthesized from a variety of sources, most historians consider the film essentially fictional, though with a strong documentary flavor.

*(New Yorker Films)*

    The documentarist—like the historian—is likely to reject these views. We arrive at truth through authentic facts, not artistic "falsehoods," he believes. Because authenticity is a documentarist's trump card, he or she is acutely sensitive to charges of inaccuracy, distortion, or fakery. Perhaps the ultimate condemnation of a documentary is to accuse it of being "fictional"—that is, too slick, contrived, and emotionally hyped up. Such movies cater to an audience's desire for drama which doesn't exist in the material. Similarly, many documentarists are suspicious of "the beautiful shot," for it tends to suggest the manipulations of the fiction filmmaker. A shaky, blurry shot of an actual murder is more emotionally moving than a carefully photographed recreation of the event, many documentarists believe, even if the filmmaker tries to reconstruct the event as authentically as possible.

    To some documentarists, then, literal truth has a beauty that transcends formal excellence. To some fiction filmmakers, on the other hand, beauty has a symbolic truth that transcends factual authenticity. The argument is an old

**9-3. *A Hard Day's Night* (Great Britain, 1964).**
*With Ringo Starr; Directed by Richard Lester.*
Even expressionist filmmakers have incorporated factual elements into their works. Lester's Beatles film is a whimsical mixture of the techniques of musicals, TV commercials, abstract films, home movies, and documentaries.

and tedious one. There are great documentaries and great fiction films, though the kind of artistry involved in each tends to be different. Perhaps Jean-Luc Godard, who has made both kinds of movies, has expressed it best:

> Beauty—the splendor of truth—has two poles. There are directors who seek the truth, which, if they find it, will necessarily be beautiful; others seek beauty, which, if they find it, will also be true. One finds these two poles in documentary and fiction.

Documentarists believe that they're not creating a world so much as reporting on the one that already exists. They are not just recorders of external reality, however, for like fiction filmmakers, they shape their raw materials through their selection of details. These details are organized into a coherent artistic pattern, although many documentarists deliberately keep the structure of their movies simple and unobtrusive: They want their films to suggest the same copiousness and apparent randomness of life itself.

Details are exploited differently in fiction films and documentaries. In

DOCUMENTARY **336**

most fiction movies, the director invents certain details to enhance the credibility of the characters and story which may or may not resemble actual people and events. The major problem of the fiction filmmaker, then, is not fidelity to external reality, but internal consistency and probability. That is, how is such-and-such a character *likely* to react in a given situation?

The documentarist tends to withhold judgment until observing how the person reacts *in fact*. Whether or not the reaction is consistent or probable, the documentarist prefers the real thing to the likely thing. For example, in any documentary dealing with the life of Robert Frost, one would expect at least one scene of the poet on a lonely road, perhaps meditating on a natural scene. But in *Robert Frost: A Lover's Quarrel with the World*, Robert Hughes avoided the probable and concentrated on what Frost actually was: a rather snappish, not altogether pleasant man, shrewd and thoroughly contemporary. The final image of the movie is not of the "celebrated contemplative poet" walking down a country road, but of a weary professional in a station wagon, driving off to another tiresome speaking engagement because he needs the income.

Most fiction films tell a story, while documentaries are primarily concerned with revealing facts, usually within nonnarrative frameworks. A cause–effect pattern is generally quite apparent in fiction films. Once the conflict is established, each subsequent scene represents a progressive inten-

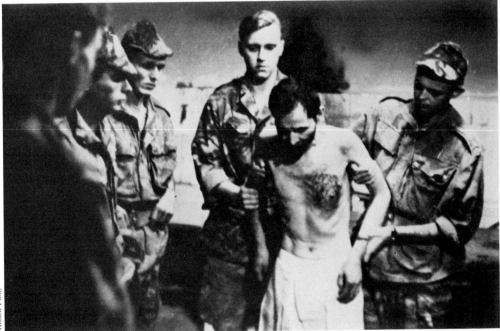

(Rizzoli Film)

**9-4. *The Battle of Algiers* (Italy/Algeria, 1967).**
*Directed by Gillo Pontecorvo.*
Many of its original audiences thought this film was a documentary compilation of authentic revolutionary footage. Its grainy images and shaky camera work produce a gripping sense of immediacy. The movie was totally recreated, and eventually Pontecorvo had to add a title to this effect at the opening of the film.

sification until the climax is reached and the conflict resolved. This cause-effect pattern of development means that the sequence of scenes is pretty much fixed by the demands of the narrative structure. One couldn't re-arrange such sequences without damaging the logic of the rising action. Of course, some fiction films are more rigorously story-oriented than others. Most of Hitchcock's films, for example, are almost exclusively structured in terms of narrative. Most French movies, on the other hand, are very loosely structured.

Documentaries tend to be thematically rather than narratively structured. The filmmaker is more concerned with presenting a problem or an argument than with telling a story. Consequently, the documentarist generally has greater freedom in arranging and structuring the materials. In many cases, the sequence of shots and even entire scenes could be rearranged with rela-tively little loss of comprehension or logic. Frequently there is no dramatic conflict in a documentary, just a given situation. Climaxes are usually not overt in factual films; the most effective argument or the most telling scene is generally saved until late in the movie, but there isn't the sense of inevitability that characterizes most fictional climaxes. Relatively few documentaries are

**9-5.** *Medium Cool* **(U.S.A., 1969).**
*Photographed and directed by Haskell Wexler.*
As an eclectic art that defies neat categories, the cinema abounds in hybrid genres. The distinctions between fiction and documentary are difficult to make in movies like *Medium Cool,* which intercuts scripted scenes with documentary footage of the 1968 Chicago political demonstrations.

*(Paramount Pictures)*

concerned with the complexities of character in the fictional sense. In fact, one of the most persistent criticisms leveled at the documentary is the preoccupation with social issues and abstract ideas rather than flesh-and-blood people. It was not until the 1960s that documentaries began to explore the ambiguities of the human personality in any great depth.

Perhaps no other type of movie is so suited to the analysis of social problems as the documentary. Many of them are concerned with exposing immediate social ills. For this reason, documentaries tend to seem dated once the problem has been solved. Only the greatest of them retain their universality long after their release date, although there are many thematically dated documentaries that are still technically brilliant. Because of their social orientation, many documentaries emphasize the interrelationships between people and their environment. Particular stress is placed on political institutions and their degree of responsiveness to the needs of citizens. Not surprisingly, many documentaries are government sponsored and are intended primarily for educational and propagandistic purposes.

Not content to analyze social problems, many documentarists also offer

(New Yorker Films)

**9-6. *Edvard Munch* (Norway, 1976).**
*Directed by Peter Watkins.*
Watkins, who is English, is an audacious innovator in form. In this work, he combines facts, speculations, voice-over narration, *cinéma vérité* "interviews," and dramatic recreations of historical events. His portrait of the great Norwegian artist Munch and his milieu has been described as part biography, part sociology, part history, part psychology, and part stylistic analysis. See also Joseph A. Gomez, *Peter Watkins* (Boston: G. K. Hall, 1980).

solutions. In the 1930s, the desire to expose abuses and suggest reform was strong, especially in Great Britain where the documentary movement was dominated by the lively Scotsman, John Grierson. It was Grierson who originally coined the term "documentary" and defined it as "the creative treatment of actuality." Grierson insisted that the documentarist must be a political and social analyst. He or she must take a position, must make a moral commitment. Grierson scoffed at the concept of objectivity in nonfiction films. The so-called objective documentary is mere newsreel, he insisted, for it only reports information and doesn't suggest causes and cures of specific social problems.

This issue of objectivity vs. subjectivity has plagued the documentary movement almost since its inception. Critics and theorists seem more preoccupied with the problem than filmmakers who generally view the issue as naive. In the late 1960s, however, it erupted into a national controversy in the United States, where the major television networks were widely criticized for their "slanted" coverage of the Vietnam conflict and the Antiwar Movement. But the problem of subjectivity is a complex one, involving epistemological dilemmas that go far beyond the confines of documentary filmmaking.

Naive viewers tend to believe that when an event occurs, the film director ought to capture it as it "really happened." The truth of the matter is that an

*(Museum of Modern Art)*

**9-7.** *Harlan County, U.S.A.* **(U.S.A., 1977).**
*Directed by Barbara Kopple.*
Documentary filmmaking can be a dangerous profession. During the production of this film, which deals with a bitter coalminers' strike for decent working conditions, Kopple and her crew were repeatedly plunged in the middle of violence. In one sequence, they are actually fired upon by a trigger-happy yahoo: the camera recorded it all. Implicit in the concept of documentary is the verb, to document—to verify, to provide an irrefutable record of an event.

event must be perceived, and the very act of perception involves an ideology—a set of moral assumptions. Relevant and significant facts must be sorted out from the vast multitude of irrelevant details. But what's relevant to one observer might seem incidental to another. The selection of "significant" details, then, is already a distortion of an actual event, like the digest of a novel compared to an unexpurgated version. Different people react differently to the same event—just as eyewitness accounts of an accident often differ. Furthermore, a person's analysis of an event will be altered by religious, ethnic, and political beliefs. A leftwing filmmaker interprets an event from a different ideological perspective than a rightwinger, yet both can sincerely believe they're portraying the event truthfully. Throughout the turbulent 1960s, for example, the three major American TV networks presented news stories of the same events, yet each tended to "see" the events from a slightly different ideological perspective. The selection of details, the use of certain angles and lenses, the style of editing, were different with each network, yet they all believed they were portraying the events responsibly and fairly.

We have seen how the form of a shot can alter its content. By exploiting certain angles and editing techniques, a filmmaker can portray a public assembly as an orderly gathering of citizens or a mass of rampaging anarchists. Objectivity, then, is an impossible goal in documentary filmmaking—at least as an absolute. Even Frederick Wiseman, among the most objective of documentarists, insists that his movies are a subjective *interpretation* of actual events, people, and places—though he tries to be as "fair" as possible in presenting his materials.

"Objectivity" and "subjectivity" are best used as relative terms. As in fiction films, the degree of distortion in documentaries ranges over a surprisingly wide spectrum. The concepts of Realism and Expressionism are almost as useful in discussing documentaries as in fiction movies, although the overwhelming majority of documentarists would insist that their principal interest

**9-8. Nanook of the North (U.S.A., 1922).**
Flaherty distrusted editing and attempted as much as possible to include all the relevant dramatic variables within the same frame. Spatial interrelationships are emphasized by deep-focus photography, and real time is preserved in the frequent use of lengthy takes. See also Arthur Calder-Marshall, *The Innocent Eye* (Baltimore: Penguin, 1970); and William T. Murphey, *Robert Flaherty: A Guide to References and Resources* (Boston: G. K. Hall, 1979).

is with subject matter rather than style. In fact, some filmmakers believe that the tension between subject matter (content) and style (form) is what gives documentaries their vitality. Albert Maysles has remarked on this artistic tension:

> We can see two kinds of truth here. One is in the raw material, which is the footage, the kind of truth that you get in literature in the diary form—it's immediate, no one has tampered with it. Then there's the other kind of truth that comes in extracting and juxtaposing the raw material into a more meaningful and coherent storytelling form which finally can be said to be more than just raw data. In a way, the interests of the people in shooting and the people editing (even if it's the same individual) are in conflict with one another, because the raw material doesn't want to be shaped. It wants to maintain its truthfulness. One discipline says that if you begin to put it into another form, you're going to lose some of the veracity. The other discipline says if you don't let me put this into a form, no one is going to see it and the elements of truth in the raw material will never reach the audience with any impact, with any artistry, or whatever. So there are these things which are in conflict with one another and the thing is to put it all together, deriving the best from both. It comes almost to an argument of content and form, and you can't do one without the other.

The documentarist, then, is faced with many of the same artistic problems as the fiction filmmaker. Needless to say, arguments over which approach is better are doomed to futility.

## Robert Flaherty and Dziga Vertov

The American Robert Flaherty is generally regarded as the father of the documentary movement and its first great realist. The history of the nonfiction film really begins with his first movie *Nanook of the North* (9-9). Actu-

*(Museum of Modern Art)*

**9-9. Nanook of the North.**
Flaherty's masterpiece has an epic scope in which humans are visually dwarfed into insignificance, specks on a vast field of ice and snow (a). But the movie is also a personal account of a friendship—between Nanook and the man behind the camera. Particularly after an amusing or daring incident, Nanook sometimes turns toward Flaherty with a winning grin of triumph (b).

(a)

(b)

ally, Flaherty began his career as an explorer and ethnologist, and in some respects his films can be considered the artifacts of his continuing exploration of remote cultures. Originally, he brought a movie camera along simply to record some scenes of Eskimo life beyond the Arctic Circle. He knew virtually nothing about filmmaking, and to the end of his career preferred a simple approach with only a handful of basic techniques.

Flaherty's method of filmmaking was almost mystical—to the annoyance of his associates, who were sometimes exasperated by his time- and money-consuming ways. Using no prepared script, he would shoot thousands of feet of film before deciding how he would use the material—if at all. His shooting ratios were very high, at least by the standards of the time. Flaherty believed that only by shooting massive amounts of footage would the theme of his film "emerge." He was hostile to the idea of imposing a structure over his materials, insisting that the rhythm of a sequence should be the same as the event in reality. The artist merely discovers what's already there—both in life and in the raw footage.

Paul Rotha, the English documentarist and film critic, suggested that Flaherty may have taken these ideas from Eskimo culture. Eskimo ivory carvers, for example, don't think of themselves as creators so much as discoverers of art objects. A piece of ivory, in their view, is a formless mass in which is hidden a given shape. The carver merely releases or "frees" this shape from its surroundings. The carving process is viewed as exploratory until the hidden subject begins to make itself apparent, at which point the artist cuts away the remaining excess materials so that the form may be viewed without obstruction. To the Eskimo, art is a process of revelation, not creation in the usual sense of the term.

Flaherty's theory of documentary art is very close to this view. Ironically, he was often accused of arrogance because of his uneconomical methods of filmmaking, when actually his attitude reflected a good deal of humility and self-effacement. To Flaherty, the integrity of the material was paramount. He

**9-10. *Man of Aran* (Great Britain, 1934).**
*Directed by Robert Flaherty.*
According to many critics of the period, the real conflict on the Aran Islands was not Man against Sea, as Flaherty stresses in this film, but lower-case conflicts—problems that could be solved, like ignorance, religious bigotry, and economic exploitation.

went to considerable lengths to avoid the superimposition of a form which was not an organic extension of the content. Suspicious of the distortions of editing, he tried to reveal his subject in and through the camera. Reality is best served through mise-en-scène, he believed, not by juxtaposing shots that chop up reality into a series of separate fragments.

Throughout *Nanook,* Flaherty employs open forms, implying that more information lies outside the frame. As in his other movies, he includes a number of sweeping pan shots to suggest the vastness of the terrain. In scenes emphasizing vulnerability, as in the blizzard sequence, Nanook's sled races precariously near the bottom of the frame, at times almost slipping into the symbolic darkness below. The unities of time and space are preserved through lengthy takes, with all the relevant variables included in a single shot. While Nanook is hunting walruses, for example, both the hunter and the hunted are kept within the same frame. Flaherty thus captures not only the distance between them, he also preserves the suspense, for with one false step Nanook could scatter the herd.

Flaherty's influence was not strong until the late 1950s when cinéma vérité became the dominant school in the documentary movement. Throughout the Great Depression, World War II, and the immediate postwar era, however, the most important nonfiction films were influenced primarily by the theories developed in the Soviet Union by the expressionist Dziga Vertov. The Polish-born Vertov was experimenting in documentary forms and theory at about the same time Flaherty was making *Nanook*. Like Eisenstein, Vertov was enthusiastic about the potential of film as an educational and propagandistic tool of the Revolution. A new society needs new forms of expression, he

**9-11. *Pumping Iron* (U.S.A., 1977).**
*With Arnold Schwarzenegger; Directed by George Butler and Robert Fiore.*
Not all documentaries are didactic. Some are just interesting, off-beat, or playful, like this affectionate exploration of the world of bodybuilders.

(*Public Broadcasting System*)

believed, and a society composed overwhelmingly of illiterate workers and peasants needs to be instructed on the workers' historical struggle and on the ideals of the Revolution. Vertov believed that documentary film could carry out this mission better than any other art form. He also believed that documentaries ought to be revolutionary in technique as well as content. "Art," he once wrote, "is not a *mirror* which reflects the historical struggle, but a *weapon* of that struggle."

Fiction movies were "aesthetic hash-hish," Vertov claimed, for they provide an escape from, not a confrontation with, reality. The raw material of the cinema must be the observable material world—real people, places, and things. Recreations of reality will inevitably falsify it, will render it fictional, even if the filmmaker sincerely tries to preserve the authenticity of the original. An actor impersonating a peasant will always strike the viewer as precisely that—not the genuine article. He condemned all acted films as opiates.

Like most expressionists, Vertov believed that filmmakers shouldn't merely record external reality, they should analyze it. They must see beneath the surface chaos of the external world in order to reveal its infrastructure— its underlying connections with the institutions of power. The revolutionary

**9-12.** *Fellini's Roma* (Italy, 1972).
*Directed by Federico Fellini.*
Total objectivity is an impossible goal in any documentary enterprise, for a director's perception of actual events will inevitably be influenced by his or her values, prejudices, and preconceptions. The choice of subject matter and the principles of selectivity are determined by what the *director* thinks is important, not necessarily what someone else might regard as essential. In this movie, Fellini makes no pretense at objectivity: as the title suggests, it's an exploration of the city of Rome as seen through Fellini's eyes which has little to do with what an average tourist might see in the city. To varying degrees, the same principle could be applied to virtually any documentary. Most critics regard Fellini's outrageously theatrical scenes, like this "ecclesiastical fashion show," as more compelling than the more objective, factual episodes in the movie.

documentarist teaches ideological lessons, explaining social and economic relationships which aren't always apparent, especially in capitalistic societies where the interests of the ruling class are best served by keeping the working class in ignorance about how the economic system works. The revolutionary documentarist reveals who produces goods, who consumes them, and who profits by them. He demystifies social institutions, exposing those that don't serve the needs of the people, praising those that do. Reality is too complex, too sprawling to be understood by those uninstructed in revolutionary ideology. Hence, the documentarist uses the actual world merely as a repository of unsystemized data.

Like Eisenstein and Pudovkin, Vertov believed that the foundation of

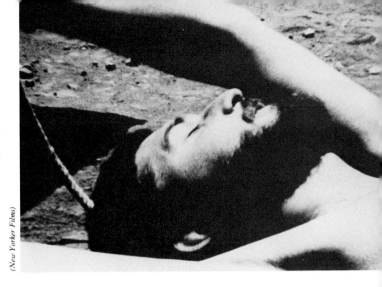

**9-13.** *Brazil: A Report on Torture* **(Chile/U.S.A., 1971).**
*Directed by Haskell Wexler and Saul Landau.*
Many documentaries are made to pierce the conscience of the civilized world about violations of human rights. In this film, seventeen witnesses re-enact the methods of torture in a modern police state.

cinematic art was montage—the art of editing. Strongly influenced by the thematic cross-cutting of Griffith's *Intolerance*, Vertov believed that montage can unite elements which are apparently unrelated in life. Editing can "contrast any points in the universe," he insisted, without regard to the restrictions of space and time. Going even beyond Eisenstein, Vertov felt that continuity in film should be *totally* thematic. Like a poet, the film artist is essentially a fuser of images, he claimed (9-14). In fact, he did little actual shooting him-

**9-14.** *The Man with a Movie Camera* **(U.S.S.R., 1929).**
*Directed by Dziga-Vertov.*
The documentary artist, according to Vertov, is a poet, a fuser of disparate images. The "cinepoet" can yoke together any elements in the universe to form new combinations, without regard to considerations of literal continuity. This whirling, lyrical dissolve is a metaphoric celebration of man's control over his technology. See also Seth R. Feldman, *Dziga Vertov: A Guide to References and Resources* (Boston: G. K. Hall, 1979).

self, believing that the art of the documentary is in the editing, not the photography. Beginning with the three-hour long *Anniversary of the October Revolution* (1918), the first Soviet feature, Vertov conducted a series of editing experiments which became progressively more radical.

Even more than Eisenstein, Vertov experimented with a metaphoric kind of montage. In *The Man with a Movie Camera,* for example, he employed an eye motif to create a startling assortment of comparisons. The human eye is likened to the camera's lens. In the opening morning sequence, we see shades lifted from windows, and doors to airplane hangars being raised like huge steel eyelids. A young woman washing herself is juxtaposed with a shot of a man washing down merchandise and with workers cleaning windows. A woman putting on a slip is compared to a photographer putting a lens on his camera. Cutting hair is likened to cutting film. Sewing machines are analogically linked with editing machines. All of these comparisons are purely visual, for the film is silent and doesn't contain a single title.

Since movies can fuse images with ease, Vertov considered cinema the ultimate poetic art. Like most Soviet directors, he also enthusiastically praised the mechanical aspects of filmmaking and considered it the ultimate technological art as well. Perhaps nothing appealed more to Soviet movie makers than this unique fusion of art with science, of imagination with material reality, of feeling with fact. The scientific properties of photography make many poetic effects possible in the cinema, Vertov believed. Unlike most documentarists, he thought that nonfiction filmmakers should use the full range of special effects that are available to the fiction film director. In his own movies, the technical variety is dazzling: Vertov uses subliminal shots merely one or two frames long, tinted stock for emotional emphasis, virtually every kind of lens and filter, fast motion, slow motion, reverse motion, freeze frames, double and multiple exposures, split screens, multiple images, even animation.

Vertov died in 1954 but his career ended 20 years earlier. Along with Eisenstein and a number of other Soviet artists, Vertov was criticized and ultimately condemned for the sin of formalism: a decadent preoccupation with technique at the expense of content. He spent most of the remainder of his life as a hack editor of government newsreels. Another poet dead.

Most documentarists have avoided the freewheeling lyricism of Vertov's techniques. Because of their undisguised subjectivity, Vertov's movies are effective only with those already in agreement with the director's views, his critics have argued. To persuade a neutral observer, a more objective presentation of factual materials must be practiced, one which presents both sides of an argument. There have been a few political documentarists who have taken over Vertov's methods, however, particularly his editing techniques and his tendency to remind audiences that what they are watching is a manipulated image of reality.

Perhaps the most effective Vertovian documentarist is the American, Emile De Antonio, whose films are polemical and unashamedly one-sided (9-15). Probably the best of these is *In the Year of the Pig,* a scathing attack on America's involvement in Vietnam. Much of De Antonio's footage was taken from archives—old newsreels, TV film clips, even still photographs. This footage is intercut—with maximum ironic impact—with interview scenes featuring antiwar spokesmen like David Halbersham, Senator Wayne Morse,

**9-15. Point of Order! (U.S.A., 1964).**
*Directed by Emile De Antonio.*
Materials which might seem politically neutral can acquire fresh ideological significance when the footage is re-edited expressively. Many documentaries in the Vertov mold, like *Point of Order!*, were photographed by relatively impartial newsreel cameramen. The political significance is conveyed by the way in which this neutral material is restructured on the editing bench. All montage films making use of newsreels descend from Vertov's theories. See also Jay Leyda, *Films Beget Films* (New York: Hill & Wang, 1964).

and Colonel W. R. Corson. Battle footage of the civilian carnage in Vietnam is juxtaposed with interviews of American leaders of both parties justifying their motives for involving the United States in "the battle for men's minds and souls." The juxtapositions in De Antonio's film are not just visual. In one sequence, for example, we see the French army ignominiously surrendering to General Giap at Dienbenphu. On the soundtrack, we hear a wittily orientalized rendition of "The Marseillaise," the French national anthem.

Ultimately, Vertov's influence has probably been greatest with fiction filmmakers and artists of the avant-garde. In diluted form, however, his editing theories influenced the documentary movement in the 1930s and 1940s, especially in western Europe and the English-speaking countries of the world.

## John Grierson and the British School

Although he personally directed only one movie (*Drifters,* 1929), John Grierson was probably the most influential figure in the documentary movement of his generation. His importance was primarily inspirational: as a teacher, publicist, producer, distributor, and organizer. Throughout his career, this crusty old warrior fought a continuing battle—wheedling, cajoling, scolding, and charming various government officials into recognizing the importance of the documentary as an instrument of public education. "I look upon the cinema as a pulpit," he once declared, "and use it as a propagandist."

For the didactic Grierson, film had to be useful—it must fulfill an important public function. He believed that documentary film was essential if a democracy hoped to survive. Only when citizens are aware of what's going on in the public sector are they likely to select the best leaders and the most responsive social programs. Grierson believed that documentary was only secondarily an art form. Throughout his career, he admired good craftsmanship and innovative techniques, but he was suspicious of anything smacking of aestheticism in documentary films: "The conscious pursuit of art carries with it, in periods of public difficulty, a certain shallowness of outlook."

In many respects, the British school can be viewed as a compromise between the traditions of Flaherty and Vertov, although Grierson expressed impatience with what he viewed as their shortcomings and excesses. With Flaherty, he had a lifelong love–hate relationship, though they liked each other personally. What Grierson admired in the American's work was his poetic delicacy, his love of natural and intimate scenes, his sincere respect for the dignity of manual labor. Grierson also felt that Flaherty demonstrated a profound sensitivity toward individuals, a quality conspicuously lacking in the Soviet cinema which tended to emphasize masses of people and communal units.

But Grierson was always dismayed by what he called Flaherty's "Neo-Rousseauism"—his romantic exoticism, his sentimentalization of a bygone era, his insensitivity to social injustice, and his glorification of the "noble savage." The problems facing the twentieth century were essentially urban and technological, Grierson insisted. These require collective and public solutions.

*(Museum of Modern Art)*

**9-16. *The Spanish Earth* (U.S.A.,/ Holland, 1937).**
*Directed by Joris Ivens.*
Many documentarists disdain the notion of objectivity. Some events, they claim, are too morally outrageous to allow for a "balanced view." In this work, the great Dutch documentarist Ivens, in collaboration with the American novelist Ernest Hemingway, exposed the mass killing of civilians during the Spanish Civil War. With the materials of slaughter provided by his cronies Hitler and Mussolini, Franco wrecked devastation on thousands of innocent Spaniards, many of them women and children. Hemingway's commentary, spoken by the novelist himself, communicates the sense of helpless terror brought on by the bombings: "Before, death came when you were old and sick. But now it comes to all in this village. High in the sky and shining silver, it comes to all who have no place to run, no place to hide."

Beautiful as they were, Flaherty's movies were simply irrelevant in solving the enormous problems facing the contemporary world.

Grierson's response to the Soviet cinema was just as ambivalent. He acknowledged the enormous technical contributions of the Russians, particularly their editing innovations. He also admired the strong sense of social purpose of most Soviet documentarists—in theory, at least, if not always in practice. Like the Russian filmmakers, Grierson insisted that the cinema is not a passive mirror of the material world, but a dynamic hammer which helps to shape reality and gives society a sense of purpose and direction.

But Grierson was sharply critical of what he believed to be an *idée fixe* of the Soviet documentary—the Revolution. So long as Russian filmmakers dwelt on this one obsession, their films were exciting and effective—in a flashy, rhetorical sort of way. But the real problems of any society, he averred, involve peacetime activities and programs. He was especially critical of Dziga Vertov, who inspired the Scotsman to new heights of indignation and wit. He duly noted Vertov's technical brilliance but condemned his "exhibitionism." *The Man with a Movie Camera* was mere virtuosity, Grierson scoffed. The shots move along so rapidly that the film seemed more like a "snapshot album" than a documentary. He dismissed Vertov's *Enthusiasm* as "all dazzle-dazzle and bits and pieces, whoopee for this, whoopee for that."

Grierson's concept of documentary tended to be pragmatic, efficient, and rational—the virtues he himself displayed in abundance. He emphasized pre-

**9-17.** *The River* **(U.S.A., 1937).**
*Directed by Pare Lorentz.*
Many documentaries are government sponsored. Lorentz's film, for example, was commissioned by the Federal Government of the United States to publicize the achievements of the Tennessee Valley Authority in curbing the disastrous soil erosion which had devastated the lives of many Americans living in the Mississippi River basin.

planning, especially in the scriptwriting stage. A certain amount of discovery and improvisation was allowable, but he didn't sanction the random experimentation of Flaherty and Vertov, neither of whom used scripts at all. Flaherty believed that documentaries were essentially creations of the camera; Vertov thought they were created on the editor's bench. Grierson, on the other hand, tended to believe that the script was the major force behind a documentary. Of course he realized that the collaborative nature of the filmmaking process doesn't always permit such easy distinctions.

In general, Grierson encouraged a problem-causes-solutions type of approach to the documentary. The films produced under his guidance tended to be brief and deliberately narrow in their themes. They dealt with specific national issues and institutions of public concern, like *Housing Problems, Coalface, Night Mail, Children at School, The Smoke Menace*—their very titles suggest their limited scope and analytical orientation.

This is not to say that British documentaries of this period are dull or conscientiously plodding. Some of them are witty, subtle, and even poetic, despite their utilitarian goals. *Night Mail*, for example, deals with a mail express train which travels from London to Glasgow, and the workers who are responsible for processing the mail along the way. The movie is rather romantic in its treatment and especially innovative in its use of sound, featuring a musical score by Benjamin Britten and a verse narration by W. H. Auden (9-18).

**9-18. *Night Mail* (Great Britain, 1936).**
*Directed by Basil Wright and Harry Watt.*
The British documentaries produced under Grierson often dealt with materials which were not intrinsically very dramatic or exciting. The success of these films was due, in large part, to their sincerity and excellent craftsmanship. See also James Beveridge, *John Grierson: Film Master* (New York: Macmillan, 1978).

Perhaps the greatest filmmaker to emerge from the British school was Humphrey Jennings, whose major work was produced during World War II. Poetic, lyrical, and inspirational in the best sense, Jennings' films are perhaps the least propagandistic of the major documentaries produced during this period. His concern was with people rather than abstract ideas, with their courage, fortitude, and determination to stand up to all the punishment the Nazi war machine could dish out. Movies like *London Can Take It, Listen to Britain,* and *Fires Were Started*—all produced during England's darkest hours—are still moving accounts of the capacity of a beleaguered nation to endure and fight on. Although the war years produced some brilliant documentaries—most notably the Nazi *Triumph of the Will* directed by Leni

*(Museum of Modern Art)*

**9-19.** *The Triumph of the Will* **(Germany, 1935).**
*Directed by Leni Riefenstahl.*
The relationship of art to morality is not simple. When Hitler was elected Chancellor in 1933, much of the German film community departed for healthier climes: most of them were Jewish, liberal, or both. Almost overnight, Germany was depleted of its finest artists. The only filmmaker of major stature who remained throughout the Nazi era was Riefenstahl. She was given virtual *carte blanche* by Hitler to make a documentary of the 1934 Nuremberg Party Convention. The result was this glorification of the Nazi mystique, a brilliantly effective piece of propaganda. It was so inflammatory that the Allied powers banned it from circulation for some years after the war.

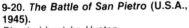

*(Museum of Modern Art)*

**9-20.** *The Battle of San Pietro* **(U.S.A., 1945).**
*Directed by John Huston.*
In contrast to Riefenstahl's grandly theatrical images and bravura style, Huston's small masterpiece is far more human and tragic in its impact. In fact, the film was not received warmly by the Pentagon, which believed that its tone of ironic bitterness, emphasizing the futility and waste of war, was virtually a condemnation of all military activity—hardly the kind of movie to inspire soldiers and civilians with a sense of the justness of their cause.

**9-21. *Divide and Conquer* (U.S.A., 1943).**
*Directed by Frank Capra and Anatole Litvak.*
Because documentaries are structured around a theme rather than a plot, the shots can be arranged with much greater freedom than in most fiction films. The famous *Why We Fight* series, which was commissioned by the U.S. War Department during World War II, consists of seven individual works. The series was supervised by Capra who did virtually no "directing" in the conventional sense. Rather, he re-edited existing footage, much of it taken from captured enemy newsreels and Nazi propaganda films. By restructuring the footage and accompanying this new continuity with an anti-Nazi commentary, Capra totally reversed the significance of the original materials.

Riefenstahl, and the *Why We Fight* series under the supervision of the American Frank Capra—few of them surpassed Jennings' achievement in terms of emotional richness, and none of them could match his delicacy.

Grierson was one of the first to recognize that a new "film generation" was emerging, one that was less oriented toward print and public speaking for its sources of information. He was able to persuade a number of high-ranking public officials that it was in the national interest to exploit the film medium as an essential channel of communication between government and citizenry. The overwhelming number of important British documentaries produced between the years of Grierson's influence (roughly from 1928 to the end of the war) were publicly funded. The concept of governmental support for the production of documentary films was also adopted in the United States during the 1930s, though Congress' funding was sporadic and tight-fisted. During the war years, all the major powers committed themselves to large-scale documentary production to boost morale.

In 1938, Grierson helped to establish the prestigious National Film Board of Canada, and in the following year he became its first Film Commissioner.

**9-22. *Fires Were Started* (Great Britain, 1943).**
*Directed by Humphrey Jennings.*
Jennings' works are impressionistic, understated, and poetic. In this film, he recounts the heroism of some English firemen within the course of a 24-hour period during the London Blitz. Unlike most wartime documentarists, Jennings minimizes political propaganda in favor of celebrating the grandeur of individuals.

*(Museum of Modern Art)*

After the war, Grierson's interests became more international. In 1947, he served as Director of Mass Communications and Public Information for UNESCO at the United Nations. During this same period, he lamented the serious decline of the documentary movement in all countries except Canada and the Communist nations of Eastern Europe. In the 1950s, he developed a greater interest in the public possibilities of television which was quickly displacing cinema as the major visual mass medium. He correctly predicted that TV would take over the main thrust of the documentary movement. In 1972, the old warhorse of the documentary movement died.

## Television and Cinéma Vérité

Some commentators see no significant difference between documentaries produced for TV and those made for the cinema. There can be considerable distinctions, both technological and aesthetic, although these tended to blur after the late 1960s. Perhaps the most important difference concerns the matter of sponsorship. Prior to TV, documentaries were either independently produced, or—as in Canada and Great Britain—sponsored by governments which exercised extraordinary restraint by allowing their film production units to go pretty much their own way. Grierson grumbled occasionally that some important subjects were considered too controversial by government bureaucrats, but, in general, no one interfered seriously with the activities of his film units.

Television is another matter. In most countries, the air waves are controlled by the government. Even in the United States, the Federal Communications Commission is empowered to regulate all major uses of this publicly owned resource. In the majority of countries, a documentary criticizing the government simply wouldn't be permitted on the air. Consequently, most TV documentaries are either nonpolitical or progovernment. In the United States, the so-called Fairness Doctrine can have a similar coercive effect, though there's considerable leeway in interpreting this regulation which postulates that every significant position ought to be given a fair hearing in the treatment of inflammable issues. The TV networks are especially sensitive to charges of distortion or slanted reporting. Whenever a documentary creates a controversy—like *Harvest of Shame* or *The Selling of the Pentagon* (both produced by CBS)—the repercussions can be severe. Almost invariably, the networks subsequently respond with caution and "self-restraint," which is really just a polite term for self-censorship.

**9-23. The Quiet One (U.S.A., 1949).**
*Directed by Sidney Meyers.*
Documentaries in the postwar period tended to be less ideological in emphasis. This movie deals with the loneliness and alienation of an emotionally disturbed youngster living in Harlem. The emphasis is not on the youth's blackness or his social environment so much as his personal needs. Meyers stresses psychological and symbolic concepts rather than social ideas or propaganda.

*(Museum of Modern Art)*

There are also significant aesthetic distinctions between television and movies. While both are visual mediums, the degree of visual density differs in each. Because of its small screen, television tends to favor detailed shots, especially closeups and medium shots. Beyond the full-shot range, the TV screen begins to lose definition, and small details get lost. A film like *Man of Aran,* with its striking extreme long shots, is likely to lose much of its power on TV. Conversely, many documentaries made for television tend to look technically inferior in the theatre. Visual blemishes that would hardly appear on the small screen are exaggerated when they're blown up for the movies.

Because of its greater effectiveness in the closer ranges. TV tends to emphasize editing rather than mise-en-scène. Linking shots together is more effective in pointing out a sequence of specific details than mise-en-scène which encourages the viewer to analyse the contents of a longer shot on his own. Most TV documentaries are not characterized by the same visual beauty found in theatrical nonfiction films, for the aesthetic resources of the long and extreme long shots must be sacrificed. As a compensation, however, TV documentaries are often more emotionally involving because of their dependence on the closer shots.

Sound is also used differently in each medium. Perhaps because many TV journalists received their early training in radio, they tend to be more dependent on language than the majority of theatrical documentarists. The continuity of many TV nonfiction films is provided by a spoken narration, not the pictures. The visuals in such documentaries tend to be *illustrative* rather than definitive. In the best theatrical documentaries, on the other hand, narration generally serves a secondary purpose—to bridge transitions, for example, or to provide abstract (that is, nonvisual) information.

In their fondness for the direct interview, TV documentaries are likely to seem tedious in the movie theatre. On television, such interviews are generally brief, but even longer interviews can hold our interest so long as what is *said* is compelling. In the cinema, interviews must be visually compelling as well or we tend to lose interest. Our eyes get bored. The most absorbing interview scenes in theatrical documentaries are generally those in which there is a tension of some kind between what the interviewee is saying and what he actually seems to be feeling. For example, *The Sorrow and the Pity* was originally made for TV (9-24). Ophuls used a great many interviews, but the most

(Cinema V)

**9-24.** *The Sorrow and the Pity* **(France/Switzerland/West Germany, 1971).**
*Directed by Marcel Ophüls.*
The problems of censorship are acute with TV documentaries, for airwaves are controlled by governments, and in most countries of the world, a documentary criticizing the government would not be permitted on the air. Ophuls' film, originally commissioned by the French television network, is a less than flattering exploration of the Resistance Movement during World War II. Because of its frankness, the movie was not permitted on the air, and Ophüls had to seek a theatrical distributor.

successful are those in which the interviewee is trying to conceal something, trying to evade the question. The straightforward interviews, on the other hand, tend to be visually dull, even though what's said is important.

Despite these technical and legal restrictions, television was responsible for producing most of the interesting documentaries in the United States throughout the 1950s and early 1960s. Edward R. Murrow's *See It Now* program for CBS was perhaps the best known and widely praised documentary series in America. But it was ABC's *Closeup!* that altered the art of the documentary. The series was inaugurated in 1960 and was produced by Robert Drew. Drew Associates employed some of the most gifted American filmmakers of the 1960s, including Richard Leacock, Albert and David Maysles, and D. A. Pennebaker.

Together, these artists launched the school of "direct cinema," or *cinéma vérité* (film-truth). At about the same time, Jean Rouch, Chris Marker, and others were experimenting with some of the same techniques and theories in France. But the French branch of cinéma vérité tended to be influenced by the subjective aesthetic of Dziga Vertov. By 1970, however, these distinctions largely disappeared. Stylistic eclecticism has been the rule ever since.

(Zipporah Films)

**9-25. *Law and Order* (U.S.A., 1969).**
*Directed by Frederick Wiseman.*
Some of the most rigorous direct cinema advocates, like Wiseman, refuse to use nonsynchronized sound. The subjects are allowed to speak for themselves, and the burden of interpretation is placed on the viewers, who must analyze the significance of the material on their own. See also Thomas R. Atkins, *Frederick Wiseman* (New York: Monarch, 1976).

Cinéma vérité is a good instance of how technology can affect aesthetics in film. Because of the need to be able to capture news stories quickly, efficiently, and with a minimal crew, television journalism was responsible for the development of a new technology, which in turn eventually led to a new philosophy of truth in documentary cinema. A lightweight 16 mm hand-held camera was perfected, allowing cameramen to roam virtually anywhere with ease. Flexible zoom lenses were devised, allowing cameramen to go from 12 mm wide-angle positions to 120 mm telephoto positions in one adjusting bar. New fast film stocks were also developed, permitting scenes to be photographed without the necessity of setting up special lights. So sensitive were these stocks to available lighting, even nighttime scenes with minimal illumination would be recorded with acceptable clarity. A portable tape recorder was invented, allowing a technician to record sound directly, in automatic synchronization with the visuals. This equipment was so easy to use that only two individuals—one at the camera, the other with the sound system—were required to bring in a news story. (This equipment is shown in 5-11.)

The flexibility of his hardware permitted documentarists to redefine the concept of authenticity. This new aesthetic amounted to a rejection of the Grierson tradition of preplanning and carefully detailed scripts. A script involves preconceptions about reality and tends to cancel out any sense of spontaneity or ambiguity. Direct cinema rejected such preconceptions as essen-

**9-26.** *The Last Waltz* **(U.S.A., 1978).**
*With The Band; Directed by Martin Scorsese.*
The French branch of cinéma vérité advocated an interventionist aesthetic—as does Scorsese in this movie. Such filmmakers make no pretense at invisibility. Instead, they speak directly to the people on-camera, and sometimes even allow themselves to be photographed with the subjects of the documentary. The result is more like a personal journal than an objective recording of events.

tially fictional: reality is not being *observed* but is being *arranged* to conform to what the script says it is. Recreations of any kind were no longer necessary, because if the members of the crew are present while an event is actually taking place, they can capture it directly, in all its sprawling, ambiguous complexity.

The concept of minimal interference with reality became the dominating preoccupation of the American and Canadian schools of cinéma vérité, at least during the early 1960s. Most of the traditional techniques of documentary film were discarded in favor of a totally aleatory approach with a strong emphasis on open forms. Attempts to alter or comment on reality were rejected as fictional. The filmmaker must not control events in any way. The cameraman was expected to record totally undirected situations. Recreations—even with the people and places actually involved—were unacceptable. Editing was kept to a minimum, for otherwise it could lead to a false impression of the sequence of events. Actual time and space were preserved whenever possible by using lengthy takes. If a closeup was required, the cameraman tended to zoom in and out, for in this way the shot was not yanked out of its spatial and temporal context. Anticipatory setups were likewise avoided, for to anticipate the contents of a shot was to impose a form on events before they actually occurred. If people or events moved, the cameraman was expected to pursue them, either by panning, zooming, tilting, or simply walking with the camera mounted on a shoulder harness.

Needless to say, the realist aesthetic of cinéma vérité tends to place enormous burdens on the cameraman. He or she must be able to make snap judgments—often in the midst of turbulent events. For this reason, many directors handle their own cameras. Leacock, Pennebaker, and Albert Maysles, for example, do most of their own shooting. The cameraman must know what to shoot, how to shoot it (that is, what type of shot to use), when to pan or zoom, and when to stop the camera entirely. Vast amounts of footage are wasted, for they often have no idea when something is going to happen, and once it does, there's no going back to get the shot if it was missed the first time. They must be patient and self-effacing, waiting and watching until they sense something important is about to take place.

Because much of the footage in these movies is caught on the run, as it were, a good many of the shots are necessarily shaky, blurred, and clumsily framed. Occasionally there are zoom-ins where the cameraman obviously expected a moment of revelation. But sometimes the revelation doesn't occur, and the camera must inch back to a looser distance. The lighting of these films is also inadequate at times, notwithstanding the highly sensitive stocks. Sound is sometimes muffled or fades into imperceptibility. Distracting street noises often drown out voices. But these blemishes were considered a part of the aesthetic of cinéma vérité—a testament, in a way, to its utter authenticity. Most of these filmmakers believe that picturesque visuals and crisp soundtracks are highly suspect: they suggest an "improvement" on reality. By sacrificing the craftsmanship associated with the traditional documentary, the direct cinema filmmakers believed they were able to capture an event with far greater immediacy and intimacy—qualities they felt took precedence over formal beauty.

In its attempt to eliminate the barriers between subject and audience, direct cinema also uses sound minimally. For the most part, nonsynchronous

**9-27. *Warrendale* (Canada, 1967).**
*Directed by Allan King.*
Because advocates of cinéma vérité
work within uncontrollable contexts,
some of the technical craftsmanship of
the traditional documentary must be sacrificed. But most of these filmmakers
would argue that the resultant intimacy
allows us to observe privileged moments
of intense poignance and authenticity—
moments which would have been impossible to capture using traditional
documentary techniques. See also Louis
Marcorelles, *Living Cinema* (New York:
Praeger, 1973).

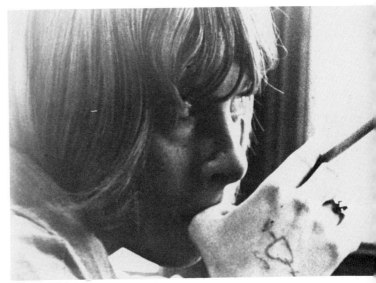

*(Museum of Modern Art)*

**9-28. *Monterey Pop* (U.S.A., 1969).**
*With Janis Joplin; Directed by D. A. Pennebaker.*
Direct cinema is particularly suited to capturing the spontaneity of events, like crisis situations and
theatrical occasions. The tremendous popularity of such performers as Joplin introduced a new
genre, the rock documentary. See also Erik Barnouw, *Documentary: A History of the Non-Fiction
Film* (New York: Oxford Univ. Press, 1974).

*(Leacock-Pennebaker Films)*

music is avoided and dismissed as a fictional technique. These artists are especially hostile to the "Voice of God" commentaries that accompanied many traditional documentaries. Narration tends to interpret images for audiences, thus relieving them of the necessity of analyzing for themselves. If narration is used, it should be used sparingly—offering only necessary factual data, and delivered in an emotionally neutral voice. Some filmmakers dispense with narration entirely. In the works of Frederick Wiseman, for example, only direct sound is employed. The people in the films are allowed to speak for themselves. Perhaps more than any American filmmaker, Wiseman insists that the ambiguities and contradictions of actual life must be preserved in documentaries. If they are too neat and clear-cut, they're probably false to reality.

Perhaps what the practitioners of direct cinema value above all is the "privileged moment"—those brief glimpses into reality that are so intimate, so genuine, that the screen seems to disappear and we feel we're in the presence of the event itself. A good example of this kind of intimacy can be seen in *The Chair*, which was made by Leacock, Pennebaker, and Gregory Shuker. The movie deals with a convicted murderer, Paul Crump, and his lawyer's at-

**9-29. *Gimme Shelter* (U.S.A., 1970).**
*With Mick Jagger (wearing scarf); Directed by David and Albert Maysles and Charlotte Zwerin.* Direct cinema filmmakers are often frustrated because they can never be certain where the action is going to occur. For coverage, many of them employ multiple cameras, as at the notorious Altamont Rock Festival of 1969 which featured The Rolling Stones (a), and an on-camera knifing in the audience (b). See also Richard Meran Barsam, ed., *Nonfiction Film: Theory and Criticism* (New York: Dutton, 1976).

(a)

(b)

tempts to have Crump's death sentence commuted to life imprisonment since
he is obviously rehabilitated. We follow Donald Moore, the lawyer, as he
desperately tries everything in his power to postpone the impending execu-
tion. At one point, he receives a telephone call informing him that some high
Church officials will issue a statement urging clemency—an important break
that Moore has been praying for. Overcome with relief, Moore silently and
thoughtfully puts out his cigarette, then, unable to control his emotions, he
bursts into tears. It's a powerful scene, so touching in its emotional impact that
it moves many viewers to tears as well.

Like most schools of documentary, cinéma vérité is better at some subjects
than others. Certainly few traditional documentaries can offer the same degree of intimacy, emotional directness, and spontaneity. On the other hand,
these techniques would be rather dull if employed on a subject like a mail
train express. In fact, even Pennebaker eventually complained that direct
cinema tends to justify itself too much on its "marvelous moments." Some
critics lamented that they were forced to endure a lot of tedious material
before arriving at these touching revelations. Footage can become mileage.

Direct cinema is most effective with materials that are intrinsically dramatic, like crisis situations in which a conflict is about to reach its climax. But
here too critics complained of the lack of aesthetic distance in such films as
Leacock's *The Children Were Watching* which deals with a highly explosive civil
rights confrontation in 1960 in the city of New Orleans. The hand-held camera captures all the fear, hatred, and tension of the situation, with angry white
bigots on one side and terrified black children and their parents on the other.
But critics complained that in such emotionally charged situations, what is
needed is sobriety, reason, and calm objectivity in the cinematic treatment, not

a whirling camera that's plunged in the middle of the most volatile confrontations. Such films encourage more hysteria, these critics argued, not rational alternatives.

In the later 1960s, rock stars and music festivals were also popular subjects for direct cinema. Feature-length documentaries like *Don't Look Back* and *Monterey Pop,* both by Pennebaker, were enormously successful at theatrical box offices, as was the Rolling Stones film *Gimme Shelter.* These movies abandoned some of the purist rigor of the early era of direct cinema. (In fact, even in the early 1960s, there was a considerable gap between the ideals and practices of the filmmakers at Drew Associates.) Editing styles became more complex, as can be seen in the elaborate flashback structure of *Gimme Shelter.* By the time Wadleigh's *Woodstock* was released in 1970, artful compositions, mul-

**9-30a. Woodstock (U.S.A., 1970).**
*Directed by Michael Wadleigh.*
**9-30b. Jimi Hendrix (U.S.A., 1973).**
*Directed by Joe Boyd, John Head, and Gary Weis.*
After 1970, the realist bias of cinéma vérité began to yield to more expressionist techniques, especially in rock documentaries. Lengthy takes, direct synch-sound, and minimal cutting were replaced by subtly composed images and stereophonic sound in such movies as *Woodstock. Jimi Hendrix* contains a number of special effects, such as showing three different views of the performer within the same frame.

(a)

(Warner Brothers)

(b)

tiple images, and sound juxtapositions of all kinds had replaced the lengthy take, direct sound recording, and blurry zoom shots. What began as a realistic movement eventually evolved into an eclectic, pragmatic attitude toward filmmaking which mixed realistic and expressionistic techniques with nonchalance.

## Further Reading

BARSAM, RICHARD MERAN, *Nonfiction Film* (New York: Dutton, 1973). A critical history.

BLUEM, A. WILLIAM, *Documentary in American Television* (New York: Hastings House, 1965). Critical history, with background on radio and print journalism.

GRIERSON, JOHN, *Grierson on Documentary*, Forsyth Hardy, ed. (New York: Praeger, 1971). Essays spanning most of Grierson's career.

ISSARI, M. ALI, *Cinéma Vérité* (East Lansing, Mich.: Michigan State Univ. Press, 1971). Major emphasis on French and American documentarists.

JACOBS, LEWIS, *The Documentary Tradition: From Nanook to Woodstock* (New York: Hopkinson and Blake, 1979). A collection of essays.

LEVIN, G. ROY, ed. *Documentary Explorations* (Garden City, N.Y.: Doubleday, 1971). Fifteen interviews with Rouch, Leacock, Pennebaker, the Maysles brothers, Wiseman, and others.

LOVELL, ALAN, and JIM HILLIER, *Studies in Documentary* (New York: Viking, 1972). Major emphasis on British documentaries.

MAMBER, STEPHEN, *Cinéma Vérité in America: Studies in Uncontrolled Documentary* (Cambridge, Mass.: M.I.T. Press, 1973).

ROSENTHAL, ALAN, *The New Documentary in Action* (Berkeley, Cal.: University of California Press, 1971). Interviews with Allan King, Albert Maysles, Charlotte Zwerin, Peter Watkins, and others.

ROTHA, PAUL, in collaboration with Sinclair Road and Richard Griffith, *Documentary Film* (New York: Hastings House, 1970). Critical history.

## 10

# AVANT-GARDE

There are three broad classifications of film: fiction, documentary, and avant-garde movies. "Avant-garde" literally means in the front rank, in advance of the main body. (The main body in this case would refer to feature-length fiction films.) The avant-garde cinema has been called many names, not all of them polite. In the 1930s and 1940s, it was known as the "Experimental Film" or the "Poetic Cinema." In the 1950s, these movies were part of the "Independent Cinema," and in America especially, they were also called "Underground" movies. In the 1960s most avant-garde films in the United States were considered part of the "New American Cinema."

### The Avant-Garde Aesthetic

By definition, avant-garde movies are produced by and for a minority. Because of their restricted appeal, they are seldom created within a commercial framework, where by necessity a film is considered at least in part a profitable commodity. Nor are avant-garde films generally considered a part of the entertainment industry as most fiction movies are. Experimental films can be exciting, witty, and provocative, but seldom are they relaxing or blandly entertaining. Many of these works are technically complex and difficult to understand, at least on first viewing. To many, they are an acquired taste. One needs to be sympathetic and tolerant in order to enter the rarified world of the avant-garde cinema.

366

**10-1. *A Trip to the Moon* (France, 1902).**
*Directed by Georges Méliès.*
A conjurer and illusionist, Méliès might be regarded as the godfather of the avant-garde. His whimsical landscapes were drawn entirely from imagination and emphasized a sense of childlike wonder. See Paul Hammond, *Marvellous Méliès* (New York: St. Martin's, 1975); and John Frazer, *Artificially Arranged Scenes: The Films of Georges Méliès* (Boston: G. K. Hall, 1979).

*(Museum of Modern Art)*

**10-2. *El Topo* (Mexico, 1970).**
*Directed by Alexandro Jodorowsky.*
Avant-garde films rarely attract large audiences, but occasionally one clicks with the mass audience. Jodorowsky's enigmatic parable of violence—he described himself as "the Picasso of violence"—appealed strongly to youthful audiences in America, and grossed more than $10 million.

*(Museum of Modern Art)*

There are almost as many kinds of experimental films as there are filmmakers. In general, however, these movies are made on small budgets because of their limited profit-returning potential. Some of them run to 6 or 8 hours in length, while others are merely a few seconds long. Most of them are under a half hour. These films are usually shot in 16 mm rather than the more expensive 35 mm which is the standard gauge for fiction films. A few experimental filmmakers have even turned to Super 8 mm in order to cut expenses.

A great many avant-garde film directors avoid courting public acceptance. Or rather, they will accept it only on their own terms. In many cases, these filmmakers reject the main body of film culture, dismissing it as glossy, false, and aesthetically dead. They are particularly in revolt against the "Big Lie of Culture," with its glib morality, its false cheer, and its refusal to explore the less "attractive" aspects of life. Many viewers are initially offended by the deliberate vulgarity and "bad taste" of avant-garde films. Shock techniques are common in these movies, for many of them are meant to jolt the audience out of its smugness. Viewers are commonly abused, ridiculed, and treated contemptuously—especially those who cling to conventional middle-class values which these filmmakers consider sterile and life-denying.

Most avant-garde films are expressionistic. These directors use film as a means for exploring beyond the surface of the material world. They aren't concerned with recording scenes from actual life, but with creating a totally imaginary universe, one that is anti-illusionist (10-3). They prefer to invent rather than discover, to present rather than represent. Many of them are preoccupied with an interior psychological reality, or with a submerged mythical existence—spiritual realms which have no counterparts in the literal world.

Independent films are generally conceived and executed by a single individual. Unlike most fiction directors and many documentarists, experimental filmmakers usually shoot and edit their own footage. To keep costs down, the collaborative aspect of the filmmaking process is kept to a minimum. Often the actors, if any, are the director's friends or family. But this necessary economy can also result in greater precision and more complete artistic control. Directors are ultimately answerable only to themselves. Hence, avant-garde filmmakers believe that their work is more personal than the average commercial movie because they make all the major artistic decisions.

Autobiographical elements are commonplace in these movies. Many avant-garde artists are primarily concerned with conveying their "inner impulses," their personal and subjective involvements with people, ideas, and experiences. Emphasis is often placed on a direct expression of emotions, and not on an objectified presentation. For this reason, avant-garde movies are sometimes obscure and even incomprehensible. The audience's engagement is not always as intense or on the same level as the artist's expression. Many of these filmmakers have evolved their own personal language and symbology. Unless the viewer is attuned to this essentially private world, these movies can seem indecipherable and out of control. However, in the best of these films—the symbolic and mythological works of Jean Cocteau, Jordan Belson, and James Broughton, for example—the necessary extra effort is rewarded.

The avant-garde cinema has excelled in treating taboo subjects—those forbidden topics that are ruled out to commercial filmmakers because of the

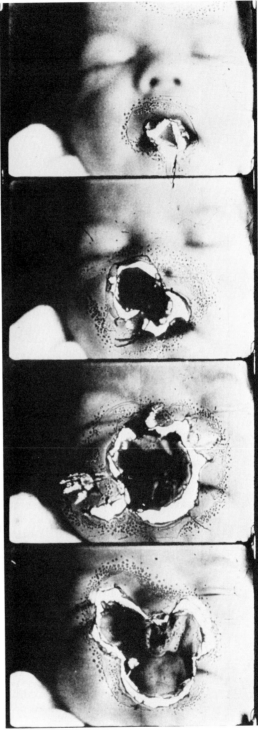

*(Anthology Film Archives)*

**10-3. *Dog Star Man* (U.S.A., 1959–64).**
*Directed by Stan Brakhage.*
Avant-garde filmmakers are often anti-illusionist—they attempt to break down the realism of an image by calling attention to its artificiality and its material properties. A movie image is printed on a strip of celluloid which can be manipulated, even violated. In this sequence, a crying baby emerges from the mouth of another crying baby. Brakhage is playing with the idea of what's "behind" a film image.

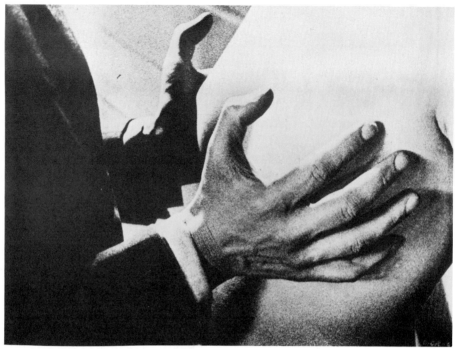

**10-4. *Un Chien Andalou* (France, 1929).**
*Directed by Luis Buñuel and Salvador Dali.*
Avant-garde movies often deal with socially taboo themes and subjects that are ignored by the popular cinema because of the problems of censorship. Human sexuality has been one of the most enduring of these themes.

problems of censorship (10-4). Many of these movies were (and still are) considered shocking, immoral, and outrageous. Political and sexual themes abound, especially the latter, which have included overt homosexuality, lesbianism, voyeurism, fetishism, bestiality, masturbation, and sado-masochism, among others. Many avant-garde films have provoked outcries of public indignation. Some have been confiscated by the police. A few have even caused riots. In fact, avant-garde artists are often delighted by such spectacles of moral outrage.

With few exceptions, avant-garde films are unscripted. In part, this is because the filmmakers shoot and edit their own footage, and are therefore able to control their material at these stages of the filmmaking process. They also value chance and spontaneity in their movies, and in order to exploit these elements they avoid the inflexibility of a preordained script. Narrative structures are rare in these films. They seldom tell a story, but tend to explore an idea, emotion, or experience in a nonlinear fashion. Shots are joined in associative clusters rather than in a logical sequence of consecutive actions.

The roots of the avant-garde can be traced to Dadaism, an artistic movement that placed a high premium on the values of irrationality and anarchy. Many avant-garde filmmakers have justified the nihilistic and uncontrolled elements in their work as an artistic reflection of contemporary social condi-

**10-5.** *The Blood of a Poet* (France, 1930).
*Directed by Jean Cocteau.*
The avant-garde films of Cocteau are among the most aestheticized, but he despised a soft, sentimental romanticism, and claimed to be a "realist." Of course his reality is not the same reality found on the average street corner. Cocteau was concerned with internal realities—the world of the psyche and the soul. He described this, his first film, as "documentary scenes from another realm." See Jean Cocteau, *Two Screenplays* (Baltimore: Penguin, 1969), which includes *The Blood of a Poet* and *The Testament of Orpheus.*

tions. In a world without order, stability, or coherence, what could be more appropriate, they would argue, than an art which stresses disorder, fragmentation, and incoherence?

Technically, the avant-garde cinema has gloried in the wide spectrum of expressionistic methods at its disposal. The images of these films are densely saturated with details. Like language in poetry, the visuals in many experimental films are highly condensed, elliptical, and often too complex to be absorbed at one sitting. Distorting lenses and filters are used with intoxicating abandon; double and multiple exposures are frequent; colors are employed nonnaturalistically; lighting effects can be startling and flamboyant; special effects are commonplace.

Avant-garde films are often cut in a furious, abrupt style. The lack of traditional story continuity in most of these movies offers maximum opportunity for juxtaposing every manner of shot, often with a minimum of logic.

Sometimes the shots zip by at a breathless rate. Actually, many experimental filmmakers delight in throwing together shots of incongruous objects. In the political satires of Bruce Conner, for example, the juxtapositions hurl head-long at a frenzied pace, the shots colliding wittily in a junk heap of newsreels, cartoon characters, nude figures, found objects, and prominent politicians.

Time and space in these films are generally subjective and psychological rather than literal. Cocteau's *Blood of a Poet,* for example, opens with a shot of a high tower collapsing. The fall is not completed until the end of the film, one hour later, when we see the tower hurling to the ground. Similarly, space in these movies is often magical and dreamlike. Objects seem to exist in a symbolic limbo of some kind. In Maya Deren's *Choreography for Camera,* for example, a dancer leaps gracefully from a wooded setting to a living room to an art museum in one fluid movement (10-21).

Very few of these movies employ synchronous sound. In the first place, the equipment used by many experimental filmmakers is incapable of reproducing sound adequately, if at all. But there are also aesthetic reasons for the avoidance of synchronization. The rebellion of the avant-garde against the

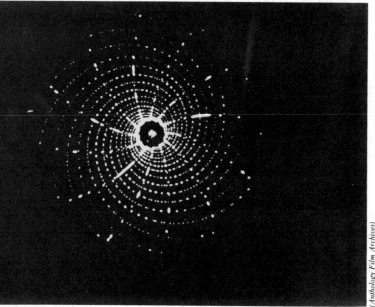

(*Anthology Film Archives*)

**10-6. *Allures* (U.S.A., 1964).**
*Directed by Jordan Belson.*
The subject matter of avant-garde movies may be personally meaningful to the artist, but often he or she makes no attempt to communicate these inner ideas to the viewer. "I think of *Allures* as a combination of molecular structures and astronomical events mixed with sub-conscious and subjective phenomena—all happening simultaneously," Belson said, adding "but there's nothing really personal in the images."

fiction feature is based in part on its "theatrical" use of sound, especially language. When sound derives from the image, an increased sense of realism is almost inevitable. But most of these filmmakers are revolting against realism in the cinema. To reinforce the unreality of their worlds, they prefer to create a disjunction between image and sound.

A few avant-garde filmmakers have even made movies without a camera. These films are composed "cinegraphically"—that is, instead of photographing images on the raw stock, the stock itself is used as a translucent medium upon which the artist paints, draws, scratches, or etches the subject matter by hand. These techniques are particularly popular with painters and sculptors who have turned to filmmaking. The Canadian Norman McLaren even created an artificial soundtrack by scratching directly on the sound portion of the film emulsion. In Brakhage's *Mothlight,* bits of moth wings, flowers, seeds, etc. were glued between layers of editing tape from which a master print was then struck. Some artists have punched holes in the film strip, glued sand to it, even grown mold on it.

Film historians generally subdivide the avant-garde into four phases: (1) the Dadaist and Surrealist periods, roughly from 1920 to 1931, based primarily in Berlin and Paris; (2) the poetic and experimental period, roughly from 1940 to 1954, and centered mostly in the United States; (3) the Underground period, from 1954 to the late 1960s; and (4) the Structuralist cinema, which has dominated the avant-garde since then. Convenient as these subdivisions are, they can also be misleading (10-7). In many respects, the avant-garde cinema can be dated from the time of Méliès at the turn of the century.

**10-7. *No. 12 (Heaven & Earth Magic Feature)* (U.S.A., 1950–61).**
*Directed by Harry Smith.*
Period classifications within the avant-garde are vague at best, for many filmmakers have continued working in a variety of idioms throughout several periods. Smith described his long career in the following manner: "My cinematic excretia is of four varieties: batiked abstractions made directly on film between 1939 and 1946; optically printed nonobjective studies composed around 1950; semi-realistic animated collages made as part of my alchemical labors of 1957 to 1962; and chronologically superimposed photographs of actualities formed since the latter year. They are valuable works, works that will live forever—they made me gray."

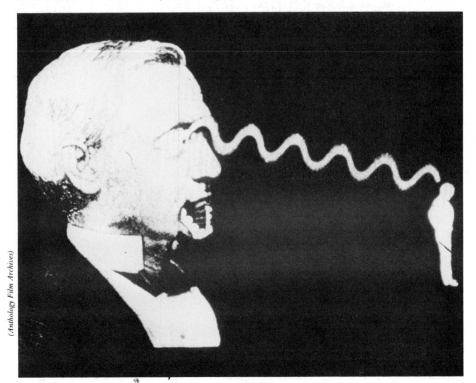

*(Anthology Film Archives)*

Although there have been periods of relatively little activity (most notably during the Depression of the 1930s), the avant-garde has never ceased to produce important new works. Furthermore, while the most famous films tended to be produced in Paris, New York, and San Francisco, the avant-garde is essentially international; important works were and still are being produced in London, Vienna, Toronto, Munich, Zagreb, and many other cities.

## Dadaism and Surrealism

The second and third decades of the twentieth century represented the most exciting period of avant-garde experimentation in the arts. The impulse to discover new modes of artistic expression was particularly fervant in Paris,

**10-8. *Rhythmus 21* (Germany, 1921).**
*Directed by Hans Richter.*
Along with a number of other German artists, Richter was a champion of the "absolute film," which consists solely of abstract shapes and designs. Insisting that movies should have nothing to do with acting, stories, or any kind of recognizable subject matter, Richter believed that film—like music and abstract painting—should be concerned with pure nonrepresentational forms.

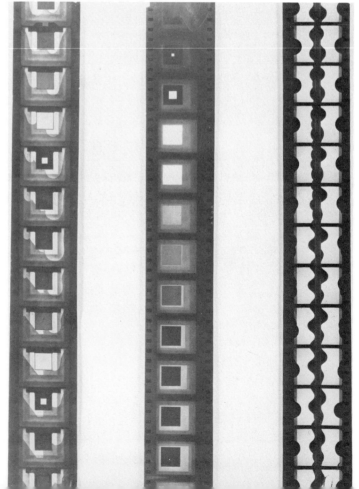

which was generally regarded as the avant-garde capitol of the world. In the plastic arts especially, the so-called Isms flourished. Perhaps the most significant of these was Cubism which developed the idea of fragmentation, not only in painting and sculpture but in literature and cinema as well. After World War I, a new tone permeated the avant-garde—one reflecting a spirit of cynicism, disillusionment, and in some cases, nihilism.

Dadaism developed from this social and artistic milieu. Painters, writers, and intellectuals formed this movement as a violent protest against "civilization," which they believed had been responsible for bringing about the Great War. Using humor, irrationalism, and outlandishness as their chief weapons, these iconoclasts wanted to tear down the scaffolding of traditional values. In their place, the Dadaists glorified individualism, hedonism, and the spirit of anarchy. They were anti-intellectual, amoral, and antiaesthetic. All social inhibitions—sexual, artistic, and personal—were dismissed with contempt. What the Dadaists valued most was an uncensored, childlike spontaneity.

The Dadaists believed that traditional culture—the "Fine Arts"—were bankrupt. Essentially Romantic revolutionaries, this cheery band of lunatics wanted to *épater la bourgeoisie* with their gleeful assault on the bastions of middle-class culture. The new movement was steeped in a subversive aesthetic: A frontal attack was launched against "decency" and "good taste" in art. The Dadaists wanted to create a wholly new art, one that was free, vulgar, funny, and fun. Art, they felt, should be a revolution for the hell of it. Needless to say, a lot of people thought they were crazy (10-9).

**10-9.** *King of Hearts* **(France, 1966).**
*Directed by Phillippe de Broca.*
The Dadaists believed that madness was liberation, and de Broca's cult classic owes much to their anarchistic spirit. The inmates of a mental asylum take over an evacuated French village during World War I. They live out their fantasies, parading in their finery, and making love whenever the spirit moves them—while the sane people are off fighting the "War to End all Wars."

(*United Artists*)

It's not hard to see why so many of them turned to movies as a mode of expression. Film, after all, was a new medium, with no real aesthetic tradition behind it and no official body of "rules" to confine its development. The Dadaists especially delighted in the crazy chase sequences in the comedies of Mack Sennett, which they thought were perfect reflections of the absurdity of life. The cinema was also eclectic, and the Dadaists, with their scorn for traditional techniques and artistic "purity," were excited by the experimental possibilities of the medium. Anything that could be photographed could be tossed into a movie, and where anything goes, nothing matters.

None of the Dadaists used narrative structures in their films, for they believed that plots are based on logic and coherence. Editing permits a filmmaker to present scenes that aren't "connected" in a sequential manner, in which there are no causes and effects. Hence, the director is able to create a world without "sense" or meaning. Indeed, the Dadaists rejected all organic conceptions of art. "There are no stories," Jean Epstein proudly proclaimed in 1921, "there are only situations without tail or head; without beginning, center, and end." This antiorganic attitude has persisted in the avant-garde to the present day. For example, one contemporary filmmaker has accumulated thousands of feet of film, and simply "slices off" some footage "like a sausage," or so he claims, whenever he wants to make a movie.

Despite the gloomy philosophical implications of Dadaism, the films themselves can be joyous, liberating, and even exhilarating. During the early 1920s, exhibitions of these movies were often more exciting than the films themselves. For example, in 1923, Man Ray, an American photographer working in Paris, was commissioned to produce a film for a Dadaist function. Ray concocted *The Return to Reason* which was made by sprinkling objects (tacks, buttons, etc.) on film emulsion. He also included shots of a female nude bumping and grinding in front of a window while sunlight and shadows made abstract patterns on her writhing torso. He hastily edited these shots together with some homemade glue. At the gathering itself, poets screamed their gibberish verses at the top of their voices, a concert of sirens and bells was performed, and Ray's film kept tearing off at the splices. The movie ulti-

(National Film Board of Canada)

**10-10. *Neighbours* (Canada, 1952).**
*Directed by Norman McLaren.*
Although McLaren is not a Dadaist, several of his movies are characterized by the same sense of irreverence, zaniness, and whimsy. Like many Dadaist films, *Neighbours* deals with a serious theme—war—in a comic manner.

mately provoked a riot, and the members of the audience went berserk by ripping up the meeting hall. All in all, as film historian Arthur Knight observed, "it was considered a very successful Dadaist evening."

Perhaps the most famous Dadaist films are René Clair's *Entr'acte* and Fernand Léger's *Ballet Mécanique,* both produced in 1924. Clair's film, scripted by the Dadaist poet and theorist Francis Picabia, was partly inspired by the chase films of Mack Sennett. A funeral procession is shown in slow motion, emphasizing the pomp and solemnity of the occasion. Suddenly the hearse breaks away, and there follows a fast motion pursuit sequence with a group of dignified bourgeois gentlemen huffing and puffing after the runaway casket. Léger, one of the original Cubist painters, was more concerned with abstraction in film. *Ballet Mécanique* consists of a series of kinetic variations (10-11), although interspersed throughout the movie are twenty-three

**10-11. *Ballet Mécanique* (France, 1924).**
*Directed by Fernand Léger.*
Best known for his cubist paintings, Léger was also a famous Dadaist filmmaker. One of the first to explore abstraction in the cinema, he created many striking kinetic effects by animating ordinary objects like crockery, dishes, and machine gears.

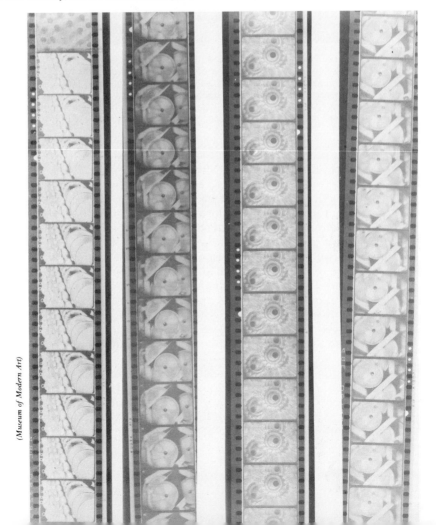

*(Museum of Modern Art)*

**10-12. Blazing Saddles (U.S.A., 1974).**
*With Cleavon Little (in hat) and Mel Brooks (being choked, right); Directed by Brooks.*
The crazy chase sequences, epic pie battles, and other forms of inspired lunacy in the silent comedies of Mack Sennett inspired the early Dadaists to even greater heights of absurdity. Film critics have noted the strong influence of these early pioneers on such later artistic loons as Mel Brooks, the Marx Brothers, Robert Downey, and Monty Python.

repetitions of the same shot of a washerwoman wearily climbing some stairs. The woman never does reach the top—which may or may not be symbolic.

In Berlin at about the same time, a number of artists were also experimenting with abstraction in film. Hans Richter, the best known of these, championed what he called the "absolute film," which has no real content, but consists of pure forms. Along with his colleagues Viking Eggeling and Oskar Fischinger, Richter insisted that film's natural affinities were not with literature or drama, but with abstract art, music, and dance. Their films contained nonrepresentational shapes, textures, and patterns, rhythmically choreographed into a kaleidoscope of shifting formal relationships. The titles of their films were often musical and deliberately neutral: Richter's *Rhythmus 21* and Eggeling's *Symphonie Diagonale* were among the first of a long tradition of abstract movies within the avant-garde movement.

Many of the original Dadaists were also prominent in the Surrealist movement, which developed in the mid-1920s and flowered at the turn of the decade. They brought with them some of the same perverse iconoclasm that characterized the earlier movement: a love of irrationality, a rejection of conventional "civilized" values, and a contempt for restraint and "good taste"

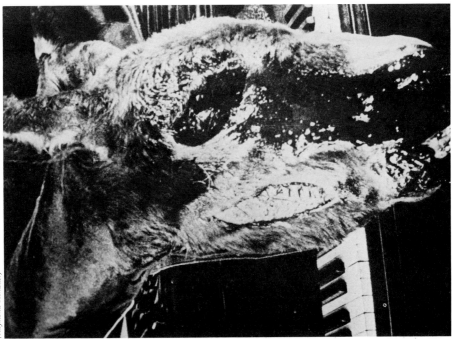

(Raymond Rohauer)

**10-13. Un Chien Andalou.**
Surrealist images—like this dead donkey draped over a piano—are weird, shocking, but not totally devoid of meaning. When asked to formulate a brief explanation of the Surrealist Movement, cultural historian Walter Strauss ventured the following: "The Surrealists, outraged by the carnage of World War I, the bankruptcy of Reason, the inhumanity of modern technology, proposed, by an attitude of rebellion, and by revolutionary commitments, to liberate man *from* Reason and from a materialistic notion of reality *toward* the 'marvelous' and toward a new spiritual notion of Surreality, by spontaneity, by surprise, by dreams, by play, by creativeness—which would once more provide access to the Unconscious, the authentic core of self, the seat of love and ecstasy, the center of desire, the source of vision, in order to integrate man with himself, with his fellow-men, with the Female, with the Cosmos." See also J. H. Matthews, *Surrealism and Film* (Ann Arbor: University of Michigan Press, 1971).

(10-13). Like Dadaism, Surrealism encompassed painters and writers as well as filmmakers. Perhaps the central figure of the new movement was André Breton, a psychologist and poet, who issued the first "Manifesto of Surrealism" (i.e., super-realism) in 1924.

But Surrealism differed from Dadaism, in tone as well as content and technique. Surrealism was more self-consciously "artistic," with a new emphasis on mystery, anxiety, and paranoia. The humor was also different. Instead of the jolly rambunctuousness of Dadaism with its sense of fun and irresponsibility, the comedy of Surrealism tended toward the grotesque and the macabre. Much of the wit in these films would now be described as black comedy, with its emphasis on sick jokes and cruelty. The Spanish-born Buñuel, for example, is ghoulishly perverse in his comic sense.

Influenced in part by Marxism, the Surrealists tended to be more serious and systematic in their rebellion. They viewed bourgeois values not only as silly, but dangerous and repressive as well. The anarchy of Dadaism was

**10-14. Production photo of *Gold Diggers of 1933* (U.S.A., 1933).**
*Directed by Mervyn Le Roy.*
The influence of Surrealism was by no means confined to European movies. Warner Brothers' Depression musicals were strongly surrealistic, thanks to choreographer Busby Berkeley (3-3) and art director Anton Grot (7-27). See also J. H. Matthews, *Surrealism and American Feature Film* (Boston: G. K. Hall, 1979).

somewhat displaced by a new leftist political orientation, resulting in a more explicit attack on capitalism and social institutions which they believed were reactionary—particularly the Catholic Church. In the 1930s, this Marxist orientation became even more pronounced, especially in the works of Buñuel.

Perhaps the major influence on Surrealism was that of Freud, whose ideas were gaining wide currency in intellectual circles of the day. Freud's theory of the unconscious, his preoccupation with dreams as a kind of subexistence with its own language, and his emphasis on sexual symbolism were to exert a profound effect on these filmmakers. By plumbing the wellsprings of the subconscious, they believed that they were revealing a truer reality, one that ultimately controls all conscious external behavior. Hence, the Surrealists preferred exploring pathological conditions rather than "normal" ones, dreams and nightmares rather than wakeful states. Many of these artists were obsessed with neurosis, hysteria, and madness.

Surrealists took a great interest in all spontaneous acts, whether it was

**10-15. *Beauty and the Beast* (France, 1946).**
*With Josette Day; Directed by Jean Cocteau.*
Above all, the Surrealists aimed at "the marvelous"—moments of concrete fancy, like a realistic fairy tale. See also René Gilson, ed., *Jean Cocteau: An Investigation into His Films and Philosophy* (New York: Crown, 1964).

(Janus Films)

primitive art, drunkenness, children's games, fantasies, or aberrant social behavior. They were particularly enthusiastic about automatism—any kind of uncontrolled artistic activity. The free association principle, which was the foundation of the literary technique of stream-of-consciousness, was incorporated in many Surrealist films. The cinema is the ideal medium for conveying the weird precision of dreams, the Surrealists believed, and most of them would agree with Dali that art is "concrete irrationality."

**10-16. *A Night at the Opera* (U.S.A., 1935).**
*With Groucho, Chico, and Harpo Marx; Directed by Sam Wood.*
The Marx Brothers are among the foremost surrealists of their era. Some critics have interpreted their movies as subversive parodies of the social chaos that reigned in the 1930s in America. See Andrew Bergman, *We're in the Money: Depression America and Its Films* (New York: Harper, 1971).

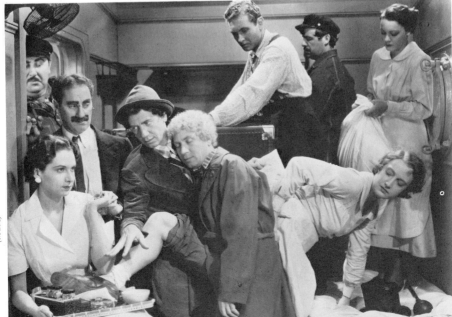

(MGM)

In general, the Surrealists were less technique-oriented than the Dadaists. Surrealism is more realistic—although only in a relative sense. Less dependent on flashy photographic distortions, the Surrealists emphasized a sense of disorientation in their *mise-en-scène*. Objects are dislocated from their ordinary contexts and placed in arbitrary, surprising locations. In *Un Chien Andalou* (*An Andalusian Dog*), for example, Buñuel and Salvador Dali placed dead donkeys on top of pianos. Nothing is explained or justified, and viewers are left on their own to try and find "reasons" for the weird tableaux and events. The Surrealists delighted in this strangeness for its own sake, and they often sneered at critical explications of their work. "Nothing in this film symbolizes anything," Buñuel and Dali perversely explained of their film—which of course doesn't contain any dog, "Andalusian" or otherwise.

*(Audio-Brandon Films)*

**10-17. *Los Olvidados* (Mexico, 1951).**
*Directed by Luis Buñuel.*
Buñuel, who is widely regarded as the finest artist of the Surrealist movement, has been influenced by Marx as much as Freud. Buñuel's movies aren't admired by orthodox liberals, primarily because he refuses to sentimentalize the effects of poverty. The youthful protagonists of this film (which is also known as *The Young and the Damned*) are economically oppressed, trapped in an urban jungle where decency is a liability. Hence, they are vicious, cruel, and violent. That's what poverty does to people, Buñuel matter-of-factly points out. To remedy the situation, we need a revolution, not pious clichés about the sanctity of the human spirit. See also Ado Kyrou, *Luis Buñuel* (New York: Simon and Schuster, 1963); Raymond Durgnat, *Luis Buñuel* (Berkeley: University of California Press, 1968); Francisco Aranda, *Luis Buñuel: A Critical Biography* (New York: Da Capo, 1976); Joan Mellen, ed., *The World of Luis Buñuel* (New York: Oxford Univ. Press, 1978); and Virginia Higginbotham, *Luis Buñuel* (Boston: G. K. Hall, 1979).

This hostility toward analysis and explication is characteristic of Surrealists, who believed that most critics were too "literary," too anxious to explain away visual complexities with language—that most analytical and rational of all mediums of communication. Indeed, many avant-garde artists still retain this prejudice against words. A good number of them tend to view the visual image as superior to language in terms of emotional impact. The medium of film criticism, of course, is words, and for this reason avant-garde artists believe that film critics are literally not speaking the same language that they are. At best, these filmmakers tend to believe that historians and critics of the plastic arts are likely to be more sensitive to their work than film critics, whose orientation is more literary and theatrical.

The Surrealists never forgot their Dadaist heritage, nor did they lose the capacity to stir up public indignation. *L'Age d'Or,* directed by Buñuel, created a riot when it was first exhibited. The film was subsequently banned, and most of the prints destroyed. The movie is a bizarre blending of Marx and Freud and is filled with scenes of savage political and religious satire, sadism, masochism, and casual cruelty.

One of the greatest of the Surrealist filmmakers was Jean Cocteau. He always maintained he was not a Surrealist, apparently because of personal differences. (The Surrealists were often squabbling with each other.) A gifted man, Cocteau also distinguished himself as a painter, poet, critic, dramatist, and novelist. He didn't neatly compartmentalize his various activities; all artists to Cocteau were "poets," whether they wrote with words, sounds, or images. Never one to disparage one art in favor of another, Cocteau felt that each form of poetic expression had its specialty. The film poet, for example, simply wrote with the "ink of light." He believed that the cinema was a first-rate vehicle for ideas, permitting the poet–director to take the viewer into realms that previously only sleep and dreams had led him to. His Orpheus Trilogy, consisting of the features *Blood of a Poet* (1930), *Orpheus* (1950), and *Testament of Orpheus* (1960), is an exploration of the mysteries of poetic creation: what a poet is, how he creates, what he creates from, what his creations do to him (10-18).

*(Films-Around-The-World)*

**10-18. *Testament of Orpheus* (France, 1960).**
*Directed by Jean Cocteau.*
Cocteau's last movie pulls out all the technical stops: it employs written language, drawings, still photographs, slow-motion sequences, double exposures, montage, reverse motion, and special effects galore. His personal friends (including Pablo Picasso) appear in a kind of testimonial. Cocteau addresses the camera, and other characters readily admit they're performing in a movie. Human statues with painted eyes on their eyelids seem both dead and alive. Graceful man-horses glide through enchanted landscapes which are populated with other exotic creatures such as this. See also Michael Gould, *Surrealism and the Cinema* (New York: A. S. Barnes, 1976).

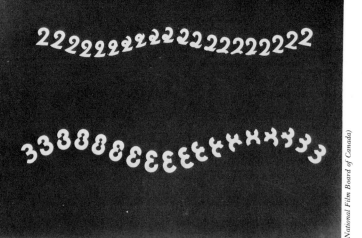

**10-19. *Rythmetic* (Canada, 1956).**
*Directed by Norman McLaren.*
A recipient of many international awards, McLaren is Canada's most prestigious filmmaker and one of the most brilliant technicians of the avant-garde. He has been engaged in experimental filmmaking for over four decades.

## The Poetic Cinema

The second phase of the avant-garde movement was essentially a period of consolidation and modest expansion. A number of excellent films were produced during this period, but for the most part, they tended to develop the themes and techniques originally explored by the Dadaists and Surrealists. During the 1930s, relatively few experimental movies were produced. Many of the filmmakers of the previous decade turned to making documentaries, which seemed a more appropriate artistic vehicle during the Depression. As the Nazis gradually seized power during this period, many of the German experimentalists began to emigrate to other countries. By the conclusion of World War II, some of the most talented European avant-garde filmmakers had moved to the United States, which partly explains the emergence of New York and San Francisco as the new avant-garde capitals of the cinema.

The influence of Freud remained strong, most notably in the films of

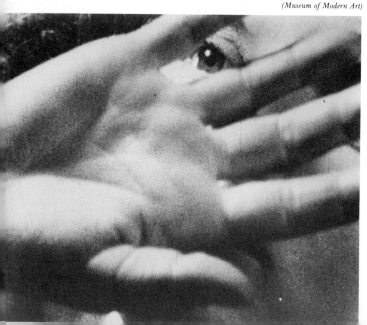

**10-20. *Meshes of the Afternoon.* (U.S.A., 1943).**
*Directed by Maya Deren.*
Like many avant-garde works of the 1940s, Deren's film is strongly Freudian in emphasis, stressing the psychopathology of everyday life. The emotionally disturbed heroine, played by Deren herself, is terrified by a series of apparently insignificant events which trigger off an increasing sense of paranoia and persecution.

Willard Maas, Sidney Peterson, and Maya Deren (10-20). Some of the psychological theories of Carl Jung were also gaining prominance, especially his emphasis on myth and ritual. Freudian and Jungian ideas were used to suggest possible motivations rather than to offer neat solutions. Explorations of the psyche were not sensationalized, although sexual frustration still figures prominantly. Unresolved anxieties, the search for identity, and the need to escape were popular themes, particularly in the works of Maya Deren who was perhaps the most influential and widely known experimental filmmaker of the period.

Deren's *Meshes of the Afternoon* was surrealist in its influence, and featured the director herself as the neurotic, terrified protagonist. There is a nightmare quality to the film, a sense of stark terror as the young woman becomes progressively more disoriented by a series of apparently trivial incidents. In her later works, Deren explored the possibilities of dance and cinema, combining the two mediums in such works as *A Study in Choreography for the Camera* (10-21), *Ritual in Transfigured Time,* and *Meditation on Violence.* These later

**10-21. *A Study in Choreography for the Camera* (U.S.A., 1945).**
*Directed by Maya Deren.*
Deren's two loves were dance and film, and in this movie she attempted to fuse them. She subtitled her work "*Pas de Deux*"—a kinetic rhapsody between camera and dancer.

films were thematically more indebted to Jung than to Freud and were rather ritualistic in emphasis.

Deren was also an important theorist of the avant-garde cinema. She wrote and spoke frequently of the advantages of the personal film over the largely standardized products being produced in Hollywood. She differentiated the poetic cinema from commercial films primarily in terms of structure. Like a lyric poem, personal films are "vertical" investigations of a theme or situation. That is, the filmmaker is not concerned so much with what's happening as with what a situation feels like or what it means. The director is concerned with probing the depths and layers of meaning of a given moment. The poetic film, then, is not concerned with movement per se, but with the "metaphysical content of the movement."

(American Federation of the Arts)

**10-22. *My Name is Oona* (U.S.A., 1969).**
*Directed by Gunvor Nelson.*
The avant-garde cinema often deals with the occult, mysticism, and archetypal experiences, like a young female's rite of passage. Throughout this movie, a girl repeats the mantra of her name in endless variation, until it becomes a magical incantation of self-realization.

Fiction movies, on the other hand, are like novels and plays—they're essentially "horizontal" in their development. Narrative filmmakers employ linear structures which must progress from situation to situation, from feeling to feeling. The fiction director doesn't have much time to explore the implications of a given idea or emotion, for he or she must keep the film "moving along." The poetic filmmaker ignores or destroys time and space, whereas the narrative director must be more careful in observing their requirements, usurping a lot of screen time.

Deren believed that in certain cases, it's possible—though very difficult—to combine these two types of structures. In the greatest plays of Shakespeare, for example, the story moves along on a horizontal plane of development. But occasionally, this forward action stops, thus permitting the dramatist to explore a given feeling within a kind of timeless void. The Shakespearean soliloquy is essentially a vertical exploration of an idea or emotion—somewhat like an aria in an opera which temporarily suspends time, space, and movement. Deren believed that, in film, such "arias" or set pieces are sometimes found in works that employ loose horizontal structures—the famous Odessa Steps sequence from Eisenstein's *Potemkin*, for example.

These soliloquies, arias, or vertical poems are what the avant-garde filmmaker tries to create without being encumbered by a horizontal narrative framework. Most poetic films are short precisely because they're emotionally condensed and narrow in scope. Since these films don't try to tell conventional stories, they are able to concentrate on the intensity of emotions, which is

(National Film Board of Canada)

**10-23. *Pas De Deux* (Canada, 1968).**
*Directed by Norman McLaren.*
This film employs a technique called chronophotography in which the movements of two dancers are staggered and overlayed by the optical printer to produce a stroboscopic effect: as the dancers move, they leave a ghostly imprint on the screen. See also Maynard Collins, *Norman McLaren* (Ottawa: Canadian Film Institute, 1977).

difficult to sustain for very long periods of time. The avant-garde cinema, then, is lyrical, layered, and simultaneous, whereas the fiction feature is distended, sequential, and (in most cases) less dense symbolically. Like poetry as opposed to prose, each kind of film sets out to do something different, and neither method is necessarily superior to the other.

Deren was also one of the key figures in publicizing the avant-garde cinema and in expanding its audiences. She spoke tirelessly to many groups across the country, urging them to form their own film societies in which personal films could be exhibited to new audiences. She booked her own works at a number of universities and art museums, and helped them form private groups where poetic films could be shown on a regular basis. Perhaps the most famous film society of this period, Cinema 16, was organized in 1947 by Amos Vogel in New York City. Throughout the 1950s, this group exhibited virtually all the important avant-garde movies produced in America. Two other famous film societies were under the auspices of the Museum of Modern Art in New York, and the San Francisco Museum of Art.

Toward the end of this phase of the avant-garde movement, a number of filmmakers were already beginning to explore themes and techniques that are more characteristic of the later Underground period. Sexual subjects began to be treated more directly, less symbolically. A new uninhibited raunchiness could be discerned in such films as Brakhage's *Flesh of Morning*, which deals

**10-24. *Fireworks* (U.S.A., 1947).**
*With Kenneth Anger; Directed by Anger.*
By the late 1940s, the avant-garde cinema was moving into a new phase, characterized by a return to some of the shock techniques of the Dada and Surrealist periods. *Fireworks*, which is filled with images of violence and male eroticism, deals with the sado-masochistic fantasies of a homosexual, played by Anger himself. See also Richard Dyer, ed., *Gays and Film* (London: British Film Institute, 1977).

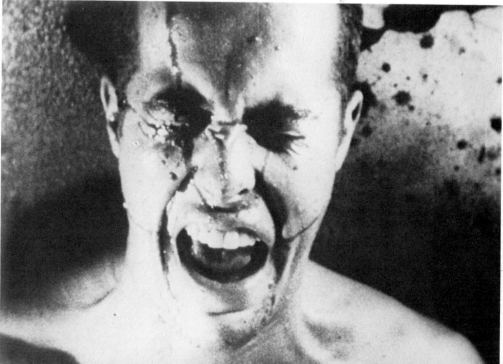

*(Museum of Modern Art)*

explicitly with masturbation. Kenneth Anger's *Fireworks* is a masochistic fantasy of a male homosexual, considerably less genteel than the majority of poetic films of this period (10-24).

In fact, a number of critics expressed alarm at this element of "perversity" which was fast becoming a dominant mode in the avant-garde. Jonas Mekas, who was to become a staunch defender of such films less than a decade later, complained of a "homosexual conspiracy" in the experimental cinema. Amos Vogel was dismayed by the obsession with crude sexuality for its own sake, which he felt characterized many of the works of the younger filmmakers. "The saleability of sex in a sexually repressed society is inevitable," Vogel observed, and he thought most of these new films were exploiting the sexual hangups of American society. They functioned merely as an artistically pretentious kind of pornography. But the avant-garde was entering a new phase in the 1950s, one which represented a return in many respects to the Dadaist heritage of anarchy, iconoclasm, and total freedom of expression. The avant-garde had grown somewhat prim since the 1930s, and the crazies were back—determined to rape the movement of its respectability.

## The Underground Phase

The Underground film represents the most prolific, stylistically varied, and controversial phase of the avant-garde movement. Beginning in the mid-1950s, hundreds of young filmmakers sprang up across the United States,

**10-25. *Skullduggery, Part I* (U.S.A., 1960).**
*Directed by Stan Vanderbeek.*
Among the most gifted political and social satirists of the Underground cinema, Vanderbeek exploits the Dadaist technique of incongruity with hilarious results. His witty "assemblages" machinegun by at a breathless clip, juxtaposing pictures of public figures with vulgar pop images.

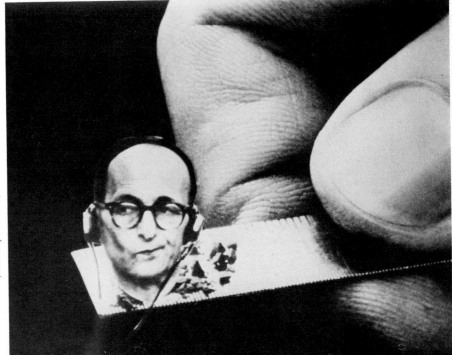

(Museum of Modern Art)

although the main concentrations were still in San Francisco and New York City. Despite harsh criticisms and persistent scorn from the film establishment, these determined nonconformists continued to make movies—some of them shrill, others outrageously comic and irreverent, a few of them profound, a great many of them inept and incomprehensible.

The turning point between the poetic cinema and the Underground phase is not easy to determine since many of the same filmmakers were active in both periods. A number of historians and critics have pointed to Brakhage's *Desistfilm* as the watershed work. Made in 1954, the movie reflected a new morality based on spontaneity, a preoccupation with youth, and an emphasis on purely sensuous elements as opposed to the more literary and psychological concerns of the previous phase of the avant-garde. The subject of the film concerns a wild teenage party which builds to an hysterical climax. Technically, *Desistfilm* established the main lines of what was to develop into a new aesthetic in the avant-garde cinema, one emphasizing "roughness" and a deliberate crudity of technique. Brakhage used a hand-held camera which bobbed, weaved, and swirled unsteadily in virtually every shot. The editing style is frantic and rapid fire, with abrupt closeups suddenly thrust upon the audience. The framing seems clumsy and unprofessional, and some of the images are out of focus.

**10-26.** *Scorpio Rising* **(U.S.A., 1963).**
*Directed by Kenneth Anger.*
This film is a mock-heroic celebration of phallic narcissism. It centers on a motorcycle gang, its essentially homosexual rituals, and its preoccupation with "masculine" emblems—leather, chains, and chrome phallic fixtures. Visually, *Scorpio Rising* has a deliberate home-movie roughness and is accompanied by a soundtrack of machismo-steeped rock 'n' roll songs of the period.

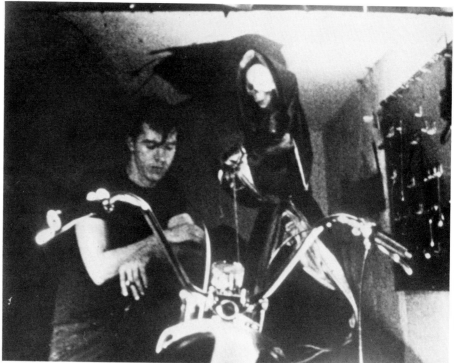

*(Museum of Modern Art)*

It was this technical crudity that aroused most of the antagonism of the critics at the time. These young filmmakers were harshly condemned for their lack of polish and their unwillingness to discipline themselves, to learn the rules of their craft. In fact, a great many of these movies were (and still are) incompetent, self-indulgent, and boring. The lighting too often has a home movie look, the cutting can be arbitrary and clumsy, the images out of focus, and the sound perfectly awful.

But in some cases, this crudity is intentional. Many of these filmmakers disdained the "costly look" which they associated with the empty gloss of most commercial movies—movies they considered "beautiful but dead." The technical crudity of these films is at least in part a kind of antiestablishment gesture of contempt, then, a badge of sincerity and independence. Furthermore, like the cinéma vérité documentarists, these artists believed that a truly spontaneous movie will inevitably be crude in places, but the honesty and directness of the shots must take precedence over technical polish. Most of these filmmakers wanted to avoid (or in some cases free themselves from) what they viewed as technical overkill. Their dislike of "discipline" was not necessarily a case of laziness, as many critics maintained, but an unwillingness to sacrifice their spontaneity, freedom, and self-expression at the sacred altar of Professionalism.

A number of these artists were competent and even gifted technicians. Marie Menken, for example, was a special-effects technician for several Signal Corps films. Brakhage has done a good deal of conventional filmmaking for various commercial organizations; and Ed Emshwiller has directed films for the conservative United States Information Agency. Emshwiller, generally acknowledged as the most gifted technician of the Underground movement, is a self-conscious and precise craftsman (10-27).

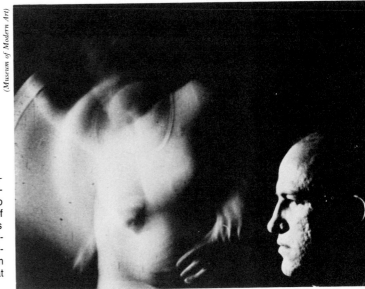

*(Museum of Modern Art)*

**10-27.** *Thanatopsis* **(U.S.A., 1960–62).** *Directed by Ed Emshwiller.* Rejecting the "costly look" of most conventional fiction movies, many Underground filmmakers wanted their works to look crude and unpolished. Some of these artists, however, didn't share this contempt for craftsmanship. While Emshwiller's movies can be wildly unconventional in other respects, most of them are photographed and edited with great skill.

**10-28.** *Juliet of the Spirits* **(Italy, 1965).**
*Directed by Federico Fellini.*
With the relaxation of censorship in the mid-1960s, the avant-garde was pre-empted of one of its most popular themes—sex. Commercial movies, like Fellini's surrealistic *Juliet of the Spirits,* began to explore human sexuality with more frankness, and often in symbolic fantasy scenes, such as this. The Underground cinema moved on to steamier sexual doings. Two of the most common subjects were homosexuality and orgiastic sex.

In the 1960s, the Underground movement flourished, and in many respects, surfaced (10-28). No longer isolated and alienated from the main cultural stream, these filmmakers now became a part of a new liberated and youth-oriented lifestyle which burgeoned during this decade. The era of sexual permissiveness, political activism, rock and pop culture, and the drug scene coincided perfectly with the themes of the Underground cinema. Most importantly, perhaps, it was a time for youth—for childlike spontaneity and even outright infantilism. "If I were you," Robert Downey wrote of his film *Chafed Elbows,* "I wouldn't let anybody over forty years old in the theatre unless they're accompanied by a teenager."

The 1960s was a decade of "doing your own thing." All of the arts assumed a new sense of improvisation, fluidity, and lack of rigor. Traditional "rules" and conventions were viewed with suspicion and even paranoia in some instances. Pop art, the Theatre of the Ridiculous, Happenings, mixed media—the new hip consciousness was found almost everywhere. Many artists were influenced by the communication theories of Marshall McLuhan, Buckminster Fuller, and the composer John Cage. The role of chance and the accidental became progressively more dominant in the arts. In the cinema, these aleatory elements could be found not only in commercial movies, but also in cinéma vérité documentaries and especially in Underground films. Brakhage was strongly influenced by theories of chance structures which had been explored originally by Cage. In *Third Eye Butterfly*, Storm De Hirsh used two simultaneous projectors so that pure chance would determine the visual juxtapositions between the dual screens.

The 1960s was also a decade of political unrest and civil protest, and a number of Underground films reflected these anxieties, often in a satirical mode. Robert Nelson's *Oh Dem Watermelons* is a witty spoof on clichés about Negroes. Watermelons serve as a symbol of black people, and to the accompaniment of corny minstrel show songs, we see these melons kicked, crushed, splattered, and even seduced! Perhaps the most effective political satirist of this period was Stan Vanderbeek, whose "assemblages" are steeped in black humor and whimsical irreverence. Movies like *Skullduggery Part I* and *Part II* feature illustrations from magazines, film clips of politicians, and all kinds of

**10-29. *Weekend* (France, 1967).**
*Directed by Jean-Luc Godard.*
Godard wanted to explode tidy film classifications by combining the conventions of fiction, documentary, and the avant-garde—even within a single movie. The apocalyptic *Weekend* includes stylized allegorical sequences, rituals, documentary scenes, a little bit of story (mostly sex and violence), lots of symbols, and quirky authorial intrusions, such as jokes, lectures, and enigmatic ruminations.

incongruous photographs which emphasize the madness of American life. *Summit* is a satire of the Kennedy–Krushchev meeting, in which Vanderbeek "animates" the actors to look like calculating robots. *Breathdeath* is an antiwar film that features, among other things, a shot of Richard Nixon with a foot emerging from his mouth.

Sex was probably the most popular theme of the Underground cinema. With the relaxation of public censorship during the 1960s, many commercial film directors also began to explore the complexities of human sexuality, and the avant-garde was thereby co-opted of one of its traditional prerogatives. The Underground responded by concentrating on sexual aberrations—at least those areas of sexuality that were considered abnormal by the middle-class majority. Homosexuality and orgiastic sex were particularly popular subjects.

One of the classic examples of this type of film is Jack Smith's paean to pansexuality, *Flaming Creatures*, which is still banned in New York State. The movie features virtually every kind of sexuality: sado-masochism, transvestism, a gang-rape of an hermaphrodite, masturbation, oral sex, and even vampirism. Twisted arms and legs writhe like serpents in a steaming pit. The

**10-30. *Dreamwood* (U.S.A., 1972).**
*Directed by James Broughton.*
Many avant-garde filmmakers are drawn to mythological materials, or, like Broughton, they create their own mythos with a private symbology. Broughton described *Dreamwood* in the following terms: "Somewhere (at the center of the world) there is an island called Animandra, or the Kingdom of Her. And somewhere in the wilds of Animandra there is a magic wood known as Broceliande, the Perilous Forest. Within this labyrinthine grove the dreamwood mysteries take place, the tests, the encounters, the rites of the Goddess in her many forms. Only a hero dares risk his life by entering this realm of the feminine powers. And most heroic is the poet, perhaps, guided as he is (and taunted) by that blessed demozel, his muse, whose name is Alchemina. Ordinary men remain safely outside in the dry meadows of their masculine games. But to the man who conquers his fear, persists in his quest and wins her favor, the Goddess of Dreamwood will reveal her greatest secret."

top of the frame decapitates many of the pulsating, swirling figures. Much of the time we're unable to distinguish the sex of the people, until their full bodies stream into the frame and their genitals are visible. There is a ritualistic quality to these frenzied activities, a kind of Black Mass in which the celebrants abandon themselves totally to the doomed ecstasy of violent sexual release. The soundtrack screeches and hisses with animal noises, mock-romantic Latin American music, rock 'n' roll, and a cacophony of tasteless commercial jingles.

Ritual and myth have always played a prominant role in the avant-garde cinema, and in the early and mid-1960s these preoccupations became even more conspicuous in such films as Brakhage's *Dog Star Man*, Bruce Baillie's *Mass*, and the works of Gregory Markopoulos who derived most of his subjects from classical Greek myths. Markopoulos' themes often revolve around homosexual love—masculine in the case of *The Illiac Passion*, feminine in *Psyche*. As early as 1948, Markopoulos made a movie, *Lysis*, based on a Platonic dialogue on friendship. Like most of his works, the film is dazzlingly edited, flipping from past to future to present with casual audacity.

**10-31.** *Lapis* **(U.S.A., 1963–66).**
*Directed by James Whitney.*
Whitney has been described as "a scientist of the soul." Influenced by Taoism and Zen Buddhism, his computer-animated films are at once mechanical, abstract, and mystical. In this movie, an Indian mandala design expands and congeals in infinite variation, creating an almost hypnotic effect on the viewer.

*(Anthology Film Archives)*

One of the finest filmmakers to be influenced by the idea of myth is Jordan Belson, whose works are only formally in the abstract tradition of the avant-garde. Belson's movies are mystical, inspired in large part by the philosophical literature of Zen Buddhism. His works have also been influenced by drug experiences, particularly mescaline and peyote, with their hallucinatory powers of expanding consciousness and their ability to induce trance-like mystical states. *Re-Entry* is generally regarded as Belson's best work. Originally inspired by John Glenn's historic penetration into space, the film is densely symbolic and mythical, although it can also be accepted as a purely abstract movie. Buddhist ideas of mystical reincarnation are likened to a spacecraft's re-entry into the earth's atmosphere. Belson used some of

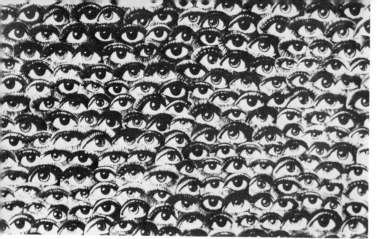

(Pyramid Films/American Federation of the Arts)

**10-32.** *Frank Film* (U.S.A., 1973).
*Directed by Frank Mouris.*
Avant-garde movies are often autobiographical and self-reflexive—they call attention to themselves, their aesthetic workings, and their creators. Mouris' film consists of magazine cutouts that he animated to illustrate the main influences of his youth. The soundtrack features two voices (both Mouris'), one listing a series of words beginning with the letter F, the other wittily recounting his life story to date.

Jung's psychological theories to structure his film. The three stages of space travel—launching, penetration of deep space, and re-entry—symbolize three mystical states: death, a limbolike suspension in the cosmic void, and rebirth. The soundtrack for the most part is synthesized electronically, and consists of eerie echoing reverberations. Included on the soundtrack are some of Glenn's actual radio messages from space, though they're deliberately distorted and incomprehensible to most audiences.

Andy Warhol was the *enfant terrible* of the Underground movement. Critics either hailed him as an audacious innovator or an outrageous fraud. Warhol's disdain for "professional" standards infuriated even other members of the avant-garde. His self-admitted indolence, his deadpan manner of saying outlandish things about—gasp!—Art, and his shrewd publicity sense alienated a good many devotees of the Underground cinema. There's a strong element of the put-on in Warhol's movies, and humorless critics—including many of his champions—often fail to discern it. Warhol himself didn't take his films very seriously. When asked why he turned to cinema after a successful career as a graphic artist, he laconically replied that movies were easier.

Warhol produced a number of films in the 1960s that were given the rather solemn appellation of the "New Realism." In fact, these movies out-Lumièred Lumière, consisting of lengthy minimal-take recordings of perfectly unspectacular events. *Eat* is a single-take 45-minute film of a man eating a mushroom. *Sleep* consists of 6 hours worth of footage showing a man sleeping. Actually, the movie is composed of only 3 hours of footage, but each reel is repeated. The camera never moves, and the editing is confined to reel changes only. Perhaps the most spectacular example of Warhol's movies that don't move is *Empire*, in which the techniques are so minimal that the film is virtually a still photograph extended in time. Warhol set up his camera and photographed the Empire State Building in a single shot that lasts 8 hours. Actual time is preserved more-or-less intact. The major event of the movie takes place when day transforms into night.

Some critics praised Warhol for the purity of his minimal techniques. His cinema is a medium of time rather than space or movement, they claimed, and by forcing us to concentrate on the minutest details, Warhol is able to create dramatic effects from the merest wisps of action. Hostile critics scoffed at such elaborate metaphysical explanations. These films are nothing but monstrous mountains giving birth to a mouse, they insisted. Like many avant-garde artists, Warhol delighted in stirring up controversy, especially within the avant-garde itself.

Stan Brakhage is perhaps the quintessential Underground filmmaker. A mystical visionary, he views the role of the artist as a kind of prophetic bard or seer. His best movies are intensely personal. Like the works of the Romantic English poet William Blake, Brakhage's films are often obscure and egocentric, saturated with private symbolism. Like most Romantics, Brakhage exploits himself as a universal symbol:

> I had the concept of everything radiating out of me, and that the more personal or egocentric I would become, the deeper I would reach and the more I could touch those universal concerns that would involve all men.

*Dog Star Man* is generally regarded as Brakhage's finest work. His technical range in this movie is very broad. The cutting is rhythmically sensuous, and there are expressionistic distortions in profusion. Multiple exposures, negative images, and many different lenses and filters are used to convey emotional suggestions. Brakhage sometimes inserts strips of black or white leader instead of photographed images to convey metaphorically the terrifying blankness of certain experiences. Point-of-view shots are frequent, and in one sequence, Brakhage shows us a scene with a point-of-view shot, then cuts to shots of internal organs, cell tissues, and the blood stream, to convey the visceral impact of the original scene.

**10-33. *The Golden Positions* (U.S.A., 1970).**
*Directed by James Broughton.*
One of the clown princes of the avant-garde, Broughton takes impish delight in lampooning human absurdities. In this shot, he zaps the prim correctness of his two ladies by presenting them in the buff. Ironically, their sagging, vulnerable flesh is the main source of their humanity.

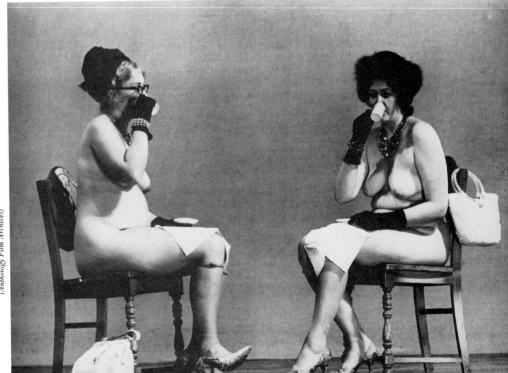

*(Anthology Film Archives)*

Structuralist cinema is indebted to its predecessors—a fusion of various influences. It's also very loosely related to the critical theory of structuralism, discussed in Chapter 11. For the most part, the movement is anti-illusionist. The subject matter of the image is either abstract or unimportant. "Film is not a vehicle for ideas or portrayals of emotion," said Ernie Gehr, a prominent structuralist. "Film is a variable intensity of light, an interval balance of time, a movement within a given space." In Gehr's films, the function of the image is to act as a formal unit of a predetermined design. The image is essentially a segment of an aesthetic system.

Structuralists also emphasize film as concrete material, rather than a medium for conveying human enactments. For this reason, this type of movie is sometimes referred to as a structural/materialist film. Many of these artists prefer a concrete subject—an empty room, a corridor, a landscape—but it's used dialectically, set in opposition to some conceptual premise. The flicker effect, created by single-frame shots, as in the works of Tony Conrad and Paul Sharits (10-34), is one such conceptual technique. Looping is another. What

*(Anthology Film Archives)*

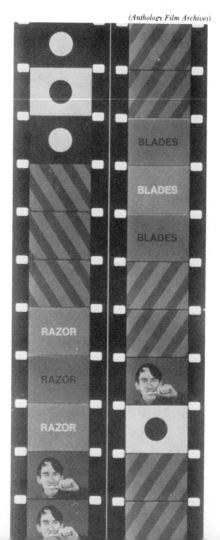

**10-34. *Razor Blades* (U.S.A., 1968).** *Directed by Paul Sharits.* In the structuralist cinema, the codes of cognition are totally self-defined. They are structured according to the principles of recurrence, dialectical polarities, time and space increments, and so on. The process of deciphering these cognitive codes and their interrelationships is analogous to the film's working itself out, fulfilling its structural destiny. In Sharits' flicker film, two images (requiring separate screens and projectors) are simultaneously juxtaposed. Each filmstrip consists of irregularly recurring images—two or three frames in duration, interspersed by blank or color frames—or purely abstract designs, like colored stripes or circular shapes. The rapid flickering of images creates a mesmerizing stroboscopic effect, testing the audience's psychological and physiological tolerance. The content of the film is its structural form rather than the subject matter of the images *as* images.

this involves is taking a short piece of film and joining it end to end so it can be repeated at variable intervals, at different speeds, and so on.

"Structuralism is a cinema of the mind rather than the eye," observed critic P. Adams Sitney. Influenced by the movements called Minimalism and Conceptualism in the plastic arts, structuralist filmmakers emphasize the shape of their movies as the principal raison d'etre. They are also influenced by systems and game theories. The subject matter—if any—is deflected by a predetermined and often mechanized concept. A film can be structured in terms of image content (concrete or abstract), duration (time and interval as structuring principles), formal juxtapositions in the editing, and so on.

Structuralists insist on the viewer's participation. The formal operations of a given film is its point, but the structuring process is discovered during viewing—it's an experience as well as a conceptual system. In George Landlow's *Remedial Reading Comprehension*, disconnected phrases are used as one of the structuring devices, and the spectator must fill in the symbolic associations the words imply. "This Is a Film About You," one of Landow's titles informs us, "Not About Its Maker." Hollis Frampton also emphasizes this participatory element in his films.

Michael Snow's *Wavelength* is one of the most written-about works of the Structuralist cinema. The film is a 45-minute forward-zoom shot, taken from the farther end of an 80-foot loft, inching almost imperceptibly toward a set of windows and the street behind them (10-35), halting occasionally when inter-

**10-35. *Wavelength* (Canada, 1967).**
*Directed by Michael Snow.*
This film has been interpreted as a metaphor of inexorability. The agonizingly slow forward zoom across a lengthy room almost imperceptibly reduces and redefines the visual field. The movement has an ultimate destination, but throughout most of the film, we can't guess what it will be; we can only wait until all other options have been eliminated. The kinetic motion is symbolic: we proceed from uncertainty to certainty, from freedom (or the illusion of freedom) to destiny. See also Peter Gidal, ed., *Structural Film Anthology* (London: British Film Institute, 1976).

*(Anthology Film Archives)*

rupted by four human events (including a death), and ending finally on a closeup of a photo pinned to the wall: waves. The film's content is multiple. It's the diminishing area of the visual field, the kinetic increments of the forward zoom, the alteration from day to night within the shot's duration, and the accompanying soundtrack, consisting of an electronic sine wave, which starts at a low intensity of 50 cycles per second and ends on a high of 1200 cps.

The film also has a metaphysical content. The camera's movement has been interpreted as a symbolic model of cognition, of the limits of perception, and the limits of human endeavor. "Most of my films accept the traditional theater situation," Snow has pointed out, "audience here, screen there." There is a dialectical tension between the human materials in the film—especially the death—and the camera's implacable forward motion. To paraphrase Snow: The zoom emphasizes the cosmic continuity which is beautiful, but tragic: it just goes on without us. On this level, the movie is a symbolic analogue, a metaphor of man's impotence in the face of an inexorable Fate.

In his book *Expanded Cinema,* Gene Youngblood explores some of the directions the avant-garde is already embarked upon and will inevitably expand. These developments include videotronics, multiple projection environments, and screenless holographic cinema in three dimensions, to mention only a few. The spectacular developments that await us in the future are likely to make previous avant-garde movements look charmingly antiquated by comparison.

## Further Reading

BATTCOCK, GREGORY, ed., *The New American Cinema: A Critical Anthology* (New York: Dutton, 1967). A collection of articles, with emphasis on the Underground cinema.

CURTIS, DAVID, *Experimental Cinema* (New York: Universe Books, 1971). A critical history, including many European filmmakers.

MANVELL, ROGER, ed., *Experiment in the Film* (London: Gray Walls Press, 1949). A collection of articles.

RENAN, SHELDON *Introduction to the American Underground Film* (New York: Dutton, 1967). Emphasis on artists of the 1950s and 1960s.

SITNEY, P. ADAMS, ed. *Film Culture Reader* (New York: Praeger, 1970). Articles and interviews.

———, *Visionary Film: The American Avant-Garde 1943–1978* (New York; Oxford Univ. Press, 1974). Critical study, with emphasis on the romanticism of the American avant-garde.

STAUFFACHER, FRANK, ed. *Art in Cinema* (New York: Arno Press, 1969). A collection of articles.

TYLER PARKER, *Underground Film: A Critical History* (New York: Grove Press, 1969). (Paper) Emphasis on the psychological, sexual, and mythic.

VOGEL, AMOS, *Film as a Subversive Art* (New York: Random House, 1975). Emphasis on the forbidden, rebellious, and blasphemous, superbly illustrated.

YOUNGBLOOD, GENE, *Expanded Cinema* (New York: Dutton, 1970). An exploration of the technological and aesthetic experiments in the avant-garde cinema, with predictions for the future.

# 11

*"Surely there are no hard and fast rules: it all depends on how it's done."*

PAULINE KAEL

# THEORY

Most theories of film are concerned with the wider context of the medium—its social, political, and philosophical implications. Theorists have also explored the essential nature of cinema—what differentiates it from other art forms, what its basic properties are. For the most part, film theory has been dominated by Europeans, especially the French. The tradition of criticism in the United States has been less theoretical and more pragmatic in its thrust. In recent times, however, American film critics have shown a greater interest in the theoretical implications of the medium, though the bias in favor of practical criticism remains strong. A theory is an intellectual grid, a set of aesthetic generalizations, not eternal verities. Some theories are more useful than others in understanding specific movies. No single theory can explain them all. For this reason, recent developments in the field have stressed an eclectic approach, synthesizing a variety of theoretical strategies (11-1).

Traditionally, theorists have focused their attention on three areas of inquiry: (1) the work of art, (2) the artist, and (3) the audience. Those who have stressed the work of art have explored the inner dynamics of movies—how they communicate, the language systems they employ. These theorists can also be divided into realists and expressionists. Siegfried Kracauer was perhaps the most influential spokesman for the theory of cinematic Realism, and the movies he cited most often were those of the Italian neorealists. The principal spokesman for the theory of Expressionism was Rudolf Arnheim. The most important artist-oriented approach is the *auteur theory,* a variant of

**11-1. *The Maltese Falcon* (U.S.A., 1941).**

*With Humphrey Bogart, Peter Lorre, Mary Astor, and Sydney Greenstreet; Directed by John Huston.*

Theory is the handmaiden of art, not vice-versa. Movies can be explored from a variety of theoretical perspectives, each with its own set of values and parameters of inquiry. One's theoretical orientation will depend in large part on what one is looking for. For example, *The Maltese Falcon* can be placed in at least seven theoretical contexts: (1) An auteur critic would regard it as a typical Huston film. (2) It could also be analyzed as a Bogart vehicle, exploiting and expanding the star's iconography. (3) An industry historian would place the picture within its commercial context—as a superior example of the Warner Brothers product of this era. (4) A genre theorist would be interested in it as a classic example of the detective thriller, and one of the first of the so-called deadly female pictures that were so popular in the United States during World War II. (5) A theorist interested in the relationship of movies to literature might focus on Huston's script, based on Dashiell Hammett's celebrated novel of the same title. (6) A stylistic critic would analyze the picture within the context of *film noir,* an important style in the American cinema of the 1940s. (7) A Marxist might interpret the movie as a parable on greed, an implicit condemnation of the vices of capitalism. Each theoretical grid charts a different cinematic topography.

expressionism. Marxist theories are prominent in Europe, the Third World, and of course the Communist bloc countries. Marxists can also be divided into realists and expressionists, although both are strongly oriented toward issues of ideology. Marxist theorists have been in the forefront in exploring how social context and the means of production can affect meaning in cinema. Structuralism and semiology were the dominant theories after 1970, and both tend to emphasize a synthetic approach, combining such concerns as genre, authorship, history, style, iconography, social context, and ideology.

## Realist Film Theories

Most theories of Realism emphasize the documentary aspect of film art. Movies are evaluated primarily in terms of how accurately they reflect external reality (1-3). The camera is regarded as essentially a recording mechanism, rather than an expressive medium in its own right. The subject matter is paramount in the cinema of Realism, technique its discreetly transparent handmaiden. As we have seen in the case of André Bazin (Chapter 4) and the example of cinéma vérité (Chapter 9), most theories of Realism have a moral and ethical bias and are often rooted in the values of Christian and Marxist humanism.

Perhaps the most comprehensive theory of Realism was put forth in 1960 by Siegfried Kracauer in his book *Theory of Film: The Redemption of Physical Reality.* Kracauer doesn't ignore expressionistic movies. He acknowledges a "formative tendency" which he traces back to the early experiments of Méliès. In general, however, he considers expressionistic movies as aberrations of the central aesthetic of cinema. The basic premise of Kracauer's aesthetic is that

**11-2. *Sounder* (U.S.A., 1972).**
*With Cicely Tyson (wearing hat); Directed by Martin Ritt.*
Kracauer attempts to carve out a mainline tradition within the cinema, and he proposes the tradition of social realism. Actually, social realism is neither a style nor a movement in the usual sense of those terms. Perhaps it would be more accurate to describe it as a set of values, both social and aesthetic, cutting across national boundaries and historical periods. For many years it was the most prestigious branch of the cinema, enjoying wide support among the liberally-educated classes of most countries. Social realism is a view from the left. Filmmakers generally assume a reformist or revolutionary perspective on the narrative materials, and explore, at least implicitly, the ways in which people near the bottom of the social heap are exploited. One of the broadest of film classifications, social realism encompasses many movements and styles, including the neorealists of postwar Italy, the films of socialist realism in the Communist countries of the world, the so-called kitchen-sink realism of the British cinema of the late 1950s and early 1960s, and many individual filmmakers who are concerned with themes of social injustice and change, like Martin Ritt.

(Twentieth Century-Fox)

film is essentially an extension of photography and shares with it a "marked affinity" for recording the visible world around us. Unlike other art forms, photography and cinema tend to leave the raw materials of reality more or less intact. There is a minimum of "interference" on the artist's part, for film is not an art of creativity so much as an art of "being there."

According to Kracauer, the cinema is characterized by a number of natural affinities. First of all, it tends to favor "unstaged reality"—that is, the most appropriate subject matter gives the illusion of having been found rather than arranged (1-18). Second, film tends to stress the random, the fortuitous. Kracauer is fond of the phrase "nature caught in the act," meaning that film is best suited to recording events and objects which might be overlooked in life—the stirring of a leaf, the rippling of a brook, a frozen instant of terror (2-28). The realistic cinema is a cinema of "found moments" (4-22) and poignant revelations of humanity (2-27B). A third affinity that Kracauer notes is indeterminancy. The best movies suggest endlessness: they imply a slice-of-life, a fragment of a larger reality rather than a unified self-contained whole. By emphasizing open forms (2-30), the cinema can suggest the same openended limitlessness of life itself.

Kracauer is hostile toward movies that demonstrate a "formative tendancy." That is, distortions and manipulations that violate these natural affinities. Historical films and fantasies he regards as tending to move away from the basic concerns of the medium. Thus, he approves of certain elements in the early semidocumentary films of Eisenstein, which use nonprofessional players, authentic locations, and natural lighting. But Kracauer condemns Eisenstein's editing practices (4-8) which distort the time–space continuum of reality. Furthermore, he disapproves of films that are propagandistic, for they impose an ideology or a single doctrine over the neutral copious-

**11-3. *Autumn Sonata* (Sweden, 1978).** *With Ingrid Bergman and Liv Ullmann; Directed by Ingmar Bergman.*
Realism is a critical term, a label. Seldom is it definitive in describing a film, because movies generally mix the conventions of realism with other aesthetic conventions. For example, most of the mother-daughter confrontations in this film are presented in a simple documentary style. But Bergman also uses a number of expressionistic devices, most notably an on-camera narrator who speaks directly to the audience, providing us with a more objective point of view, and distancing the documentary-like scenes with a kind of theatrical frame.

*(New World Pictures)*

ness of reality. He condemns outright the works of Eisenstein's later career—the "operatic" *Alexander Nevsky* and *Ivan the Terrible*. The images and events of these movies are "uncinematic," according to Kracauer. They aren't fortuitous, but arranged, synthetic, and "theatrical."

Kracauer also dismisses most literary and dramatic adaptations because he believes that literature is ultimately concerned with "interior realities,"

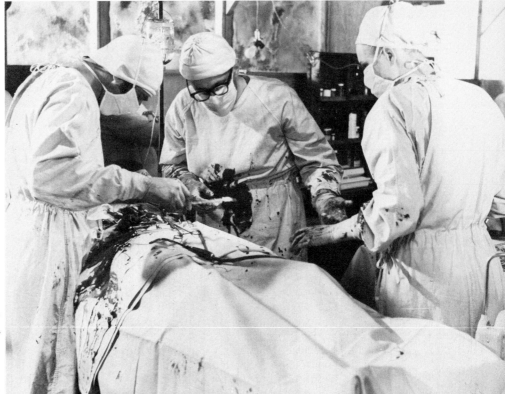

**11-4. *M\*A\*S\*H* (U.S.A., 1969).**
*Directed by Robert Altman.*
When art grows decadent, George Bernard Shaw observed, realism usually provides the cure. *M\*A\*S\*H* is a military comedy, traditionally a stylized genre, in which battle scenes, if any, are treated humorously. This movie contains no battle scenes, but we're always kept aware of the larger human stakes behind the comic chaos. For example, the surgical episodes are filled with blood, blasted limbs, and discarded corpses. Though ostensibly about the Korean War of the early 1950s, the film was photographed in a TV documentary style that reminded viewers of the Vietnam carnage unreeling each night on the evening news.

what people are thinking and feeling. There are also style clashes. If Shakespearean adaptations are performed in stylized sets, the result is mere filmed theatre, for the documentary realism of the medium is violated. If the plays are performed in natural settings (real castles, forests, and battlefields), the stylized language, the artificial costumes, and the "enclosed" world all clash with the open-ended authenticity of the locales. Adaptations from novels are permissible only when the narrative elements lend themselves to a realistic presentation. The fiction of Emile Zola, with its emphasis on slice-of-life occurrences, would be admissible in the cinema; the novels of Jane Austen, with their exquisitely filligreed plots, would not.

Kracauer tends to regard all stylistic self-consciousness as "uncinematic." The camera ought to record what *is*. When the subject matter departs from physical reality, we become conscious of the artifice, and therefore our credulity is strained. For example, historical movies tend to be uncinematic because the viewer is aware of the "reconstruction." The world of the movie is enclosed, for beyond the frame is not the endlessness of actual place and time, but the paraphernalia of a twentieth-century film crew. Similarly, in fantasy films, we become too conscious of the contrivances. Instead of concentrating on what's being shown, we become distracted by wondering how certain effects are achieved, for they have no literal counterpart in reality.

Kracauer underestimates the flexibility of an audience's response to nonrealistic movies. To be sure, it's easier for a filmmaker to create the illusion of reality if the story takes place in a contemporary setting, for the world of the movie and the actual world are essentially the same. It's also true that we're often aware of the contrivances in historical movies and fantasies, but usually when the cinematic techniques are clumsy and heavy-handed. On the other hand, there are many movies that seem saturated in the details of a remote period. Many scenes from *Birth of a Nation* look as authentic as the Civil War photographs of Mathew Brady (4-2). Kubrick's *2001: A Space Odyssey* was obviously not photographed in space, yet it's totally convincing in its *sense* of authenticity (2-2). Visconti's period films are virtually reconstructed documentaries. *The Leopard,* for instance, never betrays a sense of self-consciousness or contrivance in its use of costumes, makeup, sets, and properties (7-32). Even fantasy films like *King Kong* (3-30) and *Fantastic Voyage* (7-2) can be startlingly realistic. They present us with a self-contained "universe" which we are able to enter by temporarily forgetting the outside world of reality (11-5).

Other movies deliberately exploit the audience's double existence. As Dr. Johnson pointed out centuries ago, audiences in a theatre don't literally believe that they're watching events of a remote period. Although viewers give a kind of voluntary credence to the events on stage, they are always aware of the fact they're in a theatre, watching an artistic performance, a simulation. The same principle of aesthetic distance applies to movies.

Finally, as Pauline Kael has pointed out, audiences often enjoy the artificiality of a movie—it's part of the show. Musicals, for example, are generally pleasurable because they're *unlike* everyday reality (11-6). The same is true of most avant-garde films. In movies like *Star Wars* and *The Empire Strikes Back,* the audience derives as much pleasure from wondering how the playful special effects were achieved as from the effects themselves. In short, audiences are highly sophisticated in their responses to nonrealistic films: viewers can almost totally suspend their disbelief, partially suspend it, or alternate between extremes, according to the aesthetic demands of the world of the movie.

Certainly Kracauer's book isn't of much value in explaining why expressionistic films are so effective. On the other hand, his theory is exceptionally sensitive in explaining the effectiveness of realistic movies. The sub-

**11-5. *Star Wars* (U.S.A., 1977).**
*With C-3PO (raising hands); Directed by George Lucas.*
The world of a movie doesn't have to conform to the actual world in order to be *artistically* convincing. Viewers expect only that once the main characteristics of a screen reality are defined, the director does not violate this internal logic with inappropriate references to outside reality.

**11-6. *The Band Wagon* (U.S.A., 1953).**
*With Fred Astaire, Nanette Fabray, and Jack Buchanan; Directed by Vincente Minnelli.*
Despite its "fanciful scenery" and "stylized canvases," Kracauer admired Minnelli's film, defending its musical numbers as "outgrowths of life's contingencies." Something of an aesthetic puritan, Kracauer underrated a principal attraction of art—pleasure. For example, the witty "Triplets" number is "cinematic" not because it has anything to do with everyday reality, but because it's so superbly staged and performed.

title of Kracauer's book speaks not of the imitation or recording of physical reality, but of its redemption. To redeem something is to recover it, to rescue it from oblivion. Even realistic movies, then, go beyond everyday life in some way. They show us things we might not notice in the clutter and sprawl of life (7-4). The camera preserves fortuitous fragments from the chaos of reality, rescuing them from obscurity (1-2).

Kracauer often cites Italian neorealist films to illustrate his theories. Neorealism was one of the most influential theories of cinematic Realism. Actually, it's both a style of filmmaking and a specific film movement which

*(Contemporary Films)*

**11-7. *Open City*. (Italy, 1945).**
*With Marcello Pagliero; Directed by Roberto Rossellini.*
The torture scenes of this famous Resistance film were so realistic that they were edited out of some prints. In this episode, a Nazi S.S. officer applies a blowtorch to the body of a Communist partisan in an effort to force him to reveal the names of his comrades in the underground. The crucifixion allusion is deliberate, even though the character is a nonbeliever. It parallels the death of another partisan, a Catholic priest, who is executed by a military firing squad. See also "Italian Neorealism," edited by Luciana Bohne, in *Film Criticism* (Winter, 1979).

began in Italy during the last months of World War II. As a particularly Italian movement, neorealism was pretty much over by the mid-1950s, but as a style it spread to many other countries. In India, for example, many of the films of Satyajit Ray are in the neorealist vein, and in America, Elia Kazan and

Fred Zinnemann came under its influence. Beginning in the late 1950s, neorealism became the dominant mode in England, and lasted for nearly a decade. The earliest movies of such British directors as Tony Richardson, Karel Reisz, and Lindsay Anderson reflect both the political and stylistic biases of this movement.

Perhaps the quintessential neorealist movie is Rossellini's *Open City* which launched both the movement and the style. The film deals with the collaboration of Catholics and Communists in fighting the Nazi occupation of Rome shortly before the American army liberated the city. Reputedly, Rossellini shot some of the footage while the Nazis were actually evacuating the capital. Technically, the film was rather crude. Since good quality film stock was impossible to obtain, Rossellini had to use inferior newsreel stock; nevertheless, the technical flaws and the resultant grainy images convey a sense of journalistic immediacy and authenticity. (Many neorealists began their careers as journalists, and Rossellini himself began as a documentarist.) Virtually all the movie was shot in actual locations, and there are many exterior shots in which no additional lights were used. With the exception of the principals, the actors were nonprofessionals. The structure of the movie was episodic—a series of vignettes showing the reactions of Roman citizens to the German occupation.

Rossellini refused to idealize his characters, focusing not on heroes, but ordinary people in heroic moments. His blending of Marxism and Catholicism was historically accurate, for the Resistance was largely organized by Italian Communists, and a number of Catholic clergymen also joined the partisan movement. Rossellini's compassion for the victims of oppression was not narrowly ideological, however, for he sympathized even with those who betrayed their better instincts. The film is saturated with a sense of unrelenting honesty. "This is the way things are," Rossellini is said to have declared after the film was shown. The statement became the motto of the neorealist movement.

Within the next few years, there followed an astonishing series of movies: Rossellini's *Paisan* and *Germany: Year Zero*, De Sica's *Shoeshine*, *Bicycle Thief*, and *Umberto D*, and Visconti's *La Terra Trema*. The early works of Fellini and

*(Museum of Modern Art)*

**11-8. Shoeshine (Italy, 1946).**
*With Rinaldo Smordoni and Franco Interlenghi; Directed by Vittorio De Sica.*
André Bazin was a champion of Italian neorealism, applauding its moral fervor even more than its technical restraint. "Is not neorealism primarily a kind of humanism, and only secondarily a style of filmmaking?" he asked. The dialectical tension between the Catholic De Sica and the Communist Zavattini (the principal scenarist of this film) fused poetry with politics, feeling with fact. Interestingly, though both artists worked apart from each other, their solo achievements seldom approached the genius of their collaborations (8-6). See also Cesare Zavattini, "Some Ideas on the Cinema," in *Film: A Montage of Theories*, ed. by Richard Dyer MacCann (New York: Dutton, 1966).

Antonioni, while not generally considered a part of the neorealist movement, were nonetheless heavily indebted to it. Some directors were influenced by Rossellini's Christian humanism, most notably De Sica and Fellini. Others, particularly Visconti and Antonioni, were more influenced by the Marxist implications of *Open City*. Even as late as the 1960s and 1970s, neorealist influences could be seen in such brilliant films as Ermanno Olmi's *Il Posto*, *The Fiancés*, and *The Tree of the Wooden Clogs*.

Although there are considerable differences between these directors, and even between their early and later works, the neorealist aesthetic provided a rallying point for most of the talented Italian filmmakers of the time. Their movies tended to de-emphasize plots in favor of open-ended structures, suggesting a slice-of-life rather than clearly articulated beginnings, middles, and endings. A new honesty also characterized these films: People were pictured more frankly, "warts and all." Most of the themes revolved around the war, the Resistance, and war's aftermath: poverty, unemployment, prostitution, and the black market.

The movies avoided phony idealism and sentimentality. Complex problems weren't solved with slick solutions in the final reel. Characters were unextraordinary. Most of them came from the working and lower classes—laborers, fishermen, peasants, and factory workers. Subsidiary themes revolved around loneliness, solitude, and neglect—both personal and governmental. There was a strong emphasis on the social and political environment, which was either unresponsive or out-and-out hostile to the needs of people. Many of these movies used authentic (and usually exterior) locales, available lighting, and nonprofessional players even in principal roles. Following Rossellini's lead, these filmmakers tended to de-emphasize editing and artful camerawork in favor of long shots, lengthy takes, and open forms. Most of them strove to achieve a kind of "styleless" style.

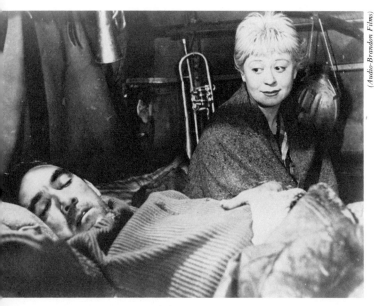

(Audio-Brandon Films)

**11-9. *La Strada* (Italy, 1954).**
*With Anthony Quinn and Giulietta Masina; Directed by Federico Fellini.*
By the mid-1950s, neorealism was displaced by a new phase in the Italian cinema, still essentially realistic, but poeticized, more psychological in its emphasis, and more aestheticized in its visual style.

The screenwriter Cesare Zavattini became the unofficial spokesman for the movement, although his strong Marxist leanings and hostility to technical artifice didn't always match up with the beliefs of his colleagues. His compassion for the plight of the underprivileged and his anti-Fascist fervor, however, were shared by all neorealists. More than any single individual, Zavattini defined the ordinary and the everyday as the main business of the cinema. Spectacular events and extraordinary characters should be avoided at all costs, he believed. Anticipating some of the methods of cinéma vérité, Zavattini claimed that his ideal movie would consist of 90 consecutive minutes from a person's actual life. Like the advocates of direct cinema, then, Zavattini believed that there should be no barriers between reality and the spectator. Ideally, neorealism should become a kind of heightened documentary; instead of *re*presenting reality, the neorealist film should *present* it directly.

Suspicious of conventional plot structures, Zavattini dismissed them as dead formulas. He insisted on the dramatic superiority of things as they really are, the texture of life as it is experienced by ordinary people. Filmmakers should be concerned with the "excavation" of reality. Instead of plots, they should emphasize facts and all their "echoes and reverberations." According to Zavattini, filmmaking is not a matter of "inventing fables," but of searching unrelentingly to uncover the implications of social facts. Thus, a whole movie

**11-10. *The Working Class Goes to Heaven* (Italy, 1975, also known as *Lulu the Tool*).**
*Directed by Elio Petri.*
The Italian cinema has remained profoundly political. Indeed, probably no other country has produced a Marxist cinema of such commanding international prestige. In addition to Petri, the Italian left (which encompasses over a half dozen parties) boasts such contemporary filmmakers as Bertolucci, Antonioni, Gillo Pontecorvo, Mario Monicelli, Marco Bellocchio, Lina Wertmüller, Franco Brusati, Francesco Rosi, and Vittorio and Paolo Taviani.

could be structured around the fact that a working couple wants to find an apartment. In a typical American film, this might constitute a minor scene, lasting some 2 or 3 minutes. But the neorealist explores the implications of this fact. Why do they want the apartment? Where did they live before? Why don't they stay there? How much does the apartment cost? Where will they get the money? How will their family react? And so on. Anticipating Kracauer, the neorealists believed that the purpose of the cinema is to celebrate the "dailiness" of events. They wanted to reveal certain details that had always been there, but had never been noticed.

These movies are generally so simple in terms of subject matter that they can seem banal when paraphrased verbally. Perhaps the greatest of them, De Sica's *Bicycle Thief*, deals with a laborer's attempts to recover his stolen bike which he needs in order to keep his job. The man's search grows increasingly more frantic as he criss-crosses the city with his idolizing, urchinlike son (6-33). After a discouraging series of false leads, the two finally track down one of the thieves, but the protagonist is outwitted by him and humiliated in front of his boy. Realizing that he will lose his livelihood without a bike, the desperate man sneaks off and attempts to steal one himself after he sends his son away. But the boy observes from a distance as his father peddles frantically to

(New Yorker Films)

**11-11. *The Tree of the Wooden Clogs* (Italy, 1978).**
*Directed by Ermanno Olmi.*
Olmi's films are steeped in the values of Christian humanism. In this movie, which was shot on authentic locations with nonprofessional players, he celebrates the everyday lives of several peasant families around 1900. For them, God is a living presence—a source of guidance, hope, and solace. Their faith is childlike, trusting, like that of St. Francis of Assissi. In a series of documentary-like vignettes, Olmi unfolds their gentle drama, extolling their patience, their tough stoicism, their dignity. Above all, he exalts the sacredness of the human spirit. For Olmi, they are the salt of the earth.

escape a pursuing mob. He is caught and again cruelly humiliated in front of a crowd—which includes his incredulous son. With the bitterness of outraged innocence, the youngster suddenly recognizes that his father is not the heroic figure he had formerly thought, but an ordinary man who in desperation yielded to a degrading temptation. Like most neorealist films, the movie doesn't offer an overt solution. The final scene shows the boy walking alongside his father, both of them choking with shame and weeping silently. Almost imperceptibly, the boy's hand gropes for his father's as they walk homeward—their only comfort a mutual compassion.

## Expressionist Film Theories

Rudolf Arnheim occupies a prominence among expressionist theorists comparable to Kracauer's among realists. Arnheim's *Film as Art* was originally published in German in 1933 when sound and color were still in their developing stages in film, but the book contains most of the tenets of Expressionism as they are still espoused. His major premise is that film art results from the *differences* between physical and cinematic reality, and that the movie director exploits the limitations of the medium—its lack of sound, color, depth, space-time continuity—to produce a world which resembles the real world only in a superficial sense. Film art doesn't consist of a reproduction of reality, but a translation of observed characteristics into the *forms* of the medium (11-12).

**11-12. *Day of Wrath* (Denmark, 1943).**
*Directed by Carl Theodor Dreyer.*
Implicit in the concept of expressionism (or formalism, as it's often called) is the supremacy of pattern over life. That is, even in films that attempt to preserve a surface realism, the volumes, weights, lines, textures, and lights are subtly coordinated within the frame to maximize their aesthetic appeal.

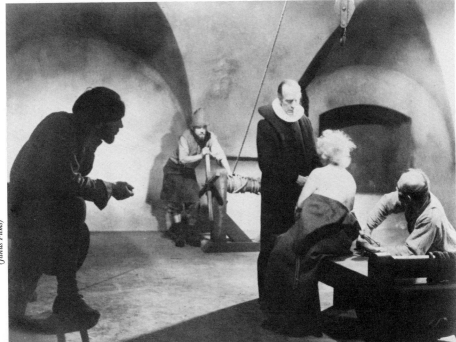

(Janus Films)

As a gestalt psychologist, Arnheim is primarily concerned with the perception of experience. His theory is based on the different modes of perception of the camera on the one hand, and the human eye on the other. Anticipating some of the theories of the communications specialist Marshall McLuhan, Arnheim insists that the camera's image of a bowl of fruit, for instance, is fundamentally different from our perception of the fruit bowl in actual life. Or, in McLuhan's terms, the information we receive in each instance is determined by the form of its content. Expressionist theorists celebrate these differences, believing that what makes photography fall short of perfect reproduction is also what makes the cinema an art, rather than a species of xerography.

Technological advancements like sound, color, and widescreen were originally viewed with suspicion, if not outright hostility by most formalists. They believed the increase in realism brought on by these technical innovations actually worked against the expressive characteristics of the cinema. Virtually all expressionists share Arnheim's belief that art begins where mechanical reproduction leaves off, that "he who vies with nature deserves to lose." This is the thesis of *The Cinema as Art,* for example, an influential book by Ralph Stephenson and Jean Debrix.

Arnheim discusses a number of examples where divergences exist between the camera's image of reality and what the human eye sees. For example, film directors must choose which viewpoint to photograph a scene from (11-13). They don't necessarily choose the clearest view, for often this does not

(Landau Distributing Co.)

**11-13. *The Servant* (Great Britain, 1964).**
*With Dirk Bogarde (forward); Directed by Joseph Losey.*
A scene can be photographed in literally hundreds of different ways, but the expressionist filmmaker selects the camera setup that best captures its symbolic or psychological implications.

emphasize the major characteristics of the scene. In life, we perceive objects in depth and can penetrate the space that surrounds most things. In movies, space is an illusion, for the screen has only two dimensions, permitting the director to manipulate objects and perspective in an artistically effective manner. For instance, important objects can be placed where they are most likely to be noticed first. Unimportant objects can be relegated to inferior positions, at the edges or rear of the image. Surprise effects can be achieved by suddenly revealing (through a pull-back dolly) what has been excluded by the frame. The frame itself is a delimiting device that has no counterpart in one's perception of the real world.

The use of lights in movies is more than merely utilitarian, Arnheim claimed. Lights can suggest symbolic ideas, can bring out essential characteristics of an object, can reveal or cover certain details, and can shift a viewer's interest from one point on the screen to another. Sound and color, if they're used, should not be employed to enhance the realism of an image, but to convey essential characteristics. The very distortion involved in recording natural sounds and colors can be exploited to emphasize symbolic rather than literal characteristics—characteristics that have no counterpart in the natural world.

**11-14. *The Warriors* (U.S.A., 1979).**
*Cinematography by Andrew Laszlo; Directed by Walter Hill.*
Style is not something tacked on to a movie—it's an externalization of the film's basic concept. Hill's stylized presentation of the life of urban street gangs is an attempt to portray not what they are, but what they want to be. The movie's style is infused with the aesthetic idioms of its characters—graffiti, sports metaphors, rock'n'roll, Day-Glo neon, formalized rites, and choreographed violence.

In real life, space and time are experienced as continuous phenomena. Through editing, filmmakers can chop up space and time and rearrange them in a more meaningful manner. Like other artists, the film director selects certain expressive details from the chaotic plenitude of physical reality. By juxtaposing these space and time fragments, the filmmaker creates a continuity that doesn't exist in raw nature. This, of course, was the basic position of the Soviet montage theorists.

Arnheim points out that there are many mechanical modes of perception in movies that have no human counterpart. We can't manipulate our eyes to approximate the camera's slow motion, fast motion, reverse motion, and freeze frames. Certainly our eyes have no real equivalents to dissolves, multiple exposures, negative images, distorting lenses and filters, and other special effects that can be created through the use of the optical printer.

The very act of photographing an object involves profound distortions of that object as it's perceived in reality. Film directors don't merely record or copy the physical world. They interpret and shape it through the camera, through the editing, and through the narrative structure which is manipulated to heighten a sense of pattern (11-15). By transforming their raw mate-

**11-15. *Scarlet Street* (U.S.A., 1945).**
*With Edward G. Robinson; Screenplay by Dudley Nichols; Directed by Fritz Lang.*
Expressionism is a concept that can be applied to a film's plot. Lang was a master of that much-maligned genre, the crime melodrama. He preferred this form because it allows a high degree of abstraction in the story, without having to make too many concessions in the name of realism. Like most of Lang's movies in this genre, *Scarlet Street* is divided into two sections, the second half paralleling the first. The tight, symmetrical story equation allows for no digressions. There are no accidents or extraneous details in this machine-like universe: Everything is relevant, especially apparent irrelevancies. The narrative structure is as inexorable as a mathematical proof.

rials in this way, they don't destroy physical reality so much as transcend it, by distilling, rearranging, and strengthening certain essential characteristics.

The problem with most expressionist theories is the same as with realist theories: There are too many exceptions. Arnheim's analysis is certainly useful in an appreciation of Hitchcock's movies, for example, or Eisenstein's. But how helpful is the theory in explaining the films of Renoir or De Sica? Even if we concede Arnheim's basic premise—that the photographic process distorts reality—we still tend to respond to realistic movies because of their similarities with physical reality, not their divergences from it. Ultimately, of course, these are matters of emphasis, for films are too pluralistic to be pigeonholed into one tidy theory. In fact, some movies—like *Citizen Kane*—have been claimed by theorists of both camps.

In the mid-1950s, *Cahiers du Cinéma* revolutionized film criticism with its concept of *la politique des auteurs* (literally, "the policy of authors"), which was put forth by the pugnacious young critic François Truffaut. The auteur theory became the focal point of a critical controversy that eventually spread to England and America. Before long, the theory became a kind of militant

**11-16. *Jules and Jim* (France, 1961).**
*With (r. to l.) Jeanne Moreau, Oskar Werner, and Henri Serre; Directed by François Truffaut.*
Above all, the auteurists emphasized the personality of the artist as the main criterion of value. Truffaut, who originally formulated *la politique des auteurs,* went on to make some of the most distinctively personal movies of the New Wave. *Jules and Jim* epitomizes his charm, warmth, and lyricism. It also embodies all that is best in the French cinema: Urbanity, wit, lightness of touch, intellectual substance, and delicacy of feeling. See also Roy Armes, *French Cinema Since 1946* (New York: A. S. Barnes, 1966) in two volumes.

*(Janus Films)*

rallying cry, particularly among younger critics, dominating such lively journals as *Movie* in Great Britain, *Film Culture* in America, and both French and English language editions of *Cahiers du Cinéma*. While there were a number of writers who rejected the theory, auteurism dominated film criticism throughout the 1960s. The movement began as a defiant gesture of contempt toward the film establishment of the time. Because of the strident tone of many of its practitioners, the auteur theory managed to offend the majority of older, more traditional critics. Even Bazin, the founder and editor of *Cahiers du Cinéma,* wrote an essay warning of the excesses of the theory as it was practiced by some of his youthful disciples.

Actually, the main lines of the theory aren't particularly outrageous, at least not in retrospect. Truffaut, Godard, Chabrol, and their critical colleagues proposed that the greatest movies are dominated by the personal vision of the director, and this dominance could be perceived through an examination of a director's total output which is characterized by a unity of theme and style. The writer's contribution—the subject matter—is artistically neutral. It can be treated with brilliance or with bare competence. Movies ought to be judged on the basis of *how*, not *what*. Like most expressionist theorists, the auteur critics claimed that what makes a good film is not the subject matter as such, but its stylistic treatment: The director dominates the treatment, provided he's a strong director, an auteur.

Drawing primarily from the cinematic traditions of the United States, the *Cahiers* critics also developed a sophisticated theory of film genre. Indeed, Bazin believed that the genius of the American cinema was its repository of ready-made forms: westerns, thrillers, musicals, action films, comedies, and so on. "The tradition of genres is a base of operations for creative freedom," Bazin pointed out. Genre is an enriching, not a constricting tradition. (See also "Story and Genre" in Chapter 8.) The auteurists argued that the best movies are dialectical, in which the conventions of a genre are held in aesthetic tension with the personality of the artist (11-17).

*(Contemporary Films)*

**11-17. *Pierrot le Fou* (France, 1965).**
*With Anna Karina; Directed by Jean-Luc Godard.*
The auteur critics were dialectical, and enjoyed fusing the conventions of opposite traditions in their criticism, and later in their movies. *Pierrot le Fou* is loosely—very loosely—based on *You Only Live Once*, a crime melodrama by Fritz Lang, one of the idols of the auteurists. Stylistically, Godard's movie is indebted to the lyrical works of Jean Renoir, another cult hero. Godard's film is also deeply personal, and explores an obsessive theme of the New Wave, *l'amour fou*—crazy, self-destructive love. See Julia Lesage, *Jean-Luc Godard: A Guide to References and Resources* (Boston: G. K. Hall, 1979).

The American auteurs that these critics praised had worked within the studio system which had broken the artistic pretensions of many lesser filmmakers. What the auteurists particularly admired was how gifted directors could circumvent studio interference and even hackneyed scripts through their technical expertise. The subject matter of Hitchcock's thrillers and Ford's westerns was not significantly different from others working in these genres. Yet both auteurs managed to produce great films, precisely because the real content was conveyed through the mise-en-scène, the editing, and all the other formal devices at the director's disposal.

The sheer breadth of their knowledge of film history permitted these critics to re-evaluate the major works of a wide variety of directors. In many instances, they completely reversed previous critical judgments. Before long, personality cults developed around the most popular directors. On the whole, these were filmmakers who had been virtually ignored by the critical establishment of the previous generation: Hitchcock, Ford, Hawks, Lang, and many others. The auteur critics were often dogmatic, in their dislikes as well as their likes. Bazin expressed alarm at their negativism. To praise a bad movie, he felt, was unfortunate; but to condemn a good one was a serious failing. He especially disliked their tendency to hero worship which led to superficial *a priori* judgments. Movies by cult directors were indiscriminately praised while those by directors out of favor were automatically condemned. Auteurists were particularly given to ranking directors, and their hierarchies could be bizarre.

The principal spokesman for the auteur theory in the United States was

**11-18. *Le Boucher* (France, 1969, also known as *The Butcher*).**
*With Stéphane Audran; Directed by Claude Chabrol.*
Taking their cue from Chabrol's seminal essay, "Little Themes," many auteur critics were suspicious of movies with ambitious themes and grand pronouncements about the human condition. Chabrol believed that the smaller the subject, the more a director could explore it in depth, that modest themes, like those traditionally found in genre films, are the richest in terms of artistic potential. This movie is a Hitchcock thriller, but without the thrills. Instead, Chabrol explores the nuances of abnormal psychology in a slow, realistic style, steeped in ironic detachment.

Andrew Sarris, the influential critic of the *Village Voice*. More knowledgable about the complexities of the star and studio system than his French counterparts, Sarris nonetheless defended their basic argument—especially the principle of tension between an artist's personal vision and the genre assignments that these directors were given by their Hollywood bosses. American and British auteurists emphasized how the director makes a silk purse of a sow's ear, how the director performs under pressure. Quite correctly, these critics insisted that total artistic freedom isn't always a virtue. After all, Michelangelo, Dickens, and Shakespeare, among others, accepted commissioned subjects. Though this principle of dialectical tension is a sound one—in the other arts as well as the cinema—some auteurists carried it to ridiculous extremes. In the first place, there is the problem of degree. It's doubtful that even a genius like Bergman or Welles could do much with the script and stars of *Abbott and Costello Meet the Mummy*. In other words, a director's got to have a fighting chance. When the subject matter sinks beneath a certain basic potential, the result is not tension but artistic annihilation.

The most gifted American directors of the studio era were *producer-directors* who worked independently within the major studios. These tended

**11-19. *Love on the Run* (France, 1979).** *With Jean-Pierre Léaud and Dani; Directed by François Truffaut.*
One of the crowning achievements of the *nouvelle vague* is Truffaut's Doinel cycle, a series of quasi-autobiographical films tracing the amorous adventures of its charming but slightly neurotic hero, Antoine Doinel. Truffaut swore that each installment would be the last. To date, the series includes: *The 400 Blows* (1959), *Antoine et Colette* (an episode in the anthology film, *Love at Twenty*, 1962), *Stolen Kisses* (1968), *Bed and Board* (1970), and *Love on the Run*, which Truffaut insisted *absolument* would be the last.

*(New World Pictures)*

to be the same artists the auteur critics admired most. But the lion's share of American fiction movies produced during this era were studio films. That is, the director functioned as a member of a team and usually had little to say about the scripting, casting, or editing. Many of these directors were skillful technicians, but they were essentially artisans rather than artists. Michael Curtiz is a good example. For most of his career he was a contract director at Warner Brothers. Known for his speed and efficiency, Curtiz directed dozens of movies in a variety of styles and genres. He often took on several projects simultaneously. Curtiz had no "personal vision" in the sense that the auteur theory defines it, he was just getting a job done. He often did it very well. Nonetheless, movies like *Yankee Doodle Dandy* and *Casablanca* can be discussed more profitably as Warner Brothers movies rather than Michael Curtiz movies. The same principle applies to most of the other Hollywood studios. In our day, it applies to films that are controlled by producers and financiers.

Other films have been dominated stars. Few people would think of referring to a Mae West movie as anything else, and the same holds true for the Marx Brothers films or the works of Laurel & Hardy. The ultimate in the star as auteur is the so-called star vehicle, a film specifically tailored to showcase the talents of a personality—but in front of the camera, not behind it.

The auteur theory suffers from a number of other weaknesses. There are some excellent films that have been made by directors who are otherwise mediocre. For example, Joseph H. Lewis's *Gun Crazy* is a superb movie, but it's untypical of his output. Conversely, great directors sometimes produce bombs. The works of such major filmmakers as Ford, Godard, Renoir, and Buñuel are radically inconsistent in terms of quality. The auteur theory emphasizes history and a director's total output, which tends to favor older directors at the expense of newcomers. Some artists have explored a variety of themes in many different styles and genres: Carol Reed, Sidney Lumet, John Frankenheimer (11-20), even the darlings of the auteurists, Rossellini and

**11-20. *The Manchurian Candidate* (U.S.A., 1962).**
*With Laurence Harvey (in clerical garb); Screenplay by George Axelrod (based on the novel by Richard Condon); Directed by John Frankenheimer.*
A weakness of the auteur theory is its tendency to gloss over the collaborative nature of the filmmaking enterprise. True, the director coordinates the contributions of others. But some of these contributions are of major significance. For example, without slighting the brilliance of Frankenheimer's direction in this movie, much of its effect derives from the story and dialogue, not to speak of the fine cast. Frankenheimer has always insisted that cinema is a collaborative art. Furthermore, he has explored a variety of styles, genres, and themes. In short, he has no consistent "artistic signature"—a major concern of auteur critics. Frankenheimer has not been one of their favorites.

(United Artists)

Hawks. There are also some great filmmakers who are crude directorial technicians. For example, Chaplin and Herzog in no way approach the stylistic fluency of Michael Curtiz, or a dozen other contract directors of his era. Yet there are few artists who have created such distinctively personal movies as Chaplin and Herzog.

Despite its shortcomings and excesses, the auteur theory had a liberating effect on film criticism. It cleared away the literary and sociological prejudices of the previous generation of critics and established the director as the key figure at least in the art of film, if not always the industry. Their emphasis on historical perspective also had a beneficial effect on film criticism, reducing the tendency to evaluate a movie only in its own terms—that is, outside its cultural and generic context. By the 1970s, the major battle had been won. Virtually all serious discussions of movies were at least partly couched in terms of the director's personal vision. To this day, the concept of directorial dominance remains firmly established, at least with films of high artistic merit.

## Marxist Film Theories

After the 1917 revolution in Russia, the new society was characterized by a proliferation of artistic as well as social experimentation. Influenced by the theories of Marx, Lenin, and Trotsky, such artistic innovators as Pudovkin, Eisenstein, and Vertov reaped a rich cinematic harvest in this permissive cultural climate. In the early 1930s, however, all experimentation came to a halt and was replaced by Stalin's monolithic theory of Socialist Realism which became the official artistic style of the Soviet Union and later of the Communist countries of eastern Europe. But whether one is discussing the radical Marxist aesthetic of Expressionism or the conservative aesthetic of Socialist Realism, these theories can be fully understood only within the wider context of the Marxist *weltanschauung* or world view.

Marxism is a political, social, and philosophical system of ideas that forms the foundation of such widely differing societies as the Soviet Union, the People's Republic of China, the disparate nations of eastern Europe, and such isolated countries as Cuba. Marxism has also exerted a major cultural influence in western Europe and the Third World. In the United States, its influence was strong during the 1930s, then faded after World War II, only to be revived in the late 1960s by the so-called New Left. Except for a few individualists like King Vidor and Elia Kazan (11-21), the influence of Marxism in the American cinema has been relatively weak—until recent times, that is. A number of contemporary American filmmakers have strong leftist leanings (11-29), and Marxism also dominates such American film journals as *Jump Cut* and *Cinéaste*. In short, Marxism is a dynamic philosophy, altering significantly from year to year and from country to country. Thousands of volumes have been written on the varying interpretations of the basic ideas of Marx, Engels, and Lenin, not to speak of the modifications of such later figures as Stalin and Mao Tse-tung. Needless to say, only the barest outline of this world view can be offered here.

Marxists believe that the fundamental basis of all human societies is economic. Those who control and consume the largest share of the material wealth form the ruling class. Marxists condemn capitalist and neocapitalist

(Twentieth Century-Fox)

**11-21. _Wild River_ (U.S.A., 1960).**
_With Montgomery Clift (center); Directed by Elia Kazan._
Kazan was a member of the American Communist Party as a young man during the 1930s depression. Though he eventually turned against Communism, he never abandoned Marxism; he merely modified it to fit his own temperament and the realities of American life. Of course yesterday's radicalism has a way of becoming today's centrism. The Marxist influence in Kazan's movies might seem less apparent from the perspective of the present. However, the following characteristics of his _oeuvre_ might be regarded as essentially Marxist in origin: (1) the use of art as a tool for social change, (2) the belief that all art is at least implicitly ideological, affirming or challenging the status quo, (3) a demystification of power: how it's actually weilded, and who it benefits, (4) the assumption that capitalism exploits the working class to further the interests of a small ruling class, (5) an identification with oppressed minorities, (6) the belief that environment largely determines human behavior, (7) a rejection of religion and the supernatural in favor of a strict scientific materialism, (8) a belief in the equality of the sexes and races, and (9) a dialectical view of history and knowledge, in which progress is the result of a conflict and ultimate synthesis of opposites.

societies because the bulk of the material wealth is controlled by a small elite, insuring its ever-increasing wealth and power by its control—either direct or indirect—over the basic means of production. The actual producers of this wealth—the workers—must be content with a disproportionately small percentage of the economic pie, leading to a diminished sense of power and self-determination. In capitalist societies, workers are "alienated" from their work, their peers, and their society because they are forced to compete economically against each other rather than cooperating in a joint effort to build a better society for all citizens. "Private property is theft," Shaw claimed, and most of his fellow Marxists would agree. This is why virtually all the means of

**11-22. *Ivan the Terrible—Part I* (U.S.S.R., 1945).**
*Directed by Sergei Eisenstein.*
Most Marxists believe that cinema, like other mass mediums, should be controlled by the government, and operated in the best interests of the people. However, the people are not always given much of a choice. Nor are the artists, who are permitted to work in this expensive medium only if they conform to the dictates of a handful of political bureaucrats who control the means of production. After Eisenstein was forced to abandon his theories of radical montage, he experimented in other expressionistic techniques, such as the operatic pageantry of *Ivan the Terrible.* But these later works met with the same official hostility, and eventually Eisenstein's career as a director was finished.

production in socialist nations are publicly owned and operated—in theory if not always in practice—in the public's best interests (11-22).

Marxists view history dialectically, and in objective materialist terms. Social structures and institutions are not mysteriously sanctioned by some cosmic outside force. They are built by *people,* who have selfish economic interests to preserve. Employing rigorously scientific and rational methods, the Marxist attempts to demystify ruling-class subterfuges, such as the concept of divine right, tradition, or social and religious fealty. Every human community has a structure of power, however much its rulers attempt to conceal it. Mysticism, religion, and all forms of philosophical idealism are dismissed as ploys to encourage workers to think in other-worldly terms rather than their material needs in the here-and-now. Marxists believe an examination of history reveals that the interests of a ruling class are always challenged by a usurping class, producing a dialectical redistribution of wealth and power.

Indeed, the optimism underlying Marxist theory is posited on the belief that history is evolving toward a classless society, in which wealth (and hence power) will be equally distributed. When genuine equality is established, individuals will be able to realize their maximum human potential: they will feel integrated with their society, not alienated from it. Economic equality will allow individuals to behave decently toward one another. Without the wasteful competition encouraged by capitalistic societies, citizens will enjoy a maximum of self-expression, freedom, and control over their own destinies.

Marxists analyze all human activity from this ideological perspective. Even those areas of life that aren't generally regarded as particularly political—like the arts—are evaluated in terms of material commodities, class, and power. Art is not politically neutral. It's produced by individuals for specific consumers. Implicit in all art, whether Marxist or not, is an acceptance or rejection of the social structure in which the art was produced. Marxist cultural critics never examine a work of art outside its ideological context, for the value and degree of truth (as they see it) of any artistic product will be

(New Yorker Films)

**11-23. *Before the Revolution* (Italy, 1964).**
*With Adriana Asti; Directed by Bernardo Bertolucci.*
Arguably the most lyrical Marxist filmmaker, Bertolucci is also among the most ambivalent. His characters are often divided in their sentiments. Some yearn for the millenium of the Revolution, yet also have a "nostalgia for the present," and all its decadent charms.

determined by who produced it and for whom. Even art-for-art's-sake, or the denial of all but purely formal and aesthetic meanings in a work of art, is viewed as a political act—that is, as an implicit acceptance of the status quo.

Marxist critics are acutely sensitive to the ideological implications of apparently neutral phenomena. Most of them are agreed that any dominant ideology in any society presents itself as the ideology of that society as a whole. This is especially true of classical cinema, as critic Daniel Dayan has pointed out. "Classical cinema is the ventriloquist of ideology," Dayan insists. "Who is ordering these images and for what purpose?" are questions classical fimmakers wish to avoid, for they want the representation to "speak for itself." Viewers absorb the ideological values without being aware of it. Marxists have also pointed out that the casting of a movie can be profoundly ideological. Players such as John Wayne (6-17), Jane Fonda (6-19), or Mbissine Therese Diop (6-28) embody political values that are intrinsic to a film's meaning. Language is ideological (5-26), as are dialects (5-27). Sets, costumes, and furnishings can convey political ideas (7-32).

Though Marxists differ over what methods and techniques are most effective in an artistic enterprise, they're in fundamental agreement that art must serve the revolution, that it must be relevant and useful in an understanding of the complexities of human nature and the nature of the material world. Some Marxists—especially the Socialist Realists—would insist that art must be overtly didactic, that it must help inculcate a revolutionary consciousness in its consumers. The major controversy among Marxist artists and theorists, then, revolves not around *what* to portray, but *how* to portray it.

**11-24.** *Antonio Das Mortes* **(Brazil, 1969).**
*Directed by Glauber Rocha.*
Marxism often fuses with nationalism, especially in the Third World. Rocha, a former journalist and film critic, was the leading figure in Brazil's short-lived Cinema Nuovo, which combined Marxist ideas with native peasant myths. Rocha presents Brazil's agonized political past in stylized epic images. Through "the aesthetics of violence" (his own term) the audience is politicized by participating in a symbolic ritual of class retribution.

Even within the Marxist fold, filmmakers can be classified as expressionists or realists. Expressionists like Pudovkin, Eisenstein, and Vertov dominated the Soviet cinema in its golden age of the 1920s. In our own time, such Marxists as Godard and Bertolucci have pursued an expressionist course in the capitalist democracies of the West. The essential argument of Marxist expressionism is: A revolutionary society must have a revolutionary art—in *style* as well as subject matter. Traditional (i.e., capitalist) art is decadent, pessimistic, cliché-ridden, and filled with stale bourgeois conventions. A truly revolutionary artist must forge a new language, one that acknowledges its own forms and its means of production (6-31).

After Stalin solidified his position within the Soviet Communist Party, he put an end to many of these notions. Eisenstein and his more daring colleagues were accused of formalism, an effete preoccupation with technique at the expense of subject matter. Many artists were condemned for elitism, producing art accessible only to intellectuals and other artists, not to ordinary citizens. Such filmmakers were chastized for their excessive individualism which was officially viewed as a bourgeois trait, totally out of keeping with the revolutionary ideals of collective action and collaboration between equals. (11-25).

**11-25.** *The Organizer* (Italy, 1963).
*With Marcello Mastroianni (wearing glasses); Directed by Mario Monicelli.*
This movie embodies many of the ideals of the Marxist cinema of realism, including the concept of historicity: portraying historical events with scrupulous accuracy, in order to show present-day audiences how basic rights were once regarded as outrageous demands by the ruling class of a given era. The film also dramatizes the dangers of individual action, and the need for a united front. Mastroianni plays a bumbling but shrewd professor who advises a group of naive textile workers on strike strategies. Their awesome enterprise is a communal effort, not the work of a single individual. The original title, *I Compagni,* means The Comrades. When the movie was shown in America, its title was changed to *The Organizer,* suggesting a more individualistic, less democratic emphasis.

In 1932, Stalin dissolved the democratically controlled workers' organizations for the arts, and virtually all artistic experimentation came to a halt. In 1934, the First Congress of Soviet Writers convened. This gathering was primarily concerned with literary forms of expression, but the same practical significance and theoretical implications applied to the Soviet cinema. Guidelines were established in which priority was given to those artistic products that were judged most useful to the state. Usefulness was defined along ideological lines, the most overtly propagandistic art generally receiving the highest priority. All film production had to be authorized in detail by a special committee to ensure "ideological correctness" and to avoid wasteful, individualistic excesses.

Abram Tertz, a pseudonymn for a writer in the Soviet Union, has written a scathing critique (banned in the U.S.S.R.) entitled *On Socialist Realism.* Under Stalin's regime, Tertz points out, the task of all Soviet artists was to portray the benevolent power of the state as the greatest good, and to scorn the temporary sufferings of the individual. Furthermore, artists were sternly warned against excessive technical and formal experimentation. The Congress of Soviet Writers, in an official decree, established Socialist Realism as the only acceptable style in literature and film. This style "demands of the artist the truthful, historically concrete representation of reality in its revolutionary development. Moreover, the truthfulness and historical concreteness of the artistic representation of reality must be linked with the task of ideological transformation and education of workers in the spirit of socialism."

In plain language, what this definition involved was the portrayal of an objective, "scientifically verifiable" reality that is independent even of the artist. Any expressions of subjectivity or distortion were condemned as perverse, individualistic, and untruthful. Needless to say, if Socialist Realism produced only the flood of boy-loves-tractor stories that dominated Soviet culture for so many years, we wouldn't take the theory very seriously. But after the death of Stalin, modifications introduced into the theory allowed for some artistically significant works, both in literature and cinema. In Poland, Hungary, and especially Czechoslovakia, there were some excellent movies produced under the aegis of Socialist Realism—though in its modified, more sophisticated form (11-26).

Georg Lukács, the Hungarian aesthetician, was one of the most persuasive—and enduring—apologists for the theory of Socialist Realism. Although he was concerned primarily with the novel, his observations could also be applied to the cinema. He expressed serious misgivings about socialist art, especially its psychological crudities. Unlike the hard-line Stalinists, Lukács rejected outright the simple-minded notion that evil could be explained away by a character's ignorance of or refusal to accept Marxist ideology. Reality is far more complex, he argued, and realistic art should likewise be more complex.

If a conflict arises over ideological correctness and objective reality, the artist's first allegiance is to reality, for otherwise how are ideological errors of judgment and fact to be corrected for future generations? Indeed, some of the best socialist films—like Forman's amusing *Fireman's Ball*—are touching precisely because of the conflict between what essentially decent people do in fact, and how they ought to behave according to strict ideology. Although

**11-26. *The Firemen's Ball* (Czechoslovakia, 1967).**
*Directed by Milos Forman.*
The so-called Prague Spring produced an extraordinary outburst of movies in the 1960s. Most of them were in the vein of socialist realism, though its more sophisticated form, with an emphasis on ambiguity, comedy, and an appealing humanism. The liberal regime of Alexander Dubcek was toppled when Soviet tanks invaded Czechoslovakia in 1968. Many of the country's finest film artists, including Forman, fled to the west in search of artistic freedom. See Josef Skvorecky, *All the Bright Young Men and Women: A Personal History of the Czech Cinema* (Toronto: Take One Film Book Series, 1971).

*(Cinema V)*

such candor as this was rare in the Marxist cinema during Stalin's reign, it became more common after 1953, the year of his death.

Like most realists, Lukács disliked any form of extremism as an end in itself, especially stylistic eccentricities. He believed that Realism was the most comprehensive artistic style, the one closest to the copiousness of the observable physical world, and hence to the scientific materialist approach of Marxism. All great fiction is essentially realistic, he claimed, even the "progressive bourgeois realism" of the nineteenth century which included Balzac, Tolstoy, and Chekhov. Lukács particularly admired how these artists portrayed their characters in a concrete social existence (see also 11-27). "It is a condition of

*(Twentieth Century-Fox)*

**11-27. *The Grapes of Wrath* (U.S.A., 1940).**
*With Henry Fonda (kneeling); Directed by John Ford.*
Because it lacks revolutionary consciousness and scientific rigor, Ford's masterpiece would probably be regarded as "progressive bourgeois realism" by most Marxist critics. They often value such works because the characters are placed in a concrete social (and by implication, political) milieu which is objectively and comprehensively portrayed.

great realism that the artist must honestly record, without fear or favor, everything he sees around him." To accomplish this goal, the artist must be objective, modest, and self-effacing, those same characteristics that were praised by such cinematic realists as Bazin, Kracauer, and Zavattini.

The shortcomings of Marxist theories might be viewed as the vices of their virtues. Their intellectual rigor, their systematic methods of inquiry,

*(John Springer Associates)*

**11-28. *Fox and His Friends* (West Germany, 1975, also known as *Fist-fight of Freedom*).**
*With Rainer Werner Fassbinder (left) and Peter Chatel; Directed by Fassbinder.*
Like his fellow Marxists, Godard and Bertolucci, Fassbinder often combines the themes of sex and politics. In this movie, Fassbinder—a militant homosexual—explores class conflicts within the gay subculture. It too has a ruling-class elite, and an underclass that's exploited sexually as well as economically. See also *Fassbinder,* edited by Tony Rayns (London: British Film Institute, 1976).

and their seriousness of purpose are all are admirable. But these virtues are not enough, and sometimes can actually obstruct the aesthetic impact of movies. The scientific jargon of Marxist criticism can be somewhat hard to take. Labels are sometimes substituted for honest analysis. Their "objective" formats of presentation are often turgid, impersonal, devoid of color and spontaneity. They can be pedantic to the point of scholasticism. Because of their materialist emphasis, Marxists scorn such "mystifications" as creativity, genius, and mystery, which they regard as "outmoded concepts." Even very gifted Marxists, like Walter Benjamin, dismissed these terms as "fascist"— which is arrant nonsense. Such critics confuse *taste*—whether personal or official—with absolute value. Marxists are also contemptuous of such seductive qualities as glamor, the irrational and the ineffable. They are notoriously insensitive to comedy, despite the fact that some of the best Marxist filmmakers—especially in western Europe—are also comic artists.

A theory is only as good as its practitioner is sensitive. Applied mechanically, Marxism, like any other theory, can seem soulless—a term Marxists would no doubt regard as a bourgeois mystification. Marxist theory is weak in dealing with such matters as tone—that most elusive of aesthetic terms. For example, a crudely mechanistic Marxist analysis of Hawks' *Bringing Up Baby* (8-15) would yield quite different conclusions than a common-sense approach. The movie deals with the desperate schemes of an idle society woman (Katharine Hepburn) in luring a dedicated scientist (Cary Grant) away from his work—to join her in amorous frolic. This is scarcely a goal that would be applauded by doctrinaire Marxists who take a grim view of social irresponsibility. Furthermore, the apolitical Hawks was born rich, attended elite schools, and was inclined to be conservative in his values. He also died richer than he was born. Armed with such knowledge, a plodding Marxist might logically

**11-29. *The Godfather Part II* (U.S.A., 1974).**
*With Robert De Niro; Directed by Francis Ford Coppola.*
A Marxist reading of a movie doesn't necessarily exclude other interpretations. John Hess has argued that Coppola comes closer to a Marxist analysis of American society than any other Hollywood filmmaker: "The film's all-pervasive theme is the warmth, strength, and beauty of family ties which, in bourgeois society, alone appear to meet the desperate need we all feel for human community. The counter theme and the real strength of the film is its demonstration that the benefits of the family structure and the hope for community have been destroyed by capitalism." See John Hess, "*Godfather II*: A Deal Coppola Couldn't Refuse," in *Movies and Methods*, edited by Bill Nichols (Berkeley: University of California Press, 1976).

(Paramount Pictures)

conclude that *Bringing Up Baby* is a perfect example of the decadence of capitalist art. Such a conclusion would not win many converts for it totally misses the film's tone, its antic air of silliness and fun (see also 6-24). The charm of Hawks' screwball comedy is found precisely in its liberating spirit of irresponsibility. In short, Marxism—like any other theory—must be relevant to the *experience* of a movie. Otherwise, it's just another collection of mechanistic formulations and dogmatic pronouncements.

## Eclectic and Synthetic Theories

Eclecticism isn't really a theory so much as a method of practical criticism. This is the favored approach of many film critics in the United States, such as *The New Yorker's* Pauline Kael, who once wrote: "I believe that we respond most and best to work in any art form (and to other experience as well) if we are pluralistic, flexible, relative in our judgments, if we are eclectic." Such critics place a movie in whatever context seems most appropriate, drawing from diverse sources, systems, and styles. Actually, almost all critics are eclectic to some degree. For example, while Andrew Sarris has been identified with the auteur theory, he is equally at home approaching a movie in terms of its star, its period, its national origin, or its ideological context.

Eclecticism is sometimes called the tradition of sensibility because a high value is placed on the aesthetic discriminations of a person of taste and discernment. Such critics are often urbane, well-educated, and conversant in the other arts. The cultural cross-references in the writings of such critics as John Simon and Stanley Kauffmann range over a wide spectrum, including literature, drama, politics, and the visual arts. They frequently allude to the ideas of such seminal thinkers as Freud, Marx, Darwin, and Jung. Sometimes these critics combine an ideological perspective—such as feminism—with practical

**11-30. Hester Street (U.S.A., 1975).**
*With Carol Kane and Steven Keats; Directed by Joan Micklin Silver.*
Eclectic critics often combine movie criticism with social movements such as feminism, exploring not only the sexual values within a film, but the ideological context of its production. Traditionally, women have been excluded from positions of power within the American film industry. (The situation is even worse in most other countries.) Some, like Joan Micklin Silver, have circumvented this legacy of discrimination by producing their films independently. Most powerful women in the industry (Pickford, Jane Fonda, Streisand) reached the top by way of the star system, where sexism is economically unfeasible. See also *Women and the Cinema,* edited by Karyn Kay and Gerald Peary (New York: Dutton, 1977).

criticism, sociology, and history, as in the criticism of Molly Haskell and Marjorie Rosen (11-30). The best eclectic critics are gifted writers, including such distinguished prose stylists as James Agee, Dwight Macdonald, and Pauline Kael. Polished writing is valued *as* writing, in addition to the ideas it conveys.

Eclectic critics reject the notion that a single theory can explain all movies. They regard this as a cookie-cutter approach to criticism. Most of them insist that an individual's reaction to a film is deeply personal. For this reason, the best a critic can do is explain his or her personal responses as forcefully as possible. But it's just an opinion, however well-founded or gracefully argued. The best criticism of this type is informative even if we disagree with its conclusions. Because personal taste is the main determinant of value in eclectic criticism, these commentators often admit to their blind spots—and *all* critics have blind spots. Everyone has had the experience of being left totally cold by a movie that's widely hailed as a masterpiece. We can't help the way we *feel*, however much our feelings go against popular sentiment. The eclectic critic almost always begins with his or her feelings about a movie, then works outward, trying to objectify these instincts with concrete arguments. To guard against personal eccentricity, they implicitly place a film within the context of a great tradition of masterpieces—that is, those works which have stood the test of time and are still considered milestones in the evolution of the cinema. This great tradition is constantly under re-evaluation. It's a loose critical consensus rather than an iron-clad body of privileged works.

Eclecticism has been faulted on a number of counts. Because of its extreme subjectivity, this approach has been criticized as mere impressionism by more rigorously systematic theorists who insist that aesthetic evaluations ought to be governed by a body of theoretical principles rather than a critic's unique sensibility, however refined. Eclectic critics are rarely in agreement because each of them is reacting to a movie according to his or her own lights rather than a larger theoretical framework, with its built-in system of checks and balances. For all their vaunted expertise and cultural prestige, eclectic critics have track records that don't always bear close scrutiny. For example, when Fellini's *8 1/2* was released in 1963, many serious critics in America dismissed the movie as self-indulgent, formless, and even incoherent. This was also the consensus of European commentators, yet in a 1972 survey of international critics, conducted by the British journal *Sight and Sound*, *8 1/2* placed fourth in their list of the ten greatest films of all time. Conversely, even good critics have pronounced a film an instant masterpiece, only to regret their impetuosity in the cool distance of time, after the movie has been long forgotten.

Eclectic critics tend to be stoical about these matters, accepting them as perils of the trade. Perhaps Pauline Kael has expressed their attitude best:

> The role of the critic is to help people see what is in the work, what is in it that shouldn't be, what is not in it that could be. He is a good critic if he helps people understand more about the work than they could see for themselves; he is a great critic, if by his understanding and feeling for the work, by his passion, he can excite people so that they want to experience more of the art that is there, waiting to be seized. He is not necessarily a bad critic if he makes errors in judgment. (Infallible taste is inconceivable; what could it be measured against?) He is a bad critic if he does not awaken the curiosity, enlarge the interests and understanding of his audience. The art of the critic is to transmit his knowledge

of and enthusiasm for art to others. (Quoted from *I Lost It at the Movies* [New York: Bantam, 1966].)

Kael and her fellow eclectics celebrate the subjective, individual element in film criticism. Others have lamented it. In the early 1970s, two interrelated cinematic theories developed partly in response to the inadequacies of the criticism of personal sensibility. Structuralism and semiology were attempts to introduce a new scientific rigor to film criticism, to allow for more systematic and detailed analyses of movies. Borrowing their methodology from such diverse disciplines as linguistics, anthropology, psychology, and philosophy, these two theories concentrated on the development of a more precise analytical terminology. Structuralism and semiology have also focused intently on the American cinema as the principal area of inquiry, for a number of reasons. In the first place, these theories have been dominated by the British and French, traditionally the most enthusiastic foreign admirers of the cinema of the United States. American movies also provided these critics with a stylistic norm—the classical paradigm. Marxists among this group have explored the implications of the capitalistic mode of production of American films. Cultural commentators have concentrated on characteristically American myths and genres.

Semiology is a study of *how* movies signify. The manner in which information is signified is indissolubly linked with *what* is being signified. There are a number of semiotic theories, most of them still in exploratory stages. The French theorist, Christian Metz, was in the forefront in developing semiology as a technique of film analysis. Using many of the concepts and much of the terminology of structural linguistics, Metz and others developed a theory of cinematic communication founded on the concept of signs or codes. The language of cinema, like all types of discourse, verbal and nonverbal, is primarily symbolic: it consists of a complex network of signs we instinctively decipher while experiencing a movie (11-31).

In most discussions of film, the shot was generally accepted as the basic unit of construction. Semiotic theorists rejected this unit as too vague and inclusive. They insisted on a more precise concept. Accordingly, they suggested the sign be adopted as the minimal unit of signification. A single shot from a movie generally contains dozens of signs, forming an intricate hierarchy of counterpoised meanings. In a sense, this book, and especially the earlier chapters, can be viewed as a classification of signs (although necessarily more limited in scope than the type of identification and classification envisioned by Metz and other semiologists). For example, each of these chapters is concerned with a kind of master code, which can be broken down into code subdivisions, which themselves can be reduced to even more minimal signs. Thus, Chapter 1 might be called a photography master code. This master would be broken down in subdivisions: shots, angles, lights, colors, lenses, filters, optical effects, and so on. Each of these, in turn, could be subdivided again. The shots, for example, could be broken down to extreme long, long, medium, closeup, extreme closeup, deep-focus. Even these relatively precise designations could be broken down further—the various types of medium shots, for example. This same principle could be applied to other master codes: spatial codes (mise-en-scène), kinetic codes (movement), and so on. Codes on language would be as complex as the entire discipline of linguistics;

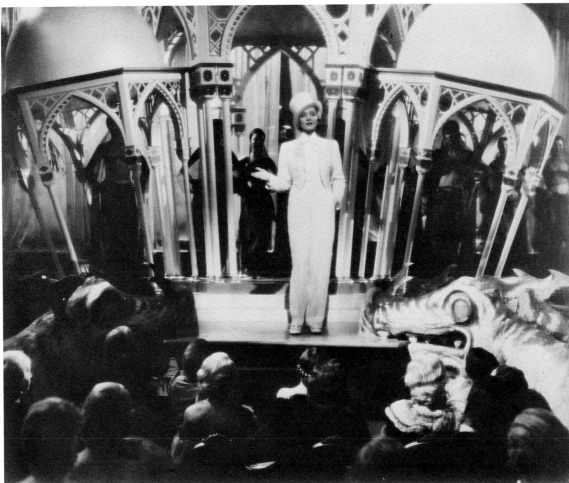

**11-31. *Blonde Venus* (U.S.A., 1932).**
*With Marlene Dietrich; Directed by Josef von Sternberg.*
Semiologists believe that the shot—the traditional unit of construction in film—is too general and inclusive to be of much use in a systematic analysis of a movie. The symbolic sign, they argue, is a more precise unit of signification. Every cinematic shot consists of dozens of signifying codes which are hierarchically structured. Employing what they call the "principle of pertinence," semiologists de-code cinematic discourse by first establishing what the dominant signs are, then analyzing the subsidiary codes. This methodology is similar to a detailed analysis of mise-en-scène, only in addition to spatial, textural, and photographic codes, semiologists would also explore other relevant signs—kinetic, linguistic, musical, rhythmic, etc. In this shot, a semiologist would explore the symbolic significance of such major signs as Dietrich's white suit. Why a masculine suit? Why white? What does the papier-mâché dragon signify? The distorted perspective lines of the set? The "shady ladies" behind the archways? The symbolism of stage and audience? The tight framing and closed form of the image? The protagonist's worldly song? Within the dramatic context, semiologists would also explore the rhythms of the editing and camera movements, the symbolism of the kinetic motions of the performer, and so on. Traditionally, critics likened the cinematic shot to a word, and a series of edited shots to a sequence of words in a sentence. A semiologist would dismiss such analogies as patently simple-minded. Perhaps an individual *sign* might be likened to a word, but the equivalent to a shot—even a banal one—would require many paragraphs if not pages of words. A complex shot can contain a hundred separate signs, each with its own precise symbolic significance. See also Christian Metz, *Film Language: A Semiotics of the Cinema* (New York: Oxford, 1974).

acting codes would involve a precise breakdown of the various techniques of signification used by players. What Metz and other semiologists envisage is an encyclopedic task of stupifying proportions.

There's no question that semiotic techniques can be valuable in aiding film critics and scholars to analyse movies with more precision. But the theory suffers some serious defects. For one thing, these are descriptive classifications only, not normative. In other words, semiotics will permit a critic to discern a sign, but it's still up to the critic to evaluate how artistically effective any given sign is within an aesthetic context. Expressionistic movies seem to lend themselves to easier classification than realistic movies. For example, it's much simpler to describe the complex mise-en-scène of *McQ* than to explicate the meanings of Chaplin's expression in *The Bank* (11-32).

**11-32a. *McQ* (U.S.A., 1974).**
*With John Wayne and Diana Muldaur; Directed by John Sturges.*
**11-32b. *The Bank* (U.S.A., 1915).**
*With Charles Chaplin; Directed by Chaplin.*
Semiology can help critics to isolate and identify signs in a movie, but not how skillfully they function within a work of art. Since the theory stresses quantification, it tends to be more effective in analyzing expressionistic films, which contain more classifiable signs. But different types of signs or codes are not compatible, and hence, qualitative judgments are difficult to make on strictly quantitative data. For example, the shot from *McQ* contains many different signs which are structured into an image of great visual complexity. Chaplin's shot, on the other hand, is relatively simple, and contains few classifiable signs other than the expression on the tramp's face. Sturges is a director of considerable skill, but he's certainly not in Chaplin's class. Yet a semiological analysis of these two works might lead to the conclusion that Sturges is the better artist, because he uses more signs in his films.

(a)

(Warner Brothers)

**(b)**

*(Museum of Modern Art)*

These signs aren't really comparable. They exist on incompatible levels. Since expressionistic signs are easier to quantify, some critics tend to value films with a greater number of signs (or at least a greater number of classifiable signs) as more complex, and hence aesthetically superior to a film with a lesser density of signs.

Another serious problem with this theory is its jargon, which often verges on self-parody. An example of this prose can be found in the Summer 1975 issue of *Screen* (p. 18), a British journal specializing in semiotics:

> The problem is to understand the terms of the construction of the subject and the modalities of the replacement of this construction in specific signifying practices, where "replacement" means not merely the repetition of the place of that construction but also, more difficultly, the supplacement—the overplacing: supplementation or, in certain circumstances, supplantation (critical interruption)—of that construction in the place of its repetition.

Communication can get pretty rarified in the arcane realms of semiology-land. Of course, taking any quotation out of context is likely to diminish communication, but the context of this quote is written in the same quaint idiom. All specialized disciplines—including cinema—have a certain number of necessary technical terms, but semiology often chokes on its own "scientific" wordiness. Even within the field, one commentator pointed out that referring to a perfectly ordinary phenomenon as "signifier" or "signified," "syntagm," or "paradigm" doesn't in itself advance social knowledge to any particular degree.

The differences between semiotics and structuralism are primarily differences in emphasis. Structuralism tends to center on practical criticism, while semiology is more abstract. As Metz pointed out, semiology is concerned with the systematic classification of types of codes in different films; structuralism is the study of how various codes function within a single structure, within one movie. Structuralists liken the analysis of a film to the reading of a text, similar to the traditional *explication de texte* used by French literary critics.

This method involves a detailed analysis of a given work in its technical complexity, accompanied by a synthesizing exposition of how these techniques produce a unified aesthetic effect.

Structuralism is strongly eclectic. The best-known structuralists are British, and they often combine the techniques of semiotics with those of the auteur theory. For example, Geoffrey Nowell-Smith's book *Luchino Visconti* is the study of a single auteur's work in which thematic and stylistic motifs are analysed. Other structural studies explore certain genres. Jim Kitses's *Horizons West,* for example, is an analysis of characteristic themes, structures, and formal elements in the westerns of Sam Peckinpah and others. Similarly, Colin MacArthur's *Underworld USA* is a structuralist analysis of gangster films, crime melodramas, and the style known as *film noir.* McArthur uses semiotic classifications in exploring the iconography of the genre films of such artists as Lang, Huston, Kazan, Wilder (11-33) and others.

**11-33. Publicity photo of *Double Indemnity* (U.S.A., 1944).**
*With Barbara Stanwyck and Fred MacMurray; Directed by Billy Wilder.*
The methods of semiology are useful in analyzing cinematic styles, such as *film noir.* This style typified a variety of American genres in the 1940s and early 1950s. *Noir* is a world of night and shadows. Its milieu is almost exclusively urban. The style is profuse in images of dark streets, cigarette smoke swirling in dimly-lit cocktail lounges, and symbols of fragility, such as window panes, sheer clothing, glasses, and mirrors. Motifs of entrapment abound: alleys, tunnels, subways, elevators, and train cars. Often the settings are locations of transience, like grubby rented rooms, piers, bus terminals, and railroad yards. The images are rich in sensuous textures, like neon-lit streets, windshields streaked with mud, and shafts of light streaming through windows of lonely rooms. Characters are imprisoned behind ornate lattices, grillwork, drifting fog and smoke. Visual designs emphasize harsh lighting contrasts, jagged shapes, and violated surfaces. The tone of *noir* is fatalistic and paranoid. It's suffused with pessimism, emphasizing the darker aspects of the human condition. Its themes characteristically revolve around violence, lust, greed, betrayal, and depravity. See also Colin McArthur, *Underworld USA* (New York: Viking, 1972).

*(Paramount Pictures)*

Structuralists and semiologists have been fascinated by the concept of a *deep structure*—an underlying network of symbolic meaning that is related to a movie's surface structure, but is also somewhat independent of it. This deep-structure can be analyzed from a number of perspectives, including Freudian psychoanalysis (8-14), Marxist economics (10-17), Jungian concepts of the collective unconscious (8-16), and the theory of structural anthropology popularized by the Frenchman Claude Lévi-Strauss.

The methods of Lévi-Strauss are based on an examination of regional myths which he believed express certain underlying structures of thought in codified form. These myths exist in variant forms and usually contain the same or similar binary structures—pairs of opposites. By collapsing the surface (narrative) structure of myths, their symbolic motifs can be analysed in a more systematic and meaningful manner. These polarities are usually found in dialectical conflict, and are in a constant state of flux. Depending on the culture analyzed, these polarities can be agricultural (for example, water vs. drought), sexual (male vs. female), generational (youth vs. age), and so on. Because these myths are expressed in symbolic codes, often their full meanings are hidden from their creators, and Lévi-Strauss believed that once the full implications of a myth are understood, it's discarded as a cliché.

A number of structuralists have explored genre films in this manner. For example, Jim Kitses, Peter Wollen, and others have pointed out how westerns

**11-34. *Young Mr. Lincoln* (U.S.A., 1939).**
*With Henry Fonda; Directed by John Ford.*
Some structuralists concern themselves with only internal signs—that is, with purely aesthetic codes found within the world of the movie. Other critics explore the significance of certain signs in relation to the external world. Such analyses are likely to combine the methodologies of a number of different theories. A much-publicized "collective" reading of *Young Mr. Lincoln* by the editors of *Cahiers du Cinéma* combined the techniques of the auteur theory (the thematic and stylistic relationship of the film to Ford's *oeuvre*), with semiology (the various signs and codes found within this particular movie), and Marxist theory (the political reasons for making the film, and the significance of its ideas in relation to the producer, studio, and period that produced it).

are often vehicles for exploring clashes of value between East and West in American culture. By clustering the thematic motifs around a "master antimony" (a controlling or dominant code), a western can be analysed according to its deep-structure rather than its plot, which is often conventionalized (and less meaningful) in genre films. Such critics have demonstrated how each cultural polarity symbolizes a complex of positive and negative traits:

| West | East |
|------|------|
| Wilderness | Civilization |
| Individualism | Community |
| Self-interest | Social welfare |
| Freedom | Restriction |
| Anarchy | Law and Order |
| Savagery | Refinement |
| Private honor | Institutional Justice |
| Paganism | Christianity |
| Nature | Culture |
| Masculine | Feminine |
| Pragmatism | Idealism |
| Agrarian | Industrial |
| Purity | Corruption |
| Dynamic | Static |
| Future | Past |
| Experience | Knowledge |
| American | European |

These techniques can also be applied to the works of a given filmmaker or even a given period. For example, the Depression movies of Frank Capra, like *Mr. Deeds Goes to Town* (1936), can be analyzed from the perspective of the two main ideologies of his era: Federalism, representing the values of Roosevelt's New Deal; and Populism, representing the values of individual enterprise. Capra's thematic concerns could be paired in the following way:

| Federalism | Populism |
|------------|----------|
| Collectivization | Individualism |
| City | Small town |
| Present | Past |
| Party machines | Participatory democracy |
| Welfare State | Self-help |
| Interdependence | Independence |
| Mass society | Communal society |
| Cynicism | Innocence |
| Materialism | Humanism |
| Sophistication | Simplicity |
| Alienation | Integration |
| European intellectualism | Yankee common sense |
| Secularism | Christianity |
| Expedience | Loyalty |
| High Art | Popular Entertainment |

**11-35. *Little Big Man* (U.S.A., 1970).**
*With Dustin Hoffman; Directed by Arthur Penn.*
Because they are in the ironic mode, revisionist genre films often reverse the symbolic values of traditional (i.e., classical) generic polarities. For example, in Penn's western, the civilized values are found primarily in the culture of the Cheyenne nation; savagery is the legacy of the white conquerers.

Semiology and structuralism have expanded the parameters of film theory considerably. Their pluralistic approach allows for much more flexibility, complexity, and depth in the critical enterprise. But structuralism and semiology are merely tools of analysis. By themselves, they can tell us nothing of the *value* of signs and codes within a film. Like every other theory, then, these are only as good as their practitioners. The writer's intelligence, taste, passion, knowledge, and sensitivity are what produce good criticism, not necessarily the theoretical methodology employed.

## Further Reading

ANDREW, DUDLEY J., *The Major Film Theories* (New York: Oxford, 1976). A helpful and clearly written exposition of the theories of such figures as Munsterberg, Arnheim, Eisenstein, Balázs, Kracauer, Bazin, Mitry, Metz, and others.

ARNHEIM, RUDOLF, *Film as Art* (Berkeley, Calif.: University of California Press, 1957). Expressionism in the cinema.

BAXANDALL, LEE, ed., *Radical Perspective in the Arts* (New York: Penguin, 1972). Marxist aesthetics, a variety of approaches.

ECKERT, CHARLES W., "The English Cine-Structuralists," and CHARLES HARPOLE and JOHN HANHARDT, "Linguistics, Structuralism, Semiology," in *Film Comment* (May–June, 1973). A useful introduction, with emphasis on the British school.

KRACAUER, SIEGFRIED, *Theory of Film: The Redemption of Physical Reality* (New York: Oxford, 1960). The most comprehensive theory of cinematic Realism.

MAST, GERALD, *Film/Cinema/Movie* (New York: Harper & Row, 1977). A demonstration of the virtues of eclecticism.

OVERBEY, DAVID, ed. and trans., *Springtime in Italy: A Reader on Neorealism* (New York: Archon, 1979). Includes pieces by Moravia, Visconti, De Sica, Rossellini, and others.

SARRIS, ANDREW, "Toward a Theory of Film History," in *The American Cinema* (New York: Dutton, 1968). A basic document of the auteur theory, written by its chief American spokesman.

TERTZ, ABRAM, *The Trial Begins* and *On Socialist Realism* (New York: Vintage, 1960). Two chilling accounts of art under Stalinism.

TUDOR, ANDREW, *Theories of Film* (New York: Viking, 1974). Includes essays on Eisenstein, Grierson, Bazin, Kracauer, auteurism and genre theory.

# APPENDIX

### North by Northwest: *The Reading Script, The Shooting Script*

There are some published screenplays that can provide a certain amount of aesthetic pleasure, though seldom as much as the finished film itself. Ernest Lehman's script for Hitchcock's *North by Northwest* is such a work, for the writing has considerable literary grace. Lehman has the novelist's gift for suggesting interior states by describing exterior events, and the dramatist's fluency with crisp, understated dialogue. In fact, the following excerpt from *North by Northwest,* like most published screenplays, is essentially a blending of the techniques of the novelist and the playwright. That is, it provides us with an essentially literary experience of the subject matter. Seldom do such reading scripts contain much technical information, such as the *découpage* of shots, their length, or the detailed contents of the mise-en-scène. Lehman's screenplay, then, provides us with a continuity of *actions* rather than the continuity of shots, which is what a shooting script contains.

Like many of Hitchcock's movies, *North by Northwest* revolves around the wrong man theme. The protagonist is an innocent man accused of and persecuted for a crime he didn't commit. In this film, Roger Thornhill (Cary Grant), a glib but charming advertising executive, is accidentally mistaken for a government agent named Kaplan. Thornhill is abducted by enemy agents, almost murdered by them, then fatefully implicated in a murder of a U.N. diplomat. Pursued by both the police and the enemy agents, he flees to

Chicago in desperation, hoping to discover the real Kaplan, who presumably will establish Thornhill's innocence. When he arrives in Chicago, he is told that Kaplan will meet him alone at a designated location. The following excerpt from Lehman's script relates what then takes place.

### Helicopter Shot—Exterior, Highway 41—Afternoon

We START CLOSE on a Greyhound bus, SHOOTING DOWN on it and TRAVELING ALONG with it as it speeds in an easterly direction at seventy m.p.h. Gradually, CAMERA DRAWS AWAY from the bus, going higher but never losing sight of the vehicle, which recedes into the distance below and becomes a toylike object on an endless ribbon of deserted highway that stretches across miles of flat prairie. Now the bus is slowing down. It is nearing a junction where a small dirt road coming from nowhere crosses the highway and continues on to nowhere. The bus stops. A man gets out. It is THORNHILL. But to us he is only a tiny figure. The bus starts away, moves on out of sight. And now THORNHILL stands alone beside the road—a tiny figure in the middle of nowhere.

### On the Ground—with Thornhill—(Master Scene)

He glances about, studying his surroundings. The terrain is flat and treeless, even more desolate from this vantage point than it seemed from the air. Here and there patches of low-growing farm crops add some contour to the land. A hot sun beats down. UTTER SILENCE hangs heavily in the air. THORNHILL glances at his wristwatch. It is three twenty-five.

In the distance, the FAINT HUM of a MOTOR VEHICLE is HEARD. THORNHILL looks off to the west. The HUM GROWS LOUDER as the car draws nearer. THORNHILL steps closer to the edge of the highway. A black sedan looms up, traveling at high speed. For a moment we are not sure it is not hurtling right at THORNHILL. And then it zooms past him, recedes into the distance, becoming a FAINT HUM, a tiny speck, and then SILENCE again.

THORNHILL takes out a handerchief, mops his face. He is beginning to sweat now. It could be from nervousness, as well as the heat. Another FAINT HUM, coming from the east, GROWING LOUDER as he glances off and sees another distant speck becoming a speeding car, this one a closed convertible. Again, anticipation on THORNHILL's face. Again, the vague uneasiness of indefinable danger approaching at high speed. And again, ZOOM—a cloud of dust—a car receding into the distance—a FAINT HUM—and SILENCE.

His lips tighten. He glances at his watch again. He steps out into the middle of the highway, looks first in one direction, then the other. Nothing in sight. He loosens his tie, opens his shirt collar, looks up at the sun. Behind him, in the distance, another vehicle is HEARD approaching. He turns, looks off to the west. This one is a huge transcontinental moving van, ROARING TOWARD HIM at high speed. With quick apprehension he moves off the highway to the dusty side of the road as the van thunders past and disappears. Its FADING SOUND is replaced with a NEW SOUND, the CHUGGING of an OLD FLIVVER.

THORNHILL looks off in the direction of the approaching SOUND, sees a flivver nearing the highway from the intersecting dirt road. When the car reaches the highway, it comes to a stop. A middle-aged woman is behind the wheel. Her passenger is a nondescript MAN of about fifty. He could certainly be a farmer. He gets out of the car. It makes a U-turn and drives off in the direction from which it came. THORNHILL watches the MAN and takes up a position across the highway from him. The MAN glances at THORNHILL without visible interest, then looks off up the highway toward the east as though waiting for something to come along.

THORNHILL stares at the MAN, wondering if this is George Kaplan.

The MAN looks idly across the highway at THORNHILL, his face expressionless.

THORNHILL wipes his face with his handkerchief, never taking his eyes off the MAN across the highway. The FAINT SOUND of an APPROACHING PLANE has gradually come up over the scene. As the SOUND GROWS LOUDER, THORNHILL looks up to his left and sees a low-flying biplane approach from the north-west. He watches it with mounting interest as it heads straight for the spot where he and the stranger face each other across the highway. Suddenly it is upon them, only a hundred feet above the ground, and then, like a giant bird, as THORN-HILL turns with the plane's passage, it flies over them and continues on. THORN-HILL stares after the plane, his back to the highway. When the plane has gone several hundred yards beyond the highway, it loses altitude, levels off only a few feet above the ground and begins to fly back and forth in straight lines parallel to the highway, letting loose a trail of powered dust from beneath its fuselage as it goes. Any farmer would recognize the operation as simple crop-dusting.

THORNHILL looks across the highway, sees that the stranger is watching the plane with idle interest. THORNHILL's lips set with determination. He crosses over and goes up to the MAN.

THORNHILL: Hot day.

MAN: Seen worse.

THORNHILL: Are you . . . uh . . . by any chance supposed to be meeting someone here?

MAN (still watching the plane): Waitin' for the bus. Due any minute.

THORNHILL: Oh . . .

MAN (idly): Some of them crop-duster pilots get rich, if they live long enough . . .

THORNHILL: Then your name isn't . . . Kaplan.

MAN (glances at him): Can't say it is, 'cause it ain't. (He looks off up the highway) Well—here she comes, right on time.

THORNHILL looks off to the east, sees a Greyhound bus approaching. The MAN peers off at the plane again, and frowns.

MAN: That's funny.

THORNHILL: What?

MAN: That plane's dustin' crops where there ain't no crops.

THORNHILL looks across at the droning plane with growing suspicion as the stranger steps out onto the highway and flags the bus to a stop. THORNHILL turns toward the stranger as though to say something to him. But it is too late. The man has boarded the bus, its doors are closing, and it is pulling away. THORNHILL is alone again.

Almost immediately, he HEARS the PLANE ENGINE BEING GUNNED TO A HIGHER SPEED. He glances off sharply, sees the plane veering off its parallel course and heading toward him. He stands there wide-eyed, rooted to the spot. The plane roars on, a few feet off the ground. There are two men in the twin cockpits, goggled, unrecognizable, menacing. He yells out to them, but his voice is lost in the NOISE of the PLANE. In a moment it will be upon him and decapitate him. Desperately he drops to the ground and presses himself flat as the plane zooms over him with a great noise, almost combing his hair with a landing wheel.

THORNHILL scrambles to his feet, sees the plane banking and turning. He looks about wildly, sees a telephone pole and dashes for it as the plane comes at him again. He ducks behind the pole. The plane heads straight for him, veers to the right at the last moment. We HEAR two sharp CRACKS of GUNFIRE mixed with the SOUND of the ENGINE, as two bullets slam into the pole just above THORNHILL's head.

THORNHILL reacts to this new peril, sees the plane banking for another run at him. A car is speeding along the highway from the west. THORNHILL dashes out onto the road, tries to flag the car down but the driver ignores him and races by, leaving him exposed and vulnerable as the plane roars in on him. He dives into a ditch and rolls away as another series of SHOTS are HEARD and bullets rake the ground that he has just occupied.

He gets to his feet, looks about, sees a cornfield about fifty yards from the highway, glances up at the plane making its turn, and decides to make a dash for the cover of the tall-growing corn.

SHOOTING DOWN FROM A HELICOPTER about one hundred feet above the ground, we SEE THORNHILL running toward the cornfield and the plane in pursuit.

SHOOTING FROM WITHIN THE CORNFIELD, we SEE THORNHILL come crashing in, scuttling to the right and lying flat and motionless as we HEAR THE PLANE ZOOM OVER HIM WITH A BURST OF GUNFIRE and bullets rip into the corn, but at a safe distance from THORNHILL. He raises his head cautiously, gasping for breath, as he HEARS THE PLANE MOVE OFF AND INTO ITS TURN.

SHOOTING DOWN FROM THE HELICOPTER, we SEE the plane leveling off and starting a run over the cornfield, which betrays no sign of the hidden THORN-HILL. Skimming over the top of the cornstalks, the plane gives forth no burst of gunfire now. Instead, it lets loose thick clouds of poisonous dust which settle down into the corn.

WITHIN THE CORNFIELD, THORNHILL, still lying flat, begins to gasp and choke as the poisonous dust envelops him. Tears stream from his eyes but he does not dare move as he HEARS THE PLANE COMING OVER THE FIELD AGAIN. When the plane zooms by and another cloud of dust hits him, he jumps to his feet and crashes out into the open, half blinded and gasping for breath. Far off down the highway to the right, he SEES a huge Diesel gasoline-tanker approaching. He starts running toward the highway to intercept it.

SHOOTING FROM THE HELICOPTER, we SEE THORNHILL dashing for the highway, the plane leveling off for another run at him, and the Diesel tanker speeding closer.

SHOOTING ACROSS THE HIGHWAY, we SEE THORNHILL running and stumbling TOWARD CAMERA, the plane closing in between him, and the Diesel tanker approaching from the left. He dashes out into the middle of the highway and waves his arms wildly.

The Diesel tanker THUNDERS down the highway toward THORNHILL, KLAXON BLASTING impatiently.

The plane speeds relentlessly toward THORNHILL from the field bordering the highway.

THORNHILL stands alone and helpless in the middle of the highway, waving his arms. The plane draws closer. The tanker is almost upon him. It isn't going to stop. He can HEAR THE KLAXON BLASTING him out of the way. There is nothing he can do. The plane has caught up with him. The tanker won't stop. It's GOT to stop. He hurls himself to the pavement directly in its path. There is A SCREAM OF BRAKES and SKIDDING TIRES, THE ROAR OF THE PLANE ENGINE and then a tremendous BOOM as the Diesel truck grinds to a stop inches from Thornhill's body just as the plane, hopelessly committed and caught unprepared by the sudden stop, slams into the traveling gasoline tanker and plane and gasoline explode into a great sheet of flame.

In the next few moments, all is confusion. THORNHILL, unhurt, rolls out from under the wheels of the Diesel truck. The drivers clamber out of the front seat and drop to the highway. Black clouds of smoke billow up from the funeral pyre of the plane and its cremated occupants. We recognize the flaming body of one of the men in the plane. It is LICHT, one of THORNHILL's original abductors. An elderly open pick-up truck with a second-hand refrigerator standing in it, which has been approaching from the east, pulls up at the side of the road. Its driver, a FARMER, jumps out and hurries toward the wreckage.

FARMER: What happened? What happened?

    The Diesel truck drivers are too dazed to answer. Flames and smoke drive them all back. THORNHILL, unnoticed, heads toward the unoccupied pick-up truck. Another car comes up from the west, stops, and its driver runs toward the other men. They stare, transfixed, at the holocaust. Suddenly, from behind them, they HEAR the PICK-UP TRUCK'S MOTOR STARTING. The FARMER who owns the truck turns, and is startled to see his truck being driven away by an utter stranger.

FARMER: Hey!

    He runs after the truck. But the stranger—who is THORNHILL—steps harder on the accelerator and speeds off in the direction of Chicago.

    Creating the shooting script was the most enjoyable aspect of filmmaking for Hitchcock. Since the beginning of his career in the 1920s, he co-authored all his screenplays, without official credit. He preferred working with only one other writer (ideally not a thriller specialist), so they could stimulate each other's imaginations. He often used novelists and dramatists as screenwriters and got them involved with the direction by explaining how he planned to shoot a sequence, what size the images would be, and so on. His pre-cut scripts are legendary. No other director worked from such precisely detailed plans. He often provided frame drawings of his shots (a technique called storyboarding), especially for those sequences involving complex editing. Some of his scripts contained as many as 600 setup sketches. Every shot was calculated for a precise effect. Nothing was superfluous, nothing left to chance. "I would prefer to write all this down, however tiny and however short the pieces of film are—they should be written down in just the same way a composer writes down those little black dots from which we get beautiful sound," he explained.

    By the time the script was finished, he knew every detail by heart, and rarely consulted the scenario during production. He compared himself to a conductor directing an orchestra without a score. He considered the actual shooting anti-climactic. For him, the creative work was over. After observing the shooting of several scenes from a Hitchcock movie, critic André Bazin marveled: "I had been watching for a good hour, during which time Hitchcock did not have to intervene more than twice; settled in his armchair, he gave the impression of being prodigiously bored and of musing about something completely different." When asked why he didn't simply let someone else shoot his movies, Hitchcock replied: "They might screw it up."

    The following excerpt is not Hitchcock's shooting script of *North by Northwest,* but perhaps the next best thing: a reconstruction of the sequence taken directly from the film by Albert J. LaValley, which appears in his volume, *Focus on Hitchcock.* Though certain elements (textures, rhythms, movements, acting nuances, etc.) in this reconstruction are necessarily lost, it nonetheless offers some useful insights about the differences between the film writer's function and those of the director. Each number represents a separate shot; drawings identified with a letter as well represent a continuation of the previous shot, though with enough new action to warrant an additional sketch. The numbers in parentheses indicate the approximate length of the shots in seconds. The following abbreviations are used: E.L.S., extreme long shot; L.S., long shot; M.S., medium shot; C.U., closeup; P.O.V., a shot taken from Thornhill's point-of-view.

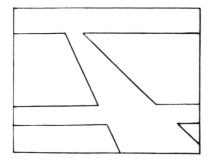

1. E.L.S., aerial. Dissolve to empty road across fields where rendezvous with KAPLAN is to take place. We see and hear bus arriving, door opening.

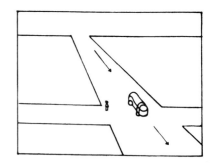

1b. THORNHILL emerges, bus leaves. He is alone. (52)

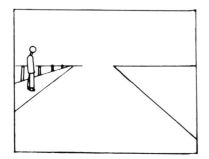

2. L.S., low angle. THORNHILL at roadside, waiting. (5)

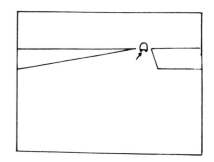

3. E.L.S., P.O.V. Looking down main road: bus going away in distance. (4)

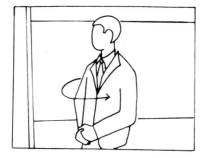

4. M.S. THORNHILL near sign, turns left to right, looking for someone. (3 2/3)

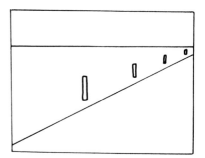

5. L.S., P.O.V. View across road, empty fields with posts. (4)

6. M.S. THORNHILL by sign, turns from right to left, looking. (3)

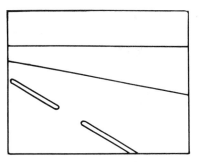

7. L.S., P.O.V. Across fields. (4)

8. M.S. THORNHILL by sign again, waiting, turns head and looks behind him. (3)

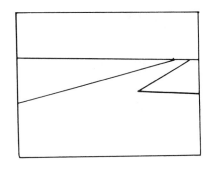

9. E.L.S., P.O.V. The field behind him, road. (4)

10. M.S. THORNHILL by sign, waiting, turning forward—long waiting feeling. (6 1/2)

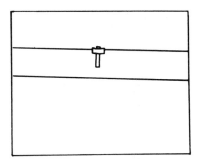

11. E.L.S. Empty landscape across road, signs, post. (3)

12. M.S. THORNHILL by sign. Turns right. (2)

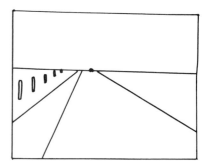

13. E.L.S. Empty main road, car coming in distance. (4)

14. M.S. THORNHILL by sign, looking at car approaching. (3/4)

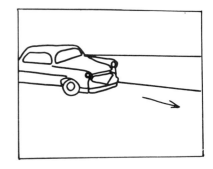

15. L.S. Car goes by fast, whizzing sound, camera pans slightly to right. (1 3/4)

16. M.S. THORNHILL by sign, moves back to left, follows car with his eyes. (2)

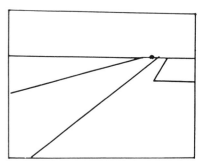

17. E.L.S., P.O.V. Road, car going, sound recedes. (4)

18. M.S. THORNHILL by sign, hands in pockets, turns from left to right. (3)

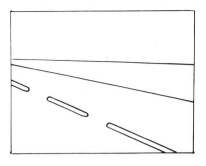

19. L.S., P.O.V. Field across road again. (3)

20. M.S. THORNHILL by sign, same pose, still looking, turns from right to left. (2 3/4)

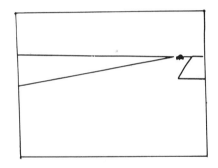

21. E.L.S. Road, car in distance, sounds begin. (3 1/2)

22. M.S. THORNHILL by sign, looking at car, no movement. (2 1/2)

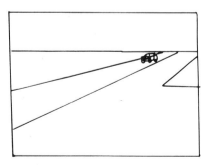

23. E.L.S. Car coming closer, sound increasing. (3 3/4)

24. M.S. THORNHILL by sign, looking at car coming. (3)

25. L.S. Car closer, rushes past, camera pans a bit to follow it. (3)

26. M.S. THORNHILL by sign, takes hands from pockets, turns left to right to follow car. (3)

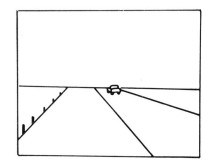

27. E.L.S. View of road, car in distance receding. (3 3/4)

28. M.S. THORNHILL by sign, waiting again. (2 1/4)

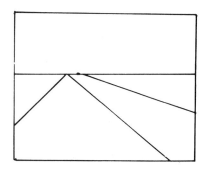

29. E.L.S. Road, truck coming; we hear its sound. (4)

30. M.S. THORNHILL by sign, sound of truck increasing. (3)

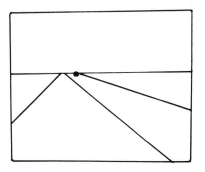

31. E.L.S. Truck coming down road, sound still increasing. (3 3/4)

32. M.S. THORNHILL by sign (2 1/4)

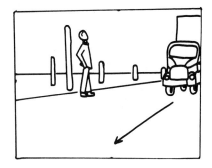

33. L.S. Truck whizzes by.

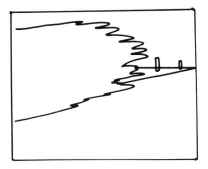

33b. Kicking up dust, obscuring THORNHILL, camera pans slightly left, and he emerges out of the dust gradually. (4)

34. M.S. THORNHILL wiping dust from his eyes, turns to right. (7)

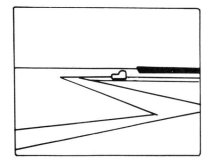

35. E.L.S. Fields across way, car coming out behind corn. (5)

36. M.S. THORNHILL by sign puzzled by car. (5)

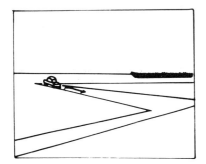

37. E.L.S. Car making turn on dirt road. (4)

38. M.S. THORNHILL awaiting car. (3 2/3)

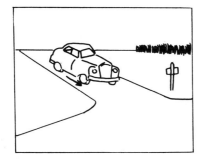

39. L.S. Car nearing main road, camera pans following it to right, a sign there. (4)

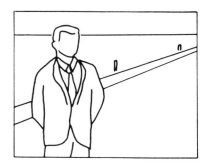

40. M.S. THORNHILL waiting to see what will happen. (3 1/3)

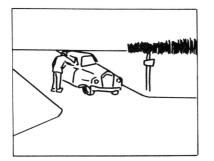

41. L.S. MAN getting out of car, talking to driver, we hear the door of the car slam. (3 1/2)

42. M.S. THORNHILL reacting, wondering, getting ready to meet this man. (2)

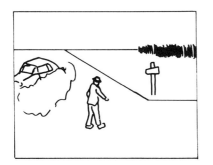

43. L.S. Sound of car turning around, dust raised, car turns around and the MAN walks towards main road opposite THORNHILL, looking back at the car leaving. (1 4/5)

44. M.S. THORNHILL, closer than previous shots, eyeing the man. (1 1/2)

45. L.S. Camera pans right slightly; the MAN goes over by the sign and turns his head to look up the road and over at THORNHILL. (4 1/3)

46. M.S. Same as 44. THORNHILL's reaction, his head tilts and he looks across the road. (3 4/5)

47. L.S. low angle. Road in the middle stretching to infinity, two men oddly stationed on either side of road, the other MAN looking up the road a bit. (7)

48. M.S. THORNHILL's reaction, takes hands out of pockets, opens coat, puts hands on hips, contemplates situation. (6 1/3)

49. L.S. Same as 45, only the MAN turns his head looking the other way. (3 1/2)

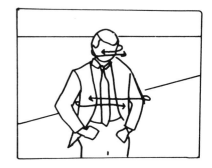

50. M.S. Same as 48, but THORN-HILL has both hands on hips now, his head looking across. His head turns up road to see if anyone is coming; he looks back, one hand on hip, other at side, at MAN across way.

50b. Starts walking across road part way. (10)

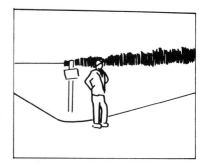

51. L.S., P.O.V. The man on the other side of road, as THORNHILL crosses, camera tracks across road part way, acting as his eyes. (2 2/3)

52. M.S. THORNHILL walks across road; synchronous tracking camera continuing movement begun in 50b.

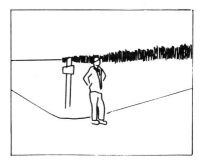

53. L.S., P.O.V. Same as 49, 51 of other MAN across road, but camera tracks in on him, acting as THORN-HILL's eyes, continues movement begun in 50b.

54. M.S. THORNHILL on other side of road, but camera tracks to continue movement of 50, 52.

54b. Camera continues tracking to other side of road until other man comes into view and THORNHILL begins to talk to him. THORNHILL's hands are a bit nervous in movement; he plays with his little finger; the other man has hands in pockets.

> THORNHILL (after a long wait): Hi! (a long pause follows) Hot day. (Another pause.)
> MAN: Seen worse.
> THORNHILL (after a long pause): Are you supposed to be meeting someone here?
> MAN: Waitin' for the bus. Due any minute.
> THORNHILL: Oh. (another pause)
> MAN: Some of them crop duster pilots get rich if they live long enough.
> THORNHILL: Yeah! (very softly) (21)

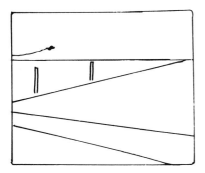

55. E.L.S. Fields with plane at great distance in far left of frame coming right. (2 2/3)

56. M.S. Reaction shot of both looking at plane.
> THORNHILL: Then . . . a . . .
> (pause) then your name isn't
> Kaplan?
> MAN: Can't say that it is 'cause
> it ain't. (pause) Here she comes
> (as he looks down the road). (11)

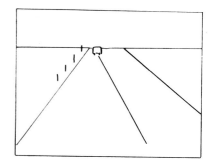

57. E.L.S. Bus coming down the
road.
> MAN: (voice off) . . . right on
> time. (2 2/3)

58. M.S. Same as 56, two talking
then looking again across road at
crop duster.
> MAN: That's funny.
> THORNHILL: (very softly) What?
> MAN: That plane's dustin' crops
> where there ain't no crops.
> THORNHILL turns to look. (8)

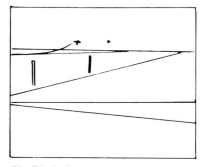

59. E.L.S. Same as 55, field with the
plane over it. (4)

60. M.S. Two men off center looking
at plane. THORNHILL's hands continue nervous movements; the other's
are in his pockets as before. Sound
of approaching bus. (3 1/3)

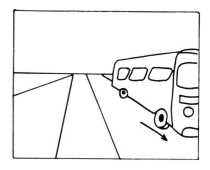

61. L.S. Bus arriving and coming
quite close to camera. (1 4/5)

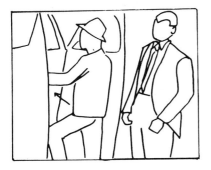

62. M.S. MAN gets on as door of bus opens and seems to shut THORN-HILL out. The bus leaves.

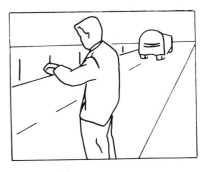

62b. THORNHILL puts hands on hips and looks across, then looks at his watch. For a second he is alone in the frame as the bus goes out of sight. (2 1/3)

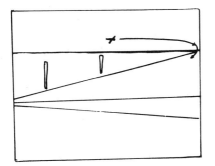

63. E.L.S., P.O.V. Same as 59, what THORNHILL sees across the road; the plane goes to end of frame and turns right, toward him. (5 1/5)

64. M.S. THORNHILL in front of road by sign, puzzled and rather innocent looking; sound of plane approaching. (2 1/3)

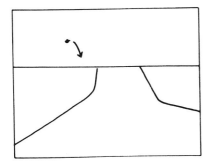

65. E.L.S. Plane coming toward camera, still far, but closer and with sound increasing. (3 4/5)

66. M.S. Same as 64. THORNHILL reacting. (2 1/4)

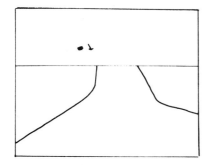

67. E.L.S. Same as 65 but plane closer and louder. (2 1/8)

68. M.S. Closer shot of THORNHILL, still puzzled and confused as plane comes at him. (4 1/2)

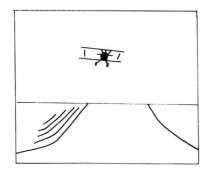

69. L.S. Plane clearly coming at him, filling mid-frame, very loud. (1 1/3)

70. M.S. THORNHILL drops, a short held shot, he falls out of frame at bottom. (2/3)

71. L.S. THORNHILL falling on ground, both arms on ground, plane behind him, he in a hole. (3 1/2)

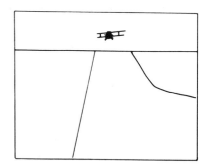

72. L.S. Plane going away from him. (3)

73. L.S. THORNHILL on ground getting up, kneeling on left knee. (3 1/2)

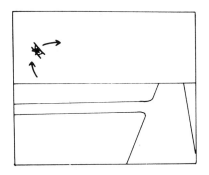

74. E.L.S. Plane going farther away and sound receding. (2 4/5)

75. L.S. THORNHILL getting up. (2 1/5)

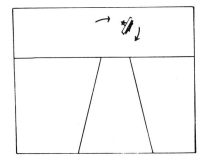

76. E.L.S. Plane in distance banking. (2 1/3)

77. M.S. THORNHILL up and about to run. (2 1/3)

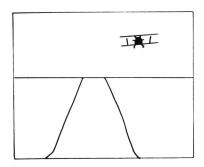

78. L.S. Plane approaching again, sound getting louder. (2)

79. M.S. THORNHILL runs and falls in ditch. (1 1/2)

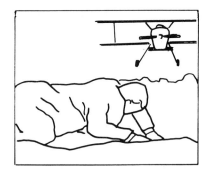

80. L.S. THORNHILL in ditch, sound of plane and bullets sprayed on him, smoke; he turns head to left and faces camera to watch when plane is gone. (5 1/3)

81. L.S. Plane getting ready again, banking. (5 1/5)

82. M.S. THORNHILL in ditch coming up, gets up on left arm, sound of receding plane. (2 1/2)

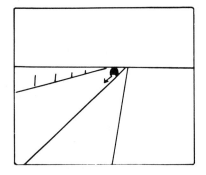

83. E.L.S., P.O.V. The road as THORNHILL sees it, car in distance. (2 1/2)

84. M.S. Same as 82, THORNHILL rising from ditch, receding plane sound. (1 1/2)

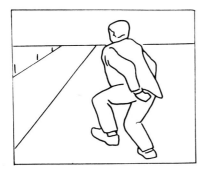

85. L.S., low angle. THORNHILL runs to road to try to stop car.

85b. He tries to flag it down. Car sounds approach and it whizzes by. (9 1/2)

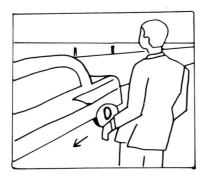

86. M.S. THORNHILL's back after turning left as the car whizzes by. (4 2/3)

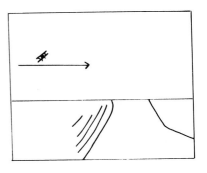

87. E.L.S. Plane in distance, sounds again. (2 1/3)

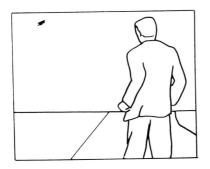

88. L.S. THORNHILL's back with plane in distance at far left coming at him.

88b. L.S. He looks at plane, turns around looking for a place to hide, looks at plane again, turns around and runs towards camera. Camera reverse tracks.

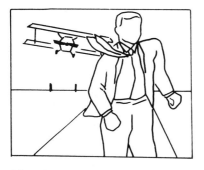

88c. THORNHILL running toward camera, camera reverse tracking. He turns around twice while running to look at plane; it goes over his head just missing him. (13 1/2)

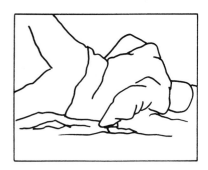

89. M.S. THORNHILL falling, side view, legs up, bullet and plane sounds. (5)

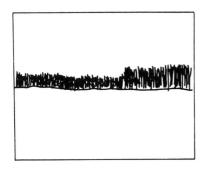

90. L.S., P.O.V. Cornfield, a place to hide. (2 1/2)

91. M.S. THORNHILL lying flat on ground, looking. (1 2/3)

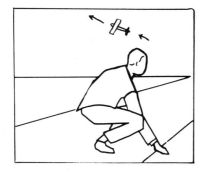

92. L.S. THORNHILL getting up, plane in distance banking again for new attack. (3)

93. M.S. THORNHILL running, turns back to look at plane, camera tracks with him as he runs to cornfield. (4 1/2)

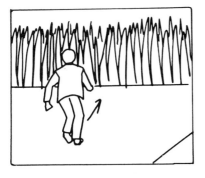

94. L.S., low angle. THORNHILL's back as he runs into cornfield; low camera angle shows lots of ground, stalks. He disappears into corn. (2 3/4)

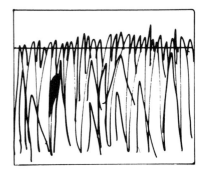

95. L.S. Picture of corn; a patch reveals where THORNHILL is hiding. The corn rustles. (2)

96. M.S. Camera follows THORNHILL down as he falls on ground inside the corn patch. He turns back to look up to see if plane is coming. A cornstalk falls; then he looks down again, up again, down again, up. (7 3/4)

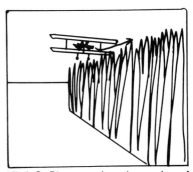

97. L.S. Plane coming along edge of cornfield and over it; it gets very loud. (4 1/2)

98. M.S. Same as 96. Corn rustles, wind from the plane blows over. THORNHILL sees he's out of danger, and smiles a bit, feeling that he's outwitted his pursuers. (15 4/5)

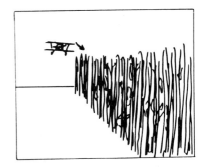

99. L.S. Plane coming in on bend, repeating pattern of 97; it gets louder. (3 1/4)

100. M.S. Same as 96, 98. THORN-HILL in corn, getting up, looking around, suddenly aware of plane in new way; he's startled that it's coming back. (4 4/5)

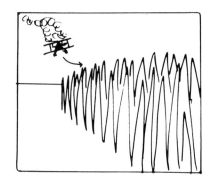

101. L.S. Plane over corn, repeating pattern of 97, only dust coming out of it; plane comes closer to camera. (7)

102. M.S. Same as 96, 98, 100; THORNHILL's reaction to dust, which fills up screen: he coughs, takes out handkerchief, camera follows him as he raises himself up and down; coughing sounds (12 1/4)

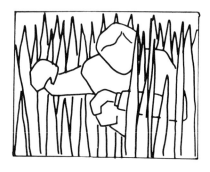

103. M.S. THORNHILL in corn, new shot; he runs towards camera trying to get out of corn; rustling corn, he looks out of field. (4 1/2)

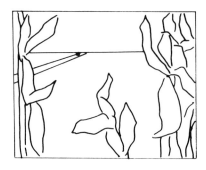

104. E.L.S., P.O.V. Out of cornfield, view of road as framed by corn; tiny speck on road in distance is truck. (2 3/4)

105. M.S. THORNHILL in corn, but he is standing; he moves forward, looks back up for plane, makes dash for the truck coming down road; he goes out of frame for moment at the end. (3 1/2)

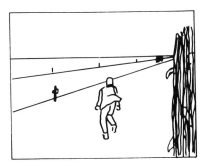

106. L.S. THORNHILL running toward truck, gets to road from corn; truck farther along the road, sounds of truck (4)

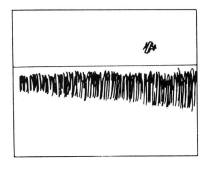

107. E.L.S. Plane banking over corn, getting ready to turn toward him; faint plane sounds; horn of truck. (2)

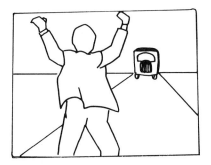

108. L.S., low angle. THORNHILL in road, truck coming, he waves at it. (1 2/3)

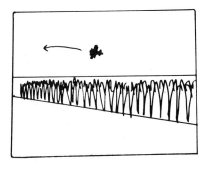

109. E.L.S. Continuation of 107, plane further left. (2)

110. M.S. THORNHILL trying to stop truck, sounds of horns, brakes. (2)

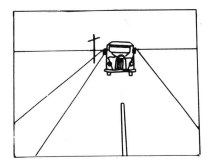

111. L.S. Truck approaching, getting bigger. (2)

112. M.S. Same as 110, but he looks at plane coming in on his left, then puts up both hands instead of one, and bites his tongue. (1 1/2)

113. L.S. Truck even closer, about fifty feet in front of camera. (1)

114. M.S. Same as 112, 110. THORN-HILL waving frantically now. (1)

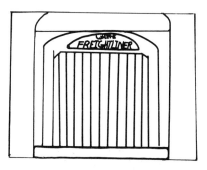

115. C.U. Grille of truck as it tries to halt; brake sounds. (1)

116. C.U. THORNHILL's face in anguish about to be hit.

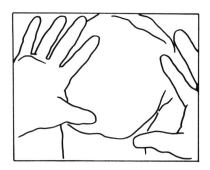

116b. His hands go up and his head goes down. (4/5)

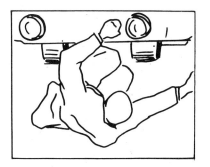

117. L.S. THORNHILL falls under the truck, front view. (1)

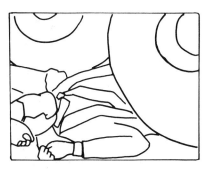

118. M.S. THORNHILL under the truck, side view. (2 1/2)

119. L.S., low angle. Plane comes toward truck (and camera). (1 3/4)

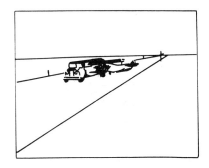

120. L.S. Plane hits truck, view from across road. (1)

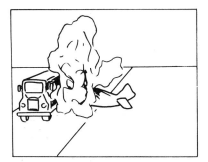

121. L.S. Truck bursts into flames; another angle of truck and plane; music begins and continues to end of scene. (2 1/2)

122. L.S. Shot of truck in flames from in front, two men scramble hurriedly from cab.
DRIVER: Let's get out of here. It's going to explode. (6 1/2)

123. L.S. Backs of men running somewhat comically to cornfield. (2)

124. L.S. THORNHILL runs toward camera from explosions of oil truck behind him. Music tends to mute explosion sounds (2 3/4)

125. L.S. Reverse angle of THORN-HILL as he now backs away from explosion. A car has just pulled to side of road, followed by a pickup truck with a refrigerator, which pulls to the side in front of it. Doors open and people get out. THORNHILL goes over and talks to them. No sounds are heard (the music continues), but we see his motions of explanation. (9)

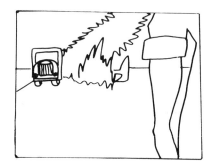

126. L.S. View of explosion in distance with close-up of farmer's arm on right. (2)

127. L.S. THORNHILL and others watch explosion. He backs away from scene to right of frame while they all move closer to the wreck as THORNHILL retreats unnoticed by them. (11)

128. L.S. Backs of others watching explosion. (6 1/3)

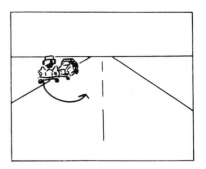

129. L.S. THORNHILL takes the pickup truck with refrigerator in back and pulls out while they are watching the explosion. (3 4/5)

130. L.S. Same as 128, but the FARMER turns, seeing his truck being taken, and shouts "Hey." (2 1/2)

131. L.S. Chase by the FARMER, bow-legged and comic; he finally stops as the truck recedes into the distance. "Come back, come back," he is shouting. Dissolve to next sequence. (15)

Of course a shooting script is no substitute for an experience of the film itself, but this shot breakdown does help demonstrate that even if Hitchcock had nothing to do with the subject matter (an extremely unlikely supposition, since it has all the earmarks of a classic Hitchcockian sequence), its effectiveness is due primarily to the director's manipulation of the materials. Hitchcock transformed Lehman's verbal description of the events into a sequence of such gripping terror that most viewers are paralyzed with fear, yet simultaneously—and paradoxically—delighted by the many unexpected shafts of wit.

To encourage us to identify with Thornhill, Hitchcock often employs point-of-view shots, thus literally forcing us to see things through the protagonist's eyes. These shots are particularly effective when combined with a tracking camera. Hitchcock exploits the emotional effects of proxemic distances with great economy: there are only two closeups in the entire sequence: the onrushing truck's grille and Thornhill's face just before he's hit by the truck. These closeups are offered in sequence to maximize the sense of physical impact. The rhythms of the editing are brilliant: the earlier shots are lengthier and seem to contain "nothing"—a deliberate attempt on Hitchcock's part to induce a sense of relaxation and then boredom in the viewer. In the climax, the staccato shots machinegun by at an explosive pace. Even with a visually uninteresting setting, Hitchcock's *mise-en-scène*—and especially his subtle use of the frame—is exemplary.

## Further Reading

LaVALLEY, ALBERT J., ed., *Focus on Hitchcock* (Englewood Cliffs, N.J.: Prentice-Hall, 1972).

LEHMAN, ERNEST, *North by Northwest* (New York: Viking, 1972).

# GLOSSARY

**Abstract film, absolute film (C).** A nonrepresentational film in which pure forms—e.g., lines, shapes, colors—constitute the only content. Abstract movies are often likened to music pieces, which similarly are "about" nothing but pure form. Usually produced independently by the filmmaker, seldom with commercial profit.

**Actor-star.** See *star*.

**Aerial shot (T).** Essentially a variation of the *crane* shot, though restricted to exterior locations. Usually taken from a helicopter.

**Aesthetic distance (C).** Viewers' ability to distinguish between an artistic "reality" and external reality—their realization that the events of a fiction film are simulated.

**A-film (I).** An American studio era term, signifying a major production, usually with important stars, and a generous budget. Shown as the main feature on *double bills*.

**Aleatory techniques (C).** Techniques of filmmaking which depend on the element of chance. Images are not planned out in advance, but must be composed on the spot by a director who often acts as his own cameraman. Usually employed in documentary or improvisatory situations.

(C) predominantly critical terms; (T) predominantly technical terms; (I) predominantly industry terms; (G) terms in general usage.

**Allegory (C).** A symbolic technique in which stylized characters and situations represent rather obvious ideas, such as Justice, Religion, Society, and so on. A popular genre in the German cinema.

**Allusion (C).** A reference to an event, person, or work of art, usually well-known.

**Animation (G).** A form of filmmaking characterized by photographing inanimate objects or individual drawings *frame by frame,* with each frame differing minutely from its predecessor. When such images are projected at the standard speed of 24 frames per second, the result is that the objects or drawings appear to move, and hence seem "animated."

**Anticipatory camera, anticipatory setup (C).** The placement of the camera in such a manner as to anticipate the movements of an action before it occurs. An anticipatory camera often suggests fatality or predestination.

**Archetype (C).** An original model or type after which similar things are patterned. Archtypes can be well-known story patterns, universal experiences, or personality types. Myths, fairy tales, *genres,* and cultural heroes are generally archetypal, as are the basic cycles of life and nature.

**Art director,** also **production designer (G).** The individual responsible for designing and overseeing the construction of sets for a movie, and sometimes its interior decoration and overall visual style.

**Art house (I).** A theatre specializing in sophisticated fare, especially classic, experimental, and foreign movies.

**Aspect ratio (T).** The ratio between the horizontal and vertical dimensions of the *frame.*

**Auteur theory (C).** A theory of film popularized by the critics of the French journal *Cahiers du Cinéma* in the 1950s. The theory emphasizes the director as the major creator of film art. A strong director (an *auteur*) stamps the material with his personal vision, even when working with an externally imposed script or *genre.*

**Available lighting (G).** The use of only that illumination which actually exists on a location, either natural (the sun) or artificial (house lamps). When available lighting is used in interior locations, generally a sensitive *fast film stock* must also be used.

**Avant-garde (C).** From the French, meaning "in the front ranks." Those minority artists whose works are characterized by an unconventional daring, and by obscure, controversial, or highly personal ideas.

**Back lot (I).** During the studio era in the U.S.A., standing exterior sets of such common locales as a frontier town, a turn-of-the-century city block, a European village, and so on. MGM boasted the largest number of back lots.

**B-film (G).** A low-budget movie usually shown as the second feature during the big studio era in America. B-films rarely included important stars, and took the form of popular *genres,* like thrillers, westerns, horror films, etc. The major studios used them as testing grounds for the raw talent under contract, and as their filler product.

**Bird's-eye view (G).** A shot in which the camera photographs a scene from directly overhead.

**Blimp (T).** A sound-proof camera housing which muffles the noise of the camera's motor so that sound can be clearly recorded on the set.

**Blocking (T).** The movements of the actors within a given playing area.

**Boom, mike boom (T).** An overhead telescoping pole which carries a microphone, permitting the *synchronous* recording of sound without restricting the movements of the players.

**Box office (G).** Literally, the ticket office of a movie theatre. Figuratively, the drawing power of a performer, genre, or individual movie.

**Cels,** also **cells (T).** Transparent plastic sheets which are superimposed in layers by animators to give the illusion of depth and volume to their drawings.

**Character roles (G).** Secondary roles in a movie, usually lacking the glamor and prominence of the leading parts.

**Cinematographer,** also **director of photography, lighting cameraman (G).** The artist or technician responsible for the lighting of a shot, and the quality of the photography.

**Cinéma vérité,** also **direct cinema (C).** A method of documentary filming, using *aleatory* methods that don't interfere with the way events take place in reality. Such films are made with a minimum of equipment, usually a hand-held camera and portable sound apparatus.

**Classical cinema (C).** A vague but convenient term used to designate the mainstream of fiction films produced in America, roughly from the maturity of Griffith in the mid-teens till the late 1960s. The classical paradigm is a movie strong in *story, star,* and *production values,* with a high level of technical achievement, and edited according to the conventions of *classical cutting.* The visual style is functional, and rarely distracts from the characters in action. Movies in this mold are structured narratively, with a clearly defined conflict, complications which intensify to a rising climax, and a resolution which emphasizes formal closure.

**Classical cutting, découpage classique (C).** A style of editing developed by Griffith, in which a sequence of shots is determined by a scene's dramatic and emotional emphases rather than by its physical action alone. The sequence of shots represents the breakdown of the event into its psychological as well as logical components.

**Closed forms (C).** A visual style which inclines toward self-conscious designs and carefully harmonized compositions. The *frame* is exploited to suggest a self-sufficient universe which encloses all the necessary visual information, usually in an aesthetically appealing manner.

**Closeup, close shot (G).** A detailed view of a person or object, usually without much context provided. A closeup of an actor generally includes only his head.

**Content curve (C).** The amount of time necessary for the average viewer to assimilate most of the information of a shot.

**Continuity (T).** The kind of logic implied between edited shots, their principle of coherence. *Cutting to continuity* emphasizes smooth transitions between shots, in which time and space are unobtrusively condensed. More complex, *classical cutting* is the linking of shots according to an event's psychological as well as logical breakdown. In radical *montage*, the continuity is determined by the symbolic association of ideas between shots, rather than any literal connections in time and space. Continuity can also refer to the space-time continuum of reality before it's broken down into fragments (shots).

**Convention (C).** An implied agreement between the viewer and artist to accept certain artificialities as real in a work of art. In movies, editing—or the juxtaposition of shots—is accepted as "logical," even though a viewer's perception of reality is continuous and unfragmented. *Genre* films contain many pre-established conventions. In musicals, for example, characters express themselves most forcefully through song and dance.

**Coverage, covering shots (T).** Extra shots of a scene which can be used to bridge transitions in case the planned footage fails to edit according to expectations. Usually long shots which preserve the overall continuity of a scene.

**Crane shot (T).** A shot taken from a special device called a crane, which resembles a huge mechanical arm. The crane carries the camera and the cinematographer, and can move in virtually any direction.

**Creative producer (I).** A producer who supervises the making of a movie in such detail that he is virtually its artistic creator. During the studio era in America, the most famous creative producers were David O. Selznick and Walt Disney.

**Cross cutting (G).** The alternating of shots from two sequences, often in different locales, suggesting that they are taking place at the same time.

**Cutting in the camera, editing in the camera (I).** The practice of shooting only what's necessary for the individual shots of a film, with virtually no leftover footage. In effect, the film is precut: The editor needs only to splice the shots in their proper sequence. A favorite method of Hitchcock.

**Cutting to continuity (T).** A type of editing in which the shots are arranged to preserve the fluidity of an action without showing all of it. An unobtrusive condensation of a continuous action.

**Dadaism (C).** An avant-garde movement in the arts stressing unconscious elements, irrationalism, irreverent wit, and spontaneity. Dadaist films were produced mostly in France in the later teens to mid-twenties.

**Day-for-night shooting (T).** Scenes that are filmed in daytime with special filters, to suggest nighttime settings in the movie image.

**Découpage (C).** From the French, "to cut up." The breakdown of a dramatic action into its constituent shots. See *editing*.

**Découpage classique,** see *classical cutting*.

**Deep focus (T).** A technique of photography which permits all distance planes to remain clearly in focus, from closeup ranges to infinity.

**Direct cinema,** see *cinéma vérité*.

**Dissolve, lap dissolve (T).** These terms refer to the slow fading out of one shot and the gradual fading in of its successor, with a superimposition of images, usually at the midpoint.

**Distributor (I).** Those individuals who serve as middle men in the movie industry, who arrange to book the product in theatres.

**Dolly shot, tracking shot, trucking shot (T).** A shot taken from a moving vehicle. Originally tracks were laid on the set to permit a smoother movement of the camera. Today even a smooth hand-held traveling shot is considered a variation of the dolly shot.

**Dominant contrast,** also **dominant (C).** That area of the film image which, because of a prominent visual contrast, compels the viewer's most immediate attention. Occasionally the dominant can be aural, in which case the image serves as a *subsidiary contrast.*

**Double exposure (T).** The superimposition of two literally unrelated images on film. See also *multiple exposure.*

**Double feature, double bill (G).** The practice, common primarily in the 1930s and 1940s in the U.S.A., of exhibiting two feature-length movies for a single admission, usually an *A-production* followed by a *B-film.*

**Dubbing (T).** The addition of sound after the visuals have been photographed. Dubbing can be either *synchronous* with an image, or *nonsynchronous.* Foreign language movies are often dubbed in English for release in this country.

**Editing (G).** The joining of one shot (strip of film) with another. The shots can picture events and objects in different places at different times. Editing is called *montage* in Europe.

**Epic (C).** A film *genre* characterized by bold and sweeping themes, usually in heroic proportions. The protagonist is generally an ideal representative of a culture—national, religious, or regional. The tone of most epics is dignified, the treatment larger-than-life. The western is the most popular epic genre in the U.S.A.

**Establishing shot (T).** Usually an *extreme long* or *long* shot offered at the beginning of a scene, providing the viewer with the context of the subsequent closer shots.

**Experimental cinema.** See *poetic cinema.*

**Expressionism (C).** A style of filmmaking which distorts time and space as ordinarily perceived in reality. Emphasis is placed on the essential characteristics of objects and people, not necessarily on their superficial appearance. Typical expressionist techniques are fragmentary editing, a wide variety of shots, extreme angles and lighting effects, and the use of distorting lenses and special effects.

**Extreme closeup (G).** A minutely detailed view of an object or person. An extreme closeup of an actor generally includes only his eyes or mouth.

**Extreme long shot (G).** A panoramic view of an exterior location, photographed from a great distance, often as far as a quarter-mile away.

**Eye-level shot (T).** The placement of the camera approximately 5 to 6 feet from the ground, corresponding to the height of an observer on the scene.

**Factory system (G).** During the studio era in America, a method of mass production based on the principle of the assembly-line, in which movies were created not by a single artist and his collaborators, but by specialized departments which performed the same function for all films produced by the studio. Except for an overseer—usually the producer—no single individual handled a movie from conception to release. The term is generally used in a pejorative sense.

**Fade (T).** The fade-out is the snuffing of an image from normal brightness to a black screen. A fade-in is the slow brightening of the image from a black screen to normal.

**Faithful adaptation (C).** A film based on another medium (usually a work of literature) which captures the essence of the original, and uses cinematic equivalents for specific literary techniques.

**Fast motion, accelerated motion (T).** If an action is photographed at a slower rate than 24 frames per second, when the film is projected at the standard rate of 24 fps, the action will appear to be moving at a faster rate than normal, and will often seem jerky.

**Fast stock, fast film (T).** Film stock that's highly sensitive to light and generally produces a grainy image. Often used by documentarists who wish to shoot only with *available lighting*. See also *slow stock*.

**Feature, feature-length film (G).** A movie of over an hour's duration, and generally under two.

**Filters (T).** Pieces of glass or plastic placed in front of the *lens*, which distort the quality of the light entering the camera, and hence the movie image.

**Final cut,** also **release print (I).** The sequence of shots in a movie as it will be released to the public.

**First cut (I).** The initial sequence of shots in a movie, often constructed by the director. Also called a *rough cut*.

**First-person point of view.** See *point-of-view shot*.

**Fish-eye lens (T).** An extreme wide angle lens, which distorts the image so radically that the edges seem wrapped into a sphere.

**Flashback (G).** An editing technique that suggests the interruption of the present by a shot or series of shots representing the past.

**Flash-forward (G).** An editing technique that suggests the interruption of the present by a shot or series of shots representing the future.

**Flash pan.** See *swish pan*.

**Focus (T).** The degree of acceptable sharpness in a film image. "Out of focus" means the images are blurred and lack acceptable linear definition.

**Footage (T).** Exposed film *stock*.

**Frame (T).** The dividing line between the edges of the screen image and the enclosing darkness of the theatre. Can also refer to a single photograph from the filmstrip.

**Freeze frame, freeze shot (T).** A shot composed of a single *frame* that is reprinted a number of times on the filmstrip which, when projected, gives the illusion of a still photograph.

**F-stop (T).** The measurement of the size of the lens opening in the camera, indicating the amount of light that's admitted.

**Full shot (T).** A type of *long shot* which includes the human body in full, with the head near the top of the frame and the feet near the bottom.

**Gauge (T).** The width of the filmstrip, expressed in millimeters (mm). The wider the gauge, the better the quality of the image. The most common gauges are 8mm, 16mm, 35mm, and 70mm. The standard in theatrical exhibitions is 35mm; in most college and museum showings, 16mm. 8mm is mostly for home movies; 70mm for big-budget spectacle films.

**Genre (C).** A recognizable type of movie, characterized by certain preestablished conventions. Some common American genres are westerns, musicals, thrillers, comedies. There are literally hundreds of them.

**High angle shot (T).** A shot in which the subject is photographed from above.

**High contrast (T).** A style of lighting emphasizing harsh shafts and dramatic streaks of lights and darks. Often used in thrillers and melodramas.

**High-key (T).** A style of lighting emphasizing bright, even illumination, with few conspicuous shadows. Used generally in comedies, musicals, and light entertainment films.

**Homage (C).** A direct or indirect reference within a movie to another movie, filmmaker, or cinematic style. A respectful and affectionate tribute.

**Iconography (C).** The use of a well-known cultural symbol or complex of symbols in an artistic representation. In movies, iconography can involve a star's *persona*, the pre-established conventions of a *genre*, the use of *archetypal* characters and situations, and such stylistic features as lighting, settings, costuming, props, and so on.

**Independent cinema, underground films (C).** An avant-garde movement which began in the U.S.A. in the mid-1950s, emphasizing film as pure form, and the filmmaker's self-expression over considerations of subject matter alone. Mostly short, non-narrative movies, produced outside the industry.

**Independent producer (G).** A producer not affiliated with a studio or large commercial firm. Many stars and directors have been independent producers to ensure their artistic autonomy.

**Intrinsic interest (C).** An unobtrusive area of the film image which nonetheless compels the viewer's most immediate attention because of its dramatic or contextual importance. An object of intrinsic interest will take precedence over the formal *dominant contrast*.

**Iris (T).** A *masking* device that blacks out portions of the screen, permitting only a part of the image to be seen. Usually the iris is circular or oval shaped, and can be expanded or contracted.

**Jump-cut (T).** An abrupt transition between shots, sometimes deliberate, which is disorienting in terms of the *continuity* of space and time.

**Key light (T).** The main source of illumination for a shot.

**Kinetic (C).** Pertaining to motion and movement.

**Leftist (C).** A political term used to describe the acceptance, at least in part, of the economic, social, and philosophical ideas of Karl Marx.

**Lengthy take, long take (C).** A shot of lengthy duration.

**Lens (T).** A ground or molded piece of glass, plastic, or other transparent material through which light rays are refracted so that they converge or diverge to form the photographic image within the camera.

**Literal adaptation (C).** A movie based on a stage play, in which the dialogue and actions are preserved more or less intact, though subtly altered by the director's uniquely cinematic techniques, like *editing*, and *mise-en-scène*.

**Long shot (G).** Includes an area within the *frame* which roughly corresponds to the audience's view of the area within the proscenium arch in the live theatre.

**Loose adaptation (C).** A movie based on another medium (usually literary), in which only a superficial resemblance exists between the two versions.

**Loose framing (C).** Usually in longer shots. The *mise-en-scène* is so spaciously distributed that the people photographed have considerable freedom of movement.

**Low angle shot (T).** A shot in which the subject is photographed from below.

**Low key (T).** A style of lighting emphasizing diffused shadows and atmospheric pools of light. Often used in mysteries, thrillers, and *film noir*.

**Marxist (C).** A person who subscribes to the economic, social, political, and philosophical theories of Karl Marx. Any artistic work reflecting these values.

**Master shot (T).** An uninterrupted shot, usually taken from a *long-* or *full-shot* range, which contains an entire scene. Later, the closer shots are photographed, and an edited sequence, composed of a variety of shots, is constructed on the editor's bench.

**Masking (T).** A technique whereby a portion of the movie image is blocked out, thus temporarily altering the dimensions of the screen's *aspect ratio*.

**Matte shot (T).** A process of combining two separate shots on one print, resulting in an image that looks as though it had been photographed normally. Used mostly for special effects, such as combining a human figure with giant dinosaurs, etc.

**Medium shot (G).** A relatively close shot, revealing a moderate amount of detail. A medium shot of a figure generally includes the body from the knees or waist up. French critics called it *le plan amèricain*, the American shot, because it's so characteristic of the classical American cinema.

**Metaphor (C).** An implied comparison between two otherwise unlike elements, meaningful in a figurative rather than a literal sense.

**Metteur-en-scène (C).** The artist or technician who creates the *mise-en-scène*—that is, the director. Used pejoratively, this term refers to a hired hand who doesn't impose his personal vision on the materials, but merely stages the action mechanically.

**Mickeymousing (T).** A type of film music which is purely descriptive and attempts to reproduce the visual action with musical equivalents. Often used in animation.

**Miniatures,** also **model** or **miniature shots (T).** Small-scale models photographed to give the illusion that they are full-scale objects. For example, ships sinking at sea, giant dinosaurs, airplanes colliding, etc.

**Minimalism (C).** A style of filmmaking characterized by austerity and restraint, in which cinematic elements are reduced to the barest minimum of information.

**Mise-en-scène (C).** The arrangement of visual weights and movements within a given space. In the live theatre, the space is usually defined by the proscenium arch; in movies, by the *frame* which encloses the images. Cinematic mise-en-scène encompasses both the staging of the action and the way that it's photographed.

**Mix (T).** The process of combining separately recorded sounds from individual soundtracks onto a master track.

**Montage (T).** Transitional sequences of rapidly edited images, used to suggest the lapse of time or the passing of events. Often employs *dissolves* and *multiple exposures*. In Europe, montage means the art of editing.

**Motif (C).** Any unobtrusive technique, object, or thematic idea that's systematically repeated throughout a film.

**Multiple exposure (T).** A special effect produced by the *optical printer*, which permits the superimposition of many images simultaneously.

**Negative image (T).** The reversal of lights and darks of the subject photographed: blacks are white, whites are black.

**Neorealism (C).** An Italian film movement which produced its best works between 1945 and 1955. Strongly realistic in its technical biases, neorealism emphasized documentary aspects of film art, stressing loose episodic plots, unextraordinary events and characters, natural lighting, actual location settings, nonprofessional actors, a preoccupation with poverty and social problems, and an emphasis on humanistic and democratic ideals. The term has also been used to describe other films which reflect the technical and stylistic biases of Italian neorealism.

**New Wave, nouvelle vague (C).** A group of young French directors who came to prominence during the late 1950s. The most widely known are Jean-Luc Godard, François Truffaut, Claude Chabrol, and Alain Resnais, who all began as movie critics at *Cahiers du Cinéma*.

**Non-synchronous sound,** also **commentative sound (T).** Sound and image are not recorded simultaneously, or the sound is detached from its source in the film image. Music, for example, is usually non-synchronous in a movie.

**Oblique angle (T).** A shot photographed by a tilted camera. When the image is projected on the screen, the subject itself seems to be tilted on a diagonal.

**Oeuvre (C).** From the French, "work." The complete works of an artist, viewed as a whole.

**Omniscient point of view (C).** In literature, this refers to an all-knowing narrator who provides the reader with all the necessary information. Most movies are omnisciently narrated by the camera.

**Open forms (C).** Used primarily by *realist* filmmakers, these techniques are likely to be unobtrusive, with an emphasis on informal compositions and apparently haphazard designs. The *frame* is exploited to suggest a temporary masking, a window which arbitrarily cuts off part of the action.

**Open up (I).** A term used in adapting a play to film, in which the action is transferred to a variety of locations, often exteriors, in order to make the story appear less stagey and confined.

**Optical printer (T).** An elaborate machine used to create special effects in movies. For example, *fades, dissolves, multiple exposures,* and so on.

**Outtakes (I).** Shots or pieces of shots that are not used in the final cut of a film. The leftover footage.

**Overexposure (T).** Too much light enters the aperture of a camera lens, bleaching out the image. Useful for fantasy and nightmare sequences.

**Over-the-shoulder shot (T).** Usually a *medium shot,* useful in dialogue scenes, in which one actor is photographed head on from over the shoulder of another character.

**Pan, panning shot (T).** Short for panorama, this is a revolving horizontal movement of the camera from left to right or vice-versa.

**Parallel editing.** See *cross cutting.*

**Persona (C).** From the Latin, "mask." An actor's public image, based on his or her previous roles, and often incorporating elements from their actual personalities as well. A persona can be exploited as a form of pre-characterization.

**Personality-star.** See *star.*

**Pixillation (T).** Also called "stop motion photography," this is an animation technique involving the photographing of live actors frame by frame. When the sequence is projected at the standard speed of 24 fps, the actors move abruptly and jerkily, suggesting primitive cartoon figures.

**Poetic cinema (C).** A term used to describe *avant-garde* movies, especially those produced in the 1940s in the United States.

**Point-of-view shot, also pov shot, first person camera,** and **subjective camera (T).** Any shot which is taken from the vantage point of a character in the film: what he sees.

**Process shot, also rear projection (T).** A technique in which a background scene is projected onto a translucent screen behind the actors so it appears that the actors are on location in the final image.

**Producer (G).** An ambiguous term referring to the individual or company that controls the financing of a film, and often the way it's made. The producer can concern himself solely with business matters, or with putting together a package deal (such as script, stars, and director), or he can function as an expeditor, smoothing over problems during production.

**Producer-director (I).** A filmmaker who finances projects independently, to allow maximum creative freedom.

**Production Code, also Motion Picture Production Code (I).** The American film industry's censorship arm. The Code was introduced in 1930, but not enforced until 1934. It was revised in the 1950s, and scrapped in favor of the present rating system in 1966.

**Production number (I).** An elaborate sequence, often in a musical, which involves a large cast and complicated technical manoeuvres.

**Production values (I).** The box office appeal of the physical mounting of a film, such as sets, costumes, props, etc. Spectacle pictures are generally the most lavish in their production values.

**Prop (T).** Any movable item which is included in a movie: tables, guns, books, etc.

**Property (I).** Anything with a profit-making potential in movies, though generally used to describe a story of some kind: a screenplay, novel, short story, etc.

**Proxemic patterns (C).** The spatial relationships among characters within the *mise-en-scène,* and the apparent distance of the camera from the subject photographed.

**Pull-back dolly (T).** When the camera withdraws from a scene to reveal an object or character that was previously out of *frame*.

**Rack focusing, selective focusing (T).** The blurring of focal planes in sequence, forcing the viewer's eye to travel with those areas of an image that remain in sharp focus.

**Radical montage (C).** A type of editing propounded by the Soviet filmmaker Eisenstein, in which separate shots are linked together not by their literal continuity in reality, but by symbolic association. A shot of a preening braggart might be linked to a shot of a toy peacock, for example. This type of editing juxtaposes shots to produce a sense of collision.

**Reaction pan (T).** Similar to a *reaction shot,* only instead of cutting, the director *pans* to a character's response.

**Reaction shot (T).** A cut to a shot of a character's reaction to the contents of the preceding shot.

**Realism (G).** A style of filmmaking which attempts to duplicate the look of reality as it's commonly perceived, with emphasis on authentic locations and details, long shots, lengthy takes, eye-level placements of the camera, a minimum of editing and special effects.

**Re-establishing shot (T).** A return to an initial *establishing shot* within a scene, acting as a reminder of the physical context of the closer shots.

**Reverse angle shot (T).** A shot taken from an angle 180° opposed to the previous shot. That is, the camera is placed opposite its previous position.

**Reverse motion (T).** A series of images are photographed with the film reversed. When projected normally, the effect is to suggest backward movement—an egg "returning" to its shell, for example.

**Rough cut (T).** The crudely edited footage of a movie before the editor has tightened up the slackness between shots. A kind of rough draft.

**Rushes, dailies (I).** The selected footage of the previous day's shooting, which is usually evaluated by the director and cinematographer before the start of the next day's shooting.

**Scene (G).** An imprecise unit of film, composed of a number of interrelated shots, unified usually by a central concern—a location, an incident, or a minor dramatic climax.

**Script, screenplay, scenario (G).** A written description of a movie's dialogue and action, which occasionally includes camera instructions.

**Semiology, semiotics (C).** A theory of cinematic communication which studies signs or symbolic codes as minimal units of signification. Influenced by the methodology and theory of structural linguistics, semiological theories are descriptive rather than normative, and are concerned with systematic identification and classification rather than evaluation.

**Sequence (G).** An imprecise structural unit of film, composed of a number of interrelated scenes, and leading to a major climax.

**Sequence shot, also plan-séquence (C).** A single lengthy take, usually involving complex staging and camera movements.

**Setup (T).** The positioning of the camera and lights for a specific shot.

**Shooting ratio (I).** The amount of film stock used in photographing a film in relation to what's finally included in the finished product. A shooting ratio of 20/1 means that 20 feet of film were shot for every one used in the final cut.

**Shooting script (I).** A written breakdown of a movie story into its individual shots, often containing technical instructions. Used by the director and his or her staff during production.

**Short lens.** See *wide angle lens*.

**Shot (G).** Those images which are recorded continuously from the time the camera starts to the time it stops. That is, an unedited strip of film.

**Slapstick (G).** A type of comedy, especially popular in the U.S.A. during the silent era, involving pantomime and broad physical actions, such as pratfalls, auto collisions, and so on.

**Slow motion (T).** Shots of a subject photographed at a faster rate than 24 fps, which when projected at the standard rate produce a dreamy dancelike slowness of action.

**Slow stock, slow film (T).** Film stocks that are relatively insensitive to light and produce crisp images, and a sharpness of detail. When used in interior settings, these stocks generally require considerable artificial illumination.

**Sneak preview (I).** A trial exhibition of a movie, usually unadvertised, in order to gauge an audience's response before the film's official release. If the reaction is unfavorable, the movie is often re-edited to conform to the criticisms—inferred or explicit—of the sneak preview audience.

**Socialist realism (C).** A *Marxist* theory of art, strongly propagandistic in its emphasis, stressing the need for the artist to portray a scientifically verifiable picture of reality which exists independently of the artist. Also known as the "Stalin School" of art, socialist realism was the official artistic style of the Soviet Union and the Communist countries of eastern Europe from the early 1930s to the mid-1950s.

**Soft focus (T).** The blurring out of focus of all except one desired distance range. Can also refer to a glamorizing technique which softens the sharpness of definition so that facial wrinkles can be smoothed over and even eliminated.

**Star (G).** A film actor or actress of great popularity. A *personality-star* tends to play only those roles that fit a preconceived public image, which constitutes his or her *persona*. An *actor-star* can play roles of greater range and variety. Barbra Streisand is a personality-star, Robert De Niro an actor-star.

**Star system (G).** The technique of exploiting the charisma of popular players to enhance the box office appeal of films. The star system was developed in America, and has been the backbone of the American film industry since the mid-teens.

**Star values (I).** The box office appeal of the stars in a movie.

**Star vehicle (G).** A movie especially designed to showcase the talents and charms of a specific star.

**Stock (T).** Unexposed film. There are many types of movie stocks, including those highly sensitive to light (*fast stocks*) and those relatively insensitive to light (*slow stocks*).

**Structuralism, cine-structuralism (C).** Cinematic theories employing various *semiological* methods to determine how certain codes and signs are synthesized in a single film, *genre,* or the works of a filmmaker.

**Story values (I).** The narrative appeal of a movie, which can reside in the popularity of an adapted *property,* the high craftsmanship of a *script,* or both.

**Studio (G).** (1) A large corporation specializing in the production and/or distribution of movies, such as Paramount, Warners Brothers, and so on; (2) any physical facility equipped for the production of films.

**Studio era (G).** That period (roughly from 1925 to 1955, but especially the 1930s and 1940s) when most American fiction movies were produced under the auspices of the big studios, such as MGM, Warner's, Paramount, and so on.

**Subjective camera.** See *point-of-view shot.*

**Subsidiary contrast (C).** A subordinated element of the film image, complementing or contrasting with the *dominant contrast.*

**Subtext (C).** A term used in drama and film to signify the dramatic implications beneath the language of a play or movie. Often the subtext concerns ideas and emotions that are totally independent of the language of a text.

**Surrealism (C).** An avant-garde movement in the arts stressing Freudian and Marxist ideas, unconscious elements, irrationalism, and the symbolic association of ideas. Surrealist movies were produced roughly from 1924 to 1931, primarily in France, though there are still surrealistic elements in the works of many directors, most notably those of Fellini and Buñuel.

**Swish pan (T).** Also known as a *flash* or *zip pan.* A horizontal movement of the camera at such a rapid rate that the subject photographed blurs on the screen.

**Synchronous sound (T).** The agreement or correspondence between image and sound, which are recorded simultaneously, or seem so in the finished print. Synchronous sounds appear to derive from an obvious source in the visuals.

**Symbol, symbolic (C).** A figurative device in which an object, event, or cinematic technique has significance beyond its literal meaning. Symbolism is always determined by the dramatic context.

**Take (T).** A variation of a specific shot. The final shot is often selected from a number of possible takes.

**Telephoto lens, long lens (T).** A lens which acts as a telescope, magnifying the size of objects at a great distance. A side effect is its tendency to flatten perspective.

**Three-shot (T).** A *medium shot,* featuring three actors.

**Tight framing (C).** Usually in close shots. The *mise-en-scène* is so carefully balanced and harmonized that the people photographed have little or no freedom of movement.

**Tracking shot, trucking shot.** See *dolly shot.*

**Viewfinder (T).** An eyepiece on the camera which defines the playing area and the framing of the action to be photographed.

**Vignetting (T).** A technique used to round off the corner edges of a movie image with a soft blurring effect.

**Voice-over (T).** A non-synchronous spoken commentary in a movie, often used to convey a character's thoughts or memories.

**Wide angle lens, short lens (T).** A lens which permits the camera to photograph a wider area than a normal lens. A side effect is its tendency to exaggerate perspective. Also used for *deep-focus* photography.

**Widescreen,** also **CinemaScope** and **scope (G).** A movie image which has an *aspect ratio* of approximately 5 by 3, though some widescreens possess horizontal dimensions that extend as wide as 2.5 times the vertical dimension of the screen.

**Wipe (T).** An editing device, usually a line which travels across the screen, "pushing off" one image and revealing another.

**Zip pan.** See *swish pan.*

**Zoom lens, zoom shot (T).** A lens of variable focal length which permits the cinematographer to change from *wide angle* to *telephoto shots* (and vice-versa) in one continuous movement, often plunging the viewer in or out of a scene rapidly.

# INDEX